THE BORZOI
HISTORY OF ENGLAND
VOLUME FIVE
1815-THE PRESENT

The Borzoi
History of England

General Editor
ARTHUR JOSEPH SLAVIN
University of California at Los Angeles

ANGLES, ANGELS,
AND CONQUERORS
Volume I: 400–1154
Joel T. Rosenthal
State University of New York at Stony Brook

THE COMMUNITY
OF THE REALM
Volume II: 1154–1485
Michael R. Powicke
University of Toronto

THE PRECARIOUS BALANCE:
English Government and Society
Volume III: 1450–1640
Arthur Joseph Slavin
University of California at Los Angeles

A CERTAINTY IN THE SUCCESSION
Volume IV: 1640–1815
Gerald M. and Lois O. Straka
University of Delaware

WATERLOO TO THE COMMON MARKET
Volume V: 1815–the Present
J. B. Conacher
University of Toronto

THE BORZOI
HISTORY OF ENGLAND
VOLUME FIVE
1815-THE PRESENT

WATERLOO TO THE COMMON MARKET

ALFRED A. KNOPF NEW YORK

J. B. CONACHER

University of Toronto

THIS IS A BORZOI BOOK
PUBLISHED BY ALFRED A. KNOPF, INC.

First Edition
987654321

Copyright © 1975 by Alfred A. Knopf, Inc.

All rights reserved under International and Pan-American Copyright Conventions. No part of this book may be reproduced in any form or by any means, electronic or mechanical, including photocopying, without permission in writing from the publisher. All inquiries should be addressed to Alfred A. Knopf, Inc., 201 East 50th Street, New York, N.Y. 10022. Published in the United States by Alfred A. Knopf, Inc., New York, and simultaneously in Canada by Random House of Canada Limited, Toronto. Distributed by Random House, Inc., New York.

Library of Congress Cataloging in Publication Data

Conacher, J B
  Waterloo to the Common Market (1815—the present)

  (The Borzoi history of England; v. 5)
  Includes bibliography and index.
  1. Great Britain—Politics and government—19th century.   2. Great Britain—Politics and government—20th century.   I. Title.
DA26.B65   vol. 5   (DA530)   320.9'42'08   74-28311
ISBN 0-394-48430-4
ISBN 0-394-31761-0 (text ed.)

Manufactured in the United States of America

To my wife
in appreciation of
her forbearance

Foreword

The volumes making up the Borzoi History of England spring from the desire the authors share to preserve for the present the excitement of the English past. To a somewhat smaller degree we also share a prejudice against the writing of a history unified artificially by an allotment of "factors" and "forces." We do not think a good consecutive history of England between the coming of the Anglo-Saxons to Britain and the British entry into the Common Market can be made by such stinting of work.

This is not to say that we dismiss the need for a concern over how five volumes by as many historians go to make one history. It is to say that we began by admitting the diverse character of our assignments. We recognized at the outset that what might be central to the history of Anglo-Saxon England might be eccentric, if given the same weight by another author, to a history of industrial England. Moreover, we began in agreement that our own gifts and interests, if followed in a disciplined way, could bring out of many volumes one book.

Professor Rosenthal's history of early English society employs a narrative technique around a political center. Yet his most basic concern is to give the reader a sense of the rudeness of life in Anglo-Saxon England.

Because Professor Rosenthal had so firm a base on which to work in Volume I, Professor Powicke agreed to concentrate his work in another direction. He set out to tell how the medieval realm was ordered. While not altogether abandoning traditional narrative, he thought it profitable to examine in detail the shape and character of the various communities that constituted the medieval realm—royal, ecclesiastical, urban, and manorial.

The aim of the medievalists was thus to establish and explain the institutions and culture in a broad way, while telling how they worked. Their working order was profoundly challenged over a period of time stretching from

Chaucer's age to that of Milton, or, reckoning politically, from Edward III's time to that of Charles I. It was my concern to describe and explain how a series of shifts in the social basis of politics led the English to reorder a turbulent commonwealth.

The efforts at establishing political, religious, and social stability undertaken by the Tudors proved more daring than durable. Professor and Mrs. Straka wished to deal with the undisputed establishment of political stability between the Puritan Revolution and England's wars to contain the expansion of revolutionary France in Napoleon's time. Where Volume III sought to base an analysis of government and society in the economic and religious life of the era, the Strakas thought it essential to tell how stability was achieved in terms narrative and political at heart. They felt they could build confidently on the descriptions already achieved in Volume III, just as Professor Powicke thought to thicken the texture of the society whose shape was defined by Professor Rosenthal.

This alternation was acceptable to all because we accepted in principle the existence of three great revolutionary situations in English history—that surrounding the Norman Conquest, another focused on the Reformation, and a third based on the transformation of a mixed commercial-agrarian society into an industrial one. It fell to Professor Conacher to take forward into our time the account of the revolution that made aristocratic England into the liberal, industrial democracy of the empire and the welfare state.

Hence this History has taken shape around two concerns: giving scope to narrative, where the story of change was itself dramatic in social terms rather than in dynastic ones; and allowing room for more analytical work, where this seemed to point to an understanding of why changes took place rather than merely what changed and how.

Our historical assumptions reveal a pluralism rather than the ideas of a "school." Our concerns and styles differ, and we hope this difference is appropriate to our problems. We felt we would work best if we marched to the drum each heard best, whether it was the steady one of ordinary people working the land and the common rhythm of factory pistons or the subtler one beating to political tunes in high places. It has been our hope thus to avoid the mere repetitive noise of texts cut to cover uniformly every aspect of society. Philosophers say nature does nothing by leaps. History, however, is constantly surprising; it is alive precisely because of its variety, its stubborn refusal of any lockstep.

Between the extremes of Alfred's tight little island and the august empire ruled by Queen Elizabeth I's heirs and successors, English history lies, a polyglot thing, nurturing our own civilization and its discontents. Since the time when Ranke spoke of national histories as a perfect guide to people's consciousness, the sense of history has profoundly altered. Yet narrative—description and analysis centered in political life as widely defined to make room for religion, economics, and popular culture—has not yielded its central place. We therefore offer this History: of a country bound in by her triumphant sea; a sepulchre for famous men; an often bleak workshop; a place that sent blacks into slavery in 1562 in a ship named *Jesus*; frankly political.

ARTHUR JOSEPH SLAVIN

Contents

LIST OF MAPS

LIST OF ILLUSTRATIONS

Introduction

The author of the final volume of this history has problems to deal with that are different from those of the earlier volumes in the series. The sources are so extensive and so varied that only a microscopic proportion have been published and the modern British historian can be familiar with only a small part of the vast mass. He is, therefore, almost entirely dependent on secondary authorities, but these are multiplying at an alarming rate calculated to make the stoutest heart despair of keeping up with the flood. Professor Josef Altholz's bibliographical handbook, *Victorian England 1837–1901*, is a highly select list of 2,500 titles of books and articles covering a mere sixty-five years of the period. Professor Alfred Havighurst is preparing a sequel to this volume on the twentieth century. These two volumes will be indispensable to the student of British history since 1815, but, of course, they make no attempt to deal with unpublished sources. Information regarding collections of private papers may be obtained from the Registry of National Archives, Historical Manuscripts Commission, Quality Court, Chancery Lane, London, England. A bibliography of books and articles on the Victorian period has been published annually in the June issue of *Victorian Studies* since 1958.

Although the historian is concerned with everything that happened in the past, his job is one of selection and of finding a pattern to make sense of the evidence he has collected. There are many approaches to choose from and the choice depends partly on the interests and views of the historian, partly on the materials available. My own view is that a general history of a period as long and complex as that covered in this book is best treated by a broad political narrative that constantly seeks to take into consideration the various economic, social, and cultural factors that mold the course of history. Even though the student's ultimate interest may lie in economic, social, or cultural history, I believe it is important for him to have some awareness of the general course of events that shaped the history of the country over the particular period under examination.

There was a time when political history tended to be considered in a vacuum, but that day is long past. The pendulum may have swung too far in the opposite direction as students have become interested in other approaches, especially in social and intellectual history; but it is even more obvious that these special studies cannot be pursued intelligently by themselves alone. Political history in its broadest sense offers a framework or a foundation from which we may build in a variety of directions, but sound political history must pay close attention to economic and social developments and the intellectual and cultural climate of the period under consideration. Professor G. R. Elton has demonstrated this point admirably in a little book entitled *Political History–Principles and Practice* (New York and London: Basic Books, Inc., 1970), which should be read by every student interested in the subject. If history is well-written there should be no complete separation of the various strands that combine to tie the present to the past.

In this book I have tried to set the stage in Chapter 1 by describing the England (and, to a lesser extent, the Britain)[1] of 1815; but this entails frequent backward glances and, consequently, some passing consideration of preceding political events, although the chapter is mainly concerned with the economy, the social structure, institutions, religion, and ideas. With the stage set it is then possible to proceed with two chapters that are mostly narratives of political events in the forty years following 1815, but since many of these events were precipitated by economic and social changes, and perhaps also by the spread of new ideas, these other themes are not forgotten. There may be an element of artificiality in treating imperial and foreign affairs separately in Chapter 4, since it means traversing at least part of the same period for a second time, but for the sake of clarity it is the sort of device to which the historian must resort. Foreign affairs tended to keep the spotlight during the decade of Palmerston's ascendancy (1855–65), so it is convenient to bring the

---

[1] Wales, conquered by the English in the Middle Ages, had virtually become part of England with the Act of Henry VIII giving her representation in the English Parliament. The English and Scottish crowns were united in 1603, and the Act of Union of 1707 completed the parliamentary union of Great Britain. Ireland, long ruled by England, but with her own parliament, had finally come into the parliamentary union of Great Britain and Ireland by the Act of Union of 1800. Socially, culturally, and administratively, however, Scotland, Ireland, and (to a lesser extent) Wales remained distinct from England. In dealing with domestic history this book will be concerned primarily with England, but a history of England must, for some purposes, become a history of Great Britain or of the United Kingdom. "Britain" is the more appropriate term in dealing with foreign relations, but cannot be used exclusively, since government spokesmen themselves talked of England and English policy. The term "United Kingdom" is more typical of the twentieth century.

political narrative in this chapter forward to the latter date. In Chapter 5 we take another look at the condition of England (or Britain), this time in the decade or so following midcentury, the high Victorian era which was so different from the Regency years that opened the book. The political narrative is resumed in the next chapter and taken up to 1880, but imperial and Irish affairs so dominate British history from then on to the end of the century that Chapter 7 combines both domestic and external themes. The beginning of a new century is again a convenient point at which to consider the economic, social, and cultural changes that have occurred in the latter half of the nineteenth century—changes that were bound to affect the course of history in the new century. The domestic history of the prewar decade is so dramatic and so complicated that it deserves a chapter all to itself, but then in Chapter 10 we must briefly retrace out steps to see how Britain got involved in the First World War, before examining her actual role in the war. The interwar years are covered by a chapter on domestic affairs and party politics, another chapter surveying the general state of the country in that period, and a third tracing the path leading to Britain's participation in the Second World War. This was one of the most traumatic experiences in Britain's long history and also merits a chapter to itself. As we approach the present in the postwar era it becomes necessary to tie all the strands together in the last two chapters dealing with the years before and after the Suez crisis of 1956.

The book closes with Edward Heath's singular achievement, Britain's entry into the Common Market, which was a goal that had eluded two earlier prime ministers, Harold Macmillan and Harold Wilson. But in Opposition, sensing the anti-Market feeling among the majority of his party, Wilson backed away from Europe and condemned the terms on which Heath had entered the European Economic Community. During the year following Britain's entry everything seemed to go wrong for the Heath Government, which clung tenaciously but ineffectively to a wage and price control policy that would not work, partly because of the general rise in world prices. In the winter of 1973–74 it was the miners who, not for the first time, precipitated a national crisis. Their case was a strong one, but the Government refused to meet their full demands, fearing that to do so would undermine the official incomes policy with which they were trying to fight inflation. The result, at first, was a slowdown in coal production as the miners worked to rule, and finally, an all-out strike that threatened to bring the British economy to its knees in a year of world-wide fuel shortages precipitated by the Middle East oil crisis. In desperation Heath dissolved Parliament and appealed to the people to back him against the miners. He lost the election and Wilson returned to office as head of a minority government, dependent for support from the Liberals and/or various splinter parties drawn from "the Celtic fringe." The new Labour Government quickly brought the coal strike to an end by granting the miners acceptable terms, thus increasing already severe inflationary pressures, and began to renegotiate the terms of Britain's participation in the Common Market. In a second election in October 1974, Wilson won an overall majority of three, promising a "social contract" with the trade unions and a referendum on Britain's membership in the Common Market within a year. Continued opposition from the trade unions and from the right wing of the Conservative party left the result problematical when the polls were counted. After all these years of knocking on the door, withdrawal from the European Economic Community would be a sad anticlimax, but prophesy is not the historian's role.

This book is based almost entirely on the work of other historians and it is impossible to begin to spell out my debt. In a book of this sort I have infrequently had occasion to indicate my sources in footnotes, and the select bibliography does not exhaust the sum of my debt. I must acknowledge my special indebtedness to Professor David Spring of Johns Hopkins, to Professor J. Slavin, general editor of the series, and to my two colleagues, Professors R. J. Helmstadter and T. O. Lloyd, who read all or most of the book in typescript and made many valuable suggestions for its improvement. Many other colleagues, too numerous to mention, helped me with particular points, for British history has a habit of running all over the globe and touching everybody else's territory. If any reader of any of my previous books finds the style of this one improved then I must attribute the improvement to an extremely zealous, but anonymous, copy editor. Finally, I should like to acknowledge the help and courtesy of Helene Kendler, the editor who saw the book through to the press.

Chapter One
ENGLAND IN 1815

History has often been called a "seamless web," because we cannot cut it off at any point in time without tearing the threads that bind it together and leaving a ragged edge. The historian, however, must begin somewhere, so he will look for turning points in the course of history, comparable to creases in the whole fabric. The year 1815 is one such point in English and in European history.

The events of that year and of the years that followed were determined by what had gone before. The men who directed England's affairs and, indeed, all their fellow countrymen had their roots in the past and were not conscious of stepping into a new era. Nevertheless, 1815 was a significant year. The battle of Waterloo, fought on June 18, marked the end of twenty-two years of war interrupted only by what amounted to two uneasy armistices; indeed, since the accession of William III, a period of more than a century, the country had faced more years of war than of peace. It had, however, been an era of remarkable social and political equilibrium, during which the English landed aristocracy had ruled with no serious challenge. The year 1815 inaugurated a century of comparative peace in which Britain[1] was involved in only one brief European war, fought on the far extreme of the Continent in the Crimean peninsula. At least the first half of the coming century would be known as the era of Pax Britannica: The Royal Navy sailed unchallenged around the globe, and Britain alone among the great powers continued to rule a large overseas empire. Spain and Austria were in decline; France seemed condemned to periodic revolutions and consequent instability; Prussia had not yet succeeded in uniting Germany; Russia, potentially strong, was remote and badly governed; the United States was laying the foundations of her future power, but had not as yet posed a serious threat to Britain's naval supremacy. Britain, with a half-century lead in the Industrial Revolution,

[1] See *Introduction*, footnote 1.

The United Kingdom
of Great Britain
and Northern Ireland

Cities over–1,000,000
500,000–1,000,000
150,000– 500,000
under– 150,000

Orkney Islands

Scapa Flow

CAITHNESS

SUTHERLAND

Hebrides

ROSS AND
CROMARTY

NAIRN
MORAY
BANFF

ABERDEEN

•Aberdeen

INVERNESS

KINCARDINE

S C O T L A N D
ANGUS

PERTH

•Dundee

ATLANTIC

CLACK-
MANNAN
KINROSS FIFE

ARGYLL

STIRLING
DUNBARTON

OCEAN

Glasgow
RENFREW

Clyde R.

EAST
LOTHIAN

Edinburgh
MIDLOTHIAN

BERWICK

BUTE

LANARK

PEEBLES

SELKIRK

AYR

ROXBURGH

DUMFRIES

NORTHUMBERLAND

Tyne R. •Newcastle

Londonderry

N.
IRELAND

LONDON-
DERRY

ANTRIM

KIRK-
CUDBRIGHT

WIGTOWN

CUMBERLAND

DURHAM •Durham

•Belfast

TYRONE

WEST-
MORLAND

FERMANAGH

ARMAGH

DOWN

Isle of Man

YORKSHIRE

L
A
N
C
A
S
H
I
R
E

•York

I R I S H

•

York

E I R E

SEA

Bradford

Leeds

Dublin

Wigan

Sheffield

LINCOLN-
SHIRE

(I R E L A N D)

Liverpool

Manchester

ANGLESEY

FLINT

CHESHIRE

DERBY

DENBIGH

NOTTING-
HAM

Nottingham

CAERNARVON

STAFFORD

MERIONETH

RUTLAND

Norwich

MONT-
GOMERY

SHROPSHIRE
(SALOP)

LEICESTER
•Tamworth
Birmingham

NORFOLK

CARDIGAN

RADNOR

WORCE-
STER

WARWICK

Coventry

NORTHAMPTON
HUNTINGDON

CAMBRIDGE

Cambridge

SUFFOLK

HEREFORD

BEDFORD

PEMBROKE

BRECK-
NOCK

Severn R.

GLOUCESTER

OXFORD

Oxford

BUCKINGHAM

HERTFORD

ESSEX

CARMARTHEN

Thames R.

London

Swansea

GLAMORGAN

MONMOUTH

Bristol

Cardiff

WILTSHIRE

BERKSHIRE

SURREY

Canterbury•

KENT

Dover

SOMERSET

HAMPSHIRE
Southampton

SUSSEX

*Strait
of Dover*

DEVON

DORSET

Isle of Wight

Brighton

CORNWALL

•Plymouth

E N G L I S H   C H A N N E L

N O R T H   S E A

was to remain for another half-century the wealthiest and most secure country in the world. At home, however, the Industrial Revolution, the basis of Britain's power in the world, would ensure that the coming century would be one of social, political, and constitutional change that would transform the state from an oligarchy into something approaching a democracy, a metamorphosis inconceivable to eighteenth-century patricians.

Had King William III, who died in 1701, been permitted to return to England in 1815, what changes would he have noticed? Suppose he had accompanied Major Cartwright on a speaking tour to the new industrial towns.[2] In the north and the Midlands he would have come across a score or more of large towns of which he had probably never heard, while he would find London to have grown beyond recognition with more than a million inhabitants. He would probably be impressed by the ports of London and Liverpool, with their acres of new docks, but he would surely be dismayed by the ugliness of the industrial towns marring the beauty of the northern countryside. These towns were generally little more than collections of great factories with smoking chimneys and endless rows of cheap, jerry-built houses. They lacked churches, schools, shops, paved streets, proper sanitation, and even adequate lighting—at night in the iron mining regions they were illuminated mostly by the eerie flames of great blast furnaces.

Had he gone on one of Cobbett's rural rides,[3] the king would have been struck by the transformation of the countryside. Even here he would have found industry's scars—mills built by mountain streams to utilize cheap water power, the shafts of new mines, and growing piles of slag—all disturbing the peace and beauty of once-secluded valleys. He might, however, have been impressed by the 2,600 miles of canals that now criss-crossed the country linking all the centers of industry, and by the speed of the mail coaches bowling along the improved turnpike roads. The journey from London to Edinburgh, which in his lifetime had taken several weeks, could now be completed in sixty hours. In the rural areas he would have noticed in particular the extent of enclosure. Open fields, which were already disappearing in his own day, were largely gone by 1815 and the countryside had a much trimmer look. Moreover, on the estates of the great landowners there was a marked increase in the size and number of stately mansions and landscaped gardens. England, he would conclude, had grown rich in the intervening century; and this conclusion would be confirmed by the opulence he would see in London's new West End, where, under the patronage of the prince regent,

---

[2] Major John Cartwright (1740–1824), a lifelong advocate of parliamentary reform, embarked on several such tours in the years 1812–15.

[3] William Cobbett's *Rural Rides* (London, 1830) described his famous jaunts around the English countryside, begun in 1821. (For Cobbett see p. 23.)

the beautiful street and park that alone gave luster to his name were taking shape, and the genius of Nash was constructing rows of elegant town houses that are still London's pride today.

Allowing our visitor to return to his grave, let us examine in more detail some features of England in 1815. Economic historians have long debated the reasons for the great increase in population in the preceding half-century. Some have attributed it primarily to the rising birth rate, while others have emphasized the falling birth rate. The rise in the birth rate has been explained by improvements in the diet of mothers, by a demand for child labor that enabled a child to contribute to the family earnings from the age of five or six, and by the earlier marriages that were encouraged by better job opportunities and changes in social customs. All these explanations are, however, a matter of speculation and open to various objections. There is similar controversy over the reasons for the fall in the death rate. Improvements in sanitary conditions do not make a very convincing explanation for a reduction in working-class mortality at this date, but there is some evidence that the introduction of vaccination around the turn of the century helped to reduce the death rate from smallpox, which had been one of the most fatal diseases in the eighteenth century. It has also been pointed out that catastrophic losses from plague and famine had ceased to be a common phenomenon in western Europe in the later eighteenth century; in England the disappearance of famine could be attributed to agricultural improvements.[4]

There is also some debate on the relationship between the population increase and the Industrial Revolution. The two were undoubtedly related and stimulated one another, but it would be an oversimplification to say they were cause and effect. Too rapid a population growth could have been a drag on industrial expansion, as is the case with some of the developing countries of today. Nevertheless, it may be said that both the Industrial and Agricultural Revolutions made possible the continued population expansion of the nineteenth century.

The basic class structure of England in 1815 was similar to what it had been for several centuries, but class divisions were becoming more pronounced and there were notable changes within classes. E. P. Thompson, in his monumental study of the subject,[5] sees the working class only just emerging with an identity of its own during the years 1790–1820. Undoubtedly the rigors of the early years of the Industrial Revolution and the political repression of the period of what he calls "counterrevolutionary wars" did much to create a class consciousness, at least among the more articulate spokesmen for the

---

[4] For a summary of the latest research on this controversial issue see M. W. Flinn, *British Population Growth, 1700–1850* (London: Macmillan, 1970).

[5] *The Making of the English Working Class* (New York: Pantheon, 1964).

industrial workers; but Thompson is less convincing when he argues that "the working people were forced into political and social apartheid during the wars." Other historians have emphasized the innate spirit of deference in the English masses that enabled the old governing classes to retain control for so long. It is doubtful that class antagonisms were quite as widespread as Thompson suggests, but the contrast between the ever-growing opulence of the rich and the hardships of the poor was never sharper.

There was little change in the composition of the landed aristocracy, numbering some 27,000 families in 1803, who had run the country unchallenged since the seventeenth century, except that the English lay peerage, the upper crust of this class, had increased from 174 in 1760 to 287 in 1803.[6] This class ranged from a few dukes (who owned estates as large as 50,000 acres bringing them a rental income of as many pounds)[7] to typical landed gentlemen with estates of 1,000 to 3,000 acres. Although the more rustic squires had little to do with the great nobles, there were no fixed social barriers within this landed class of "gentle blood" who lived on the incomes from their estates, most of which were rented to substantial tenant farmers. The latter, along with freeholders of yeoman stock, who owned their own land, formed the rural middle class.[8] Much of the farmer's gross income went in rent to the landlord, who was in turn responsible for capital improvements. In contrast to the poor Irish tenants, English farmers were a prosperous class. They employed servants, who lived in the farmhouse, and landless agricultural laborers, who generally lived in mean cottages with no more than a garden patch to tend in their spare time.

In accordance with the system of primogeniture, the estates of the English landed aristocracy were passed on intact to eldest sons, although the head of a family always had some responsibility for providing for the maintenance of its other members. Younger sons looked mainly to the professions—the church, the army and navy, the law, and government service at home and abroad—

[6] See Harold Perkins, *The Origins of Modern English Society 1780–1880* (London: Routledge & Kegan Paul, 1969), p. 20, quoting Patrick Colquhoun, *A Treatise on Indigence* (1806). There were five ranks in the peerage: duke, marquess, earl, viscount, and baron. All English male peers had a hereditary right to a seat in the House of Lords on coming of age. Sixteen Scottish and 28 Irish peers were elected to sit in the House of Lords. Irish peers not so elected were eligible for election to the House of Commons.

[7] Prior to 1931, when Britain went off the gold standard, the £ sterling was worth $4.82, but in the nineteenth century the purchasing power of this amount was of course very much greater. Obviously, it is difficult to compare the value of money between different periods of time in which great changes in the standard of living have occurred.

[8] According to Patrick Colquhoun, a contemporary demographer, there were 160,000 freeholders in 1803 and another 160,000 tenant farmers, but many of the freeholders rented additional land and so themselves became tenants.

but many younger sons of the lesser gentry must have gone into business or emigrated. The professions were one of the bridges between the middle and upper classes, for with the possible exception of the army they were open also to the better-educated sons of the middle class; more than one famous Lord Chancellor, the top office in the legal profession, was a lawyer of obscure origin.

The middle classes were far more numerous and spanned a wider scale of gradations than the nobility and gentry, who socially outranked them; the urban middle class, in particular, were much less homogeneous than their country cousins. They ranged from the great merchants and bankers of London and Liverpool, the owners of the larger textile mills of Manchester and Leeds, and the ironmasters of South Wales and the Midlands to the shopkeepers and publicans in provincial towns. The small tradesmen was as far removed from the wealthy factory owner as the small squire from the great duke, but again there were no fixed social barriers that could not be mounted by an ambitious, successful man, and many of the great captains of industry or their fathers had modest beginnings. The line between the wealthy middle classes and the gentry might be crossed in the course of a generation, either by marriage or education, or by a change in the family's way of life. The elder Peel, a cotton manufacturer, and the elder Gladstone, a merchant and plantation owner, were two of the richest men in the country early in the nineteenth century; yet they were never completely assimilated, although both became owners of large landed estates, were elected to parliament, and were raised to the rank of baronet. Their sons, however, who were educated at Eton and Oxford with the sons of the nobility, who entered parliament immediately after graduating, who married into the landed classes and lived on their own estates, and who never participated in their fathers' businesses, were accepted with little question. Thus, ever recruiting from below, the English ruling class maintained its vitality.

The great majority of people in town and country belonged to the working class, but within it the range of gradations was considerable. The more successful master artisans in some of the older skilled trades—such as Francis Place, the tailor, and William Lovett, the cabinetmaker—were closer in standard of living to the lower middle classes than to the mass of workers whose cause they espoused.[9] There were also numerous skilled workmen in various industries, such as wheelwrights, shipwrights, cutlers, leather dressers and brass founders, to name a few, while the engineers who built the machines, the canals, the roads, and the bridges emerged as a new profession. Many trades, however, lost stability and security as new methods or new markets undermined one calling and created openings in another. In the late eighteenth

[9] For Place and Lovett see pp. 19 and 52.

century few artisans were better off than the handloom weavers, but in the early nineteenth century they became one of the poorest and most depressed groups of all industrial workers.

The data regarding the standard of living of the working classes at this time are as complex and as inconclusive as those regarding the increase in population. Some groups undoubtedly suffered a loss while others appeared to win at least temporary material gains, but the Industrial Revolution accentuated the ups and downs of the business cycle, thus adding the threat of frequent unemployment to a working class with no reserves to tide them over periods of depression. We may also note the depressive psychological effect, especially for those of rural background, of living in drab and confined quarters in large industrial towns, which offered little or nothing in the way of amenities. During the war years the per capita consumption among the working classes of wheat bread, meat, and beer probably declined, as did their share of the national product, in comparison with the landed and professional classes.

It must be admitted that the life of the majority of those in the working classes throughout the first half of the nineteenth century was, by any civilized standards, bleak and often painful. Below the skilled artisans, or "aristocracy of labor," as they are called, there was such a diversity of occupations and conditions that it is difficult to generalize about them. Descriptions of the lot of the working people are equally varied, depending on many factors, including where they lived and whether times were good or bad or their employers brutal or humane. According to the Factory Commission Report of 1833, the average work day in Coventry and Birmingham was only nine or ten hours, but in Leicester, Nottingham, and Manchester it was twelve hours. Some factories worked a fourteen-hour day, and there are stories of children having to get up before five in the morning to reach the factory on time. The state of the old, small mills was starkly described in the same report: "dirty; low-roofed; ill-ventilated; ill-drained; no conveniences for washing or dressing; no contrivance for carrying off dust or other effluvia; machinery not boxed in . . ." Women and children comprised a large proportion of the factory operatives, and it was the ill-treatment of children that most shocked contemporaries when the horrors of the industrial system were finally revealed before government commissions in the thirties and forties. Many children, forced to work such long hours and often treated brutally by those whom they were assigned to help, suffered permanent injury.

The economic unit tended to be the family. In good times the combined family income might be quite sufficient to meet the necessities of life, but after such long hours of labor there was little time for leisure. Accidents and illness, all too frequent, could spell disaster in homes where they struck; and when trade was bad, widespread unemployment brought hunger and destitution to many. Factory hands and miners often had to take part of their pay in food from the employer's "truck shop" at his prices. In bad times those who dealt with the local shopkeeper often ran into debt, from which it was difficult to extricate themselves. Until there was effective government regulation, much later in the century, the poor also suffered seriously from the adulteration of food and beverages by unscrupulous shopkeepers. Some of the workingman's troubles were of his own making, and drunkenness remained a serious social problem throughout the nineteenth century.

Housing conditions varied greatly. Some employers provided four-room houses at reasonable rents, but in the larger industrial towns housing conditions were generally horrendous. In both Liverpool and Manchester it was reported that between forty and fifty thousand people were living in cellars without adequate drainage. Whole rows of jerry-built houses lacking proper ventilation were put up back to back. Indoor plumbing was unknown and chamber pots were often emptied into the streets, which were unpaved and unlighted. To many twentieth-century minds, the unsanitary conditions in which the mass of the population lived until the latter half of the nineteenth century are beyond comprehension. Cholera, in particular, was the great ravager even into the 1840s. Agricultural laborers, who were still the largest single group in the work force, might have had better-situated and more picturesque cottages than those of the factory operatives, but inside their cottages it was apt to be just as dank, cold, and crowded. Agricultural laborers were paid lower wages, existed at an even lower standard of living, and, since most were employed on an annual basis, were by no means protected against unemployment. Some of them also had to walk long distances to their work, because of the reluctance of some landlords to have more than a minimum of cottages on their estates.

There had been little change in the English form of government in over a century. It was nominally monarchical but essentially oligarchic, as it had been since the Revolution settlement of the seventeenth century. The ministers governed, but they could not ignore the prejudices of the king or the demands of Parliament. They performed every executive act in the king's name and could only legislate and raise taxes through the agency of Parliament. If the king was young and active, as George III had been half a century earlier, his views on high policy had to be respected. In 1815, however, he was an old man and had long been mentally ill; the prince regent, who would in 1820 become George IV was indolent and essentially a negative force in the machinery of government. The ministers came mostly from the small ruling class of landowners and were themselves members of the House of

Lords or the House of Commons. They were chosen partly because of their acceptability to Parliament and partly because of their power to control it, although this power had been reduced as a result of economic and administrative reforms first begun in the late eighteenth century and continued by Lord Liverpool, prime minister from 1812 to 1827. In 1815 there were no longer enough placemen left in the House of Commons to ensure support of the Government. Many of the country gentlemen were highly independent in their attitude, supporting the Government only when they wanted to, so Liverpool was constantly dependent on a floating majority. He was a past master at courting and conciliating various groups or factions, such as the Grenvillites and the Canningites, by appointing their leaders to coveted offices. But the basic reason for the Government ministers' long stay in office, according to W. R. Brock, was that "to a majority of members the continuance of the Tory Government was of the first importance."[1]

With the exception of the short-lived Coalition Ministry of 1805-6, the party of the younger Pitt had been in office since 1783 and would remain there until 1830. Pitt had not acknowledged the designation Tory and indeed disliked the concept of party. His disciples were nevertheless now generally known as Tories, accepting the name that, for the greater part of the eighteenth century, had been suspect because of the Jacobite associations of an earlier age. The name Tory was also used to describe the party in power in those years because Fox and his followers, heirs of the Rockinghamites, had appropriated the name of Whig and claimed they were the defenders and exponents of true Whig principles. Moreover, in the days of the French Revolution Pitt's party was very clearly the party of church and king, so Tory became a natural appellation. Party lines were still indistinct and party discipline loose, but Government and Opposition both had their whips, and both on occasion summoned party meetings. There remained, however, some independent country gentlemen, sixty-eight according to one estimate, who were potential but unreliable Government supporters.

The great majority of the 658 members of the House of Commons, both Whigs and Tories, were landowners or their relatives in the professions, many of them closely connected with the nobility. There were, however, close to a hundred members representing the "commercial" interest (banking, commerce, and manufacture), not including landowners with business interests such as coal mines. Many of these businessmen were the owners of "rotten" or "pocket" boroughs—parliamentary boroughs with so few voters that the owner controlled the elections, taking, if he wished, a seat in parliament for himself.

The division between Tory and Whig, Government and Opposition,

[1] *Lord Liverpool and Liberal Toryism* (1941), p. 101.

therefore, was not in terms of economic interests, since most members of Parliament came from the same class. The Tories were essentially concerned with preserving the status quo in church and state, that is, with preserving the privileges of the landed and commercial interests against the egalitarian ideas of the French Revolution, and those of the established Anglican Church against the threats of Roman Catholics, Dissenters, and freethinkers. Consequently, they favored protective Corn Laws and were opposed to parliamentary reform and, most of them, to Catholic emancipation.

The Whigs, being in opposition, could afford to take a larger view of things. Since the 1790s they had paid at least lip service to parliamentary reform, and since the Irish Union they had been strong champions of Catholic emancipation in the spirit of their tradition of religious liberty. They also had a good record, during the darkest days of political repression in the nineties, for defending the freeborn Englishman's right to free speech. Except, however, for a small group of left-wing radicals known as the Mountain, the Whigs were aristocratic in outlook, lacking the fervor to crusade for the causes they nominally espoused. Their leader, Lord Grey, in his youth had been a spokesman of the advanced Friends of the People; but for years, since ascending to the House of Lords, he had withdrawn from active politics and had left the Whigs largely to their own devices. In 1815 they had no more than 130 members in the House of Commons. They were looked upon as indolent and unpatriotic by the Tories and with suspicion by the more advanced middle- and working-class radicals, as yet mostly outside the House.

The truth was that the House of Commons had long ceased to be a representative body. It was ridden with anomalies crying out for reform, but the French Revolution had frightened the dominant landed classes, who refused to do anything to upset the status quo. Many new towns were without any representation and many old ones were run by closed corporations that excluded the mass of the population. Some places no longer having any population at all continued sending two members to Parliament, which meant, as we have seen, that the members were the nominees of the local landowner. Indeed, there were 148 English boroughs, almost all returning two members each, where the number of voters was so few that the seats were controlled by the so-called borough owners, who owned most of the property to which the franchise was attached. The advanced working-class radicals demanded "manhood" (i.e., male) suffrage, but most of the middle classes would have been content with some extension of the franchise and a redistribution of seats giving proper representation to the industrial towns and London.

Elie Halévy, the celebrated French historian of nineteenth-century England, maintains that, despite an oligarchic system of government and years of

THE BLESSINGS OF PEACE OR THE CURSE OF THE CORN BILL.

Illustrated by George Cruikshank, English caricaturist and painter of the nineteenth century From Drawn and Quartered, published by Times Newspapers Ltd., 1970.

political repression, England in 1815 was essentially a free country. This seems a paradoxical statement, but the people actually had a number of significant rights. They had the right to petition Parliament, and the constant use of this privilege had helped to persuade that conservative body to abolish the slave trade in 1809. Already for some years the indefatigable Major Cartwright had been traveling around the country collecting petitions for the reform of Parliament itself. The right to hold public meetings, often used for launching parliamentary petitions, was another traditional freedom. This practice had been severely curtailed during the war, but it was now revived on a larger scale than ever. Although the franchise in most constituencies was limited, the first stage of voting took place at open meetings addressed by the candidates. Many who were not entitled to vote attended, expressing their views in their reception of the candidates and in the initial show of hands. To visitors from more autocratically governed European countries, English elections may have seemed to contain the elements of a riot, and Halévy points out that even the right to riot was a part of England's tradition, based on the seventeenth-century belief in the ultimate right of rebellion among a free people. Of course, the governing class did not encourage such views, but their power to control the boisterous mob was limited by lack of an effective police force and the people's hatred of standing armies. The Gordon riots in the 1780s were the worst of such outbreaks. Generally the authorities took the view that the wisest policy was to ride out the storm, although the revolutionary events in France and the great growth of the size of the British army during the long period of war inclined them for a time to meet threats of riot with force.

The English system of government was antiquated. The main concern of the central administration was the maintenance of the army and navy and of the judicial system, the conduct of foreign relations, the provision of a rudimentary postal system, and the collection of revenues. The majority of the civil service were employed in the collection of customs and excise taxes, the main source of revenue. Those in power at this time were reactionary, but the government was not effectively despotic, since its powers were so limited. Britain lacked the bureaucracy essential to the Continental type of despotism, in which the state could attempt any sort of close supervision of the lives of the people. The weakness of the government was accentuated by the division of its power with the local authorities, but this was an amicable arrangement, since the same classes provided leadership in the provinces as at Westminster. The country was ruled by a landowning aristocracy, the majority of whom were more at home on their estates than in the capital. Each county had its Lord Lieutenant—usually a peer and one of the largest landowners in the county—who normally held office for life, although

in those grimmer parts of England and Wales where the church of England was scarcely known. Although the total active adult Methodist membership was only about 200,000, it provided a leaven that undoubtedly influenced the society of that and later generations.

The success of the Methodists lay in the combination of religious enthusiasm (sometimes carried to unfortunate extremes) and efficient organization. Their influence was spread beyond their own ranks by the activities of individual members in their communities and also by the stimulus the movement provided for the older dissenting sects, and eventually reached even to the established church. The Baptists and Congregationalists borrowed from the Methodists forms of organization and adopted the revivalist approach that had made Methodism so effective in gaining converts. Even more significant, perhaps, was the evangelical revival within the Church of England, for not all the Anglican clergy inspired by revivalist fervor left the establishment. Initially there was much opposition to Methodism from the dominant Erastian High Church party that had long dominated the bench of bishops. By the end of the eighteenth century, however, the evangelicals had become a powerful reforming force within the establishment, supported by a large and devout lay body drawn from the middle and part of the upper classes. Such statesmen as Wilberforce and some ministers in Liverpool's Cabinet even brought the evangelical outlook to the topmost ranks of church and state.

By the early nineteenth century religion was probably a more vital force in English life than at any time since the Puritan revolution. Yet by now English society was essentially pluralistic, and other forces besides religion helped mold its character and beliefs. In the area of economic thought the ideas of Adam Smith (1723–90) and his many disciples of the classical school of political economy had largely undermined the old mercantilist doctrine and were preparing the way for acceptance of the free trade policy that would characterize the Victorian era. In the view of the classical economists, economic activity was properly governed by the laws of supply and demand. Consequently, they developed their famous doctrine of laissez-faire deprecating state intervention in this sphere for purely economic reasons[2]. Lord Liverpool, the prime minister, William Huskisson, President of the Board of Trade in the 1820s, and several of their colleagues accepted much of Adam Smith's philosophy. They began the long process of shaking off the bonds of mercantilism, but the Corn Law of 1815 still provided complete protection of British agriculture.

[2] Lord Robbins in *The Theory of Economic Policy in English Classical Political Economy* (New York: St. Martin's Press, 1952), argues that the doctrinaire aspects of the laissez-faire principle have been exaggerated.

Related to the classical economists were the Benthamites, disciples of Jeremy Bentham (1748–1832), who accepted most of the economic ideas of the former school but went beyond them in their sweeping approach to social institutions. They were known as Utilitarians, because utility was their measuring rod in all their moral judgments of laws, customs, and institutions. Their overall objective was the greatest happiness for the greatest number of people. Adam Smith identified as the Deity's the unseen hand directing the laws of supply and demand, but Bentham and most of his followers were rationalists and freethinkers. Bentham's views were zealously propagated by James Mill (1773–1836) and other admirers (including, in the next generation, John Stuart Mill), initially in the pages of the *Edinburgh Review* and later, more completely, in those of the *Westminster Review*. The latter was a radical Benthamite organ set up in 1824 to confront the old aristocratic periodicals, the Tory *Quarterly* and the Whig *Edinburgh Review*. In the generation that followed 1815 Bentham, as interpreted by his disciples, was the main inspiration of the middle-class Radicals, who were beginning to gain a foothold in Parliament as the gadfly left wing of the Whig-Liberal party. As we shall see, the reform of the law and of institutions—including Parliament—that took place in the next quarter-century owed much to the prodding of the Benthamites, whose influence extended far beyond their own ranks, but who perhaps reflected the temper of the time as much as they molded it.

Utilitarianism was by no means, however, the only intellectual force in the England of 1815. Paradoxically, this was also the age of Romanticism. Sir Walter Scott (1771–1832), the most popular novelist and poet of the day, had stirred new interest in the Middle Ages (long discredited as Catholic and barbarous by a Protestant country), thereby helping to inaugurate the Neo-Gothic revival. William Wordsworth (1770–1850) and Samuel Taylor Coleridge (1772–1834) had quickly lost the revolutionary ardor of their youth; but Coleridge, influenced by Hegel and the German philosophers, had offered to more enlightened Tories a social philosophy of noblesse oblige that rejected the harsher aspect of the utilitarian creed. This led John Stuart Mill (1806–73), the foremost Benthamite philosopher of the next generation, to modify considerably the doctrinaire ideas of his father. The second generation of Romantic poets, Shelley and Byron, presented a more radical critique of contemporary society, but Byron's fervent desire to revive the glories of ancient Greece in a new Greek national state represented an element in nineteenth-century English liberalism differing sharply from that of the sober, calculating Benthamites.

Finally, what of the working classes? What attraction did these conflicting ideas have for them—or were they developing a political and social philosophy of their own? The Methodists, as we have seen, made many converts within this section of the population, but the leaders of Methodism, Wesley and his eventual successor, Jabez Bunting (1779–1858), were extremely conservative in their political outlook and unwilling to see their religious revolution extended to the political and social sphere. Nevertheless, many of their followers did just this; with them the moral fervor inspiring their spiritual lives understandably turned their thoughts and energies to social justice. Thus, among working-class leaders of early nineteenth-century England we find some with the religious zeal of Methodism and the older dissenting sects rubbing shoulders with others raised in the freethinking Jacobin tradition of the 1790s. The working classes were still concerned mainly with political rights and the remedying of social and economic grievances. Richard Carlisle (1790–1843), an outspoken champion of working-class causes and of the battle for freedom of the press, was more an anarchist than a socialist; but some socialist ideas are to be found in the writings of Thomas Spence (1750–1814), a disciple of Tom Paine's, who went further than his mentor in attacking the principle of private property; his followers were the most militant working-class radicals in the years after Waterloo.

At the opposite extreme was Francis Place (1771–1854), often regarded as the most influential spokesman for the working classes of this time. As a journeyman tailor in the late eighteenth century, Place had endured suffering and privation and had been active in the London Corresponding Society in the 1790s. Later, having prospered as a master tailor, he became associated with the middle-class Benthamite Radicals, whose views he generally accepted. As an active member of the Westminster election committee he helped to secure the election to Parliament of such Radicals as Sir Francis Burdett. In 1824 he was to play an important role in the legalization of trade unions by the repeal of the hated Combination Laws. Yet trade union leaders and other ardent working-class spokesmen suspected Place's doctrinaire economic views, his readiness to collaborate with the middle classes, and his preference for pulling wires behind the scenes rather than making emotional public appeals.

More typical, perhaps, of working-class militancy in those somber days were the nameless men in the army of "King Ludd," the legendary machine breaker, who roamed the northern and midland counties at night, breaking up the hated new knitting frames in Nottinghamshire and larger machinery in factories of uncooperative owners in Lancashire and Yorkshire. Once explained as an irrational reaction to hunger and hardship, Luddism has recently been interpreted as a valiant, if hopeless, effort to resist the new business philosophy of laissez-faire and to maintain the old paternalism of the statute of artificers (an Elizabethan labor code). "What was at issue," according to E. P. Thompson, "was the 'freedom' of the capitalist to destroy the customs of the trade, whether by new machinery, by the factory system, or by unrestricted competition, beating down wages, undercutting his rivals, and undermining standards of craftsmanship."[3]

Among those commanding large working-class audiences in these times, the most popular were three men of middle- or upper-class origin who had thrown in their lot with the masses. William Cobbett (1763–1833), a stout English patriot of yeoman stock and something of a Tory romantic, was opposed equally to Jacobinism in France and to the Industrial Revolution in England. After serving in the army, he established himself as a bookseller and journalist in England and, for some years, in the United States. Soon after his return to England, where in 1802 he started his famous paper, the *Political Register*, he became disillusioned by the corruptness of the existing social and political system; he came out as an ardent champion of reform and the restitution to the people of their rights and a way of life that they had supposedly lost. Except for the brief period from 1817 to 1819, when, fearing arrest, he fled the country, Cobbett spent the rest of his life propagating these ideas in the press and on the platform. He was extremely self-centered and often outrageous in what he said and wrote about other people, but his style was always colorful and his sentiments warm-hearted. No journalist was more widely read or beloved by the masses.

Henry Hunt (1773–1835) was a well-to-do gentleman farmer by origin. He was a handsome man with a powerful voice and a marvelous platform presence that made him the greatest popular orator of his day. He was very vain and lacked the solid qualities of a successful political leader. But in his unrelenting demands for parliamentary reform in many speeches to vast audiences all over the country, he awakened a sense of political awareness in the masses and aroused public opinion to the point where it could no longer be ignored. Cobbett and Hunt were both demagogues with many personal failings, and neither was qualified to provide constructive leadership. Yet in a period of reaction and repression Cobbett and Hunt both helped in their different ways to voice the woes of the inarticulate masses and to stir in them a political consciousness that might otherwise have grown more slowly or taken a less fortunate direction. They occupied the middle ground between the extremism of Spence on the left and the middle-class radicalism of Place on the right.

Robert Owen (1771–1858) was unique among Radical reformers of this period. He was a successful businessman whose "model" mills and planned community at New Lanark, outside Glasgow, attracted visitors from all over the country and abroad. Owen was convinced that the happiness of mankind could be achieved if those in authority would only improve the environment in which men worked and lived. He developed this theory in

[3] *The Making of the English Working Class*, p. 549.

his *New View of Society*, published in 1813. It was only after his proposals were ignored by fellow industrialists and cautious ministers that he turned his back on the upper classes and devoted the rest of his life to utopian schemes for the betterment of working-class conditions. These included an experimental colony at New Harmony, Indiana (1824–9), an experiment in equitable labor exchanges (1832–3), and an attempt to unite all the trade unionists in a Grand National Consolidated Trades Union (1834). All Owen's projects after New Lanark ended in failure, but today British Socialists and the flourishing British cooperative movement regard him and his followers as pioneers in a new social tradition.

England in 1815 was a land of contrasts. To the world and her own ruling class she was wealthy and powerful, the center of a great empire that straddled the globe and that promised even greater expansion. Perceptive observers, however, recognized in her social and political problems that could gnaw the nation like a cancer or, perhaps, that would lead to an explosive revolution. The history of England during the next century would consist largely of a gradual (though incomplete) amelioration of these unhappy conditions. It would bring no millenium, but it would avert the worst dangers that might have arisen.

Chapter Two
REACTION AND REFORM

It is easy to condemn the government of Lord Liverpool for its reactionary record in the years immediately following Waterloo and the end of the Napoleonic Wars; but historical figures and institutions must be judged relative to their times. Although Lord Liverpool's ministry was undistinguished, it lasted twice as long as the six preceding ministries, which had rapidly succeeded each other in the first eleven years of the century. Moreover, its members showed a capacity for working together under an able, if colorless leader. It was this ministry that won the generation-long war against France and Napoleon and through its foreign secretary, Lord Castlereagh, played a large part in shaping the peace settlement which would remain largely intact for half a century.

Lord Liverpool (1770–1827) was the son of Charles Jenkinson the first earl, one of the younger Pitt's most trusted colleagues. He had been brought up by his father in the Pitt tradition. He was lacking in social graces, but as a member of all Tory ministries since 1793 had proved to be an honest, conscientious, and hard-working administrator, a disciple of the new political economy and a good colleague who inspired the respect of his associates. Although not a hidebound reactionary, he was naturally conservative, disposed to administrative and economic reform, but too ready to give in to pressures from more reactionary colleagues. In the popular view, one of the worst of these was Lord Castlereagh (1769–1822), an Irish peer, who, as Government leader in the House of Commons, bore the brunt of public hostility after 1815. Actually, Castlereagh was less reactionary than some of his associates. His conduct of foreign affairs was enlightened, and, as an old disciple of Pitt's, he always supported the policy of Catholic emancipation. But he was an ineffective speaker in the Commons, and he made no effort to conciliate public opinion in defending the Government's policies. The real reactionaries in the Cabinet, whose opinions guided the Government's repressive domestic policy, were two older men, Lords Sidmouth and Eldon. Henry Addington (1757–1844), first Viscount Sidmouth, came from much the same social background as Liverpool and Castlereagh, although his father was a doctor. He had been a close friend of Pitt's and speaker of the House of Commons (1789–1801), but he was a failure as prime minister (1801–4). He was instinctively opposed to reforms implying changes and, as Home Secretary, most involved in carrying out the Government's policy of political repression. John Scott (1751–1838), first Earl Eldon, was the son of a Newcastle coal dealer. When a young man he had eloped with an heiress and then quickly risen to the top of the legal profession by his wits. Though the law was his whole life (he was Lord Chancellor for twenty-six years), he left his court encumbered with great quantities of unfinished business. This occurred because he persisted in raising the ultra-Tory objection to any change in things that he regarded as sacrosanct. Little in the way of domestic reform or sympathetic appraisal of the social problems that faced the country could be expected of a Cabinet dominated by such men as these.

In Castlereagh's eyes, and probably in those of his colleagues, the most immediate problems in 1815 were in foreign affairs, and here the Government's record was best. Castlereagh was one of Britain's great foreign secretaries. Although his was an extension of the policy of Pitt, whom he regarded as his mentor, he showed greater expertise in conducting it and was on the whole more successful. He had been one of the architects of the grand alliance that had defeated Napoleon, had participated in the negotiation of the peace treaties that followed the war, and had played a leading role at the Congress of Vienna, which met from October 1814 to June 1815. There he came to know intimately the rulers of the various European states and their ministers, especially Emporer Francis I and Count Metternich. His reputation was probably higher in Europe than in England; his policy was naturally one of protecting British interests, but he saw these in a European context. The objectives he sought for Britain were fourfold: the maintenance of the balance of power; the neutrality of the Low Countries (the Netherlands); the preservation of the maritime rights that Britain had long asserted in war; and, in deference to strong feeling on the subject recently developed at home, the abolition of the slave trade. With Napoleon, the chief threat to the balance of power in Europe, removed, the preservation of that balance seemed synonymous with the preservation of peace. If Russia should threaten to upset it, Castlereagh was prepared to stand up to the Czar. He saw the settlement as a means of preserving peace through a just equilibrium and was unmoved by the national pretentions of the Serbs, Italians, Belgians, or Norwegians, although he did make some limited pleas for the Poles. The Czar got his way pretty well in Poland, but Prussia was conciliated by acquisitions in

Germany, and Austria by the maintenance of her position in Italy. In the second Treaty of Paris, France was pushed back from the Rhine and required to pay an indemnity and suffer an army of occupation; but on all these points Castlereagh was a moderating influence, anxious that France should be left with no legitimate grievances. To this end, he and Wellington saw to the withdrawal of the army of occupation within three years. It was Castlereagh, also, who successfully urged the restoration of the Bourbons on the basis of a constitutional monarchy and who welcomed France back into the Concert of Europe.

British objectives in the Low Countries were secured, at least for the time being, by the unwise transfer of the Austrian Netherlands (Belgium) to the Dutch kingdom, with guarantees for the Belgian minority. The question of maritime rights, on which the European powers differed from Britain, was excluded from the conference agenda, but Castlereagh succeeded in getting token assent to abolition of the slave trade, which was to be effected gradually by direct treaties. As the only naval power among the allies, Britain had acquired most of the overseas possessions of France and Holland during the war. Her main objectives in Europe attained, Britain could afford to be magnanimous in returning many of these, but she retained the Cape of Good Hope in South Africa; Trinidad, St. Lucia, and Tobago in the Carribean; Mauritius in the Indian Ocean; Malta in the Mediterranean; and Heligoland in the North Sea, as well as a temporary protectorate over the Ionian Islands in the Aegean.

The project on which Castlereagh personally set the greatest value (and in which one detects a sense of mission on the part of this otherwise cold and detached diplomat), was the extension by formal treaty in November 1815 of the quadruple alliance that had defeated Napoleon. This was a means of enforcing the peace terms imposed on France. His special contribution to the treaty was the agreement that the four powers would meet at fixed periods to consult upon their common interests and to consider measures for the maintenance of the peace of Europe. His Cabinet colleagues were not enthusiastic, and the congress system was short-lived, but historians have seen in it the germ of the idea that became the League of Nations in 1920 and the United Nations in 1945.

Castlereagh dismissed Czar Alexander's proposals for a Holy Alliance as "a piece of sublime mysticism and nonsense," but he persevered, although with growing despondency, in supporting the congress system, to which France was soon admitted. Five conferences were held between 1818 and 1822, but at each it became more apparent that Britain had little in common with the autocratic governments of the Eastern powers. Russia, Prussia, and Austria wanted the alliance as an instrument for intervening in the internal affairs of lesser states, such as Naples, Spain, and Portugal, who were faced with popular constitutional movements. Castlereagh resolutely refused to commit Britain to such proposals, which, he said, were incompatible with international law and "directly opposed to the political and constitutional system of Great Britain." As he told the House of Commons, "... the House of Hanover could not well maintain the principles upon which the House of Stuart forfeited the throne." The failure of the congress system was probably a factor in the mental breakdown, on the eve of the Conference of Verona in 1822, which ended in his suicide.

Castlereagh's funeral procession was greeted by jeers and hoots from onlookers outside Westminster Abbey, where he was buried, and by biting obituaries in Radical papers. This reaction was as much the result of general bitterness over the repressive domestic policies of the government he represented as the unfair identification of him with European despots. Undoubtedly, the Liverpool administration was faced with formidable problems at home. Agricultural prices began to collapse at the end of the war and then to skyrocket due to crop failures in 1816. Merchants failed to find the markets they had expected to be open to them after the removal of Napoleon. Thousands of disbanded soldiers and sailors flooded an unstable employment market. No government of that day would have been capable of solving such problems, but the Tory administration made the situation worse in its legislation and administration by acting from class-conscious motives and showing no sympathy for the suffering masses. Upper-class fears and prejudices were quickly catered to by the passing of the Corn Law of 1815, which excluded the import of foreign cereals until prices became inordinately high. This was followed by the Government's surrender to the House of Commons in abolishing the wartime income tax, leaving a heavy burden of indirect taxation on the poor. Early nineteenth-century radicals had failed to anticipate this possibility in their fierce opposition to the income tax, which seemed to them to encourage government expenditure. More controversial among the ruling classes was the return to specie (gold) payments, which was finally affected by Peel's Currency Act of 1819. In this instance the Government listened to the advice of economists rather than to the prejudice of those landowners who feared the effect of deflation on agricultural prices.

The period 1812-20 was one of prolonged social tension almost unparalleled in English history. There was acute suffering among the people and an alienation between governors and governed that boded ill for the future. As we have noted, even before the war was over the Luddites, in 1811 and 1812, had attempted the systematic destruction of machines and factories in some northern and midland counties. In 1816 unemployment and high food prices brought nationwide rioting and severe repression. The demand for a radical reform of Parliament that would displace the existing oligarchy was promoted anew by the three demagogues—Cobbett in his *Political Register*, Hunt on the public platform, and Cartwright in the Hampden clubs he founded zealously in the provincial towns. In November 1816, Hunt addressed a giant meeting held at the Spa Fields in the environs of London. Part of the crowd attending a second meeting in December was diverted by a few revolutionary Spencean extremists; they looted a gunsmith's shop, killing the owner, and marched into the City,[1] ostensibly to attack the Tower of London; but by nightfall they were dispersed. The leaders were arrested and charged with high treason, only to be acquitted the following year by juries shocked at stories of the Government's use of spies as *provocateurs*.

In January 1817, a convention of Hampden clubs was held in London to demand manhood suffrage. The meeting was inconclusive and revealed splits among the reformers, but a national convention of this sort reflected the widespread dissatisfaction with the existing state of affairs. Sidmouth acted by planting spies among the agitators and issuing instructions to local authorities, but the Government hesitated to initiate unpopular legislation until the attack on the coach of the prince regent gave them a pretext. Most of the repressive legislation of the 1790s had lapsed, but now some of it was revived. It included an act suspending habeas corpus for six months (later extended to a year) and the Seditious Meetings Act, placing stringent restrictions on public meetings. The London agitators were temporarily muted, but in the meantime trouble was brewing in the provinces.

In March the half-starved weavers of Lancashire organized a hunger march on London, known as the March of the Blanketeers, since each participant was armed only with a blanket. All these wretched men wanted was relief from privation, but, alarmed by stories of armed insurrection, the authorities dispersed the marchers before they had proceeded very far. More serious was the so-called Pentridge Revolution of June of the same year. There is evidence that a fairly large subversive organization had spread through Lancashire, Yorkshire, and the Midlands. This group looked to London for leadership, which was provided mainly by Oliver, a notorious government spy. A rising was premeditated for June 9, but on the 6th a meeting of Yorkshire leaders was surprised by the authorities. Oliver was allowed to escape, and almost immediately the *Leeds Mercury* made journalistic history by revealing the story of his machinations. The rising was abandoned everywhere except in Derbyshire, where the local captain, Jeramiah Brandeth, gathered three hundred men at Pentridge to march on Nottingham. They were quickly rounded up by a company of Hussars, but not before one man

[1] The City of London was an administrative enclave in the heart of Greater London.

had been killed. Brandeth and two others were tried and executed and thirteen others sentenced to transportation. But the Government's use of *provocateurs* had angered the public, and prosecutions elsewhere failed or were not pressed. In the latter half of the year, improved economic conditions and a good harvest that lowered the price of bread helped bring about a temporary calm.

The failure of the Pentridge rising and the popular sympathy created by the spy revelations directed the working-class movement back along constitutional lines, although it kept itself distinct from middle-class radicalism. The latter, while attacking the privileges of the aristocracy, was more concerned with reduction of taxes and abolition of the Corn Laws and was more moderate in its approach to parliamentary reform. Nevertheless, in 1818 Bentham came out in favor of universal suffrage, and in 1819 there were signs of reconciliation between working-class reformers and the more progressive manufacturers in Lancashire and Yorkshire. Meetings were held in the north demanding parliamentary reform and the repeal of the Corn Laws, and in July a huge assembly in Birmingham protested that city's lack of representation in Parliament by electing the Radical Sir Charles Wolesley as its "Legislatorial Attorney and Representative." Wolesley's arrest deterred other unrepresented cities from following suit; instead, a mass demonstration for parliamentary reform was planned for August 16 at St. Peter's Fields, outside Manchester. To ensure order, contingents from the surrounding country were drilled, and on the fateful day 60,000 or more marched onto the field, with alarmingly good discipline, to hear Orator Hunt address them. The local authorities, sure of support from the Home Office, called in the military, both the regulars and the yeomanry (mounted militia). When Hunt arrived the magistrates ordered his arrest and instructed the yeomanry to clear the field. This was done in the most callous and inept way with a quite unnecessary loss of life. Within minutes the peaceful, well-dressed multitude was turned into a terrified rabble, frantically seeking an escape from horses' hoofs, soldiers' sabers, and the terrible press of numbers. Eleven people were killed or mortally wounded, and hundreds more were injured. Characteristically the Government supported the action of the local authorities, but large numbers of moderates and liberals throughout the country were shocked at what was soon called the "massacre of Peterloo." This wave of sympathy may well have helped to prevent the aggrieved working classes from taking the road to revolution. Peterloo was undoubtedly a stepping-stone toward the Great Reform Act of 1832. The Government's immediate response, however, was more repression in the form of the notorious Six Acts, which further restricted public meetings and freedom of the press, forbade military drilling, and provided for seizure of arms. The Government also took an unusual step in dismissing Lord Fitzwilliam, the Whig Lord Lieutenant of Yorkshire, for chairing a public meeting denouncing the brutality of the troops at Manchester.

The final act in this turbulent second decade of the century had the character of farce that might have turned into tragedy. Early in 1820 a small group of Spenceans, the Spa Field ringleaders, who in 1817 had escaped a charge of high treason, plotted in a Cato Street hideout to free the country from tyranny by murdering the entire Cabinet when they assembled to dine. Unfortunately for the plotters, a spy in their midst, after helping to promote the plot, revealed all. Thistlewood and four of his associates suffered for their foolhardiness on the gallows, and the remaining five were transported. Their action had aroused only revulsion, and for the next decade reformers refused to consider the use of force.

For a variety of reasons the social and political climate gradually began to change in the third decade of the century. The accession of George IV (1762–1830) to the throne in 1820 could not have been the cause, since he had warmed no hearts as prince regent during the last ten years of George III's life. He was a selfish, dissipated spendthrift and probably one of England's most unpopular kings, frequently hissed and booed at when he appeared in public. In this age of sharp political satire, Charles Lamb had lampooned him while he was still prince regent:

By his bulk and by his size
By his oily qualities
This (or else my eyesight fails)
This should be the Prince of Whales.

For sponsoring Regency London and, more doubtfully, for sponsoring the Brighton Pavilion, he is credited with some artistic taste. Having inherited most of his father's prejudices but not their corresponding redeeming qualities, he could make life difficult for his ministers; fortunately, his natural indolence left them a reasonable amount of freedom. His reign began with a scandal that was a great embarrassment to the Government, a godsend to the Opposition, and a diversion from the grimmer problems that had faced the country in the preceding twelve months. The new King's wife, the German Princess Caroline, had for years been separated from her husband and living on the Continent in rather dubious company. Now she returned to England to demand recognition as Queen. In the tradition of Henry VIII (but without his winning ways), the King asked his ministers to secure him a divorce through an act of Parliament. Public sympathy for Caroline, enkindled by some Whig politicians, was immediately aroused, and the ministers, in danger of defeat in the House of Commons, were forced to withdraw their bill. The following year the Queen died, but her popularity with the fickle public had already begun to wane.

The gradual evaporation of the worst aspects of postwar reaction was probably due to some temporary economic improvement after 1820 and the replacement of several of the more reactionary ministers by more liberal men, although the pliable Lord Liverpool remained as prime minister for another seven years. George Canning (1770–1827) was a contemporary of Castlereagh, but a lifelong rival and different in many respects. The quarreling of the two had led to Canning's withdrawal from office in 1809. He returned to a minor post in 1816, but was overshadowed by his former enemy until Castlereagh's untimely death gave him the Foreign Office and the lead in the House of Commons. Like Castlereagh he favored Catholic emancipation and opposed parliamentary reform, but his approach to public affairs was very different. Castlereagh, as we have seen, was respected by his colleagues and by foreign diplomats; but he was a poor speaker and aloof in manner, making no effort to conciliate public opinion either inside or outside the House. On the other hand, Canning, while often offensive to colleagues and abhorred in foreign chancelleries as a "world scourge" (to use Metternich's phrase), was a brilliant orator and courted public approval by the liberal and nationalistic tone of his speeches. The change in foreign policy after Castlereagh's death was not as abrupt as it may have appeared on the surface. Castlereagh had known that his policy of working closely with the autocratic rulers of Russia, Austria, and Prussia had failed before Canning closed the door on the congress system with a bang. Canning opposed, but was unable to prevent, French intervention on behalf of King Ferdinand against the Constitutionalist party in Spain. Britain's main interest was in the former Spanish colonies, with which British trade had increased greatly since the turn of the century. Canning made it clear to the French governments that Britain would not tolerate extension of French intervention to these colonies and received an assurance on this point from the French ambassador in October 1823, two months before the proclamation of America's Monroe Doctrine. The two complementary pronouncements were made separately, although Canning would have preferred united action with the American government. The natural sequel was British recognition of the Spanish American republics, despite the objections of the King and some of the right-wing Tories. "I resolved that if France had Spain," Canning boasted, "it should not be Spain 'with the Indies.' I called the New World in to redress the balance of the Old." In Portugal Canning gave more positive and effective aid to the Constitutionalist party, which was legitimately in office but threatened by Spanish intervention in aid of the Queen's uncle, Dom Miguel.

Canning sent a small British expedition to Portugal, and the pretensions of Dom Miguel and the absolutists were thwarted.

Despite widespread English sympathy for the Greeks, Canning was more cautious about supporting the Greek rebellion against Turkey, which had begun in 1821. In 1827, in the Treaty of London Britain, Russia and France agreed to intervene jointly on behalf of the Greeks, and when the Turks refused their proposals an allied fleet sank the combined Turkish and Egyptian fleets in the Battle of Navarino, a turning point in the Greek war of liberation. Before the battle was fought, however, Canning was dead. Within a few months the direction of British policy had fallen into the more cautious hands of Wellington and Aberdeen. In the end Greek independence was secured by Russian and French rather than British arms, although the conference at which it was finally affirmed was held in London in 1830.

Although Canning was the dominant minister from 1822 to 1827 and indeed was prime minister for a few months in 1827 before following Lord Liverpool to the grave, the real liberalizing of the Government was in the domestic sphere. This was mainly the work of William Huskisson (1770–1830), a protégé of Canning's, who became president of the Board of Trade, and Robert Peel (1788–1850), former Chief Secretary for Ireland, who was Home Secretary from 1822 to 1830, except for a few months in 1827. Huskisson was a firm believer in the political economy of Adam Smith. With the support of Liverpool and of Frederick Robinson (1782–1859) at the Exchequer, he began a great housecleaning. He got rid of many obsolete statutes, reducing customs duties, canceling bounties, modifying the old Navigation Acts, and generally moving in the direction of free trade, a major objective of the classical economists. In the same spirit Peel's Act of 1819 provided for exchange on demand of Bank of England notes for gold. Similarly, in 1824 Joseph Hume (1777–1855), a Radical M.P., with the assistance of Francis Place obtained the repeal of the Combination Acts, restoring the legal position of trade unions (although a second act in 1825 put further restrictions upon them).

The most important reforms of this period were those initiated by Peel in the field of law and penology. These went in the direction of Bentham and his disciples, and on one occasion Peel even consulted the old Utilitarian philosopher, but Peel's approach was pragmatic and not ideological. Such reformers as Sir Samuel Romilly (1757–1818) and Sir James Mackintosh (1765–1832) had for years campaigned against the harshness of English criminal law. In 1823, overcoming Eldon's inevitable objections, Peel obtained passage of acts repealing the death penalty for more than a hundred crimes and giving judges more discretion in imposing sentences. In 1826 he launched a series of measures intended, he said, "to break the sleep of a century" by consolidating the criminal law and eliminating much statutory deadwood. He rejected the Benthamite idea of a complete code, but he did put English law on a new basis by repealing 278 old acts and replacing them with 8 new ones. In 1829, having returned to the Home Office under Wellington, he consolidated the law of forgery, again repealing many archaic statutes. Peel's revisions covered three-quarters of all criminal offenses, and in a few short years he had reduced a mass of archaic legislation to "a handful of intelligible statutes," to quote his modern biographer. "Between the law books of George III and those of William IV," Professor Gash observes, "there was now a great divide."[2]

Along with reforms in criminal law came reforms in prison and police administration. Peel's Gaols Act of 1823, passed over Eldon's opposition, consolidated former legislation, introduced principles of enlightened prison administration, provided for the establishment of jails in all counties and large towns, and regulated their discipline and sanitation. In 1829, after long investigation and research, Peel's Metropolitan Police Act was passed. It was a revolutionary measure, replacing most of the old, inefficient police authorities in the London area with a central authority under two commissioners responsible to the Home Office. The new police comprised a force of some thousand officers and men with headquarters at Scotland Yard, and provision was made to extend the system to provincial cities. Initial suspicion of these "Peelers" (as they were first called) soon gave way to respect, illustrated by the friendlier and more enduring sobriquet of "Bobbies."

The most contentious issue in the fourteen years following the peace of 1815 was that of the Catholic emancipation. It divided the Tory party and gave the Whigs one of the few constructive planks in their program. This may seem strange, since there were so few Catholics in England and none in the House of Commons, but it was the direct result of forcing Ireland into parliamentary union with Britain. Pitt had made a commitment to the Irish Catholics that, if they supported the union, he would bring in legislation granting them seats in Parliament. He had been forestalled by the religious prejudice of George III, but many of his Tory associates felt bound by his commitment. To this moral obligation was added a political motive: The Ireland of Daniel O'Connell (1775–1847) could not be governed unless Irish Catholics, the majority of her population, were given some constitutional recognition.

O'Connell, an accomplished lawyer, was a big man with a splendid voice, boundless energy and great leadership ability. He persuaded the Irish to present their political claims in an orderly and peaceful manner. By calling

---

[2] Norman Gash, *Mr. Secretary Peel: The Life of Sir Robert Peel to 1830* (Cambridge, Mass.: Harvard University Press, 1961), p. 487.

attention to the sizable number of oppressed Catholics while at the same time repudiating violence, he anticipated the methods of Mahatma Ghandi and Martin Luther King in the next century. O'Connell's Catholic Association was organized with the help of the priests in every parish. The organization extracted a "rent" of a penny a week from its mass membership, which produced an income of £1,000 a week and, before long, substantial capital investment. O'Connell soon became the uncrowned king of Ireland and a formidable force to the authorities. Thanks to his legal skill he succeeded in circumventing their efforts to outlaw his association.

Eventually his opponents were faced with an impasse. Even before O'Connell had organized his followers, Protestant champions of emancipation such as the Irishmen Gratton and Plunkett, the Radical Burdett, and Canning himself had introduced into both houses of Parliament bills or motions to give the Catholics the vote. Eight such measures were introduced between 1812 and 1827 and a number, including a bill of Canning's in 1822, passed the Commons only to be defeated in the Lords. Victory might have been expected when Canning became prime minister in 1827, but his premature death intervened, and little could be hoped for from a ministry dominated by Wellington and Peel, both lifelong opponents of emancipation. But this was the hour that O'Connell chose to strike. Although a Catholic, he presented himself in 1828 as a candidate for a by-election in County Clare against the popular Vesey Fitzgerald. His overwhelming victory indicated that in a general election O'Connell's forces would sweep large areas of the country. The Lord Lieutenant, head of the English administration in Ireland, realized it would no longer be possible to govern unless emancipation was adopted. Although personally opposed to the policy, Wellington, now the prime minister, looked at the situation with a soldier's eye and concluded that retreat was necessary. The government's defenses were weakened further by passage of a private bill introduced by the young Whig member, Lord John Russell. The bill repealed the Test and Corporation acts, which had helped to bar Dissenters (non-Anglican Protestants) from sitting in the House of Commons. Peel threatened to resign, for he had long opposed emancipation, partly because of his Protestant evangelical background and partly because of his experiences as Irish Secretary in Dublin Castle. There he had acquired what became lifelong distrust and dislike of O'Connell, which had once almost led to a duel. Wellington convinced Peel it was his duty to stay and bring in a bill for emancipation. This measure was enacted in 1829 and made Peel forever suspect in the view of the ultra-Protestant wing of the Tory party. For the next ninety years a block of Irish members would be an indigestible element in the English body politic.

Except for one brief interlude, the followers of the younger Pitt, now known as the Tory party, had been in office for almost half a century. The party had been dedicated to maintenance of the status quo in church and state, but by the time George IV died in 1830, the Tories were showing signs of disintegration. Under Huskisson the liberal wing, followers of Canning, had withdrawn from the Wellington ministry and were in touch with the Whigs, some of whom had joined Canning's brief ministry. The ultra-Tories had lost faith in Peel and Wellington for what they saw was a betrayal of the Protestant cause. Some, equating a more representative Parliament with a more Protestant one, consequently changed their attitudes on reform.

With the end of the wars, the demand for parliamentary reform—that is, for extension of the franchise, abolition of rotten, or pocket boroughs, and representation for the new industrial towns—had been renewed outside of Parliament. In the Commons several recently elected younger Whigs took up the cause. Notable among them were John Lambton (1792–1840), Lord Grey's son-in-law and the future Lord Durham, and Lord John Russell (1792–1878), scion of the Whig house of Bedford, both of whom introduced reform bills and motions throughout the twenties. The failure of a proposal to transfer to Manchester a seat from the small, corrupt borough of Penryn precipitated the resignation of the Canningites from the Wellington ministry in 1828. The passage of Catholic emancipation in 1829 seemed to clear the way for a concentrated drive for parliamentary reform. In the session of 1830 much time was spent in debating the subject. A redistribution bill introduced by Lord John Russell was defeated, but it had obtained support from Canningites and ultra-Tories as well as from Whigs and Radicals. Outside Westminster, Thomas Attwood (1783–1856), an eccentric Tory banker, organized the Birmingham Political Union, which would play a leading part in the battle that was about to be joined.

On June 26, 1830, George IV died. He was succeeded by his brother William IV (1765–1837), a rather foolish man, but less objectionable and prejudiced than the dead king. The succession necessitated an election, and for the first time in more than a century the Government in office failed to control the results. So hazy were party lines at this time, however, that the outcome could not be predicted. When Parliament met the ministers were defeated by a vote on the Civil List (an annual bill to authorize payment of salaries and pensions) of 233 to 204. Sixty-two members on whom they had counted for support voted or paired against the Government. Wellington's resignation was inevitable. This almost unprecedented loss of a general election by a ministry in office is explained partly by the drying up of patronage following the administrative reforms of the past quarter-century and partly by the divisions in the Tory party over Catholic emancipation and Wellington's inept leadership. At a time when demand for parliamentary reform was at its height and an obvious factor in the electoral defeat of the Government, Wellington had chosen to flout public opinion by stating publicly that he considered the British system of representation perfect and incapable of improvement.

In November 1830, Lord Grey formed what was in effect a Coalition Ministry, pledged to parliamentary reform. It included four Canningites and one ultra-Tory as well as Grey's radical son-in-law, Lord Durham, and the brilliant but erratic lawyer-politician, Henry Brougham (1778–1868), one of the most powerful advocates of reform, who became Lord Chancellor and was thus exiled for life to the House of Lords. Although committed to reform the new ministry was the most aristocratic of the century, and when a bad harvest brought on agricultural riots the ministry was as resolutely repressive as any of its predecessors. Grey had undoubtedly grown conservative during years of disillusionment in Opposition, but he had not completely forgotten the ardor of his youth. In the decade of repression after Britain's declaration of war on revolutionary France, he had dared to introduce a parliamentary reform bill. He may have seen a reflection of his old enthusiasm in his son-in-law, whose influence over him was considerable. He appointed Durham chairman of a committee of four, including Russell, entrusted with the responsibility of drafting a bill. The choice of this committee and the growing reform demands outside the House—spurred, in part, by the successful constitutional revolution of 1830 in France—guaranteed that the changes proposed would be significant. The committee went further than had been anticipated, but on all points except the secret ballot the Prime Minister supported their recommendations. The more conservative ministers such as Lord Melbourne, the Home Secretary, and his fellow Canningite Lord Palmerston, the Foreign Secretary, reluctantly agreed.

When Russell announced the proposals to the House of Commons in March 1831, members were incredulous. All boroughs with less than 2,000 inhabitants were to lose both seats, and those having between 2,000 and 4,000 would forfeit one seat. This measure would eliminate rotten boroughs and give more representation to densely populated parts of the country. If the bill passed, men with a traditional guarantee of membership in the House of Commons for themselves or their protégés would lose it overnight and become dependent to a varying extent on popular election.

The division on the second reading of the bill, the debate on its principle, was passed by only one vote, and on a subsequent amendment introduced by the Opposition in the committee stage the Government was defeated. Lord Grey demanded and obtained from the King a dissolution of the House of Commons. In so doing, he took advantage of the elastic feature of the English constitution allowing ministers, with the approval of the crown, to appeal at any time to the electorate in an attempt to improve their position in the Commons. The country was strongly in favor of the bill, and the issue influenced elections to an unprecedented extent even in small constituencies. In order to be elected, most candidates had to declare their support for reform. The Government thus increased its strength by 140, a majority that ensured the passage of a second reform bill, which was quickly introduced. The Tories, however, still had a majority in the House of Lords, and there the bill was defeated in October. Public indignation, which had been mounting steadily, was intense; serious riots broke out in Bristol, Derby, and Nottingham with some loss of life. New political unions came into existence throughout the country, and for the first time the danger of some sort of revolution, if the popular will was brooked, became possible. Some moderate Tory peers, the Waverers, began to seek a compromise from the ministers, who decided in December to placate the public. They recalled Parliament and introduced a third bill, counting on moderate Tories to cooperate. If worst came to worst, they hoped the King would create enough new peers to ensure a Government majority. Early in the new year Grey discussed this idea with the King and eventually obtained a reluctant assurance that he would so act if necessary. After passing through the Commons the third bill went to the Lords in April and passed its crucial second reading.

On May 7, however, a hostile procedural amendment was passed against the Government, indicating that the bill was in danger. The King, who had never been enthusiastic for reform, now turned against his ministers on pressure from his family and members of the court. When Grey approached him he refused to carry out his promise to create peers, so the Government resigned. The Duke of Wellington agreed to form a ministry, but was prevented from doing so by the refusal to cooperate of Sir Robert Peel, his senior colleague in the House of Commons. Although by now Peel realized a reform measure was inevitable, he persisted in his unwillingness to be responsible for it. During these famous "days of May" the attention of the whole country was focused on the political crisis. Public opinion was roused as it never had been by a political issue. The political unions redoubled their efforts, and mass meetings to demand reform were organized throughout the country. The leaders of the agitation in London and Birmingham were in close liaison. Joseph Parkes (1796–1865), a radical solicitor, claimed all Birmingham had joined the union and that at a meeting numbering 100,000 people, the general determination was to withhold taxes until the bill was passed. Parkes headed a Birmingham deputation that met, in a Covent Garden tavern, with leaders from other cities and Francis Place and his London colleagues. It was agreed they would avoid violence, but by holding demonstrations would force most of the troops to remain in London. They would also precipitate an economic crisis by creating a run on the banks for gold. Placards with the message "To Stop the Duke Go for Gold" were prepared. The moment it was learned Lord Grey had returned to office the demand for gold ceased, but Francis Place cautioned Sir John Hobhouse, a moderate Radical minister, that if any doubt remained alarm would commence again and panic would follow. Hobhouse was warned that if the duke came into power mass uprisings would begin in the provinces, towns would be barricaded, and business would be brought to a halt. Apparently, detailed preparations for such eventualities had been made in Birmingham. But the return of Grey to office and the King's reluctant agreement to appoint peers as a last resort averted the crisis. In the end the appointments were unnecessary; moderate conservative peers preferred to pass the bill rather than have their House inundated by the addition of so many new members.

It is difficult to say to what extent passage of the Reform Act was due to the activities of middle-class radicals in marshaling public opinion in London, Birmingham, and other centers. Certainly, James Mill and such Benthamite associates as Parkes and Place had sought from the beginning to intimidate the Government by sparking dangerous popular reaction with inflamatory press accounts and public meetings and, in the final stages, by offering more direct threats. Their ability to follow through was problematical, but their activities did give credence to the arguments of the Whigs' parliamentary spokesmen, such as T. B. Macaulay (1800–1859), the most powerful advocate of reform in the Commons, that failure to pass this just and moderate measure would result in even graver dangers. Macaulay emphasized the great contribution that the middle classes had made to the remarkable material progress the country had enjoyed and the anomaly of excluding them from parliamentary representation. In passing the bill the legislators undoubtedly acted, as usual, from mixed motives—a grudging admission of the justice of these claims and fear of the consequences of rejecting them.

The reform effected by the Act of 1832 was twofold. First, it increased the number of voters from about 500,000 to over 800,000 by introducing a uniform franchise to all householders paying their own rates (local taxes) and £10 in rent annually, as well as to certain tenant farmers in the counties. This extension only enfranchised one out of every seven adult males in the United Kingdom (one out of five in England). It affected mainly the middle classes, excluding some of the lower middle classes where rents were low and including a few skilled artisans where rents were high. The rejection of the secret ballot ensured the continued influence of landlords over new tenant voters in the counties. The Whigs had argued plausibly that there could be no harm in giving the respectable, hard-working people the vote, and that it was only right they should have it. The Tories, with equal perspicacity, had pointed out that the £10 dividing line was artificial and that demands for its further reduction would be impossible to withstand, a forecast that proved later to be true. The Great Reform Bill, as it was called, was not a democratic measure, but it made possible, even likely, the coming of democracy.

More attention probably was paid to the redistribution aspects of the act. As finally revised, it provided for the withdrawal of 143 seats from the smaller boroughs (both seats from 56 pocket boroughs and one seat from another 31 small boroughs). Of the 143 seats released, 65 were distributed among the English counties, another 65 went to English boroughs (many of them previously unrepresented), and 13 were given to Scotland and Ireland.

From the viewpoints of nineteenth-century working-class reformers and twentieth-century democratic society, the Reform Act of 1832 was a moderate, even a disappointing, measure. Indeed, the Whigs argued that their reform would preserve and not destroy the country's social heritage, and modern historians, such as Norman Gash, have emphasized the element of continuity in the political system after the passage of the Reform Act. Nevertheless, in the context of British parliamentary history it proved to be a dramatic break with the past, perhaps the most radical step in the whole history of Parliament, and certainly the most momentous event since the Revolution of 1688. Not only did the Reform Act wipe out about one-quarter of the existing English and Welsh seats in the House of Commons—it is difficult to imagine a modern legislature doing this to itself—but it set a precedent for inevitable further rationalization that in the long run justified the Tories' worst fears.

Apart from its long-term implications, the Reform Act of 1832 had several more immediate political consequences. Although in some constituencies local influence was still valuable, now that all members had to take a larger number of voters into consideration, they were much more susceptible to the influence of public opinion and elections took on a new significance. As a result, party organization became more important, although for another generation it was loosely structured by modern standards. Each party established a political club as an informal party headquarters, the Carlton Club for the Tories and the Reform Club for the Whigs and their Radical allies, who first proposed this innovation. Both parties appointed political agents and systematically undertook the work of registering potential supporters. In all this the Tories (who under Peel's leadership assumed the less offensive name of Conservatives) took the lead. After his party lost heavily in 1832, in the first election after the Reform Act, Peel realized they would have to adjust to new conditions or perish.

The Reform Act also had constitutional implications. The power of the king had waned as the patronage at his disposal had been reduced, and now it was apparent that the chief responsibility of the ministers was not to the king but to the House of Commons. In 1834 King William virtually dismissed his Whig ministers, but when Peel was unable to obtain a majority at the ensuing election (as Pitt had done in a similar case in 1783) the King was forced to bring the Whigs back to office. The will of the recently elected Commons, thus, prevailed over the whim of the King. Having been forced to pass legislation to which they were opposed, the House of Lords was also in a different position. Theoretically, the same pressures could be used at any time, although it was eighty years before this actually occurred.

Finally, it may be observed that the development of cabinet government (as described in Walter Bagehot's *English Constitution*, first published in 1867) was a direct result of the Reform Act of 1832. The Cabinet as an institution had been evolving for more than half a century before its promulgation, but previously it had been responsible primarily to the king. Henceforth the Cabinet that had the confidence of the Commons and of the voters could not effectively be removed.

Chapter Three
PARTY POLITICS
AND SOCIAL UNREST

The first reformed House of Commons was elected after the passage of the Reform Act of 1832 and met in early 1833. In its membership it differed less from its predecessor than might have been expected. The number of Radicals increased only to fifty or sixty—less than a tenth of the whole House—supplemented by some thirty-nine followers of O'Connell. There was some change in the atmosphere of the House, as the Radicals and the Irish made it a noisier and more unruly body; but the majority of its members continued to be drawn from the same classes as before. The landed interest lost nothing; there was as yet no appreciable increase in the representation of business interests, and Dissent was scarcely represented at all, although a large proportion of the new voters must have been Dissenters. Many old members who had previously sat for rotten boroughs simply turned up as representatives of the new constituencies, for they came from a leisured class traditionally inclined to parliamentary politics.

The position of many old members was, however, changed in the new Parliament, now that they had to consider more seriously the feelings of the electors to ensure their own return at subsequent elections. The new Parliament was not a radical or democratic body, but it could not stand still. Since an aroused public had succeeded in forcing the old Parliament to reform itself against its will, the resulting reformed Parliament would have to progress still further along the road of reform. Thus it was that the Whig aristocrats, many of whom would have been quite content to sit back after the exertions of the past two years, became responsible for several other major reforms before relapsing into apathy. The most important of these was an act abolishing slavery throughout the British Empire, completing the humanitarian crusade begun by Wilberforce years before. It was a generous measure in that the freedom of the slaves in the British colonies, mostly in the West Indies, was bought by the British taxpayers, since payment of £15 million, later raised to £20 million, was voted to compensate slave owners. The reform was a triumph for the forces of morality, but it had an adverse effect on the economy of the British West Indies. The slaves won freedom but not prosperity; free-grown sugar of the British West Indies had to compete with slave-grown sugar of rival suppliers, and the years in which it would enjoy a protected market in the mother country were numbered.

Royal commissions were used frequently and effectively in this period, for the commissions were dominated by experts, whose knowledge led to practical reform proposals. A demand for factory reform was referred to such a commission, which accepted the principle that regulation of working hours should be confined to those of minors, but made the enlightened stipulation that factory inspectors be appointed to implement the new regulations. The Factory Act of 1833 prohibited employment of children under nine years of age, and it limited the laboring hours of children under thirteen to forty-eight a week and of young persons under eighteen to sixty-nine a week. The act proved in part defective, but the all-important provision of a factory inspectorate laid the basis for effective regulation in the future. Another royal commission was appointed to investigate the breakdown of the old system of poor relief. Administration of relief had remained virtually unchanged since the late sixteenth century until, at the end of the eighteenth century, many parishes had adopted the controversial "Speemhamland" system, supplementing the low wages of agricultural workers from the "poor rates" (local taxes).[1] The voters, who were all ratepayers, were eager for a change in the law that would reduce the burden of rates. The result was the Poor Law Amendment Act of 1834, which rejected "outdoor" relief in the form of indiscriminate handouts. Instead, all seeking relief were required to enter the local workhouse, maintained by a union of neighboring parishes. Conditions in the workhouse (quickly dubbed Bastilles and graphically described by Charles Dickens in *Oliver Twist*) were deliberately made as harsh as possible—families were separated and the food allowance kept to a bare minimum—to deter the poor from applying for help except as a last resort. The new system did lead to an overall reduction in the poor rates, but at the cost of much human misery and degradation. Moreover, it was quite unsuited to industrial towns, where large numbers were often thrown out of work temporarily by "trade" conditions over which they had no control, and it was soon found impossible to abandon completely the practice of "outdoor" relief. From the beginning the system was denounced by humanitarians, but with some modifications it survived into the twentieth century.

[1] Articles by Marc Blaugh in the *Economic History Review*, vols. XXIII and XXIV (1963 and 1964), indicate that the criticism of the old Poor Law made by the Commissioners was ill-founded and highly contentious.

In addition to the three measures thus effected, Brougham, the Lord Chancellor, effected several useful legal reforms. An attempt also was made to deal with Irish grievances. The Irish Church Act of 1833 fell short of the demands of O'Connell and the Radicals and even the advanced party in the Cabinet. It did, however, force substantial reforms on the established Anglican Church of Ireland, an anomalous institution that had been imposed for almost three centuries on a predominantly Roman Catholic people.

Cumulatively all these reforms were a surprising achievement for a government in the process of falling apart. The more conservative ministers had little heart for the reform program, and, when in 1834 Lord John Russell publicly declared his belief in the legitimacy of appropriating Irish church revenues for other purposes, four of them resigned (and later joined Peel). This blow from the right was soon followed by an even more serious one from the left. When the Government proposed the Irish Coercion Act, O'Connell attacked the bill as betraying an agreement he had made, unknown to the Prime Minister, with some of the ministers. The result was the resignation of Lord Althorp, Government leader in the Commons, and then of Lord Grey himself. After some hesitation the unambitious Lord Melbourne, a former Canningite and one of the most conservative members of the Grey ministry, accepted the King's invitation to him to succeed Grey as prime minister. He induced Lord Althorp to return to his post, but some months later the death of Althorp's father forced him to leave the House of Commons for the Lords. The King refused to accept Melbourne's proposal of Lord John Russell to be Althorp's successor and as a result forced the Prime Minister's resignation. The Conservatives came into office temporarily, but they failed to obtain a majority in the subsequent election. The King had to recall Melbourne and to accept Russell as leader in the Commons.

Melbourne's majority was much smaller than Grey's, and his ministry, never strong, became progressively weaker as the years passed. Melbourne's lack of zeal for reform was negated in part by the energy of Russell. Further reforms were achieved, notably the extensive Municipal Reform Act of 1835, which abolished 178 oligarchic and corrupt municipal corporations and replaced them with new bodies. The new municipal councils were elected by all the ratepayers, a much more democratic franchise than the parliamentary one. A similar measure had been passed for Scotland in 1833, and, after much difficulty, a more conservative one was passed for Ireland in 1840. This was the last of the great Whig reforms, but there were also some less dramatic, yet useful, innovations made, such as the introduction of penny postage (at the urging of Rowland Hill, a crusader for an improved postal service) and the allocation of small grants to support charity schools for the poor. A Prisons Act introduced some penal reforms and provided for a central inspectorate, while a Marriage Act and a Burials Act removed two of the worst grievances of the Dissenters by ending the Anglican monopoly in these areas. The Irish were partially placated by the so-called Lichfield House compact, as a result of which O'Connell was consulted about government appointments in Ireland, a step of obvious significance. Finally, on the recommendations of a predominantly clerical commission appointed by Peel in 1835, several important acts effected reforms in the Church of England.

The list of significant reform legislation passed in the thirties is impressive. But it is only the top of the iceberg. In every session throughout Queen Victoria's long reign, which began in 1837, the modern bureaucratic edifice continued to be built in a series of miscellaneous acts of Parliament, many of them amendments to previous acts, all adding to the structure brick by brick.

Historians readily acknowledge the significance and range of the reforms of this period, but find it difficult to explain the phenomenon. After a century of inaction, what had sparked this legislative and administrative outburst, which began in the 1820s with the reforms of Peel and Huskisson and reached its zenith in the mid-thirties? Many factors had combined to kindle the flame although individually none was strong enough to do so. The two most important were probably evangelicalism and Benthamism. The evangelical revival, both inside and outside the established church, had awakened in Christians of all classes an awareness of social wrongs, especially when these were a bar to spiritual development. The stimulus toward abolition of slavery was undoubtedly evangelical, and some evangelicals, such as Lord Ashley (later Lord Shaftesbury), fought to alleviate harsh working conditions in England. The Factory Act of 1833 was the result of Ashley's pressure on the government, although it was not quite the measure he had intended. The drafting of the report of the royal commission and of the subsequent legislation was largely the work of Edwin Chadwick and other Benthamites. It was their influence that led to the creation of a factory inspectorate and the restriction of the act to minors (according to the laissez-faire principle, which presumed that adults could best look after themselves). The Benthamites were less directly involved in the abolition of slavery, but, naturally, they favored a reform that would implement Bentham's principle of seeking to increase the greatest happiness for the greatest number.

The evangelicals and the Benthamites were strange allies—the one inspired by spiritual, the other by material considerations. In this respect their philosophies were diametrically opposed, but for practical purposes they often worked together. The Poor Law, however, was uniquely a Benthamite conception, embodying their ideas of efficient administration. It was even based on the greatest happiness principle, since its intention was to force the poor to help themselves, while simultaneously reducing the burden of taxation on the rest of the community. The evangelicals, unconcerned with laissez-faire, were shocked at the callousness of the measure and many of them joined in the unsuccessful outcry for its repeal. Since they had friends in high places, the influence of the evangelicals in some areas is undisputed, but their interests were narrower than those of the Benthamites. Historians differ as to the effectiveness of the Benthamites. Among politicians their creed was accepted fully only by the Philosophical Radicals, a small group, of whom none except Sir William Molesworth in the 1850s ever held Cabinet Office.

It has been argued that much of the reform of the period was self-generating, that new officials appointed to administer new institutions pressed for further refinements to improve them. But this still does not explain the primary source of the movement. Perhaps reform had already been in the air, the inevitable result of industrialization and all it implied, but had been postponed by reaction to outside events. The legislative changes did no more than match the great social and economic changes begun in the latter half of the eighteenth century, and they would have come earlier and more gradually had it not been for the political reaction created by the revolution in France. Once the fear aroused by those events had faded, the dam was removed and the reform movement was in full flood, carrying along with it whatever ministers were in office. Many of the reforms undertaken partially fitted into the program of the Benthamites, who rationalized and justified what was being done, whether or not they were actually responsible for it; but the full logic of their arguments was not acceptable to the politicians, who were never prepared to go as far as the philosophers wanted. One historian sums up Bentham's importance in "the foresight, the clarity, and the logic with which he expounded those truths which other forces far stronger than his own ideas would bring to pass."[2]

Paradoxically, the supposed age of laissez-faire, when the principles of the classical economists were accepted by most reformers, was also an age of growing state intervention. The economists, while generally advocating laissez-faire, admitted that there were areas in which the state had to intervene. The Benthamites, or Utilitarians, as they were also called, in subscribing to the principles of the economists, were concerned that where the state intervened it should do so efficiently. This was undoubtedly their major contribution. It is best illustrated by the wide-ranging activities of Edwin Chadwick, Bentham's former private secretary, who was appointed to various royal

[2] David Roberts, "Jeremy Bentham and the Victorian Administrative State," *Victorian Studies*, II (1959), 207.

commissions and drafted much of the new legislation. He became secretary to the Poor Law commission and later a member of the Board of Health, two bodies he was instrumental in creating. Chadwick was prepared to increase the power of the state in an effort to centralize improvement of public health, but he was constantly thwarted by resistance from private companies and local authorities.

The coming of the railway posed another challenge for the state. The state assumed some regulatory responsibility, but less than had been recommended by W. E. Gladstone, the young President of the Board of Trade (and normally a champion of the economists), in his bill of 1844. The adoption of penny postage in 1840 is a good example of the empirical approach of ministers in extending the scope of government activity. With Rowland Hill pushing hard in this matter and persuasive arguments supporting the proposal, which would obviously benefit many people, it was done despite the economists.

As the framework of society became more complex state regulation expanded continuously in a variety of fields. Most of it was piecemeal, initiated by advice from administrative officials such as factory or sanitary inspectors, and occasioned little parliamentary debate. Over the years a great body of administrative regulations was built up, much as a coral reef is formed. This legislation governed such diverse matters as police, prisons, prostitutes, lodging houses, hackney cabs, railways, shipping, the medical profession, education, and so on, all greatly increasing the supervisory power of the central government; the Merchant Shipping Act of 1854, which was passed with relatively little parliamentary debate, contained 200 pages of regulations.

Relatively speaking, the reform achievement of the 1820s and 1830s was substantial, but not from the point of view of the poor, or even of the mass, of the working classes, who remained incapable of guiding their own destiny. From the viewpoint of the economic historian, the period is one of extraordinary and sustained economic expansion, but, unfortunately, it was characterized by a series of short business cycles with deep troughs in the years 1826, 1829, 1832, 1837, 1842, and 1848 that produced temporary unemployment on a large scale. This situation was often aggravated, prior to the repeal of the Corn Laws, by bad harvests and high grain prices. Economic historians have compiled indexes showing (1) the fluctuations of the business cycle, ranging from deep depression, with an index of 0, to major peak, with an index of 5, and (2) similar fluctuations in wheat prices, from an index of 0, representing abnormally high prices, to an index of 5, representing abnormally low prices. These two indexes have been combined to construct the "social tension chart" reproduced below, which indicates years when the combination of unemployment and high prices was worst. In the first half of the nineteenth century peak years were 1812, 1819, 1829–32, 1838–41, and 1848, i.e., years associated with the Luddite riots, the Peterloo massacre, the reform bill agitation, and the three Chartist movements. Thus, the graph dramatically illustrates the close connection at this time between social tension and bad economic conditions.[3]

SOCIAL TENSION CHART

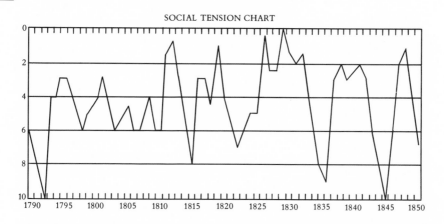

The politically-minded working classes were disillusioned with the results of the Great Reform Act, which left most of them without the vote, and which produced middle- and upper-class parliaments insufficiently concerned with their particular problems. Early experiments in trade unionism following the repeal of the Combination Acts soon collapsed, including Owen's Grand National Consolidated Trades Union, which briefly claimed membership of some half a million. These unions mushroomed too quickly, lacked financial resources or educated leadership on a local basis, and were often hamstrung by the counter-organizations of employers, who locked the unionists out from their mills and forced employees to sign a "document" pledging not to strike. The authorities showed no sympathy for trade unionists, and six leaders of a small agricultural union in Tolpuddle, Dorset, were sentenced to transportation to Australia for administering illegal oaths. The "Tolpuddle martyrs" were an extreme example of what early trade union leaders faced, causing them to be regarded in retrospect as heroes of the English trade union movement.

The failure of these early trade unions turned the working classes back on the track of direct political action. In 1836 the London Workingman's Association was founded in London by Henry Hetherington (1792–1849) and

[3] See W. W. Rostow, *British Economy of the Nineteenth Century* (Fairlawn, N. J.: Oxford University Press, 1948), pp. 123–4.

William Lovett (1800–1877). From its deliberations sprang the idea of a national charter embodying the six major political demands of the working classes: annual parliaments, universal adult male suffrage, vote by ballot, removal of property qualifications for members of Parliament, payment of members, and equal electoral districts. The movement spread rapidly throughout the country and linked up with the revived Birmingham Political Union. It soon fell under the domination of the strange figure of Feargus O'Connor (1794–1855), a small Irish landowner who had joined the working-class cause in England. O'Conner had a great platform presence and could influence an even wider audience through his popular newspaper, the *Northern Star*, which distributed the Chartist gospel in 50,000 copies a week. Nationwide meetings, attended with great enthusiasm, were held to collect signatures. A great Chartist convention calling itself the People's Parliament met in London and prepared the petition for presentation to Parliament. The convention was adjourned to Birmingham, where it fell under the domination of more extremist elements, who alienated many earlier supporters of the movement. Thomas Atwood, then a Radical member associated with the movement, introduced the petition into the House of Commons in July, but it was summarily rejected by a vote of 235 to 46. The first Chartist movement dissolved soon after the arrest of some of its leaders. It had been weakened by divisions between those opposed and those advocating physical force. One sorry attempt at armed force was made in what was supposed to be a national rising; a few thousand armed colliers headed by John Frost, a draper and ex-magistrate, marched on Newport, in Wales. They were quickly overcome and their leaders condemned to death, a sentence later commuted to transportation for life.

With many of the movement's leaders in jail, the first surge of Chartism subsided by the end of 1839—but hunger kept the spirit of the movement alive. A National Chartist Association was formed in 1840, almost entirely controlled by O'Connor, who now broke with Lovett and Bronterre O'Brien, the movement's "first theorist." A second Chartist petition was presented to Parliament in 1842 but was rejected as emphatically as the first, after a short debate in which Macaulay warned the House that universal suffrage would be fatal to the constitution. As times improved O'Connor and his association concentrated their efforts on implementing a plan to bring workers back to the land. This was, in fact, a forlorn attempt to reverse the whole trend of the Industrial Revolution of the preceding century. With the return of bad times in 1847–48, however, one last effort to pressure Parliament was organized and signatures were collected for a third petition, which was presented on Parliament after a mass demonstration on Kennington Common.

There was some apprehension on this occasion, since it was the year of revolution on the Continent. Special constables were enrolled in London and elsewhere, troops were brought into the capital, and the Chartists were forbidden to march across the river to Westminster. O'Connor, himself now an M.P., meekly accepted these restrictions and brought the petition, loaded into three cabs, to the House. The petition had 1,900,000 signatures appended to it, but evidently many, such as "No Cheese," "Pug Nose," and "Victoria Rex," were spurious. Parliament treated it no more seriously than its predecessors, and the Chartist movement dissolved as good times returned in the following years. O'Connor died not long afterward, and most of his younger lieutenants turned their energies in other directions. Some undertook the organization of new trade unions that were to prove more successful than the earlier ones, while others started a consumers' cooperative movement that has flourished ever since. The Chartist movement ended in complete failure because of its divided and muddleheaded leadership, weak organization, and lack of adequate resources. Its demands were not taken seriously by the contemporary ruling class, but less than a century later five of the six points were met. The real significance of the movement lay in what it did to create a feeling of working-class solidarity and to remind the ruling classes that the masses were not to be ignored. Many of the men who helped to form the new unions and the Labour party at the end of the century recalled the aspirations of their parents in the Chartist movement, which rapidly came to be regarded as a great chapter in British working-class history.

Chartism was not the only popular movement of those years. Throughout the thirties and forties many of the factory workers organized themselves into "short time" committees to demand a limitation of working hours. They received much support from a number of Tory evangelicals such as Richard Oastler (1789–1861), a land agent; Micheal Sadler (1780–1835), a banker; and Lord Ashley, later known as Lord Shaftesbury (1801–1885), who gave his whole life to the pursuit of humanitarian causes. The powerful agitation stirred up by Lord Ashley and his friends led to the appointment of royal commissions to investigate conditions in both the factories and the mines. Their reports, published in the early forties, so shocked public opinion that the government was forced to take action to ameliorate those conditions. The same forces, led most vehemently by Oastler and Joseph Stephens (1805–1879), the Methodist clergyman, campaigned strenuously, but with less success, against the new Poor Law.

The most powerful and successful pressure group of the day, however, was the Anti-Corn Law League, founded in 1839. Local associations of businessmen, all fanatical freetraders and firm believers in laissez-faire, had preceded it in Manchester and other cities. From the beginning the league was highly organized and, in contrast with the Chartists, in possession of ample funds to spread its propaganda. This was done by the organization of public meetings and the distribution of tracts denouncing the inequity of the Corn Laws, blaming them for keeping the price of bread high, especially in time of shortage, to the advantage of a small group of aristocratic landowners and at the expense of the mass of the population. The League argued that repeal of the Corn Laws would effect the only real help that could be given to the poor. But there is reason to believe that the businessmen behind it were more interested in promoting their own exports by creating new markets in the wheat-supplying countries and by reducing at home the cost of labor, which was expected to fall with the cost of living. The most outstanding national orators of this movement, who preached it inside Parliament and out, were Richard Cobden (1804–1865), a small Manchester businessman of yeoman origin, and John Bright (1811–1889), a more substantial Rochdale cotton manufacturer and a Quaker. Owing to their zeal and oratorical prowess, Cobden and Bright preached with great effect. For they believed implicitly in their cause and promoted it with the moral fervor of true missionaries, but they were only the two most distinguished advocates of a large and determined army of militant businessmen who were tired of the aristocratic rule of the landowners.

The demand for the repeal of the Corn Laws presented a quandary to the Whig ministers. Almost all of them came from the landed interest and supposed with Huskisson and Peel that the social and political necessity of protecting that interest made an exception to any general arguments in favor of free trade. Since the elections of 1835 and 1837, however, the forces of the Government and those of the Opposition had been more evenly balanced and the Whig ministers made more dependent upon the support of their Radical allies, who were all freetraders. Some more enlightened members of the aristocratic class had accepted the free trade philosophy. They considered it absurd for a manufacturing and commercial nation to keep the price of food artificially high and believed that with proper development British agriculture could remain competitive. Such a view was held by Charles Villiers (1802–1898), member of a noble family, who in 1838 introduced a motion to inquire into the Corn Laws. He repeated the motion annually until victory was acheived. In 1839 it won the support of more than half of the members on the Government's benches, but Lord Melbourne remained adamant in his opposition to any change. In 1841, in the face of growing unrest among their own followers and recurrent deficits in the budget, the liberal wing of the Cabinet, under Russell's leadership, decided on a general reduction of customs duties, including those on sugar, and on the replacement of the sliding scale on corn with a low, fixed duty of eight shillings a quarter. Exploiting the widespread antislavery feeling, the Conservative opposition defeated a motion for the reduction of the duty on foreign (slave-grown) sugar. This was followed by the passage of a want-of-confidence motion in the Government by one vote. Instead of resigning, the Government advised the Queen to dissolve Parliament, but was badly defeated in the ensuing general election, which gave the Conservatives a majority of seventy-six seats.

The strength of the Whigs had been on the decline ever since their return to office in 1835. They had been unable to improve their position in the general election following the accession of the young Queen Victoria in 1837, and two years later they had resigned after a defeat in the House of Commons. They had once more returned to office when Peel failed to form a Government, owing to the Queen's refusal to dismiss the Whig Ladies of her Bedchamber. From 1839 to 1841 they remained in office on suffrance and their eventual defeat was not surprising. It was due in part to deep and long-standing divisions within their ranks, to the negative leadership of Lord Melbourne, to their financial incapacity (as demonstrated in a series of deficit budgets), and to the weakness of their party organization. There were, however, more positive reasons than these for Peel's victory.

Parties in opposition have more time and inclination to repair their electoral machinery than those in office, a factor that favors backward and forward swings of the electoral pendulum. The Tories, who in 1833 faced extinction, had particularly strong reasons for putting their house in order despite the disinclination of many to accept the implications of the Reform Act. It was Peel's great achievement during this period that he persuaded them to do so. He even went so far as to sanction the use of the term Conservative party to replace the old name of Tory. In his Tamworth manifesto of 1834 he made it clear that he accepted the Reform Act as "a final and irrevocable settlement" and that under his leadership the Conservative party would accept a program of moderate reform. He refused to pander to every popular whim that radical agitators might drum up or to abandon "the respect for ancient rights, and the deference to prescriptive authority" so dear to the true conservative. "But," he wrote, "if the spirit of the Reform Bill implies merely a careful review of institutions, civil and ecclesiastical, undertaken in a friendly temper, combining with the firm maintenance of established rights, the correction of proved abuses, and the redress of real grievances, in that case, I can, for myself and my colleagues, undertake to act in such a spirit and with such intentions." As a result, Peel supported most major reforms of the period in principle while preserving the right to criticize them in detail, and refused any support to the noisy wing of his party demanding the repeal of the new Poor Law.

Under Peel's leadership the party also improved its electoral organization, although he left the details to Francis Bonham (1785–1863), his capable party manager. The Carlton Club was founded in 1832 and became an unofficial party headquarters to which most active party members of both houses belonged. At the constituency level, local Conservative associations and, in some places, Conservative operative societies were formed and efforts made to see that all potential Conservative voters were properly registered. Attention to these details undoubtedly contributed to the electoral success of 1841, but the most important factor was probably the shift in the attitude of a large section of the newly enfranchised middle classes. They wanted no further changes, they were frightened by the demands of the Chartists and Radicals, and they were disillusioned with the incapacity of the aristocratic Whigs. Such men looked for good government from the more businesslike Sir Robert Peel.

The Conservative party was socially more homogeneous than the coalition of Whigs, Liberals, Radicals, and Irish repealers they had ousted from office, but they too had their divisions, although these had been less dangerous in opposition. There were an indeterminate number of ultra-Tories opposed to all change in church and state who had never reconciled themselves to the Reform Act and who still blamed Peel for "betraying" them on Catholic emancipation. Then there were a smaller number of so-called Tory Radicals, who demanded the repeal of the obnoxious Poor Law and favored social legislation to ameliorate the lot of the oppressed urban poor. Their view of society was paternalistic, and they tended to despise and mistrust political economists, factory owners, and everything associated with the Industrial Revolution. The most articulate espousal of these ideas came from a small group of young aristocrats who called themselves Young England. Their inspiration was Benjamin Disraeli (1804–1881), the strange young novelist, who, after failing to get elected as a Radical, entered Parliament as the protégé of a Tory aristocrat. Disraeli was something of an adventurer (or, at best, was always acting a part), but he had genuine contempt for the doctrinaire approach to politics of the economists and the Benthamites. He was a strange mixture of cynicism and romanticism, and the latter was the main strain in the short-lived Young England movement.

There was, however, a strong corps of Peelite Conservatives, who shared Peel's views on the necessity of moderate reform and who respected the dicta of the economists. It was from their ranks that Peel largely chose his ministers. There were clearly also many rank-and-file party members who accepted Peel because of the ability that set him far above his colleagues. They might find some of his ideas hard to swallow, but he had brought them into office and promised the country the strong government that had been lacking under the Whigs.

Peel was too reserved and aloof—he was basically a shy man—to make a popular party leader, but he had a well-earned reputation as a parliamentary debater and could present the most complicated bills or budgets with remarkable lucidity. His real forte, however, was in the Cabinet, where he had a moral authority greater than any other prime minister of the century. He chose his ministers, especially the young ones, with great discernment, but he kept a sharp eye on all departments and was prepared to take responsibility for everything the Government did. He was concerned particularly with the Government's fiscal policy and personally presented the 1842 and 1845 budgets to the Commons. These proved the Government's greatest achievement, for Peel resumed the work begun by Huskisson, which the Whigs had failed to tackle—removal of most of the anomalies of the old mercantilist system by a thorough revision of tariffs. This included abolishing duties on hundreds of items, removing other restrictions, and putting an end to all export charges. Peel also lowered duties on the remaining items, on the principle that lower duties would mean increased imports of necessities and hence no loss in revenue. To make up temporarily the losses he hoped eventually to recover by increased trade, he reintroduced Pitt's income tax, which had been abandoned after the war. In general, Peel accepted the arguments of the economists in favor of free trade, but for political reasons he made three important exceptions: colonial sugar, colonial timber, and corn (i.e., cereals). The latter was the foundation of the country's landed wealth, which had been protected since the seventeenth century. He did make some concession to opponents of the Corn Laws by introducing a new sliding scale that allowed foreign corn in more easily when prices were high, but he did not accept Russell's proposal for a small fixed duty. This was as much a compromise as his party would swallow, and many Conservatives went this far without enthusiasm.

Peel was also responsible for the Bank Act of 1844, which, although it has been criticized for its rigidity, fixed the pattern of British banking for the rest of the century. In the field of social reform, Peel and his colleagues were inhibited by their acceptance of the principles of the political economists, so they resisted Lord Ashley's demands for a ten-hour bill to limit working hours in the textile industry. They did, however, secure a Factory Act in 1844. It went further in restricting the hours of young people than the Act of 1833, but religious animosities unfortunately prevented an intended provision of schools for factory children. An attempt by Lord Ashley to turn this bill into a ten-hour bill led to a serious division in the party, but Peel took a firm stand and got his way. Public opinion, shocked by conditions in the mines, revealed in the report of a royal commission (again produced through pressure from Lord Ashley), secured the passage of a Mines Act, prohibiting women and young children from working underground. Peel's critics were also nettled by his attempt to placate the Irish by increasing the annual grant, first made by Pitt, to the Maynooth seminary. There were 137 votes against the measure, which was passed only with the help of Liberal votes.

All these years the Anti-Corn Law League kept up, both in and out of Parliament, their campaign for the repeal of the Corn Laws. Listening to the arguments of their parliamentary spokesman in the spring of 1845, Peel whispered to a colleague beside him, "You answer them, for I cannot." Sooner or later he would have to attack the anomaly of protected corn in what was becoming a free-trade economy. The day of decision was hastened by a blight in Ireland in the autumn of 1845. It destroyed the greater part of her potato crop, upon which most of that part of the United Kingdom depended for sustenance. Peel sensed this as his opportunity; it seemed iniquitous to retain restrictive duties on food imports when a large portion of the population was faced with starvation. He proposed to his Cabinet a suspension of the Corn Laws, but the majority were not ready to take such a fateful step.

Lord John Russell, the leader of the Opposition, with a large number of freetraders among his followers, had less difficulty in revising his own policy. In November, without consulting his colleagues, he published his famous Edinburgh Letter demanding immediate repeal of duties on all cereals. Peel recalled his Cabinet and, finding them divided in opinion, resigned from office. Russell, however, was unable to form a government, ostensibly because of Lord Grey's objection to the inclusion of Lord Palmerston as Foreign Secretary, so Peel accepted the Queen's request that he return. All the ministers except Lord Stanley, soon to become the leader of the Protectionists, now agreed on the necessity of repeal no matter what the political cost. Another great free-trade budget was devised, which provided for the abolition of the duty on wheat and other cereals. This was too much for the majority of Peel's followers. Their opposition was led by Lord George Bentinck, (1802–1848), scion of a noble family and hitherto a silent backbencher more interested in horses than in politics.

The brains and debating skill of the opposition, however, were those of his inscrutable friend, Benjamin Disraeli. Initially, Disraeli had lacked social and political connections, and his early career was not very creditable. But with his pen and his colorful personality he made his way into society at an early age and, once in Parliament, revealed his aptitude for parliamentary debating. His novels Coningsby and Sybil, although jejune in plot and structure, were very successful satires of post-1832 politics, showing a sympathetic understanding of the social problems that had precipitated the Chartist movement. Although by 1841 he had already made his mark,

I would here call your attention to the nature of employment in the coal mines; an employment which, from the manner it is still conducted, may be regarded a relic of the base feudalism just described, and which in the nineteenth century continues to excite our disgust and compassion. I know of no mode by which the nature of that labour can be better presented to your notice than by the following simple extracts from evidence of the witnesses themselves.

[Janet Cumming.]

Janet Cumming (No. 1), 11 years old, bears coals:

I gang with the women at five and come up at five at night; work *all night* on Fridays, and come away at twelve in the day. I carry the large bits of coal from the wall-face to the pit-bottom, and the small pieces called chows in a creel. The weight is usually a hundredweight; do not know how many pounds there are in a hundredweight, but it is some weight to carry; it takes three journeys to fill a tub of 4 cwt. The distance varies, as the work is not always on the same wall; sometimes 150 fathoms, whiles 250 fathoms. The roof is very low; I have to bend my back and legs, and the water comes frequently up to the calves of my legs. Have no liking for the work; father makes me like it. Never got hurt, but often obliged to scramble out of the pit when bad air was in.

[Girl carrying Coals.]

Isabella Read (No. 14), 12 years old:

I am wrought with sister and brother; it is very sore work. Cannot say how many rakes or journeys I make from pit-bottom to wall-face and back, thinks about 30 or 25 on the average; distance varies from 100 to 250 fathoms. I carry a hundredweight and a quarter on my back, and am frequently in water up to the calves of my legs. When first down, fell frequently asleep while waiting for coal from heat and fatigue. I do not like the work, nor do the lassies, but they are made to like it. When the weather is warm there is difficulty in breathing, and frequently the lights go out.

Agnes Moffat (No. 23), 17 years of age:

Began working at 10 years of age. Work 12 and 14 hours daily. Can earn 12s. in a fortnight, if work be not stopped by bad air or otherwise. Father took sister and I down; he gets our wages. I fill five baskets; the weight is more than 22 cwt.; it takes me five journeys. The work is o'er sair for females. Had my shoulder knocked out a short time ago, and laid idle some time. *It is no uncommon thing for women to lose their burthen* [load], *and drop off the ladder down the dyke below.* Margaret M'Neil did a few weeks since, and injured both legs. When the tugs which pass over the forehead break, which they frequently do, it is very dangerous to be under a load. The lassies hate the work altogether, but they canna run away from it.

[Load dropping on ladder while ascending.]

* The former *arleing* of infant colliers and bearers, in consequence of a payment made to their parents is very different to the binding of colliers and bearers now practised: and a bounty for each paid to their parents at the time of their christening, agreeably to the custom and feudal kind of laws on the subject then still remaining in force.

Excerpted from ROYAL COMMISSION REPORT ON CONDITIONS IN THE MINES, 1842

Disraeli was refused office by Peel, who suspected him of being a charlatan. After this, with nothing to lose, Disraeli became daringly independent. Time after time he attacked Peel and his policies from a seat behind Peel's back, but with different arguments than those of the Whig-Liberal Opposition. It was the complaint of Disraeli and those Tories who listened to him that Peel's conservatism was simply "Tory men and Whig measures." Disraeli's philippics against Peel in the Corn Law debate of 1846 rallied the Protectionist Conservatives in their rebellion, but made Peel's friends his eternal enemies. The Corn Laws were repealed with Liberal votes in the Commons and with the influence in the Lords of the Duke of Wellington, who argued, as usual, that the Queen's government must go on. But no sooner was the issue settled than the Protectionists joined the Opposition on another issue to turn the Government out of office.

The more fanatical protectionists and free traders both regarded Peel's action in repealing the Corn Laws as a great surrender, but Peel completely rejected this charge. He and a minority of enlightened landowners were firm believers in what they called "high farming." In their view, the expenditure of capital to improve the land by proper drainage and the use of fertilizers would result in a great increase in productivity. Thus, any fall in prices could be more than compensated for by increased production. Peel believed (as did Cobden) that the repeal of the Corn Laws would be a prod to British agriculture to put its own house in order in the face of foreign competition, and he coupled repeal with provision for governmental loans to enable landowners to undertake the necessary renovations. A large section of the landed interests, however, remained obdurate in the conviction that they had been betrayed.[4]

Lord John Russell became prime minister in June 1846 under exceptional circumstances. His party was in a minority in the House of Commons until the general elections of the following year, but the Conservatives were so bitterly divided that each side was determined to keep the other out of power. Although the Protectionists had put Russell in office by their vote on an Irish coercion bill, Peel preferred to keep him there rather than risk a Protectionist government under Stanley and the return of the Corn Laws. A sufficient number of Peel's former colleagues and supporters followed his lead to secure Russell's position, but many became restive in their unnatural middle position. Some, such as the young Gladstone, argued privately that a Protectionist government might be the best way to clear the air, for they were confident that free trade could not be defeated.

[4] See D. C. Moore, "The Corn Laws and High Farming," *Economic History Review*, 2nd ser. XVIII (1965), 544–561.

The rivalry of Russell and Palmerston colored the history of the Whig-Liberal party and indeed the whole political history of the period, from Russell's first attempt to form a ministry in 1845 to Palmerston's death in 1865. Palmerston was the senior by seven years and had longer official experience, but it was never forgotten that he served his early years in a Tory ministry. As the younger son of a duke of Bedford, Lord John Russell's credentials as a Whig leader were indisputable. Melbourne made Russell leader of the House of Commons from 1835–1841, and Russell succeeded without question to the premiership when the Whigs returned to office in 1846. Palmerston was then content to return to the Foreign Office, but, as we have seen, he was determined to go his own way and never showed Russell the respect owed to a prime minister. In his eyes "Johnny" was always someone to be put down. In almost every way the two were opposites. Russell was small and generally in poor health; Palmerston was tall and handsome, strong and active. Russell was thin-skinned and introspective, irascible and stand-offish. Palmerston (at least on the surface) was bluff and hearty, ready to hit hard in a fight but also ready to forget. Although not popular early in his career, Palmerston was the more successful in cultivating the press and popular opinion during the years of their rivalry. Cartoonists depicted him as a jovial John Bull type with his top hat at a rakish angle, while the diminutive Johnny Russell generally appeared as a thin-lipped little urchin. Both men were happily married, Russell twice; but Palmerston married late in life after a long, gay bachelorhood. Palmerston had no children of his own, while Russell, the father of six, was always anxious to withdraw to the bosom of his family. As one of the great political hostesses of her day Lady Palmerston did much to promote her husband's political career, but the political influence of Russell's second wife was less fortunate. Both Palmerston and Russell were men of superior intelligence; but Palmerston was the man of action, Russell the intellectual, a great reader and himself the author of various books. Both were aristocratic in their views, but Russell was the more liberal-minded and genuine reformer, although more often antagonizing the Radical wing of the party by his manner. Their views on foreign policy were not dissimilar, for both were strong patriots, convinced of the superiority of British institutions and of Britain's right to encourage other nations to adopt constitutional government on the British pattern.

Although he obtained a nominal majority in the election of 1847, Russell's position remained weak because of divisions within his own party and the alienation of his Irish supporters with the passing of the foolish Ecclesiastical Titles Act of 1851. This was a law forbidding Roman Catholic bishops to assume territorial titles in the United Kingdom. Russell's Radical supporters were annoyed by the aristocratic complexion of his government and at his initial failure to meet their demands for further parliamentary reform. In 1851 a majority from his own party defeated him in the House of Commons on the reform issue, but Lord Stanley, the Protectionist leader, was too weak to form a government, and Russell struggled on. In the course of his long political career Russell was associated with most of the major reforms of the day, but the record of his ministry proved undistinguished. With Peel's support he continued the movement toward free trade by reducing the duties on foreign sugar, even though it might be slave grown, and by repealing the Navigation Acts, or what remained of them. His government also accepted Fielden's Ten Hour Factory Bill—passed during Ashley's absence from the House—and was responsible for the first Public Health Act, which, despite its defects, recognized the state's responsibility in this area.

But Russell's ministry failed to deal successfully with the greatest problem it faced, that of famine in Ireland. For three successive years, 1845–47, the potato crop failed, resulting in a disaster unparalleled in the history of the British Isles since the Black Death of the fourteenth century.[5] The provision of relief measures was quite inadequate, almost a million people may have died of starvation and disease despite the heroic efforts of private relief organizations, notably the Quakers. A million and a half, many of whom died on the way, migrated to the colonies or to the United States. By 1851 the population was 6,500,000 instead of the 9,000,000 it would have been had the famine not occurred. The misery and suffering of the Irish defies description, and their losses were proportionately greater than those of any nation in a modern war.

The death toll would have been still greater without the intervention of the state and of private charity, but by modern standards more might have been done. The reason for forbearance was not lack of concern but the limited view of the day as to what the state might do. As conditions got worse the Whig government was forced to assume greater responsibility and eventually to set up soup kitchens, following the example of private charity. At the peak of the famine almost a million people were receiving outdoor relief, while close to that number were being maintained in the workhouses; in August 1847 some three million were being fed daily in government soup kitchens. Over £8 million was expended by the treasury for famine relief but most of this was in the form of loans to local authorities, which were later remitted when the income tax was extended to Ireland in 1853. Much of the money spent on relief schemes was wasted because of restrictions on its expenditure and the inability of many of the starving recipients to work. The forebodings of the economists were partly realized by the tendency of

[5] Cf. Arthur Joseph Slavin, *The Precarious Balance: English Government and Society, 1450–1640,* Borzoi History of England Series, III (New York: Knopf, 1973), pp. 9–13.

the poor to leave the land for employment on nonproductive government projects. An examination of the correspondence of the Prime Minister and his colleagues acquits them of any charge of callousness or indifference. Their failing was, rather, a lack of imagination, but it is doubtful that any other contemporary government would have had more success in wrestling with this dreadful problem.

The end of Russell's ministry early in 1852 came suddenly; it was the result of a difference with his Foreign Secretary, Palmerston, which we will consider later. The political situation was complicated because of the curious state of parties at the time. Russell had alienated most of his former Irish supporters and failed to win full confidence of the Radicals. His breach with Palmerston, who had some personal following, was too much for him when Palmerston joined the Opposition against a Government militia bill. The Peelites, who, fearing a Protectionist ministry, had helped to keep Russell in office, failed to come to his rescue on this occasion. Since the death of Peel they had remained even more independent, for Gladstone and Sidney Herbert, their virtual leaders in the House of Commons, did not believe the Derbyite or Protectionist Conservatives would be capable of restoring the Corn Laws. Most of the Peelites (who only numbered between forty and fifty), although they detested the Protectionist leaders, hoped (because of old ties) for an eventual reunion of the Conservative party. Only a few were as yet prepared to join formally with the Liberals despite their semi-alliance of the past six years. But the avid Protectionists, who were mostly ultra-Protestants as well, had no use for the liberal-minded Peelites, who favored free trade and, to a lesser extent, religious toleration.

The Protectionist Conservatives under the leadership of the former Lord Stanley, who had just inherited his father's earldom and the title of Lord Derby, lacked able and experienced leaders in the House of Commons, since almost all Peel's ex-ministers remained loyal to him and his tradition. Indeed, as we have seen, Stanley had been unable in 1851 to form a government. But he could scarcely decline to try a second time, and so he put together a ministry of nonentities, which quickly became known as the "Who Who Ministry." (It appears that when Derby whispered the name of each unknown minister to the Duke of Wellington in the House of Lords, the deaf old duke responded in his shrill, high-pitched voice, "Who? Who?") Disraeli became leader in the House of Commons and Chancellor of the Exchequer. At first he questioned whether he possessed the qualifications for the office, but Derby casually reassured him, saying, "They will give you the figures."

The Peelites decided to give the new Government tentative support, providing it avoided controversial legislation and held an early election. As a result, the Peelites and the Irish Independents (alienated by Russell's

Ecclesiastical Titles Act) held the balance between the two main parties. The Peelites still held off final judgment until presentation of Disraeli's budget when the new Parliament met in the autumn, but they already had been antagonized by the unfriendly attitude of the Protectionists in the summer elections. When, early in December, Disraeli eventually introduced a budget designed to compensate the agricultural interest, the Peelites joined the Liberals in rejecting it as unorthodox. The result was the resignation of the first brief Derby-Disraeli ministry.

Since Russell had been defeated earlier in that year and seemed no longer in control of his party, the Queen sent for Lord Aberdeen, a Peelite peer, who succeeded in forming a Coalition Ministry of Peelites and Liberals. It was an extraordinary achievement, since the Peelites had a corps of only forty-odd members in the House of Commons (although they hoped—as it proved, with good reason—to get a fair amount of independent Conservative support). It was surprising that the Whig Liberals, who supplied more than five times as many votes, should have accepted such a lopsided arrangement which denied some of their leaders the chance of office. In fact, Russell had always been short of talent in making ministerial appointments and had often sought to recruit Peelites into his ministry. Now the shoe was on the other foot. Russell was no longer strong enough to form a government; Palmerston had not yet got control of the party in the Commons; Lord Lansdowne, the Whig leader in the Lords, was too old and ill to take the first place. The amiable Lord Aberdeen, a ward of the younger Pitt who had never sat in the Commons or taken much part in partisan politics, became prime minister by default. He insisted, however, on bringing four ex-colleagues into the Cabinet with him and in giving important offices to several friends who had formerly served under Peel. It was a high price for the Liberal party to pay, but in the long run they stood to gain, since the larger Liberal mass would eventually absorb the much smaller Peelite remnant.

In its first year the Coalition surprised its critics and even its own supporters. Old political rivals worked well together and developed in office a mutual respect. Lord John Russell, who became Government leader in the House of Commons, was the only minister consistently to create difficulties, and in doing so he alienated most of his old Whig colleagues. Palmerston magnanimously joined the ministry of his former critic, accepting the Home Office, although continuing to influence the formation of foreign policy. The strong man of the new Government turned out to be Gladstone. As Chancellor of the Exchequer he introduced in 1835 a budget that won warm praise from the economists for the way it extended Peel's fiscal policy and settled, for the time being, the vexing question of the income tax. A compromise India Act temporarily resolved another outstanding problem by further reducing the power of the East India Company and introducing competitive entrance examinations into the Indian Civil service. Gladstone attempted to promote the same principles with an investigation of the home civil service. The result was the Northcote-Trevelyan report. But the Government fell from office before the sweeping reforms it advocated could be implemented.

In the year 1854 everything went wrong. With the exception of an important act reforming Oxford University (largely Gladstone's work) and a useful Bribery Act, almost all major Government measures were thwarted, including a parliamentary reform bill and a second attempt at Jewish emancipation, both promoted by Russell. The reason for these failures is chiefly explained by the advent of the Crimean War. Mismanagement of the war led to the downfall of the Government and the consequent postponement of the final absorption of the Peelites by the Liberal party. To understand these developments, however, we must turn to consider the course of foreign and imperial affairs.

Chapter Four
PAX BRITANNICA
IN THE AGE
OF PALMERSTON

The first half of the nineteenth century was a time of unparalleled change and development in British domestic history, but it was also a period when Britain played a unique role in world affairs. These years have been called the Pax Britannica. Britain's navy was preponderant and for more than a half-century following the peace settlement of 1815 her worldwide empire had no rival. It was little wonder that mid-Victorians became smug and self-confident and were not loved abroad. Let us look first at the extent and nature of the British colonial empire during this period.

Imperial and Colonial Policy, 1815–1865

The loss in 1783 of the thirteen American colonies was a severe blow to the British Empire. Yet by 1815 the empire was larger in both population and territory than it had been thirty years earlier. The British North American colonies of Upper and Lower Canada, the Maritime Provinces, and Newfoundland were still underpopulated but slowly growing, and American expansionist attempts in Canada had been halted in the War of 1812. To the far west the Hudson's Bay Company held by royal charter the vast northern tract from the bay to the Pacific. British West Indian possessions in the Caribbean were increased by the acquisition of several islands from the French and the Dutch. On the mainland of South America the boundaries of British Guiana were extended, while in Central America there remained the colony of British Honduras and a shadowy claim to a protectorate over the Indians of the Mosquito Coast that was later to lead to difficulties with the United States. Since the seventeenth century Britain had held a few forts in west Africa that were to be important in suppressing the slave trade, a task that kept the Royal Navy busy in the years of the Pax Britannica. In South Africa, Cape Colony had been taken from the Dutch, primarily for

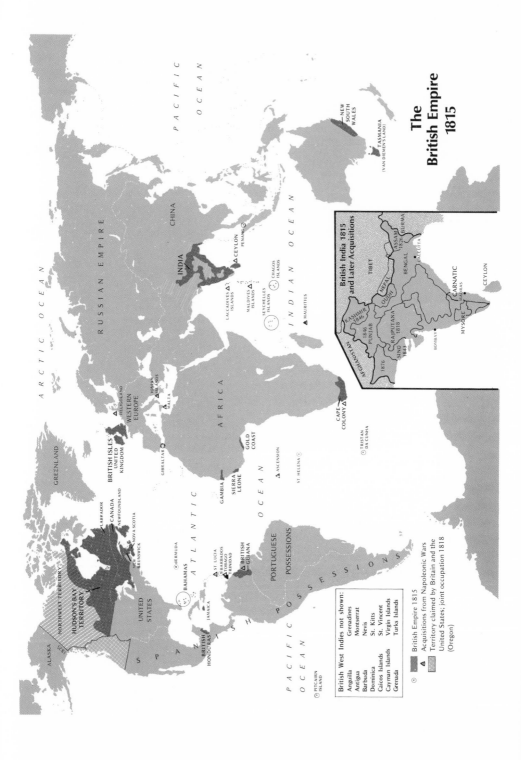

The
British Empire
1815

British India 1815
and Later Acquisitions

British West Indies not shown:
Anguilla   Grenadines
Antigua   Montserrat
Barbuda   Nevis
Dominica   St. Kitts
Caicos Islands St. Vincent
Cayman Islands Virgin Islands
Grenada   Turks Islands

British Empire 1815
Acquisitions from Napoleonic Wars
Territory claimed by Britain and the
United States; joint occupation 1818
(Oregon)

use as a naval station on the route to India. It proved one of the few parts of the continent suitable for European settlement and was the base from which grew the later Union of South Africa. British control of India had been greatly extended during the Napoleonic Wars. By 1815 Britain ruled directly or indirectly all the southern part of the peninsula as well as Bengal and its hinterland to the northwest, and the frontiers continued rapidly to stretch toward their natural limits in the Himalayan mountains. In the peace settlement the strategic island of Mauritius in the Indian Ocean had also been acquired from France, and Ceylon was ceded by the Netherlands. In the Pacific the vast island continent of Australia had become a British possession and a small penal colony had been established in New South Wales in 1788. British supremacy closer to home was guaranteed by retention of the strategic Mediterranean naval bases, Gibraltar and Malta; of more doubtful value, the island of Heligoland had been acquired in the North Sea, off the coast of Germany. With the exception of India this vast empire was governed from the Colonial Office under the Secretary of State for War and Colonies, who appointed the colonial governors in the name of the Queen and gave them their instructions. India was the responsibility of the Board of Control, presided over by another cabinet minister. Its administration was shared with the East India Company, which retained most of the patronage after losing its trading monopoly in 1813 and ceasing its trading operations entirely in 1833.

In the decades following 1815 there was little inclination on the part of the British government or of public opinion to continue a policy of colonial expansion. The cost of administering and defending the empire was already high and, in the absence of imperial competition in these years, there was less temptation toward further empire building.[1] Nevertheless, there is a momentum in the growth (and decline) of empires that is difficult to check. The men on the spot had reasons for extending the frontiers that Whitehall could not control from a distance. This was particularly true in India, which had its own army and its own revenue. Communication with England was inadequate, at least until the completion of the telegraph in 1870, and the governor general had extraordinary power. The expansion of British rule in India toward the natural frontiers of the subcontinent went on unabated partly by the extension of protection to weak native princes who were glad to surrender sovereignty for security, partly by the conquest and annexation of warlike neighbors. The conquest of the Punjab in 1846–49 brought the frontiers of British India up to Afghanistan, while at the same time a protectorate was established over the neighboring state of Kashmir. British rule,

[1] It has been suggested that the doctrine of free trade was the basis of a form of economic imperialism in this period when British trade spread far beyond the flag. See J. Gallagher and R. Robinson, "The Imperialism of Free Trade," *Economic History Review*, 2nd ser., VI (1953), pp. 1–15.

either direct or indirect, now stretched over 2,500 miles from Travancore in the south to Kashmir in the north and some 2,000 miles from Sind in the west to Assam in the east.

Attacks by the kingdom of Burma on the east led to war and annexation in 1824 of part of the Burmese coast. A second war, arising from mistreatment of British merchants, ended with the occupation in 1852 of the rest of Burma's littoral. The Dutch East Indian colonies had been returned by the peace treaties, but Britain remained in possession of Malacca, on the Malaysian mainland, which was formally ceded by the Dutch in 1824. Meanwhile in 1819 Sir Stamford Raffles negotiated a treaty with the sultan of Johore, giving Britain the island of Singapore. These new possessions were the base of future penetration into Malaya and of extensive trade in that part of the world.

Following the abolition in 1833 of the East India Company's monopoly, private British merchants sought access to the challenging new Chinese market. They were less discreet than the Company had been and looked directly to the British crown for protection. They quickly incurred the hostility of the suspicious Chinese authorities, who regarded all foreigners as barbarians. In 1839 the Chinese government took strong measures against British merchants involved in the opium trade, hitherto connived in by local authorities in Canton. Intervention by the British superintendent on the scene led to hostilities and the bombardment of Canton by a British fleet. The British government supported the high-handed action of its representative for the war was about more than opium. The basic British demand was for the right to trade and recognition as an equal sovereign power, a concept quite foreign to contemporary Chinese thinking; but eventually in 1842 the Chinese signed a peace treaty opening certain ports to British merchants and ceding to Britain the island of Hong Kong. A second, more extensive war sparked in 1856 by a similar incident led to further concessions by the Chinese and the acceptance of foreign diplomatic representatives at Peking. The South Pacific islands now called New Zealand were acquired in 1840 by a treaty negotiated with the Maori chiefs. This step was taken reluctantly by the British government on pressure from the missionary interest to forestall French occupation and the advent of French Catholic missions. The islands proved suitable for European settlement and colonies flourished in the following decades, but at the cost of an unhappy war with the native Maoris. In Australia new colonies appeared, either independently or as offshoots of New South Wales. Among the latter, Tasmania, first settled in 1804, became a separate colony in 1825, Queensland in 1826, and Victoria in 1834. Founded independently were the West Australian Swan River settlement, in 1829, and the colony of South Australia, in 1836.

Across the Indian Ocean the frontiers of Cape Colony were being continually extended, again at the price of native wars as new settlers arrived; Natal, on the east coast, was annexed in 1843 and organized in 1856 as a separate colony. To avoid British rule many Dutch settlers (or Boers, as they were known) had withdrawn into the interior and set up the independent Orange Free State and the Transvaal, which were recognized by conventions signed in 1852 and 1854.

The philosophical foundation of the first British Empire was mercantilist; the purpose of empire was to increase the strength and prosperity of the mother country. The colonists, however, brought across the seas the concept of the rights of freeborn Englishmen. They were not satisfied to be told that these rights were preserved in the imperial parliament in the mother country, where they had no direct representation. This paradox had led to the loss of the original thirteen American colonies, but Britain's new colonies sprouting around the globe in the next half-century were too small and defenseless to make such a challenge. Nevertheless, three schools of thought burgeoned in this period that combined to some degree to undermine the traditional mercantilist concept of empire.

First there was the missionary interest, promoted by the active and influential evangelicals. All cabinets in the early nineteenth century had evangelical spokesmen. One was Charles Grant, the first Lord Glenelg (1778–1866), who was president of the Board of Control from 1830 to 1835 and Colonial Secretary from 1835 to 1839. In the evangelical view, the purpose of empire was the spread of Christianity. As we have seen, the missionary interest was responsible for the annexation of New Zealand as well as the abolition of slavery, which had serious repercussions in the West Indies. Evangelicals also sided with natives opposing white settlement, especially in South Africa. Although far from successful, they put at least some brake on the expansion of settlement and won some protection of the rights of natives.

A more positive force was that of the so-called Colonial Reformers, a radical group anxious to apply Benthamite principles to colonization. The leading exponent of this school was Edward Gibbon Wakefield (1796–1862), who in his writings developed a theory of systematic colonization. His schemes, designed to supply colonies with capital and labor in proper proportions, proposed sale of crown lands to settlers and subsidization of their emigration by the mother country. Wakefield's ideas were partially adopted by the South Australia Company in the 1830s and carried still further by the New Zealand Company in the 1840s, although eventually the crown took over responsibility for both colonies. The Colonial Reformers, favoring development of colonial self-government under overall imperial control, were instrumental in inspiring the Durham Report of 1839.

The most important force undermining the old colonial system was the antimercantilist philosophy of the classical economists. As it happened, Adam Smith's *Wealth of Nations* had been published in the same year as the outbreak of the American Revolution. Half a century later its teachings had been widely accepted by those of the British governing class with any interest in economic matters. The erosion of mercantilism begun by Huskisson in the 1820s reached its final stage with the repeal of the Navigation Acts in 1849. By that time many statesmen were beginning to question the viability of empire. In a free-trade world it was difficult to justify colonies as an economic advantage to the mother country. Indeed, the "Little England" radicals of the Manchester school argued that the cost of defense made overseas settlement an expensive luxury. They believed the sooner colonies became independent, the better for all. Many statesmen also saw independence as inevitable, but few were anxious to precipitate it. Their reluctance arose partly from a sense of responsibility and partly, no doubt, from a natural human reluctance to surrender territorial power.

In this political climate colonial demands for autonomy, or "responsible government," as it was called in British North America, met little resistance. Nevertheless, minor rebellions against governing cliques in Upper and Lower Canada were needed to bring matters to a head. It was Lord Durham of Reform Bill fame who visited Canada after the rebellions of 1837 with several Colonial Reformers on his staff and penned the famous report setting forth (admittedly in guarded form) the principle of responsible government. When the Whigs returned to office in 1846 under Lord John Russell, with the third Lord Grey at the Colonial Office, the principle was finally put into practice, first in the British North American colonies and almost immediately afterward in Australia, followed by New Zealand in 1856 and Cape Colony in 1872. It may be noted that the same British statesmen who promoted self-government in the colonies had brought about parliamentary reform at home, which in effect gave responsible government in the United Kingdom itself. There was an anomaly in the theory of responsible government that worried constitutional theorists: The crown might be advised in opposite directions by colonial and imperial ministers. However, imperial ministers refrained from interfering in the internal affairs of colonies, although on occasion they were tempted to do so; and colonial ministers did not at first press for autonomy in external relations, which instead came gradually over the next century. But the self-governing colonies were quick to assert their fiscal independence at an early stage.

Despite the money, time, and energy devoted to administration and defense of this far-flung colonial empire, it did not arouse great interest either among the public or the politicians. The post of Colonial Secretary, which was separated from the War Office in 1854, frequently changed hands and was often no more than a stepping-stone in ministerial careers—four Victorian prime ministers held it at one time or another. India was another matter; it fascinated Victorians in a way that the temperate-zone colonies never did and the office of governor general was one of the most prized at the disposal of the crown. Great pride was taken in Britain's extraordinary achievement of subjugating and ruling this vast subcontinent, and few questioned her right to do so. It was generally supposed that British rule was a boon for the Indians, bringing peace, justice, public works, and Western enlightenment. Some governors general, such as Lord Bentinck in 1828–1835 and Lord Dalhousie in 1848–1856, although they ruled as austere autocrats, were undoubtedly great reformers according to their own lights. They set up judicial, financial, administrative, and educational procedures along Western lines. They built railways, canals, telegraph lines, and irrigation systems, abolished slavery, and attacked such unsavory native customs as suttee (the burning of widows) and thuggee (a murder cult). There was, however, a gulf between the rulers and the ruled, and the sensitivities of the Indians were too often ignored. Except in the native states, which remained under their princes, there was no element of self-government on the higher level; moreover, by Dalhousie's doctrine of lapse the number of native states was decreasing as princes died without immediate heirs and their territories came under direct rule. All higher offices in the civil service and the army were held by Europeans, although 85 percent of the rank and file of the army were natives.

The high-handed policy of the foreign rulers, and in particular the failure to appreciate the importance to Hindu soldiers of religious taboos, provoked the bloody Indian Mutiny in 1857. It came as a great shock to Britain and was suppressed with much severity. Unhappily, unforgettable atrocities were committed by both sides. The mutiny led to a reorganization of the Indian government by the India Act of 1858. This act completely eliminated control by the East India Company, made the cabinet minister responsible for India a secretary of state, advised by a council, and turned the governor general into a viceroy, further exalting that office. Amnesty was granted to most of the mutineers, the proportion of white troops in the Indian army was increased, the pace of material progress was stepped up, and a new penal code was introduced. But the gulf between the handful of Europeans in India and the native inhabitants was widened by bitter memories of the mutiny.

Foreign Policy, 1830–1865

By and large, early and mid-Victorians were more interested in foreign than in colonial affairs, although the two were, of course, connected. Relations with the United States were obviously governed by the

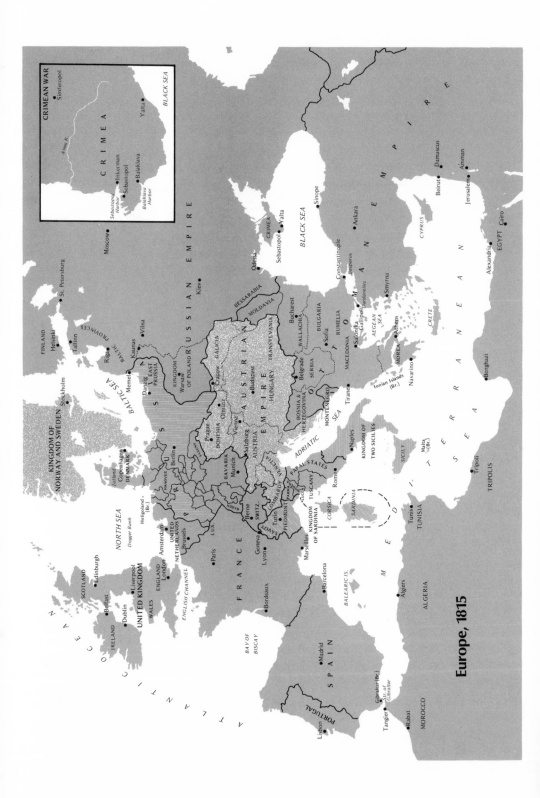

Europe, 1815

attitude of that country toward British North and Central American possessions, while relations with Russia were always colored by the supposed
threat that Russia in Asia offered to India. As we have seen, British policy in
the dozen years following 1815 was shaped by two brilliant foreign secretaries, Castlereagh and Canning, who differed much in temperament and
methods, but not in objectives. The making of policy in the next generation
was dominated by Lord Palmerston, the disciple of Canning, and to a lesser
extent by Lord Aberdeen, the disciple of Castlereagh.

Henry Temple, Viscount Palmerston (1784–1865), is one of the most fascinating figures of the nineteenth century. He inherited an Irish peerage
(which allowed him to sit in the Commons) and large landed estates from
his father, while on his mother's side he was the grandson of a wealthy merchant, the kind of amalgam that had put Britain where she was in the world.
He attended both Edinburgh and Cambridge universities and in 1807 was
elected to the House of Commons, where he remained for fifty-eight years.
From 1807 to 1828 he was Secretary at War, a routine office concerned
mainly with army estimates, the duties of which he performed with compe-
tence and industry. He was a handsome and dashing young man, something
of a "regency buck," who in these years seemed to cut a greater figure in
society than in politics, as may be judged from his nickname "Cupid." A wit
once called him the illegitimate brother-in-law of Lord Melbourne because
of his attachment to that peer's sister, to whom eventually Palmerston was
happily married after the death of her first husband, Lord Cowper. It was as
a friend and colleague of Melbourne that Palmerston entered the Grey
ministry in 1830 as foreign secretary, a post he held, except for a few months,
until 1841 and resumed under Russell from 1846 to 1851. As prime minister,
1855–1858 and 1859–1865, he continued to influence foreign policy until the
end of his long life.

Palmerston was bluff and genial, hard-hitting but magnanimous, and active
to his last days, whether at his desk, in the saddle, or at the dinner table (where
he continued to eat gargantuan meals). His attitude and manner are wonder-
fully reflected in his letters and dispatches. Always written in a strong, bold
hand, their style is straightforward and to the point—although, to judge by
his political career, he was probably more calculating than he appeared on
the surface. By his own standards he was an excellent foreign secretary in
that, more often than not, he got his way. He was well-informed and clear-
minded, although inclined to oversimplify situations to suit his own pre-
dilections. He drove his staff and ambassadors with a tight rein and generally
succeeded in bullying his colleagues and the crown into accepting his views.
He was, however, high-handed and overconfident, too blustering with
foreign diplomats and too ready to antagonize foreign chancelleries. His

basic objectives in foreign policy were those of his predecessors—maintenance of the balance of power and the integrity of the Low Countries, protection of British nationals and British commerce abroad, and suppression of the slave trade, which he promoted vigorously. He attached too much importance, however, to the concept of British prestige abroad and demanded shrilly to be consulted and to advise (and consequently, to meddle) in the affairs of other countries. In particular he loved to pose as the champion of liberal constitutional government against the forces of absolutism, although he never indulged in crusades except against the slave trade, and was a conservative opponent of democracy at home. He once said that "the independence of constitutional states never can be a matter of indifference to the British Parliament or, I should hope, to the British public," adding that he considered constitutional states as "the natural Allies of this country." He avowed that England had no eternal allies and no perpetual enemies, but he was always suspicious of Russia, contemptuous of Prussia, cool to Austria, and solicitous of Turkey. He paid lip service to the idea of an entente with France, but readily forgot it when he suspected a divergence of interests.

Palmerston may have lacked some of Canning's eloquence as an orator, but he defended his policies robustly in the House of Commons, never more effectively than in the 1850 Don Pacifico debate, when he argued that British subjects should be able to enjoy the protection of the British crown anywhere in the world just like ancient Romans, who could boast "*civus Romanus sum*." He went further than Canning in removing the wraps of secrecy from diplomatic negotiation. By the publication of innumerable "blue books" of diplomatic correspondence he kept the public informed of (and sympathetic to) his policies. As a young man Palmerston had not been a popular figure, but as "Cupid" gave way to "Lord Pumicestone" he became more adroit in obtaining support, especially through cultivation of the press. His forthright admonitions to foreign rulers and stout assertion of Britons' rights appealed to the growing chauvinism of the public. "With his dyed whiskers and red face," A. J. P. Taylor has written, "Palmerston exemplifies British self-confidence and bounce."

But this was the Palmerston of later years, depicted in *Punch* as a jaunty old gentleman with a straw in his mouth. In the 1830s he was only beginning to restructure British policy according to his own image. His first and perhaps greatest achievement was his part in the establishment of the new state of Belgium. In the peace settlement of 1815 Holland and Belgium had been united as the kingdom of the Netherlands. But the Belgians had never really accepted the terms of the union or the rule of the Dutch king, William. Stimulated by the July revolution in France, which had put Louis Philippe on the French throne, the Belgians rose in 1830 and set up a provisional

government. Following an appeal for assistance from the king of the Netherlands Wellington had called a conference of the powers in London, but his
government had fallen by the time it assembled. Consequently Palmerston,
as the new Foreign Secretary, became chairman of the conference. More than
anyone he was responsible for the final settlement recognizing the independent new kingdom of Belgium, with the new crown bestowed on the neutral
Leopold of Saxe-Coburg. The Eastern powers agreed reluctantly; a rebellion
in Poland had tied the hands of the Czar, who had been the most inclined to
intervene on behalf of the Dutch king. The French strongly supported Belgian claims, but tried also to benefit themselves. It was this Palmerston determined to prevent. He successfully vetoed the candidacy of Louis Philippe's
son for the Belgian throne and the annexation of Luxembourg by France.
Moreover, after Anglo-French intervention had forced the withdrawal of
the Dutch, he compelled the French also to withdraw their own army by a
threat of war. The new French government was in no position to take the
risk, and Palmerston had his way. Belgian independence was achieved and
guaranteed by the five powers, and the ambitions of France in this sensitive
area were forestalled.

In handling the Belgian question Palmerston learned two lessons that for
better or worse would color his future conduct of foreign relations. One was
the value of Britain's navy (he used it twice to restrain the Dutch) and the
other the advantage of firmness. "You don't stave off war or stop demands
by yielding . . . from fear of war," he concluded.

The labyrinthine course of Palmerston's policy in the Iberian peninsula
during his sixteen years in the Foreign Office scarcely repaid his investment
in time and energy. By and large he followed Canning in supporting the
movements for constitutional government in Spain and Portugal against intervention from the Eastern and absolutist powers; but for all his watering of
the ground, liberal institutions in both countries failed to take root. In 1834
he proposed a quadruple alliance of Portugal, Spain, France, and Britain, the
four nominally constitutional governments in western Europe, but with
little result. The entente between Britain and France, begun by their joint
solution of the Belgian question, grew strained in a clash of interests in the
Near East, and on Palmerston's return to office in 1846, it foundered on the
rocks of the Spanish marriages unwisely arranged by Louis Philippe to
establish his family in Spain. Nothing was gained from the marriages, and
Louis Philippe earned Palmerston's illwill for the few remaining years of
his reign.

No problem preoccupied Palmerston more during his years in office than
the Eastern Question, which stemmed from the disintegration of the Ottoman Empire through Turkish misrule of predominantly Christian subjects.

In Palmerston's view it was in Britain's interests to shore up the weak Turkish government against Russian encroachment, for once Russia was established in Constantinople the whole balance of power in that part of the world would be shifted. Thus in 1832 when the sultan of Turkey was threatened by his unruly vassal, Mehemet Ali, the pasha of Egypt, Palmerston was anxious to come to his aid, but the Cabinet vetoed any such action while the Belgian question was still unsettled. The result was unilateral Russian intervention on behalf of the sultan, who in 1833 signed the Treaty of Unkiar Skelessi, giving Russia special privileges. As a result of this development, of Russia's bloody suppression of the Polish revolt, and of Russian incursions on the frontiers of Persia and Afghanistan, Anglo-Russian relations deteriorated in the 1830s. When in 1839 Mehemet Ali again threatened Turkey, this time by the extension of his power through Syria to the Persian Gulf, both the czar and Palmerston saw the advantage of working together through the so-called Concert of Europe. Palmerston was concerned with Mehemet Ali's threat to new overland routes to India. France, regarding Egypt as her special sphere of influence, declined to participate in any action against Mehemet Ali, but Britain, Russia, Austria, and Prussia agreed on joint support of Turkey. This involved British naval operations on the coast of Syria and a serious rift in the entente with France, which was agreed to with great reluctance by the pro-French, anti-Palmerston wing of the Whig Cabinet. The quadruple agreement, signed by Britain and the Eastern powers in London in 1840, closed the Straits of the Dardenelles to all but Turkish warships in peacetime and provided for the subjugation of Mehemet Ali. It effectively put an end to Russia's special position in Turkey under the Treaty of Unkiar Skelassi, which was allowed to lapse. France's participation in the Straits Convention was only secured in the following year, after Mehemet Ali had been forced to abandon his pretensions. For the time being the danger of Russian domination of the Near East was averted, but at the price of a rift in Anglo-French relations.

In Anglo-American affairs, Palmerston took a strong line against the United States in the McLeod case. McLeod was a crew member of a Canadian vessel that had chased an American gun runner into American waters at the time of the 1837 rebellion in Upper Canada. An American citizen was killed in the incident, and sometime later McLeod was charged with murder after boasting of his exploits in a New York bar. He was released for lack of evidence, but by that time Palmerston had handed over the Foreign Office to Lord Aberdeen, Peel's Foreign Secretary, leaving a legacy not only of bad relations with France and the United States, but also of war in China and Afghanistan.

Aberdeen's policy, which he pursued with limited success, was one of pacification. Through his friendship with Guizot, the French foreign minister, he worked hard to restore the entente cordiale with France, promoting friendly visits between the British and French courts and reaching what he thought was agreement over the marriages of the Spanish queen and her sister. Nevertheless, the suspicions of the public and of many in high places in the two countries died hard. French animosity was aroused by the alleged intrigues of the British ambassador at the Greek court, while British hostility was stimulated by French military activity in North Africa. British opinion was even more inflamed by the arrest of an English Protestant missionary in Tahiti, a French protectorate, but eventually the affair was resolved satisfactorily by the French king.

Anxious to improve British relations with the United States, Aberdeen sent Lord Ashburton in 1842 to negotiate a treaty settling the long-contested boundary between Maine and New Brunswick. To Palmerston's disgust Britain accepted a large part of the American claim, which left a wedge of territory between Quebec and New Brunswick in American possession. American sectionalist factions were antagonized, however, by Aberdeen's proposed treaty to abolish the slave trade and by his readiness to give de facto recognition to an independent Texas. He even discussed with France a joint guarantee for Texas, but this came to nothing, and when Texas was annexed by the United States in 1845 Britain made no objection. By this time the main bone of contention was the Oregon boundary. British fur traders had been established at the mouth of the Columbia River since early in the century, but in the election campaign of 1844 Polk was promising to extend the boundary north to the 54th parallel. Aberdeen resisted this pressure, but just before leaving office concluded a compromise treaty setting the international boundary along the 49th parallel to the coast and leaving all of Vancouver Island to Britain.

The return of Palmerston to the Foreign Office in 1846 meant more diplomatic storms, first with France over the Spanish marriage embroglio (see page 79), and later with the Eastern powers in the aftermath of the revolutions of 1848. Palmerston was no revolutionary, and during that year he did his best to preserve European peace and to localize the crises. His quick recognition of the new French republic had a stabilizing influence, but he readily gave asylum to Louis Philippe and Guizot. Although rejoicing at the downfall of his old enemy, Metternich, he showed no enthusiasm for the resurgence of Italian nationalism and suggested compromises with respect to Austrian rule there. He had no sympathy for Austria, but he was unwilling to disturb the balance of power in that area and permit substitution of French for Austrian influence. He made no attempt to support the Hungarian Revolution or to oppose Russian intervention, but when the crisis was over he condemned Austria's drastic actions during the suppression of the revolt. When Russia and Austria attempted to force Turkey to return the Hungarian refugees who had escaped into that country, he joined France in urging Turkey to refuse and sent a fleet to the Dardenelles to stiffen Turkish resistance.

In the early thirties, shortly after first becoming Foreign Secretary, Palmerston had been instrumental in placing Otto of Bavaria on the new Greek throne. Otto's failure to accept British guidance thereafter was undoubtedly a factor in Palmerston's espousal in 1850 of the exaggerated claims against the Greek government of Don Pacifico, whose house had been ransacked by an Athenian mob. Pacifico was an unpopular Portuguese moneylender who claimed British citizenship because he was born in Gibraltar. Palmerston took up the case without sufficient investigation and unnecessarily damaged Anglo-French relations by first accepting France's offer of mediation and then imposing a settlement on Greece by show of force. His action in this case was condemned in the House of Lords, but upheld after a famous debate in the House of Commons, despite the combined attack of Peelites, Manchester school radicals, and Conservatives. Queen Victoria and her husband, Prince Albert, had long resented Palmerston's methods of conducting foreign policy, his failure to show them dispatches, his use of provocative language when addressing foreign governments, and his gestures of disdain towards them. Lord John Russell, who was jealous of Palmerston's primacy, was ready to accommodate them by removing his rival from the Foreign Office, but Palmerston's victory in this debate forced Russell to postpone such action.

In 1851 Palmerston objected to demands from Russell and the Queen that he avoid provoking the Austrian government by refusing to receive Kossuth, the Hungarian nationalist hero then visiting England, although eventually he gave in to the combined pressure of all his Cabinet colleagues. A few days later, however, he received a delegation of radical working men, who applauded him for standing up to the absolutist powers and who, to the indignation of the Queen, made the most uncomplimentary references to the rulers of Russia and Austria. In December Palmerston finally overstepped himself by privately assuring the French ambassador of his satisfaction with Louis Napoleon's coup d'état at the very moment the British ambassador in Paris was rigidly following the Foreign Secretary's instructions to maintain a neutral position. Russell immediately agreed to the Queen's demand for Palmerston's dismissal, but six weeks later was himself overthrown when Palmerston had his "tit for tat," as he called it, by joining the Opposition to defeat Russell's Militia Bill. Palmerston would never again serve under Russell or hold the seals of the Foreign Office, but except during the two brief interludes of Conservative government under Lord Derby, he was a major influence on British foreign policy until his death.

Within a year Russell and Palmerston were once more in office together in the Coalition Ministry of Lord Aberdeen. The former was government leader in the House of Commons and briefly, Foreign Secretary; the latter, rather incongruously, was Home Secretary. Both greatly affected foreign policy throughout the life of the ministry, which almost immediately ran into difficulties with the reopening of the Eastern Question. Czar Nicholas I of Russia was jealous of recent Turkish concessions to the upstart Louis Napoleon with respect to Christian places of worship in the Holy Land. Nine years earlier he and his chancellor, Count Nesselrode, had visited England and discussed with Lord Aberdeen, then Foreign Secretary, Anglo-Russian cooperation in the event of the collapse of the Turkish empire. He now thought the time had come and looked mistakenly for support from a government headed by Aberdeen. He sent a mission to Constantinople under Prince Menshikov, a bullying diplomat, to demand similar concessions with regard to the holy places for Orthodox Christians and recognition of a Russian protectorate over the Orthodox subjects of the sultan. Against Aberdeen's better judgment, but on the urging of Russell and Palmerston, the British government had just sent the anti-Russian Stratford Canning (1786–1880), recently entitled Lord Stratford de Redcliffe, back to Constantinople, where he was reputed to have great influence. Stratford helped settle the issue of the holy places, but encouraged the Turks to resist the other Russian demands. As a result Russia broke off diplomatic relations with Turkey and occupied the principalities of Moldavia and Wallachia, semi-autonomous Turkish provinces at the mouth of the Danube over which the Russians had some treaty rights. In the months that followed Stratford managed to restrain the Turks from going to war with Russia while the powers sought a solution to the impasse. In June, following the diplomatic breach between Turkey and Russia, Aberdeen, under Cabinet pressure led by Russell and Palmerston, reluctantly agreed to sanction a joint movement of the British and French fleets into the Aegean, as a warning to the Russians and a sign of support to the Turks. In July a conference of ambassadors was held in Vienna under Austrian auspices. The conference endorsed the French compromise proposal known as the Vienna Note. Russia agreed to its terms, but the Turks refused because their own proposals, which arrived late in Vienna, had been ignored. From this point the situation deteriorated despite a series of proposed compromises considered by both sides. The outbreak of nationalist riots in Constantinople led Aberdeen, in defiance of the Straits settlement, to agree to the dispatch of the British and French fleets through the Dardenelles to protect Allied property in Constantinople and to safeguard the Sultan. The czar, anxious to avoid war with Britain and France, met the Austrian emperor at Olomouc (Olmütz) and agreed to a not unreasonable solution proposed by the Austrian minister, Buol. The war party in the British Cabinet, however, led by Palmerston and Russell, overruled Lord Aberdeen and insisted on the rejection of the Austrian proposal, although Lord Clarendon (1800–1870), the Foreign Secretary, continued fruitlessly to seek other solutions. By this time Turkish patience was exhausted; shortly afterward the Porte[2] declared war, attacking Russia's positions across the Danube. The Russians retaliated by sinking a Turkish naval squadron in the Black Sea port of Sinope. Goaded by a bellicose press, the British public was incensed at the so-called "massacre of Sinope." Britain and France then sent Russia a virtual ultimatum requiring her to neutralize the Black Sea. The Russians refused, and with the breakdown of another round of negotiations, Britain and France declared war on Russia in support of Turkey at the end of March 1854.

The ensuing Crimean War has, with some reason, been judged unnecessary. It was ironic that a government with so much talent (at various times four of its members were prime minister and five were foreign secretary) should have failed so dismally. The fact is that the Government's policy fell between two stools. If Lord Aberdeen had had his way war could have been avoided. He would have told the Turks they rejected the Vienna Note at their peril, or he would have accepted the czar's later agreement to the Olmütz proposal. The majority, in the Cabinet led by Russell and Palmerston backed by public opinion, would not pay the price. Their fear of Russia was exaggerated, their confidence in Turkey's ability to reform herself unrealistic. Yet if the Palmerstonians had been free to act from the beginning, the Russians might have been persuaded that war was inevitable if they pressed their original demands, and they might have drawn back before it was too late. Originally, Clarendon agreed with Aberdeen; but as time went on his distrust of the Russians led him closer to the position of Palmerston and Russell. By the time war was declared, the entire Cabinet—except for Aberdeen—was convinced of its justice. The prime minister should have resigned, but he feared that to do so would further postpone the chance of peace, and he believed that since the war had been declared, it must be won.

Palmerston welcomed the war. He saw it as an opportunity to settle longstanding differences with Russia, and it must be added that the public felt as he did. Years of peace and prosperity had made the British proud and bellicose despite warnings from such peacemongers as Cobden and Bright, two

[2] Porte refers to the government of the Turkish empire. It derives from the term *Sublime Porte* (i.e., High Gate), the name given to the palace gate at which justice was administered in ancient times.

of the most unpopular men in the country because of their opposition to the war. Many Radicals supported the conflict because of their detestation of Russian absolutism. France, Britain's old enemy, was accepted as an ally, even under the leadership of a Napoleon. As in the case of Belgium, an important consideration in British eyes was that France should not be allowed to intervene alone. Louis Napoleon, not yet sure of his position, was only too anxious to strengthen it with an English alliance. Before long he was exchanging friendly visits with Queen Victoria and Prince Albert, who at first had been hostile to the usurper of their friend Louis Philippe's throne. Enthusiasm for the war was never as great in France as in Britain, although in the long run France, with her greater military resources, had to bear the brunt of the fighting.

The diplomacy of the Crimean War was as complex as that of its antecedents. No country was more concerned in its outcome than Austria, who prior to the war had joined the Western Allies in putting pressure on Russia, but had refused to take part in the hostilities despite negotiations to that end throughout the war. Austria, desperately anxious to avoid war but not to break with the Allies, sought to escape a decision by mediating a settlement. In the summer of 1854 Austria demanded Russian withdrawal from the principalities, the occupation of which was the original raison d'être of the war. Russia reluctantly complied, and Austria, with the agreement of Turkey, occupied them herself for the duration of the war. She never entered actual hostilities against Russia, although in December she did sign a defensive alliance with Britain and France; she was greatly concerned with the outcome, but in her weak military and financial position dared not commit herself to arms. Throughout the war, however, she worked closely with the Allies in an attempt to force Russia to come to terms. The first result of this protracted diplomacy was the Four Points, stating the basis on which the Allies were prepared to make peace. But initially Russia rejected them, and a subsequent peace conference in Vienna in the spring of 1855 was equally abortive.

Other diplomatic crises were overshadowed by the main course of the war and have consequently received little attention from historians.[3] Greek sentiment was naturally pro-Russian, and Greek volunteers were crossing the Turkish frontier to join insurgent forces of their compatriots in Thessaly and Epirus who had risen against their Turkish rulers. Britain and France, as allies of Turkey, demanded the cessation of this activity, and when the Greek government failed to comply, the Allies sent an occupation force to Athens, which forced a change of government, and remained until the end of the war.

[3] See J. B. Conacher, "Lessons in Twisting the Lion's Tale: Two Sidelights of the Crimean War," in Michael Cross and Robert Bothwell, eds., *Policy by Other Means: Essays in Honour of C. P. Stacey* (Toronto: Clarke, Irwin & Co., 1972), pp. 77–94.

The force was predominantly French, but it was the old story of the British government not being ready to sanction French intervention alone. The paradoxical result was that Lord Aberdeen's government engaged on this occasion in far more drastic action against Greece than had Palmerston in his handling of the Don Pacifico case a few years earlier, which Aberdeen had so severely condemned.

Anglo-American relations also deteriorated during the Crimean War, for different reasons. British suspicions were at first aroused by rumors of American intentions to seize Cuba, Santo Domingo, and the Sandwich Islands (Hawaii); but the real trouble spot was Central America. The Clayton-Bulwer Treaty of 1850 had failed to settle differences in this area, for Britain continued to maintain her position in British Honduras and, for the time, her alleged protectorate over the Indians of the Mosquito Coast. A state of semi-war had developed between two rival communities in this region, one American and one British. The latter, known as Greytown, was bombarded and destroyed by an American war sloop when the inhabitants refused to pay an American demand for reparations for injuries done to an American diplomat. The British government reacted strongly against what Lord Clarendon in a stiff dispatch declared to be an outrage "without parallel in the annals of modern times." Palmerston went as far as suggesting that Britain seize Alaska "to forestall the bargain between Nicholas and the Yankees." He even suggested that, with her naval predominance, Britain could sack American seacoast towns if necessary. In the end the storm blew over, but a final settlement did not come until 1860, when Britain at last abandoned her claims to the Bay Islands and the Mosquito Coast protectorate.

Palmerston's breezy proposal in the summer of 1854 that Britain take on the United States as well as Russia is an indication of the overconfidence with which Britain entered the Crimean War. Initial preparations, it is true, were impressive. A strong Anglo-French naval force entered the Black Sea even before the war began and guaranteed Allied control of that area for the duration. A British army of 25,000 was assembled at Malta before the declaration of war and shortly afterward sent to Gallipoli to join an equivalent French force. Extra rations, clothing, and medical facilities were provided, and the British soldiers were equipped with the ultramodern Minée rifle, which had just been introduced. However, the fundamental flaws in Britain's military system could not be overcome by energetic dispositions on the eve of battle. The British peacetime army was essentially a force of garrisons spread around the world, with a very limited reserve kept in England. There was no system of conscription to ensure a supply of recruits in time of war, and pay and living conditions were so bad that only the poorest or most desperate elements in the population would enlist. Most officers in infantry and cavalry regiments were from the upper classes and lacked proper professional training. Commissions and early promotions were usually purchased, and higher appointments were almost invariably based on seniority alone. Thus nearly all the senior officers sent to the Crimea were Peninsular War veterans. The General Officer Commanding was Lord Raglan (1788–1855), a worthy but incompetent old man who had been many years in Whitehall and had seen no active service since 1815. The organization of the army was incredibly complicated. The Secretary of State for War and Colonies was responsible for its disposition, the Secretary at War for its financing, the Commander in Chief for training and discipline, the Home Secretary for the militia, the Chancellor of the Exchequer for the commissariat, and the Master General of the Ordnance for provision of arms and ammunition and other supplies of war. There had been little change in the organization, equipment, or training of the army since the Napoleonic Wars, largely because of the baleful influence of the Duke of Wellington, who had strenuously resisted all attempts at reform. It was not surprising that when this cumbersome machine was first tested in large-scale operations against a European army it began to fall apart.

The immediate purpose of the Allied expeditionary force was to support the Turks against the Russians on the lower Danube and, in the event of Turkish defeat, to defend Turkey against Russian invasion. The French and British armies therefore advanced from Gallipoli to positions in Bulgaria on the shores of the Black Sea, where they soon began to suffer heavily from cholera and dysentery. Shortly after their arrival, however, the Russians withdrew from the principalities, and the Allied armies were left without a target. After some consideration, but with little information, the decision was made in London and Paris to send the combined force by sea to the Crimean peninsula to seize the important naval base of Sebastopol.

The British and French army commanders doubted the wisdom of the order, but they accepted it and made their plans accordingly. Assembly in the Black Sea of adequate transport for an army of 50,000 to be landed over open beaches was a logistical achievement, but tactical planning was minimal.

The British and French were saved from disaster by the greater incompetence of the Russians, who failed to oppose their landing. The greatest hardships the invaders suffered were fever and the inclement weather. They landed in late summer heat and immediately started marching south towards Sebastopol with insufficient transport. They first made contact with the enemy drawn up on high ground on the far bank of the Alma River. A battle ensued on the following day, but there was no coordination between

the two Allied armies. The French attacked first on the right flank, ineffectively. Eventually Raglan ordered his divisions to advance in a straight line
across the river and up the hillside to the Russian positions, which were finally
taken by sheer courage and will power. Allied casualties were heavy, however,
and the victory was not followed up immediately. The Russians thus had time
to prepare defense works on the landward side of Sebastopol. When the
Allies eventually invested the city by a long circular march around it, the
enemy was ready and resisted a siege from land and sea that was to last a year.
Twice during the autumn the Russians sallied out to counterattack, and both
times the British took the brunt of the blow. The first was aimed at the
British base at Balaklava, a battle which witnessed the heroic but purposeless
charge of the Light Brigade, the result of a misunderstood order. Although
the Russians failed to take Balaklava they blocked a key road, which greatly
circumscribed British operations in the ensuing winter. The second battle at
Inkerman, just outside of Sebastopol, was a bloody affair with heavy losses
on both sides. The arrival of French reinforcements finally forced the Russians
to withdraw. After that the main enemy was the weather. In mid-November
a severe hurricane turned the Allied encampment into a shambles and sank
most of the supply ships, leaving the armies for the time being without many
necessities. To make matters worse heavy rains made impassable the seven
miles of road between the little port of Balaklava and the British positions
outside Sebastopol. For the rest of the winter the chief concern of the Allied
armies was survival. A high proportion of the British army was hospitalized,
but the hospitals—overcrowded, understaffed, and for long without essential
supplies—were no better than charnel houses, even those back at the base
near Constantinople.

In the long run most of these conditions were remedied. The commissariat,
which on peacetime civilian basis was incapable of supplying a large army in
a distant theater of war, was transferred from the Exchequer to the War
Office, and the War Office was separated from the Colonial Office. Florence
Nightingale was sent out with the first female nurses to look after the sick
and wounded at the base of operations; eventually needed medical supplies
arrived. An electric telegraph was laid to the Crimea and a railway was constructed from Balaklava to the front. Materials were sent for the building of
hutments and a transport corps with mules was organized. Warm winter
clothing was available in good supply by spring. The only items still lacking
were reinforcements and efficient leadership. Raglan died under the strain,
but his replacement was little improvement. The British army outside
Sebastopol never fully recovered; the French, with their greater military
reserves, bore the brunt of the siege from then on to the surrender of the
citadel in September of 1855.

It was not until the following spring, however, that the Russians agreed to terms of peace, which were finally settled in the Treaty of Paris. This provided for the neutralization of the Black Sea (a severe blow to Russian prestige), the internationalization of the Danube, and the virtual independence of the principalities (the modern state of Rumania), with some cession of Russian territory at the mouth of the Danube. Turkey in turn made meaningless promises of reform and guarantees of good treatment of her Christian subjects. The immediate objectives of the war were obtained; Turkey was temporarily propped up, Russia temporarily stopped from upsetting the balance of power in the Balkans. The creation of modern Rumania was an incidental and lasting result. Russia, however, was left with a grudge, and it was not to be expected that the Black Sea clauses would last indefinitely. Moreover, British military prestige had been weakened and the need for army reform made manifest. The navy had fared better, for in addition to maintaining the two-thousand-mile communication route between England and the Crimea, it had successfully closed the Baltic Sea to the Russians for the duration of the war—although in the eyes of critics, opportunities here had also been missed through inadequate leadership.

The Crimean War was the first modern war to be covered by newspaper correspondents in the field. The most effective of these was William Russell of *The Times*, whose scathing dispatches revealed to a bewildered and embittered public the sad state of their armies in the field. *The Times* also published numerous accounts from private letters of junior officers supplied by their relatives, describing the terrible conditions under which the army carried on the siege. A great public outcry arose against the Government and the Radical, John Roebuck (1801–1879), introduced a motion in the House of Commons—passed by a large majority—demanding a commission of inquiry. Lord John Russell refused to defend the Government and resigned office before the motion was debated. As soon as it was passed the Government resigned, although most of the steps required to correct the numerous deficiencies had already been taken. Lord Derby was unable to form a government, as was Lord John Russell, whose credit with his old colleagues was completely destroyed. In the end Lord Palmerston, now the most popular politician in the country, undertook the task of reconstituting the previous ministry, except for Lord Aberdeen and the Duke of Newcastle, his unfortunate war minister. Most of the other Peelites withdrew when Palmerston agreed to accept the Roebuck commission of inquiry, but its report had negligible effect. The change of ministry made little difference to the prosecution of the war, except that it was perhaps prolonged by Palmerston's determination to teach the Russians a lesson. To the end he refused to realize the limit of British resources for this sort of operation. He took full credit, however, for the successful conclusion of the war and remained firmly entrenched in office.

Palmerston was seventy years old when he became Prime Minister. Although head of a Liberal government his outlook on domestic affairs was essentially conservative. The followers of Lord Derby were in disarray, and many were content to keep the conservative and popular "Old Pam" in office. Palmerston's main challenges came from his own side of the House. Foreign affairs continued to be his chief preoccupation, and here some of his Peelite and Radical allies were his severest critics.

Although the Liberal-Peelite coalition had temporarily collapsed because of the exigencies of war, it was by no means a complete failure. The Aberdeen administration had been a reforming one, and its Peelite members had taken the lead, although the Duke of Newcastle was an unfortunate choice for the War Office in wartime. While the coalition lasted Whigs and Peelites worked together harmoniously and with mutual respect, except for Russell, who antagonized all his colleagues by his restless ambition. The breach in 1855 was accidental and temporary, and none of the Peelites who held office under Aberdeen ever returned to the Conservative party. Their contribution to the Liberal Party that was emerging from its Whig crysalis was substantial.

In the later stages of the Crimean War relations with the United States again became strained over a maladroit British attempt to recruit reinforcements for the British army in that country. The American government made a great issue of the matter and eventually required Crampton, the British minister, to leave. As the crisis developed the British Government sent naval and military reinforcements to North America, but a complete diplomatic break was avoided through the intervention of moderates in the Cabinet. The Government's decision not to retaliate undoubtedly was influenced by mounting criticism on their own side of the House, led by the curious combination of Roebuck, whose motion had virtually put Palmerston in office, and Gladstone, who had broken with the new Prime Minister over it.

The following year, 1857, Palmerston's critics were once more aroused by the *Arrow* incident. Relations between Britain and China, such as they were, had been strained since the first China War of 1842. In the autumn of 1856 the Chinese authorities seized the lorcha *Arrow*, which had once had British registry, and imprisoned several of her crew. On the demand of the British consul at Canton the crew were released, but the Chinese refused to apologize, whereupon Canton was bombarded by a British naval squadron. The Palmerston government upheld this questionable action when the news reached England. They were defeated, however, on Cobden's motion for an inquiry, which was passed by a combination of Conservatives, Peelites,

Radicals, and Lord John Russell, who had again broken with Palmerston. Palmerston immediately called an election and was returned to office. The complacent British electorate were not greatly interested in Chinese affairs and were certainly not shocked by this incident. Lord Elgin was sent to China as an envoy with a force of British and French troops and the diplomatic support of other powers. The Chinese agreed to open diplomatic and commercial relations with the Western world, but before the treaties were ratified hostilities were resumed as the result of the murder of some members of a British and French truce party. As a result Peking was occupied in 1860, and the Chinese emperor's winter palace was burned down in retaliation. In the nineteenth century Pax Britannica truly encircled the globe.

In 1858 Palmerston ran into unexpected trouble because of an attempt on the life of Louis Napoleon by Orsini, an Italian revolutionary. When the French government discovered the assassination had been planned and the bomb made in England, they sent a sharp protest and demanded a tightening of British law governing such matters. Palmerston ignored the dispatch, but met the French demands by introducing the Conspiracy to Murder Bill, which was supported by the Opposition on its first reading. On the second reading, however, a Radical member, Milner Gibson, introduced an amendment deploring the Government's failure to object to the offensive French dispatch. This was passed by the same combination from both sides of the House that had defeated the Government in the previous year. It was ironic that Palmerston should be attacked by men like Gladstone, Cobden, and Bright for not upholding the honor of England, but this time they succeeded in driving him from office.

Lord Derby again succeeded in forming a minority government, this one a little stronger than the first and lasting a little longer. With help from the opposite side of the House it succeeded in passing the India Act of 1858 and, to the annoyance of some of its own supporters, resolved the long-standing Jewish claim of a right to sit in the House of Commons, by allowing each House to choose the form of its oath of office. This annulled the veto of the House of Lords, which had long opposed legislation excusing Jews from taking the prescribed oath. On the matter of parliamentary reform, however, the Government failed; nor could it secure a majority in the subsequent election. Eighteen months in opposition tamed Palmerston's arrogance and brought the various Liberal elements together again in a portentous caucus meeting in Willis' Rooms. Russell and Palmerston each agreed to accept the leadership of the other, depending on which the Queen called. Derby's minority government was defeated on a want-of-confidence motion and, unable to find a satisfactory alternative, the Queen reluctantly recalled Palmerston to form a government. The leading Peelites, who were still politically active, accepted office, but this time in a clearly Liberal ministry, with Milner Gibson representing the Radicals.

Gladstone returned to resume his work of fiscal reform at the Exchequer. He saw there was no longer a role for him in the Conservative party, and he was too active and energetic to spend a lifetime in fruitless opposition. Moreover, he had found an issue in foreign policy on which he agreed more with Palmerston and Russell (now Foreign Secretary) than with Derby. The cause of Italian unification was espoused by this formidable trio despite the doubts of the court and of some of their colleagues. The Derby government had remained neutral in the war Austria still fought against Piedmont (Sardinia) and France to maintain her position in Italy, but Conservative sympathies were Austrian. The Liberal government's support to the aspirations of Piedmont and later to the unification of all Italy under Victor Emmanuel was tempered only by fear of French hegemony in Italy.

Under Russell's direction British policy was aimed at persuading Austria and France to refrain from interfering in Italian affairs. Russell wanted the Italians themselves to settle the question of unification, which eventually they did. Louis Napoleon proposed joint opposition to Garibaldi's intended crossing from Sicily to take over the kingdom of Naples in the name of Victor Emmanuel. The British government refused and backed the Italian patriot. Garibaldi's subsequent entry into Rome produced a welcome breach between France and Piedmont, and Russell hastened to pen a famous dispatch proclaiming full British endorsement of the unification of Italy, with suitable references to the precedent of the Glorious Revolution of 1688. Britain had given little more than moral support to the Italians, but the latter remembered this with gratitude, and the Government had the satisfaction of seeing the cause it favored both popular and successful.

Britain's attitude to France was ambivalent throughout 1859–60. Public opinion was anti-French and desirous of strengthening Britain's defenses, a goal Palmerston was always ready to support, though it meant serious differences with Gladstone at the Exchequer. On the other hand, Palmerston encouraged Cobden and Gladstone to work out a reciprocal trade treaty with France that was conducive to improved relations. The negotiation of the trade treaty marked the growing bond between Gladstone and the Manchester school. The latter looked to Gladstone to promote free trade, reduce taxation, and curb Palmerston's appetite for expensive foreign and military adventures. All Radical groups applauded Gladstone's decision to abolish the tax on paper imports, which they had always regarded as a tax on knowledge. Palmerston was opposed to this reform and was happy to see it defeated in the House of Lords, despite the convention in the Lords of noninterference in fiscal matters. But Gladstone was determined not to be beaten. The following year he included the measure in a comprehensive Budget Bill, dealing with other taxes, which Palmerston and the Lords grudgingly accepted. Gladstone was becoming the idol of the left-wing Liberals and "Old Pam" gloomily prophesied strange doings when he was gone and Gladstone had his place.

Foreign affairs continued to preoccupy the Government throughout the early sixties. The American Civil War posed problems on which public opinion in Britain was divided. It might be supposed that traditional British opposition to slavery and the slave trade, championed for so long by Palmerston, would have assured Britain's sympathy for the North. But this was not so, partly because secession, not slavery, was the issue over which the war began. Moreover, anti-British feeling and protectionism were more prevalent in the North than the South. On the whole, the British upper classes tended to sympathize with the Southerners (although there were notable exceptions), but there was strong sympathy for the North and the antislavery cause from members of the working classes and some of the middle class, such as Cobden and Bright. Officially the Government was neutral; the ministers resisted the temptation to offer mediation, which would have been resented by the American government as a recognition of the Confederacy's claim to independence. The situation was complicated by Britain's dependence on large supplies of raw cotton from the Southern states and, to a lesser extent, wheat from the North. The Confederates hoped to precipitate British intervention by stopping cotton supplies even before the Northern blockade became effective, but this hope was not realized. Britain had an oversupply of raw cotton at the beginning of the war and, although the suspension of further imports eventually brought a shortage and consequent unemployment in the cotton industry, new sources of supply were developed and Lancashire survived. Gladstone was much impressed, however, by Lancashire's endorsement of the Northern cause despite local industrial distress, which disposed him toward further extension of the franchise to the working classes.

Two incidents in the course of the war disturbed Anglo-American relations. The British government strongly objected to the seizure of two Confederate agents, Mason and Slidell, from the British steamer *Trent*, but the dying Prince Consort, who had always been pro-Union, persuaded Russell to modify his dispatch. The American government avoided a rupture by releasing the captives. More serious was the British failure to prevent the sailing of the commerce cruiser *Alabama*, which had been built in England for the Confederacy. American damage claims for losses caused by this and two other vessels, which were considerable, clouded Anglo-American accord for some years after the war was ended. They were settled when the Gladstone government agreed to arbitration in the Treaty of Washington of

1871. Eventual payment of compensation by Britain in 1872 helped to heal the rift created by the war.

British policy in Europe was less successful in the last years of the Palmerston era. In 1863 a Polish rebellion against Russian rule evoked much sympathy in Britain and France. The British and French governments both attempted to intervene on behalf of the Poles, but Palmerston and Russell had no intention of committing Britain to war on this issue and ultimately abandoned the efforts Lord Derby described as "meddle and muddle." Napoleon could do nothing alone and resented Britain's failure to cooperate. On Britain's misguided attempt in 1864 to intervene in the Schleswig-Holstein matter, a smoldering crisis burst into flame. The kings of Denmark had long ruled the duchies of Schleswig and Holstein, the former partly and the latter predominantly German-speaking. In 1863 there was strong German reaction to the Danish king's action to incorporate Schleswig into Denmark. Palmerston announced in Parliament that aggressive interference in Danish concerns would have repercussions in more places than Denmark. Prussia had been ineffective in European affairs since 1815, and Palmerston had always been contemptuous of the German states. He therefore underestimated Bismarck, the new Prussian minister, who persuaded Austria to join in military intervention that resulted in the Danish War of 1864. Lacking French support Britain was incapable of coming to Denmark's aid, and an international conference in London in June of that year proved fruitless. Denmark was defeated and forced to surrender the duchies to the triumphant German powers. The age of Palmerston had given way to the age of Bismarck, and the following year "Old Pam" disappeared from the scene. He died two days before his eighty-first birthday. The assumptions that underlay Palmerstonian foreign policy were no longer valid, and for the rest of the century Britain played a less flamboyant role in European diplomacy. Her position as an imperial power remained intact, however, and indeed was considerably enhanced in the great competition for empire that characterized the late Victorian era.

Chapter Five
ENGLAND
AT MIDCENTURY

Political and constitutional history is governed by chronology —all events that concern the historian are related to each other within a rigid time sequence that consequently dictates the order of their presentation. This is less true in social and economic history, where (with some exceptions) individual episodes are relatively unimportant, and the historian is concerned with the totality of what has happened over varying periods of time. The economic, and even more often, the social, historian is concerned with generalizations in which the time element is approximate. Generalizations (for example, those involving the rise of the middle class) crop up from century to century, although their contexts may vary greatly. The task of the social historian is fraught with hazard. In the past some of the most popular have painted beautiful pictures based largely on prejudice and imagination. The modern social historian's materials force his findings to be more tentative, less categorical, and frequently less exciting to read. Nevertheless, an overview of the social, economic, and intellectual climate of any period is necessary to make sense of its political history, even though the full picture may elude our grasp.

The first century of the Industrial Revolution clearly increased national wealth, with unequal benefits for different classes. In the interim there had been a long period of growing pains and much suffering for the masses, but by the 1850s the positive results were becoming more obvious. In the jargon of the modern economist the British economy had reached the takeoff point. To understand the changes that had taken place we must examine some demographic and economic statistics. The population of England and Wales had doubled between 1801 and 1851, rising from 8,882,960 to 17,927,609 in this half-century despite heavy emigration during much of the period. In the three decades following 1850 the British birth rate was at its maximum with 35 births per 1,000 population annually. The greater part of the population increase was urban. By the census of 1861 about 11 million of the 20 million people in England and Wales lived in some 781 towns. Liverpool by this time had 444,000, Manchester 358,000, and Birmingham 296,000, although all three had numbered less than 85,000 in 1801. "If nothing else had happened in the first half of the nineteenth century," Dr. Kitson Clark has written of the phenomenal population increase, "this alone would have secured that Victorian England was decisively different in a hundred ways from Georgian England in 1800."[1]

By pre-Industrial Revolution standards Britain was now a highly industrialized country, but by modern standards most industry was still on a small scale. Out of 5,000 employers in 15 important trades reporting in the 1851 census, only 755 employed 100 men or more, and the majority of these were cotton manufacturers. According to the census of 1851 there were 527,000 workers in the cotton industry, as against 284,000 wool workers, 219,000 coal miners, 28,000 iron miners, 80,000 engaged in processing iron, 48,000 engine and machine makers, and 442,000 engaged in the building trades. Agriculture was, however, still by far the greatest source of employment, engaging 1,790,000 as farmers and agricultural laborers, as many as those employed in all kinds of manufacture put together. Another 1,039,000 people were engaged in domestic service; it was an age when every family of any standing at all in the community had at least one servant and the wealthier nobility employed virtual armies to staff their large country houses and town mansions. British agriculture, after some distress in the thirties and forties, enjoyed some share in the national prosperity of the fifties and sixties before the great slump of the seventies. The completion of enclosure, further technical progress in drainage, the use of new machinery and fertilizers, the spread of railways, the commutation of tithes, and the influx of gold all contributed to make the quarter-century following the repeal of the Corn Laws a "golden age" or, perhaps more accurately, an "Indian summer" of British agriculture.

The remarkable growth of railways in the forties and fifties favorably affected all forms of industry and commerce, except those associated with stagecoaching. Indeed just as the growth of canals characterized the first half-century or more of the Industrial Revolution and were an all-important factor in its development, so did the construction between the thirties and the sixties of an extensive railway network characterize this later stage of the Industrial Revolution and give the period the name of the Railway Age. Steam engines had been used in the late eighteenth century to pump out mines, and Richard Trevithick (1771–1833) had invented a steam carriage in 1801 and, in 1804, a railway locomotive to haul loads at the Penydarren

[1] G. Kitson Clark, *The Making of Victorian England* (London: Methuen & Co. Ltd., 1962), p. 66.

ironworks. Ten years later George Stephenson (1781–1848), a colliery engineer, also designed a steam locomotive and then proceeded to build a colliery railway. Stephenson's locomotive was adopted by the proprietors of the Stockton and Darlington Railway, the first commercial railway, which was opened in 1825. Over the next few decades Stephenson, his son Richard, and a corps of self-made engineers solved the innumerable technical problems that faced the early railway builders, and showed great perseverance and ingenuity in constructing giant viaducts and drilling long tunnels to overcome the geographical hazards of the far-from-level British countryside.

The accomplishment was great despite haphazard planning, initial differences in gauges, excess financial speculation, and opposition from some landowners. All railways had to be authorized by acts of Parliament, of which there were 121 in 1845 and an even greater number in 1846. Gladstone's Railway Act of 1844 governed regulation of railway charges and provided for cheap penny-a-mile trains daily on most lines, general supervision by the Board of Trade (replaced temporarily by the Railway Board 1846–51), and even possible purchase of railways by the state (an event that did not take place until a century later). Railway contracting became a major industry, employing some 188,000 men by 1848. Large firms such as Thomas Brassey's built railways on four continents and exported rails and locomotives as well. Large quantities of capital were invested, not always profitably, in railways in the United Kingdom. There was much wild speculation and, in 1847, a serious crash, but building continued until one of the best railway networks in the world was completed in the latter part of the century. By 1835 only 500 miles of railway had been built. This figure jumped to 2,148 by the end of 1844, to 8,054 by 1854, to 12,789 by 1864, and to 16,449 by 1874. The number of passengers soared from 27.7 million in 1844 to 490 million in 1875. The economic and social consequences were incalculable. All sorts of goods were handled more economically; perishable garden produce was more widely sold; coal costs in some areas were cut in half; labor became more mobile. Holiday resorts and excursion trips widened the horizon of thousands of the lower classes to whom travel was a new experience, while for the upper classes the railway greatly facilitated the growing fashion of the boarding school.

The steamship barely antedated the railway locomotive, but it displaced the sailing ship much more slowly than the latter did the stagecoach. In 1833 the first steam crossing of the Atlantic was made by the *Royal William* in twenty-five days, although the *Savannah* had made auxiliary use of steam in 1819. There were only 771 steamships registered in 1840, with a combined tonnage of 87,928. By 1860 the figures had risen to 2,000 ships with a tonnage of 454,327, and by 1874 to 4,033 with a combined tonnage of 1,870,611; but

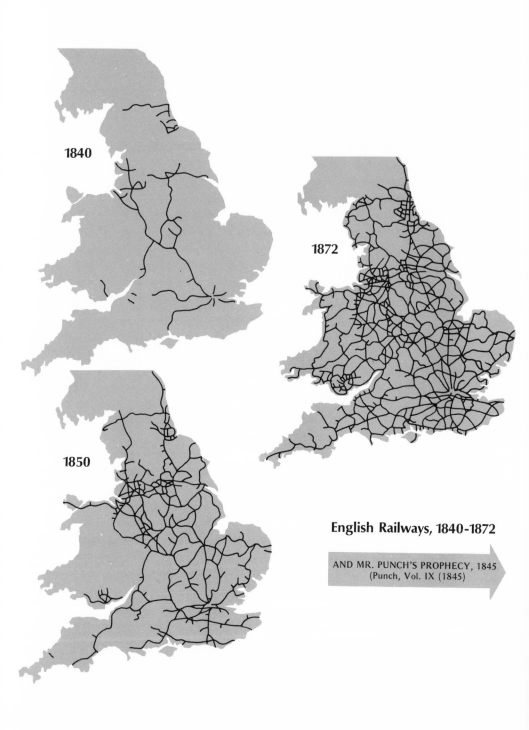

1840

1872

1850

English Railways, 1840-1872

AND MR. PUNCH'S PROPHECY, 1845
(Punch, Vol. IX (1845)

A RAILWAY MAP OF ENGLAND.

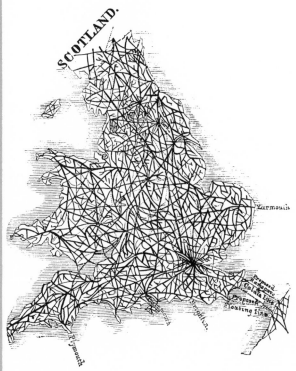

Proposed lines..............

WE are not among those who like going on with the March of Intellect at the old jog-trot pace, for we rather prefer running on before to loitering by the side, and we have consequently taken a few strides in advance with Geography, by furnishing a Map of England, as it will be in another year or two. Our country will, of course, never be in chains, for there would be such a general bubbling up of heart's blood, and such a bounding of British bosoms, as would effectually prevent that; but though England will never be in chains, she will pretty soon be in irons, as a glance at the numerous new Railway prospectuses will testify. It is boasted that the spread of Railways will shorten the time and labour of travelling; but we shall soon be unable to to go anywhere without crossing the line,—which once used to be considered a very formidable undertaking. We can only say that we ought to be going on very smoothly, considering that our country is being regularly ironed from one end of it to the other.

in that year the number of sailing ships was still five times as great as that of the larger steamships and their combined tonnage was more than double.

The rapid extension of the electric telegraph, first at home and then around the world, had great implications in international trade, diplomacy, and journalism. Direct telegraphic communication with the Black Sea area was achieved in the Crimean War; after earlier failures the first transatlantic cable was successfully laid in 1866 by the *Great Eastern* (the largest ship built in the nineteenth century), and a direct line to Bombay was completed in 1870, bringing the Indian government under closer control of Whitehall. In 1869, in face of much criticism, Gladstone's government turned the telegraph system over to the Post Office.

Expansion of trade was a natural corollary to these developments, and during this period British trade exceeded that of France, Germany, and Italy combined. Exports rose from approximately £70 million to £200 million between 1850 and 1870. The textile industries still maintained the lead, and in 1850 cotton and woolen goods formed 60 percent of British exports. The value of cotton goods and yarn exported in 1840 amounted to £24,669,000, increasing to £71,416,000 in 1870. Exports of woolen goods and yarn increased more than fourfold in the same period. The most spectacular increases were in the export of coal, iron, and steel, which increased by tenfold in these years. The output of iron trebled between 1839 and 1860, and steel manufacture developed rapidly with the introduction of new processes by Bessemer and Siemens, although Britain never enjoyed the preeminence in steel production that she once did in iron.

Imports increased even faster than exports, but the adverse balance was made up by payments for shipping services and the return on foreign investments. Net income from such investments grew from £6,000,000 in the early forties to almost £50,000,000 in the early seventies. Indeed in the period 1851–1881 a total of £1,000,000,000 was invested overseas.

The material progress of the mid-nineteenth century is nowhere better illustrated than in the government-sponsored Great Exhibition of 1851. It was warmly promoted by the Prince Consort and consequently patronized with enthusiasm by the Queen, who visited it forty times. Victoria kept a special Exhibition journal from May 1, the day it opened, which she called "one of the greatest and most glorious days of our lives," to October 14, the day it closed, when she wrote: "It looked so beautiful I could not believe that it was the last time I would see this wonderful creation of my beloved Albert's."[2] Exhibits from all over the world were imaginatively housed in a giant prefabricated glass house in Hyde Park, which *Punch* felicitously called the Crystal Palace. British manufacturing and engineering skills were dis-

[2] C. R. Fay, *Palace of Industry, 1851* (New York: Cambridge University Press, 1951), p. 69.

played to their best effect, but the artistic side of these displays was more dubious.

The Exhibition of 1851 helps mark the great transformation in British society of the mid-nineteenth century. The element of barbarity never far under the surface of eighteenth-century civilized life lasted well into the first half of the nineteenth century. Life was cheap, and there seemed little the masses could do to better their lot. Exciting changes took place in the first half of the century; reforms were mooted and achieved on a scale hitherto unknown, keeping pace, in some respects, with the technical achievements of industry. But society was still raw; armed revolution remained a possibility (as, for instance, in 1832); social unrest was a fearsome reality in the age of the Chartists when the upper classes felt the need to protect their homes with their own resources. For instance, in 1842 Peel sent arms and ammunition for the defense of his family in Drayton Manor; yet it was unthinkable that Palmerston would consider fortifying his country house at Broadlands when he was Prime Minister fifteen years later. By the 1850s the press gang had gone; dueling was an anachronism; the thief was no longer hung on the gibbet, although public executions were not abolished until 1868; the police-man was now a familiar figure both in London and the provincial towns. Railway transportation had made maintenance of public order much easier; indeed, it had been a factor in bringing Chartist rioting under control. Of course some vestiges of the old predilection for rioting remained, but the occasions were few and far between and, on the whole, there was little threat to the maintenance of public order in the second half of the century.

The quarter century following the failure of the third Chartist petition was undoubtedly one of ever increasing economic prosperity and of reduced social tension, but it is difficult and dangerous to make sweeping generaliza-tions about the lot of the working classes as a whole. Some of the worst con-ditions in the factories and mines had been ameliorated by legislation, but long hours and hard work were still the order of the day for those fortunate enough to be employed and employable. The coming of the railway was, as we have seen, a boon to the working class and Gladstone's Railway Act of 1844 required the provision of third-class accommodation on all lines at the rate of a penny a mile. Britain's towns and cities became more livable in the second half of the century as city fathers, despite the conflicting range of local authorities and the traditional opposition of local authorities to central con-trol, began to develop civic pride and a readiness to spend money both on drainage and on the improvement of amenities such as parks, libraries, public buildings, and hospitals.

The provision of adequate housing for the working classes remained an almost insoluble problem with the rapid growth of population. In particular

SPECIMENS FROM MR. PUNCH'S INDUSTRIAL EXHIBITION OF 1850.

(TO BE IMPROVED IN 1851).

From Punch, Vol. 18 (1850), p. 145.

the density of population near the center of the larger cities made crowding inevitable, and large, once-fashionable houses became slum tenements teeming with human life. Courts sprang up in the centers of large city blocks where once there had been gardens or coach houses behind the rows of fine mansions of an earlier period, and here congestion and filth were accentuated. In the newer industrial towns back-to-back houses, rapidly deteriorating, were still lived in, but local authorities were starting to forbid the building of new ones. Indeed, local authorities were beginning to set basic building standards that, in time, would lead to some improvement; in London large slum areas were cleared away to make room for the broad, main thoroughfares that characterize central London today, and for the numerous stations and railway yards that form a ring around the inner city. The better sort of working class houses that were being built were four-roomed, two up and two down with a small attic. Large blocks of flats began to appear, mainly in London, for the first time in the 1840s--later than in continental cities—many of them put up by philanthropic bodies such as the Peabody Trust (endowed by the wealthy American merchant, George Peabody). These buildings, known as model dwellings, were well-built with running water and proper ventilation, but they were too few in number to go far towards solving the housing problem. In the country some socially conscious landlords built model cottages that were great improvements over the typical agricultural laborers' hovels, but again, in insufficient numbers to meet the need.

Water closets were only beginning to appear in working class homes, and outside privies remained common until late into the century with a variety of unpleasant methods of disposing of their contents. Gas was used for street lighting, home lighting, and cooking by the middle and upper classes, but for the most part the working classes remained dependent on candles and paraffin lamps, small ranges or open fireplaces, and the baker's oven down the street.

Although the wealth of Britain increased greatly in the mid-Victorian years, it seems that the working classes still failed to get their share of the increase to which they contributed, except in the improvement of public facilities. Wages increased, but so also did prices, and it was not until the later 1860s that there is good evidence of a rise in real wages, i.e., in terms of what they could buy. The longer periods of prosperity, however, meant less unemployment and steadier income. In 1867, according to a contemporary authority, the average weekly wages of skilled artisans ranged from twenty-eight to thirty-five shillings a week; metal workers, the better-paid male textile workers, seamen, and others averaged twenty-five shillings a week; miners, coal heavers, railway workers, tailors, and the poorer-paid textile workers, twenty-one to twenty-three shillings a week; fishermen, police, messengers and porters, horsekeepers, and the like, fifteen to twenty shillings a week; farm laborers and general laborers, fourteen shillings a week; and soldiers, pensioners, and silk workers, only twelve shillings a week. A shilling could buy three two-pound loaves of bread, or two to three pounds of meat. Working class rent was likely to cost between two and three shillings a week.

The wages of women and young people were much lower than those of men. Approximately a quarter of the female population over the age of fifteen worked in these years, but they were concentrated in a limited number of occupations. The census of 1851 lists 905,000 in domestic service, 635,000 in textiles, 227,000 women in agriculture, and 146,000 as "washerwomen, manglers, etc.," but only 19 as commercial clerks. The numbers engaged in domestic service and in the textile industries continued to rise but the number employed in agriculture dropped steadily after midcentury. Large numbers of boys and girls under fifteen continued to be employed in many industries and a commission of inquiry in the 1860s came to the conclusion that often their own parents were their worst exploiters. Gradually the laws protecting children were extended (thanks largely to the efforts of Lord Shaftesbury) and, in the 1870s, the number of children in employment began to fall as a system of national education was developed.

There was some improvement in the hours and conditions of work in the third quarter of the century; the Saturday half-day became common and four additional public holidays were authorized in the 1870s. Shop assistants, domestic servants, "self-employed" domestic workers, casual laborers and employees in some small industries remained unprotected and open to exploitation by unscrupulous employers. Much industrial employment remained hazardous (especially in the mines and on the railways, where accidents were frequent), but limited progress was made in the development of health and safety standards.

Below the ranks of the working classes who were in regular employment there was a residuum of poor people who rarely or never worked as a result of some incapacity, of being work-shy, or of pure bad luck. Some turned to crime and some to begging and at times they might have done quite well living by their wits. But most lived grey, empty lives below the poverty line, saved from starvation by private charity or the poor law. In bad times the numbers in this condition were greatly increased with the rise of unemployment. A great deal of money was expended in personal and institutionalized charity, possibly as much as £7,000,000 in 1870 in London alone. It is difficult to measure either the amount or the effect of this charity, but it was spread very unevenly and open to endless abuse.

It was estimated that some 17 percent of the population of England and Wales received poor relief for varying periods in the year 1850, a figure that decreased to 9 percent in 1879. Poor Law expenditures in England and Wales between 1850 and 1875 ranged from just below £5,000,000 to £8,000,000 a year, but this was no measure of the extent of pauperism. About half of the Poor Law expenditure went to "outdoor relief" and only about one-fifth to maintenance in the workhouse, despite the intention of the Poor Law Act of 1834. An increasing amount—10.2 percent in the early 1870s—was spent on the maintenance of lunatics, and the remainder was spent on staff and buildings. The mid-Victorian workhouses were usually well-built and not prisonlike as has been suggested. There were still some scandals in their administration, but many, especially the larger ones, were sensibly and humanely run with "extras" for special occasions.

On the whole, we may conclude that there was some general improvement in the lot of the British working classes in the third quarter of the century, in contrast to the turbulence and disappointment of the preceding decades. A new generation of leaders turned their backs on direct action of the Chartist variety and devoted their efforts to the development of effective trade unions. Most earlier unions had failed because they were either small and clandestine or had mushroomed without establishing a firm base. A more conservative type of union, organized on a national basis, emerged in the 1850s, chiefly among the more skilled trades. The gradual extension of popular education and of the new Mechanics Institutes providing centers of adult education across the country produced a more educated and practical leadership.

The Amalgamated Society of Engineers, founded in 1851, and the Amalgamated Society of Carpenters, which followed a few years later, exemplified the new type of conservative craft union. By levying rather high dues they built up substantial reserves, which were used to provide sickness, accident, and unemployment benefits for their members. They also acted as bargaining agencies, but only turned to strikes as a last resort. Their leaders, such as William Allen of the engineers, Robert Applegarth of the carpenters, and George Odger of the London Trade Council (another innovation), were men of strong character and marked business ability, who gradually won the respect and confidence of the Victorian middle and upper classes. "Self-Help," the title chosen for one of the best-selling books of the popular author, Samuel Smiles, was the keynote of the day, reflected in the growth of this kind of trade unionism, of cooperatives, and of various new benefit societies, although as yet such associations were largely limited to the upper crust of the working classes. In 1870 there were only some 400,000 union members in England, but the unions had already formed a loosely-knit Trade Union Congress that has met annually since 1868.

It is not difficult to imagine what England looked like at midcentury—a country bustling with activity, a country of ever-expanding red-brick cities and black-plumed factory chimneys, but also of rich, trim farmland, all bound together by new rails of steel and surrounded by a sea thronged with ships of both sail and steam. The contrasts between wealth and poverty, beauty and degradation, were still discernible to the perceptive onlooker, but the general atmosphere was one of confidence and optimism. England was riding the crest of the wave; no country in the Old World could equal her wealth, prosperity, and apparent political stability. On the surface, at least, an air of respectability pervaded English society, from the elegantly dressed ladies and gentlemen in their carriages, to the numerous clerks, small trades-men, and skilled artisans, most of whom were quite content to ape their social betters. Abject poverty was largely out of sight in city slums penetrated by few who did not live there, or in more remote parts of the countryside. But just above the line of utter poverty masses of town and country workers lived short, gray lives marked by hard work and few comforts.

It is more difficult to understand the postulates on which this society was built and the values which governed it than it is to assess and account for its stability. We may begin by examining the state of religion, for a count was taken of church attendance in England and Wales on the last Sunday in March, 1851. From this it was calculated that some 7.25 million people attended at least one service. Of these 3,773,474 were Anglican, 3,234,685 Dissenters, and 252,873 Roman Catholics. What was alarming to the com-pilers of the census and of contemporary opinion was the conclusion that, after allowing for absence on account of age, health, or duty, over 5 million people stayed away who were free to attend, and these were almost all from the working classes. The figures depict the strength and the weakness of organized religion in Victorian England. At no time since the Reformation, with the possible exception of the years of the Puritan Revolution, had the upper and middle classes been so punctilious about religious observances. One sees this in the intensity of debate on religious topics in Parliament and press; in the increased sale of religious literature; in the widespread practice of family prayer and Bible reading; in the very strict observance of Sunday, with often two or three attendances at church services; and with the great increase of church and chapel building that characterized the first half of the century. In 1801 the number of places of worship in England and Wales was 15,080, increasing to 22,413 in 1831 and 34,467 in 1851. But new churches barely kept pace with the rapid rise in population and never succeeded in closing the gap created in the late eighteenth century by the growth of indus-trial towns with practically no church facilities. A large proportion of the working-class population were virtually heathen with no knowledge of the Christian religion, judging from evidence in royal commission reports on conditions in factories and mines in the 1840s. Obviously, the population shift and the growth of churchless industrial towns had contributed to the decline of working-class church membership. But connected to this was a feeling of class alienation, a disinclination, among the working classes, to join congregations where class differences were all too visible, especially in cases where workers lacked clothes suitable for church attendance.

All this was a matter of grave concern to zealous churchmen of the Victorian era and great efforts were made to cope with what proved an insoluble problem. The half-century following 1815 was a period of reform unparalleled in the history of the Church of England; especially during the thirties and forties, when Peel and the Whig ministers set up an Ecclesiastical Commission to force the church to put its house in order. This reduced the worst abuses arising from absenteeism, pluralism, maldistribution of revenues, and lack of training facilities. In the years 1831–51 more than two thousand new churches were built at a cost of some £9 million, much of it raised by private subscription; and many more old churches were restored. Prior to this time there were no Anglican seminaries, and only a third of the clergy were university graduates. Between 1846 and 1876 eight theological colleges were founded, and the Anglican clergy increased from 17,320 in 1851 to 21,663 in 1881. The creation and financing of new parishes nevertheless posed grave difficulties (often raised by vested interests), and many of the lower clergy remained poorly paid. During the same period large sums were also raised for home and foreign missions and for the building of schools and charitable institutions. There was more vitality in the Anglican Church in the middle of the nineteenth century than there had been a century before, and the bulk of the clergy had a keener sense of vocation.

The religious fervor of churchmen in these years was unhappily marred by fierce differences within the established church and with the other Christian churches. It is paradoxical that a religion founded on love should throughout its history have produced bitter feelings between those who differently interpreted its teachings, but the violence of these controversies arose from a strong sense of conviction as to where the truth lay. Toward the issue of religion Victorians cannot be charged with the sin of indifference. Within the church the major split was between the High and Low Church parties. The Low Church party, which was the more numerous (especially among the laity), drew much religious inspiration from evangelicalism. Nobody better reflected their best and their worst features than Lord Shaftesbury; narrow and bigoted in his religious views, he was still a champion of moral and social reform. The Low Churchmen were ultra Protestant and intensely anti-Catholic, greatly exaggerating the threat to England of the Roman Catholic religion. Their fierce antagonism was fanned by the Tractarians, the extremists within the High Church party, who in the Catholic tradition extolled the power of bishops and emphasized the essential Catholicism of the Anglican Church and, consequently, the continuity with pre-Reformation days. The ground was perhaps prepared for this movement by revived interest in the Middle Ages stimulated by such romantic writers as Sir Walter Scott. The High Church party later embarked on a revival of Catholic ritual that, in seeming to challenge the official prayer book, brought the anger of Low Churchmen to a white heat. The original Tractarian movement, however, which began in Oxford in the 1830s under the inspiration of such distinguished clerics as Pusey, Keble, and Newman, was essentially aimed at restoring a full knowledge of Christianity and its proper practice through the study of the writings of the early Church Fathers of the fourth and fifth centuries. Ninety Tracts in all were published by this zealous band of Oxford dons, and these were widely read and heeded by large numbers of the Anglican clergy. The Low Church, however, were up in arms against the allegedly Catholic interpretations of these tracts, and Newman's *Tract 90*, seeking to reconcile the Thirty-Nine Articles of the Elizabethan church settlement with Catholic teaching, went too far for the episcopal authorities, who brought the series to an end.

The majority of the Tractarians remained loyal members of the Anglican Church to the end of their lives and left on it an imprint that is felt to this day. Others, however, including John Henry Newman (1801–1890) and Henry Manning (1808–1892), future Roman Catholic cardinals, concluded that there could be only one true church, and that it was the Roman one. Most of them were ordained clergymen of the Church of England, and their conversion to Rome created a sensation in an age when religion was regarded very seriously and Roman Catholicism looked upon with distaste. The shock was as great as if an important group in the hierarchy of Britain's Labour party today were to renounce their old allegiance and join the Communist party.

A third faction existed in the Victorian church—the Broad Church party —precursors of the liberal Christianity of the twentieth century, who reacted against doctrinal dogmatism. Their views are to be found in a volume entitled *Essays and Reviews*, published in 1862, which the High Church violently attacked as subversive of true religion, but which would be read today with little surprise by any serious student of Christian theology. Nevertheless, it was not a very long step from the Broad Church position to skepticism, which became increasingly common among educated people in the latter part of the century. In the views of the High Church, the Broad Church, in their efforts to seem reasonable and in tune with the times, gave away too much and undermined the Christian position. In 1847 Lord John Russell nominated Dr. Hampden, a Broad Church theologian, as Bishop of Hereford. The appointment was strongly opposed by the High Church, who suspected

Hampden's liberal views on baptismal regeneration. The incident led some of them to question the wisdom of church control by the state. Their fears were enhanced by the decision of the judicial committee of the Privy Council denying the right of the High Church Bishop of Exeter to question on doctrinal grounds the appointment of a clergyman named Gorham to a living in his diocese. The widespread excitement aroused by these incidents illustrates the intense preoccupation of the Victorians with religious problems.

An interesting disclosure of the census of 1851 was that Dissenting services rivaled those of the established church in terms of church attendance. Indeed, their chapels had increased sevenfold in the half-century and accounted for the greater share of church construction of that period. The largest of these churches and the one that most dramatically increased its membership was the Wesleyan Methodist, from which the Primitive Methodists and other groups had splintered off. The other independent or congregational churches, as well as the Baptists, had also increased their numbers and activity, although most of the Dissenting churches began to experience setbacks after 1850. The Wesleyans, who formed the right wing of Dissent, long remained under the conservative and dictatorial sway of Wesley's eventual successor, Jabez Bunting, who once declared that Methodism was "as much opposed to democracy as to sin," an attitude that finally brought grave divisions into the society. Two groups whose important influence was not reflected in their small membership, were the Unitarians and the Quakers. The former were the intellectuals of Dissent, the latter, the philanthropists. The Unitarians produced many leaders of municipal government, including, later in the century, Joseph Chamberlain, mayor of Birmingham and ultimately a national political leader. The beliefs of the Quakers precluded their active participation in politics; but this rule became less rigid, as is evident in the career of John Bright, the most famous nineteenth-century Quaker whose religious convictions were an inspiration for his politics.

The Anglican gentry ruled the countryside in England and Wales, but the Municipal Corporations Act of 1835 gave control of local government in many large industrial towns to Nonconformist businessmen. Only a handful of Dissenters got into Parliament before the second Reform Act of 1867, and even in 1868 they numbered only sixty-three. Nevertheless, a large proportion of the newly franchised "ten-pound" voters were Dissenters, and their views carried considerable weight at election time. This may be seen in their wholehearted participation in the Anti-Corn Law League and in their fierce opposition to any legislation favoring Anglican schools, which unhappily helped to delay the introduction of national education in England. Although expansion of the Dissenting Church slowed after the middle of the century their political voice became shriller, partly owing to the activity of Edward Miall, editor of the militantly radical weekly, *The Nonconformist*, and founder of the Anti-State Church Society, precursor of the Liberation Society founded in 1853.

The Roman Catholic minority in England at the beginning of the nineteenth century was very small and rather aristocratic in that it was centered around a number of landowners, whose families had remained loyal to the old religion at the time of the Reformation, and those over whom they had local influence. They had lived obscure lives, cut off from participation in national political life, until the passing of the Catholic Emancipation Act in 1829. Until the French Revolution had forced them to build their own seminaries, their priests had been trained abroad; and their church in England had been organized on a mission basis. In the nineteenth century, with penal laws repealed and their numbers considerably increased by both poor Irish immigrants and distinguished Anglican converts, their position was greatly changed. In 1850 a papal bull, couched in language English Protestants found offensive, reorganized the Roman Catholic Church in England into sees under bishops with territorial titles, including Nicholas Wiseman (1802–1865), as Cardinal Archbishop of Westminster. The Catholic community weathered the storm, which culminated in Lord John Russell's ineffective Ecclesiastical Titles Act (see p. 61); but they were made painfully aware of their unpopularity in what was still an intensely Protestant country. There was a wide social gulf between the old English Catholics and the new Irish Catholic immigrants, but the challenge of numbers was met by a doubling of the number of clergy and of churches in the two decades following the census of 1851.

In the first half of the nineteenth century education was still closely associated with religion and was claimed by many as a prerogative of the established church. Appointments at Oxford and Cambridge long remained the preserve of the Anglican clergy, and religious tests for students were only removed in 1854 and 1856 in the face of strong objections. (Science laboratories were not built at these universities until the fifties and sixties.) All the great public schools, in reality private boarding schools, to which the upper classes sent their sons to be educated, were Anglican, and all the headmasters inevitably were clergymen. The motto of the most devoted Victorian headmasters, all Anglican clerics, was "godliness and good learning," but the latter meant the classics; as late as 1864 a royal commission deplored the lack of instruction in history, modern languages, and science. The avowed objective was character building, and in this regard emphasis was put on organized games and strict observance of the sportsman's code of fair play.

The elementary education of the poor was left mainly to voluntary religious societies, which depended initially on private subscriptions, but beginning in 1833 received government grants providing they filled certain basic requirements. The grants, which were gradually enlarged, were administered by a committee under the Lord President of the Council, and in 1856 a separate department of education was instituted. A school inspectorate was formed to ensure standards of teaching, and teacher training colleges were set up. But differences over the role of the church postponed the establishment of a national system of education, although various royal commissions were appointed to investigate education, and a number of abortive bills were introduced in Parliament.

Victorian conventions put restrictions on Victorian writers and the intelligentsia, to which they submitted with good grace but these did not reflect lack of imagination or versatility. Letters and ideas flourished; books and periodicals of every description were sold and read on a scale never before equaled. It was an age of great literary vitality and boasted a remarkable number of writers—poets, novelists, historians, philosophers, and critics—whose names are still renowned. They included such poets as Tennyson, the Brownings and Swinburne; such novelists as Dickens, Thackeray, George Eliot, and the Brontës; such literary and art critics as Matthew Arnold and Ruskin; such historians as Macaulay, Hallam, and Froude, and a little later, Maitland, Stubbs, and Maine; such political philosophers as J. S. Mill and Carlyle, to name only a few. Paradoxically, the majority (except perhaps the historians) were skeptics, who for the most part accepted the strict moral code of Victorian society but no longer shared the religious faith of their middle- and upper-class contemporaries.

Two of the most influential thinkers of the day—both agnostics as well as earnest moralists who appealed to the idealism of their contemporaries—were Thomas Carlyle (1795–1881) and John Stuart Mill (1806–1873). These two men were friends, but very different in temperament, background, and outlook. Carlyle never completely escaped his Scottish Calvinist upbringing, but was much influenced by the German idealistic school of philosophy. His unique style was vivid and volcanic, combining the moral fury of an Old Testament prophet and the mordant wit of more modern times. He idealized the past, championed the role of the strong man or hero in history, denounced industrial society and its values, extolled imperial expansion, and held democracy in contempt. He would have been shocked to learn it, but in many ways his ideas foreshadowed twentieth-century fascism. Mill, whom Gladstone dubbed "the saint of rationalism," was more representative of his times, although many of his ideas were in advance of his age. A child prodigy, he was brought up by his stern, unbending father in the narrow school of Benthamite utilitarianism, described in his fascinating *Autobiography*. Although he never repudiated the ideas of Adam Smith and Jeremy Bentham,

THE HUB OF THE CITY, 1851

he later broadened his horizons and was influenced by other schools of thought, especially by Coleridge and other Romantic writers. As a result, he humanized and ameliorated the doctrines of the older Benthamites and economists. His great essay "On Liberty" remains to this day one of the wisest treatments of the subject.

Despite the neglect of science and mathematics in the English system of education there was a growing interest in science outside of the universities, and some English scientists, most of them self-educated, made important contributions to international knowledge in this field. John Dalton (1766–1844), Michael Faraday (1791–1867), and James Joule (1818–1889) were important pioneers in the modern study of physics and chemistry, Dalton in the determination of atomic weights, Faraday in the investigation of electricity, and Joule in developing the theory of the conservation of energy. In the 1830s Charles Lyell (1797–1875) published his *Principles of Geology*, which upset Biblical belief in an instant Creation by indicating the great age of the earth and its slow geological development. Still more startling were the ideas of Charles Darwin (1809–1882) in his epoch-making *Origin of the Species by Natural Selection* published in 1859, which developed the theory of biological evolution. Although this theory was compatible with a belief in Christianity, it seemed initially to offer a dangerous challenge to the orthodox Christian churches. Inevitably, it was seized upon as a weapon, by freethinkers such as Herbert Spencer, to attack the credibility of the Christian religion. It was rejected unthinkingly by such redoubtable Christian spokesmen as Bishop Wilberforce. Newman's more subtle mind was less offended, since he was convinced that truth was indivisible, a view that pointed to the direction in which the reconciliation of science and religion might be sought.

In 1861, when Queen Victoria's beloved Prince Albert died prematurely, she had been on the throne for twenty-four years. Her name was already being used to describe the age in which she ruled, as different from the regency period in which she had been born as night from day. Despite a diversity of economic, religious, and intellectual activity, the characteristic common to most leaders in every walk of Victorian life was moral earnestness. It was shared by believer and agnostic, by mill owner and artisan, by Liberal and Conservative. In the front ranks of public life Palmerston and Disraeli were the two exceptions who managed to flourish without it—the one a lone survivor of regency days, the other an outsider who rose to the top by his wits, but who lacked the confidence of the majority of his followers during much of his career partly because he failed to satisfy them in this all-important respect. To later generations, especially that of satirist Lytton Strachey,[3] Victoria and the Victorians seemed a very

_____
[3] *Queen Victoria* (1921); *Eminent Victorians* (1928).

stuffy lot. The way they dressed and furnished their houses appeared to sustain this view. Their solemn adherence to social proprieties and conventions, their refusal to speak out on such "delicate" subjects as sex, suggested a dull uniformity of ideas and lack of intellectual vitality that was far from the fact. For all their conventionality the Victorians were a creative lot. They may seem to have been smug, but they sowed the seeds of change that leads to progress. The term "Victorian," insofar as it denotes the characteristics we have been considering, was not applicable to the whole reign of the Queen, who outlived most of her contemporaries. As we shall see, by the time she died many supposed Victorian verities were being questioned or openly discarded. The third quarter of the nineteenth century may be considered the high noon of the Victorian era and perhaps, indeed, of England's long history.

Chapter Six
GLADSTONE AND DISRAELI

The decade 1855–1865 was one of political doldrums, although below the surface new ideas were fermenting that burst into life in the decade that followed. No great legislative reforms mark these years (unless we count the Divorce Act of 1857 as such), but piecemeal reform continued almost unnoticed on momentum generated by the administrative revolution of the preceding decades. Once the state had undertaken the task of social regulation and appointed inspectors for factories, mines, schools, sanitation, and other areas of social concern, the process of adding to and amending existing regulations went on almost automatically, even in a nonreforming era. It has been well described by W. L. Burn in a book appropriately called *The Age of Equipoise*.

After Lord Melbourne, Palmerston was probably the most conservative nineteenth-century leader of the Whig-Liberal-Radical coalition. Yet ironically, a distinct Liberal party was beginning to emerge during these years. Like the Conservatives, the majority of Liberals still came from the landed and leisured classes, but an increasing number of businessmen were to be found in Liberal ranks. The important developments, however, were taking place in the constituencies, where more people were becoming politically minded. The backbone of Liberal support was to be found in the provinces, the middle classes, and the ranks of Dissent, the latter introducing into politics the so-called "Nonconformist conscience." The upper level of the working class, which tended to model itself on the middle class and adopt its values, consequently identified with the emerging Liberal party. New Liberal clubs and registration associations in the sixties united the various elements in the constituencies. A new type of Radical also began to appear, typified by such men as W. E. Forster, Sir Charles Dilke, and later, Joseph Chamberlain. These men were less attached to the old Manchester school ideas of laissez-faire and "Little England," and would drive the Gladstonian Liberal party along a new path of reform. Despite his Tory origins, Gladstone was destined to be the leader of the new Liberalism once Palmerston and Russell had disappeared from the scene. This meant that in the new Liberalism there would also be an important Peelite element combining moral values with a pragmatic, utilitarian approach to government.

During the early sixties Cobden and Bright looked to Gladstone more and more as the minister most likely to accept and promote their views, although his outlook was broader than theirs and eventually his liberalism went further. Gladstone's political philosophy was influenced by Edmund Burke as well as by his strong religious convictions. He always cherished a great respect for the past, for inherited institutions, and the existing social hierarchy. With Burke he also shared a love of freedom and of justice, but he had a more optimistic temperament, perhaps because he lived in more settled times. He was thus readier to believe in the possibility of righting the wrongs that afflicted society, by improving, but not rejecting, existing institutions. As Chancellor of the Exchequer in Peel's tradition, he sought to keep expenditure to the minimum and make taxation more equitable by reducing or abolishing taxes on necessities. In this capacity he began for the first time to meet working-class leaders who came to him with their requests. He was much impressed by their sobriety and earnestness, to which he catered by instituting postal savings accounts where working men and trade unions could deposit small savings at suitable interest. In these years he began receiving invitations to address large working-class audiences. It appears speaker and listeners were mutually impressed, although neither fully understood the other. Audiences were captivated by his striking platform presence, his flashing eye, his wonderful voice, his eloquence, and his sincerity. He was gratified by their response, their obvious sense of responsibility, and their good humor. He was soon persuaded that such men deserved the franchise, and he said as much in a parliamentary speech in 1864. Although the assertion was hedged with typical Gladstonian qualifications, it was said that it ensured him the future leadership of the Liberal party.

The Radical wing of the Liberal party had long been demanding the secret ballot and some extension of the franchise, and since the late forties there had been almost annual reform motions. After his humiliating defeat on the reform motion of 1851 (see p. 62) Lord John Russell, the sponsor of the Great Reform Bill of 1832, had promised he would himself introduce a bill to extend further the 1832 franchise. He did this in 1854 with Peelite support, but was forced to withdraw the measure because of national preoccupation with the Crimean War. In 1860, following the fiasco of Disraeli's abortive Reform Bill of 1859, Russell made another attempt, but there was little response. Absorbed in the intricacies of the Italian question, he again allowed his bill to lapse.

The demand for parliamentary reform was muted in the early sixties, but by 1864 John Bright and others had renewed the cry with the formation of the Reform Union, joined a year later by the more left-wing Reform League. The success of Garibaldi's democratic nationalists in Italy, and of the North in the American Civil War, stimulated political activism in Britain, as did the business recession of 1866. But there was an accidental element in the success that came to the reformers in 1867, largely explained by political developments in Parliament. Parliamentary reform had not been a major issue in the election of 1865, but many Liberal candidates were committed to it, including a new batch of intellectual radicals such as J. S. Mill, G. O. Trevelyan, Henry Fawcett, and Thomas Hughes. The death of Palmerston shortly after the election transformed the situation. Russell, now in the House of Lords, succeeded him briefly as prime minister, and Gladstone took the lead in the House of Commons. Russell, nearing the end of a long career, was anxious to climax it with a second reform act, and Gladstone, now a convert to reform, was ready to prepare a moderate measure. The result was the Liberal Reform Bill of 1866, which proposed to enfranchise 400,000 new voters by extension of the borough franchise from £10 ratepayers to all householders who paid at least £7 annual rent and a more limited extension of the county franchise. The eligibility requirement was put at £7 because it was calculated that a lower figure would have made the working class the majority of the electorate. Gladstone admitted the Government was not prepared to go that far, but he appealed to the Commons to welcome the new voters "as you would welcome recruits to your army or children to your family." Forty-eight Liberals, nicknamed by Bright "the Cave of Adullam," ignored the plea and secured the defeat of the bill by joining the Opposition in support of an amendment restricting the franchise to those who paid their own rates. Since a large proportion of the poorer working-class tenants "compounded" with the landlords to pay their rates, this was a serious restriction. The most effective spokesman for the Cave was Robert Lowe (1811–1892), who made the position of the bill's opponents clear when he callously asked, "If you want venality, if you want ignorance, if you want drunkenness, and facility for being intimidated . . . , where do you look for them in the constituencies? Do you go to the top or to the bottom?" The majority of the House did not really want a reform bill, and since the Government was unwilling to call another election so soon after the previous one, they resigned.

The defeat of the bill and Lowe's indiscreet language were just what the reform movement needed to stir up public opinion. In the course of the summer numerous meetings throughout the country were addressed by Bright and other reformers. The Queen and her new ministers were upset when the railings around Hyde Park were knocked down after police had refused to allow its use for such a meeting. A number of people were injured and the flower beds damaged before the crowd adjourned to Trafalgar Square. The demonstration was a warning of what might happen if the reform issue was ignored. Queen Victoria pressed on her new government the need for another reform bill, a proposal to which Derby and Disraeli assented. By this time there were plenty of rank-and-file Conservatives who saw that reform must be settled and that their party might as well get the credit.

After a good deal of chopping and changing, the Cabinet, on pressure from their back benches, decided to gamble on a "household suffrage" bill giving the vote to all householders who paid their own rates, but this was to be balanced by "plurality of voting" (additional votes), quickly called "fancy franchises," for people with additional educational and financial qualifications. Even so three ministers resigned, of whom one, Lord Cranborne, the future Lord Salisbury, became the bitterest opponent of the bill. Nevertheless, they could not kill this bill as Lowe and his "Adullamites" had killed its predecessor the year before, because the Opposition was not with them. The Liberals supported the Conservative bill in principle, but insisted on a series of amendments that completely transformed it. The period of residence was reduced from two years to one, certain lodgers were given the vote, the "fancy franchises" were eliminated, and the county franchise was extended. The most important amendment of all, introduced by Hodgkinson, a Liberal backbencher, required all householders to pay their own rates with the result that all the "compounders" were turned into ratepayers and the number of new voters was doubled. Disraeli accepted all these amendments rather than lose credit for the bill; his party went along with him, sometimes, one suspects, not realizing the full implications of what they were doing. Passage of the revolutionary Hodgkinson amendment was perhaps assisted by the Government's failure to prevent another mass meeting in Hyde Park the previous week. Thus amended, the Reform Act of 1867 went far beyond the moderate Liberal bill of 1866. The total electorate was increased from 1,358,000 to 2,477,000, with the majority of electors drawn for the first time from the working class. There was also a limited redistribution of seats to larger centers of population, but in this respect the measure bore no relation to 1832. At the end of the debate Cranborne pointed out that Gladstone had demanded ten changes when the bill was first introduced, and that he had secured every one of them. This was true to a point, but the Liberal leader had failed to persuade the left wing of his party to accept an amendment giving the vote to compounders paying £5 rent annually. Reluctantly he had been forced to accept the radical proposals to abolish compounding and thus enfranchise all householders. Passage of the amended bill may have been a moral victory for Gladstone, who had first introduced a reform bill in the previous session, and who had insisted on extensive amendment of the Conservative measure. But politically his position seemed weaker, for he had been repudiated by both the right and the left wings of his party in two successive sessions, while Disraeli had succeeded in carrying almost all his party with him. Disraeli's policy has been described as one of consistent opportunism, but he continually outmaneuvered Gladstone and won a considerable political victory that strengthened his position in his own party. Their acceptance of such a wide extension of the franchise is surprising, but it was based on an underlying assumption about the submissiveness of the working classes that subsequent elections seemed to bear out.

Gladstone, as Disraeli observed, was "terrible on the rebound." In the following session he took up the cause of Irish Church disestablishment, united his party on this issue, and defeated the Conservatives under Disraeli, who had now succeeded Derby as prime minister. In the following election Gladstone led the Liberals to a decisive victory by winning a majority of 112 seats. That long-lived generation of Palmerston, Russell, and Derby, who had begun their political life in the days of the prince regent, passed the great Reform Bill of 1832, and dominated British politics between the Reform Acts of 1832 and 1867, had at last come to an end. The age of Gladstone and Disraeli had indeed dawned during the Reform Bill debates, although these two formidable antagonists had both been active in politics for three decades.

Few men have caught more vividly the imagination of contemporaries and subsequent generations, and the contrast between these two was striking. Both were commoners who rose to the top by their own endeavors and abilities, but Gladstone's background and rise in political and social position was the more conventional. His father was a very prosperous Liverpool merchant who had bought his way into the landed establishment and won a baronetcy in recognition of his wealth and social position. As a result, young William's education and preparation for life at Eton and Oxford, where he had a brilliant career, were the same as those of the landed aristocracy among whom he made his friends. Disraeli was the grandson of a Sephardic Jew who had settled in England in the eighteenth century. His father was a man of letters and comfortably off, but the family were not wealthy and Disraeli never went to a great public school or attended university. Gladstone was brought up in a strict evangelical atmosphere and, although he later turned to the High Church, his religious convictions were always the greatest driving force of his life. Disraeli's father was a skeptic, but on the advice of a friend he had his son baptized an Anglican for worldly reasons. While Disraeli respected the role of the church in society and for political reasons was its champion, there is no evidence that religion ever meant much to him. To his credit, however, he took pride in his Jewish ancestry, for which he suffered politically, although religion alone was no bar to entering Parliament.

Although four years younger than Disraeli, Gladstone entered Parliament four years earlier thanks to the influence of the Duke of Newcastle, father of his close friend, Lord Lincoln. Disraeli made his own way, partly through success as a writer, partly through friendships he made after penetrating the literary and social world. After several unsuccessful attempts to enter Parliament as a Radical he managed in 1837 to be elected as a Conservative, thus starting his parliamentary career on the same benches as Gladstone. His extravagance in dress and manner and his spendthrift ways contrasted sharply with the earnest sobriety of his future rival. The contrast was equally marked in their physical appearance and attainments. Gladstone, with striking stature and a robust constitution, was a man of tremendous physical energy, which he indulged in the singular pastime of cutting down large trees on his estate. Disraeli, a man of slight frame and poor health, was naturally indolent and hated unnecessary exercise. Both men wrote extensively throughout their careers, but Disraeli confined himself largely to fanciful novels or political tracts, while Gladstone ranged over a wider variety of erudite subjects— theology, classics, history, and literature—aiming at a more select audience. A contemporary cartoon shows them back to back in a bookshop. "Hmmm, flippant!" snorts Mr. G. as he glances at Disraeli's most recent novel; "Ha, prosey!" sneers Mr. D. as he picks up Gladstone's latest work on Homer.

Both men enjoyed a happy married life, one of the few things they shared in common; but Disraeli married late (after a series of rather scandalous affairs) and had no children, while Gladstone, who married earlier, was the dominant and active father of a large family. Ironically, the adventurer Disraeli in his old age became the favorite of the Queen and a distinguished member of the House of Lords; Gladstone, for all his early high connections, was in his later years detested by the Queen and most of the aristocracy, but affectionately known as "the People's William." Disraeli was a curious mixture of romantic and cynic, a combination that drove him toward Conservatism, but politically he was essentially an opportunist. Gladstone was by instinct conservative in his respect for rank and authority, but his strong moral sense made him see politics as a means of righting wrongs and overcoming injustices and thus drove him to become a liberal reformer. "I was brought up to distrust and dislike liberty," he once said toward the end of his long life. "I learned to believe in it. That is the key to all my change."

The Liberal party under Gladstone's leadership won the election of 1868 by a large majority of 385 seats to 273 for the Conservatives, and the popular vote of 1,408,000 to 884,000 was even more striking. Not all the new voters got onto the registers in time for the election, but evidently those who did voted overwhelmingly for Liberals. For thirty to fifty of the seats that the Liberals won from the Conservatives their success was probably due in large part to the support of the predominantly working-class Reform League. The working class did not get much out of their vote, but the action of the League was less a betrayal by their leaders, as Marx and Engels suggested, than a reflection of the extent to which Liberal ideology dominated working-class political thinking at the time. Probably still more important to the victory was backing from Nonconformist voters supporting Gladstone's platform of Irish Church disestablishment.

In view of the fact that Ireland was Gladstone's main concern during all four of his ministries, it is curious that he only took the question up seriously at this late stage in his career. One biographer has suggested that it was his sense of timing. Hitherto he had allowed himself to be preoccupied with other matters—the welfare of the church, fiscal reform, Italy, and, more recently, parliamentary reform. Now he sensed the time was ripe to deal with Ireland, although the Irish problem had been chronic for as long as he could remember. He naturally condemned the recent Fenian violence but reminded English audiences that it reflected real grievances in Ireland. Traditionally these had been threefold: religious, economic, and political. The penal laws and political discrimination on religious grounds no longer existed, but the predominantly Roman Catholic Irish people had long been forced to accept an Anglican established church with very large public revenues. The main Irish economic grievance lay in the inequitable land system. Long ago all the land had been confiscated by the English Protestant conquerors, and as Catholics, the vast majority of native Irish had not been allowed to own land until the late eighteenth century. Unlike their counterparts in England, the landlords, about a third of whom were absentee, were generally unconcerned with capital improvements and were little more than rent gatherers. There was such competition for land in this heavily populated country that the estates were carved into many small holdings. The tenant farmers had to make all their own improvements, but since they lacked sufficient capital, the standard of agriculture was low. The poorest tenants were cottiers who cultivated a small plot of land which they paid for by their labor. The tenants were at the mercy of the landlords with respect to raising of rents and evictions, and until Gladstone's time had no legal recourse against them. The political grievance, which was related to the other two, was enforced parliamentary union with Britain. Under O'Connell the Irish had long demanded the repeal of the Act of Union. This claim was soon to be pressed again by two exceptional members of the Protestant ascendancy, Isaac Butt and Charles Stuart Parnell, as a demand for Home Rule, but some time would elapse before Gladstone could take up that challenge.

Gladstone formed a strong reforming ministry. Besides himself it contained five other Peelites: Edward Cardwell, Robert Lowe, H. A. Bruce, the Duke of Argyll, and later Roundell Palmer (1812–1895), who as Lord Selborne became Lord Chancellor. At least six Cabinet members were of middle-class background, two of them originally Quaker businessmen, but there was also a strong nucleus of Whigs led by old Lord Clarendon at the Foreign Office, who was succeeded on his death in 1870 by Lord Granville. Gladstone devoted his main efforts to Irish legislation, for on forming the ministry he had said, "My mission is to pacify Ireland." But he gave full support to his colleagues in their extensive legislative program, and few ministries achieved the number of important legislative reforms as Gladstone's did in its five years in office.

Gladstone himself drafted and piloted through the House of Commons in 1869 a complicated bill to disestablish and disendow the Anglican Church in Ireland. More than half the revenues were to be turned over to the church as compensation and the remainder expended for secular purposes. The bill was fiercely resisted in the House of Lords, although, on urging from Queen Victoria, the moderates prevented it being thrown out altogether. Nevertheless the Lords' amendments were unacceptable to the Commons and an impasse threatened to occur between the two branches of the legislature, which was finally settled by the good sense of the moderate Conservative peers and the concession by the Government of an additional compensation of approximately one million pounds. The Irish Church Disestablishment Act put an end to a long-standing Irish grievance and made the Anglican Church in Ireland a healthier and more viable institution.

In the following year Gladstone turned his attention to the more difficult problem of Irish land and found the landlord an even more entrenched vested interest than the Church to attack. Twenty-five years earlier Peel's Devon Commission had revealed how Irish landlords commonly exploited their tenants, by forcing them to make their own improvements and then raising rents or evicting without compensation. Gladstone's first Land Act of 1870, introduced despite reluctance in his own Cabinet and with damaging opposition in the House of Lords, provided for compensation for evicted tenants who had made improvements. The act was to apply even in an eviction for nonpayment of rent if the courts considered the rent "exorbitant." Since the courts rarely made such rulings the provision was of no great benefit to tenants. The legislation was of historic importance, however, because it was the first time the British Parliament recognized that Irish tenants had any rights. It was the beginning of a series of Land Acts that would eventually make the tenant the owner of his land, and there were indeed clauses in this bill, introduced on pressure from Bright, providing for the beginning of tenant purchase.

The most important domestic reform of the Gladstone government was the Education Act of 1870, primarily the work of W. E. Forster (1818–1886). England lagged behind every major Western nation in the lack of a national school system. As we have seen, this was primarily due to religious differences between Anglicans and Nonconformists. Nevertheless the public demand for a national system of education was growing. It was promoted by a National Education League, founded in Birmingham by prominent Dissenters including Joseph Chamberlain, and a National Education Union made up mostly of supporters of church schools. Since the majority of children in the country were attending some 1,500 voluntary schools, mostly Anglican and already receiving public grants, the Government decided to build a national system on this nucleus. These schools were now to receive government grants provided they accepted public inspection, accepted children without discrimination, and exempted non-Anglicans from compulsory religious instruction. In parishes lacking facilities school boards were to be created and new schools opened, to be supported by government grants, local rates, and fees. The fees were to be paid by the local board in hardship cases. As a result of Nonconformist protest an amendment was added prohibiting the teaching of any catechism or religious formulary in board schools; but Nonconformists still criticized the act as too favorable to Anglicans. It was passed only with the help of Conservative votes, since many Liberals abstained or were opposed.

The bill was a landmark in English education and remained the basis of the system until well into the twentieth century. (Subsequently Conservative ministries made school attendance compulsory and free.) Other educational reforms included a similar act for Scotland and an act permitting changes in the trust deeds of several thousand endowed schools.

While the Irish and educational reforms were being enacted, Edward Cardwell (1813–1886) had embarked on an extensive and long overdue program of reform at the War Office. By further reducing the colonial garrisons abroad Cardwell considerably lowered military expenditure, but by introducing better terms of service and a system of linked battalions connecting garrisons abroad with home depots he considerably increased the efficiency of the army. At the same time he brought the office of Commander in Chief with his headquarters known as the Horse Guards (the building in which it was located) directly under the jurisdiction of the Secretary of War, thus eliminating much duplication and division of authority. Cardwell's reform necessitated great tact in view of the resistance of the Queen and her cousin, the Duke of Cambridge, who for many years as Commander in Chief was an obstacle to modernization. More remarkable was Cardwell's success, in the face of intense opposition from the House of Lords and the officer class generally, in abolishing the purchase of commissions. When the

House of Lords defeated the purchase bill, Gladstone supported Cardwell by arranging to terminate the system by a royal warrant. This was perfectly legal, since permission to sell commissions had first been authorized by warrant; but the Lords were then forced to accept another bill providing payment of compensation to those officers who had purchased their existing commissions. It was a common sense reform essential to the formation of a professional army and was consequently supported by professionally-minded officers, such as Colonel Sir Garnett Wolseley (1833–1918). But it was un-popular with the upper classes because it eliminated one of their privileges, and with the Radicals because of the considerable expense of compensation. *Punch* hit the right satirical note, however, with a notice addressed to "gallant but stupid" young gentlemen. "You may buy Commissions in the Army up to the 31st day of October next," they were told. "And after that you will be driven to the cruel necessity of deserving them."

Selborne's Judicature Act of 1873 was in the same genre of institutional reform. The inadequacies of the English system of law were brilliantly satirized in the pages of Dickens and other Victorian novelists. In fact piece-meal reform had been going on for half a century, but this was probably the most significant single measure. It retained the circuit system and the refer-ence of appeals to London, but it brought all the courts into one system, set up a single Court of Appeal for England and Wales, and authorized common-law courts to apply the system of equity where relevant. This measure was supplemented by a second Judicature Act, passed by the Conservative government in 1875, for law reform tended to be a nonpolitical issue. Another reform in the same general category, long desired by Gladstone since his sponsorship of the Northcote-Trevelyan Report of 1854, was the adoption of competitive entrance examinations in the Civil Service, a policy introduced by Robert Lowe as Chancellor of the Exchequer. It is interesting to note that these three important institutional reforms in the army, the judi-ciary, and the civil service were all the work of Peelite members of the cabinet—Cardwell, Selbourne, and Lowe.

A significant reform in the Radical tradition was the Ballot Act, a measure long resisted by the landed aristocracy as likely to decrease their political influence. The Lords defeated the first attempt in 1871, but Gladstone forced the bill through in 1872. The act, which for the first time provided for voting by secret ballot in parliamentary elections, greatly reduced the chances of intimidation at elections, but this was no longer so serious a matter since the electorate had been enlarged by the second Reform Act.

The government was less successful with the problem of trade unions. Upper- and middle-class hostility had been accentuated by incidents of violence connected with small trade unions in Sheffield and elsewhere, and a few years earlier a royal commission had been set up to investigate the matter. With the help of Frederic Harrison and Thomas Hughes the commission brought in a report surprisingly sympathetic to the trade union movement. The government implemented its proposals in the Trade Union Bill of 1871 that gave unions full legal recognition and, consequently, the protection of the courts. This was a great boon to the unions but, unfortunately, it was accompanied by the Criminal Law Amendment Act that made picketing illegal and consequently undermined the right to strike. Any credit the Government won through the Trade Union Act was lost by the second measure.

In response to growing demand for temperance legislation from Nonconformist supporters of the Liberal government, the compromise Licensing Act of 1872 regulating the hours of public houses was passed despite opposition from liquor interests and a certain Anglican bishop, who asserted he would rather "have England free than England sober." Other reforms included repeal of the Ecclesiastical Titles Act of 1851; the abolition of all religious tests at Oxford and Cambridge, except in schools of theology; virtual abolition of imprisonment for debt; and establishment of a Local Government Board, a precursor of the Ministry of Health, in an ineffectual attempt to coordinate supervision of local government.

In foreign affairs the policy of Gladstone's ministry was the reverse of Palmerston's. As Foreign Secretary Lord Clarendon attempted in 1870 to mediate the quarrel between Prussia and France, but he died on the eve of the Franco-Prussian War. His successor, Lord Granville (1815–1891), was less effective, although both Prussia and France were persuaded to guarantee the neutrality of Belgium. When Russia took advantage of the war to repudiate the Black Sea clauses of the Treaty of Paris of 1856, the British government merely arranged a conference of the signatory powers, which met in London in 1871 to give legal acknowledgment to the *fait accompli*. Gladstone was more indignant at German annexation of Alsace-Lorraine, but failed to persuade his Cabinet to make a formal protest. The most significant action of his ministry in foreign affairs was the negotiation of the Treaty of Washington, which resolved outstanding differences between Canada and the United States and agreed to international arbitration of the *Alabama* claims. The public thought the American demands exorbitant and were angered by the Geneva court's decision against Britain in 1873. But the Government, following their principle of peaceful settlement of international disputes, paid the $15,000,000 award.

The first Gladstone ministry was epoch-making in the range of its reforms. It catered to the diverse elements in the newly evolved Gladstonian Liberal party, which included philosophical and Manchester school radicals, Peelites, and Nonconformists. The ingredients of Gladstonian liberalism were manifold, but one characteristic derived from Gladstone was the attempt to apply the Christian ethic to the solution of political problems. The Whig influence was apparent in limitations imposed on such reforms as the Land Act; but without the Whigs many reforms would not have passed the House of Lords. Even so, some measures were controversial enough to stir strong opposition from vested interests and sometimes bitterly disappoint the Government's own supporters. This was particularly true of the Education Act, which failed to satisfy the Nonconformists; and the Criminal Law Amendment Act, which antagonized the working classes, despite the benefits derived from the Trade Union Act. The Licensing Act antagonized publicans and their patrons without satisfying the temperance people; acceptance of the *Alabama* arbitration enraged the belligerent element of the public. The ministry was showing signs of exhaustion by 1873, when Disraeli wittily described the Government front bench as a row of extinct volcanoes. A third Irish reform measure, Gladstone's Irish Universities Bill, was defeated because it satisfied neither Irish Catholics nor English Protestants. Gladstone resigned, but Disraeli refused to form a government, and the Liberals struggled on until the dissolution of Parliament early in the following year. A number of minor scandals, one of which led to Gladstone's assumption of the Exchequer and preoccupation with narrow fiscal problems, further accelerated the deterioration of the Government's fortunes. Despite their achievements (in part because of them) the Liberals were badly defeated in the election of 1874, losing about 140 seats of which over 50 went to the new Irish Home Rule party.

There were positive as well as negative reasons for the Liberal defeat. In 1870 Disraeli had appointed an able and aggressive young lawyer, John Gorst (1835–1916), as party agent and allowed him considerable authority. Gorst, who believed a popular base for the Conservative party had been opened in the large urban areas by the 1867 Reform Act, systematically set about organizing all the constituencies. He developed the efficient Conservative Central Office and brought under its roof the recently formed National Union of Conservative Associations, a loosely knit federation of local associations. His party machine was a factor in winning the election, but Disraeli also made his contribution. Following his defeat of 1868 he had been less active politically and had resumed his lucrative career as a novelist with the publication of *Lothair* in 1870. In these years his leadership was seriously challenged, especially by Tory peers. But he asserted it successfully in 1872 by taking the offensive in Parliament and by giving two important speeches at the Crystal Palace in London and the Free Trade Hall in Manchester (where he spoke for more than three hours, sustained by large quantities of white brandy that passed for water). The controversial Gladstone government was an ample target for his shafts, but he also contrasted it with the objectives that a Conservative government would follow under his leadership, namely, "... to maintain our institutions, to uphold the Empire, and to elevate the condition of the people." The first point was to be expected from a Conservative leader facing the innovations of the existing Liberal administration and the republican speeches of some of its radical supporters, such as Sir Charles Dilke. The second indicated that Disraeli had picked up the Palmerstonian torch discarded by Gladstone, but it also hinted at imperial expansion in the years to come. The third revived the memory of Young England and a belief in the Tory workingman for whom the Reform Act of 1867 was supposedly passed.

If Disraeli had been a character in a Victorian novel, a philanderer, and a speculator as a young man, careless in his company and his debts, the sins of his youth would inevitably have brought him to a bad end. The reality, in fact, was otherwise; nor would he have thought to abjure his past and thus make his story acceptable to the moralist. With luck, help from admiring friends, a fortunate marriage, natural ability, and an inner drive that negated his outward indolence, he managed to overcome all obstacles and, as he said to "reach the top of the greasy pole." It has been said of him that he seemed to place obstacles in his own path for the sheer pleasure of getting over them. Now at last he was prime minister with a strong majority behind him; but he was also in his seventieth year, his health was poor, and his beloved wife was dead. He refused, however, to allow these disabilities to prevent him enjoying both the realities and the trappings of power. Always stimulated by female society, he fell in love in his old age with two sisters, Lady Bradford and Lady Chesterfield, both of them grandmothers. Although perhaps more attached to the former he proposed to the latter, who had the advantage of being a widow. She refused, but the friendship continued. The hundreds of letters he wrote to the two of them are valuable sources of information about his ministry and incidentally reveal the casual way in which he treated state secrets. With a little more restraint he also charmed Queen Victoria ("the Faery," he called her, despite her weight), to whom he wrote intimate and witty letters such as she received from no other prime minister during her long reign. Victoria had not liked Gladstone, who treated her as an institution rather than a woman, and she responded warmly to Disraeli's flattery. It has been suggested that he manipulated her for his own ends, but the influence was by no means all one way.

Disraeli formed a strong Cabinet, although it was small and aristocratic. It included as Foreign Secretary the young Lord Derby (1826–1893), whose views on foreign policy unfortunately tended to be Gladstonian; as Indian Secretary, Lord Salisbury (1830–1903), who succeeded later to the Foreign Office; and as Colonial Secretary, Lord Carnarvon (1831–1890). Lord John

Manners, a friend from Young England days, went to the Post Office; and Sir Stafford Northcote (1818–1887), once a private secretary of Gladstone's, to the Exchequer in the Peelite tradition. It was magnanimous of Disraeli to offer and of Salisbury to accept office after the latter's bitter criticism of Disraeli's Reform Bill in 1867, but they soon forgot their differences and to the credit of both developed a mutual respect. Disraeli also recognized a new element in the Conservative party by making Richard Cross (1823–1914), the middle-class Lancashire solicitor, Home Secretary and a little later W. H. Smith (1825–1891), the railway bookstall magnate, First Lord of the Admiralty (to the amusement of Gilbert and Sullivan, who caricatured him in their operetta *Pinafore* as the "Ruler of the Queen's Navee").

Disraeli had no large-scale legislative plans when he came into office, to the surprise of Cross, one of his most energetic new ministers, but he appointed some men with ideas and gave them his support. Thus in the first three years, mostly in 1875, the ministry was responsible for a good deal of social legislation, the area in which Gladstone's ministry had been least productive. The most important and positive measures lay in the area of labor. The Employers and Workmen Act introduced by Cross gave employees the same status as employers in contract law and avoided the old invidious terms "master" and "servant." The Trade Union Act amended the law of Conspiracy in favor of trade unions and, on the urging of the Liberal, Lowe, repealed the Criminal Law Amendment Act of 1872, removing the main bar dividing working men from the Liberal party. The Factory Act reduced the hours of labor in textile factories from 60 to 56½ a week, forbade full-time employment of children under fourteen and their part-time employment under ten. The Education Act, concerned mainly with bolstering the position of the church schools, required school certificates for working children between the ages of ten and fourteen and, on pressure from the other side of the House, adopted the principle of compulsory attendance. The Public Health Act was built on previous acts, especially those of 1866 and 1872, but proved an important piece of codification. The Food and Drugs Act contained regulations against adulteration, although it lacked suitable enforcement measures. The River Pollution Act was a step in the right direction, but limited in scope. The Artisans Dwelling Act was a landmark in public housing, yet in itself had limited results. Dr. Paul Smith, in his book *Disraelian Conservatism and Social Reform*, argues that the significance of these measures has been exaggerated, and that most were relatively uncontroversial and supported by the Liberals, with little consequence to party politics. The Conservative legislators were in the pragmatic Peelite tradition and by no means paternalistic in their viewpoint. They took care not to interfere with the laws of political economy or the rights of property, and much of the legislation was permissive rather than mandatory. Disraeli gave Cross support when he needed it, but took no part in producing any of the legislation, an aspect of government that had little interest for him.

Disraeli's main preoccupation during his six years in office was with foreign and imperial policy. Like Palmerston he was an activist, and his chief concern was the maintenance abroad of British prestige, which he considered to have suffered under Gladstone. He was less insular in outlook than Palmerston, and on the surface more cosmopolitan, but in fact he was much less knowledgeable. His approach to foreign and imperial policy was emotional and romantic, as can be seen in his bill naming the Queen Empress of India and in his melodramatic manner of purchasing the Suez Canal shares of the bankrupt khedive of Egypt. (Disraeli's action in this case was wise, however, since it prevented the canal, used predominantly by British ships, from falling entirely into French hands; but on the short-term loan for the purchase he agreed to the payment of exorbitant interest to his friend Baron Rothschild. The resulting degree of British control of the canal has been exaggerated, but acquisition of the shares was a good financial investment until the canal was nationalized in 1956 by Colonel Nasser.)

In 1874 Disraeli's chief concern was "to reassert Britain's power in Europe." The main challenge was the reopening in a new form of the old Eastern Question. Turkey's misrule of her Christian subjects in the Balkans continued after the Crimean war and led in 1875 to revolt in the provinces of Bosnia and Herzegovina in the far northwestern corner of the Turkish empire. Panslav sympathy with the rebels was strong in Russia and the neighboring independent states of Serbia and Montenegro, which declared war on Turkey in 1876. Austria, on the other hand, was jealous of Russian pretensions in the Balkans and anxious to maintain the status quo, unless the rebellious provinces should chance to fall into her own lap. The threat of an Austro-Russian conflict undermining the recently formed *Dreikaiserbund* of the emperors of Austria, Germany, and Russia led to a meeting of those three powers and promulgation of the Berlin Memorandum of May 1876. This offered a reasonable solution to the Turkish problem and was quickly adhered to by France and Italy. But Disraeli persuaded his Cabinet and his reluctant Foreign Secretary, Derby, to reject the memorandum as hostile to Turkey, although his real reason was the failure of the three powers to consult Britain first. In any event, a nationalist coup in Turkey guaranteed nonacceptance of the Berlin proposal. However, the British action and the dispatch of a British fleet to Besika Bay, near the entrance of the Dardenelles, obviously encouraged the Turkish resistance.

In June unrest in the Turkish empire spread to Bulgaria, resulting in a barbaric massacre of some 15,000 Christians by the Turks. Disraeli was unmoved by these events, since he regarded moral considerations as irrelevant to foreign policy decisions, but they caused him temporary political embarrassment when a spontaneous wave of public opinion sprang up to denounce them. Although remaining in Parliament, Gladstone had retired the year before from the Liberal party leadership and took no part in the early stages of this agitation. Yet it appealed to him as the sort of moral response to public affairs in which he believed, and before long he was drawn into taking its lead with the publication of a famous pamphlet entitled *The Bulgarian Horrors and the Question of the East*, which sold 200,000 copies in a month. This was followed with public speeches to large audiences and, when Parliament met, with resolutions in the House of Commons (to the embarrassment of the Whig leaders, Granville and Hartington, who had temporarily succeeded him in the leadership of the party). "You talk to me of an established tradition and policy in regard to Turkey," Gladstone told the House of Commons. "I appeal to an established tradition, older, wider, nobler far —a tradition not which disregards British interests, but which teaches you to seek the promotion of these interests in obeying the dictates of honour and justice." This approach was incomprehensible to Disraeli who as Lord Beaconsfield had just withdrawn to the upper house on account of ill health. He dismissed the agitation as the work of "priests, poets, and historians" and denounced Gladstone as "that unprincipled maniac—extraordinary mixture of envy, vindictiveness, hypocrisy, and superstition."

In December a conference of the powers in Constantinople failed because of Turkish obduracy, despite the success of Salisbury, the British representative, in establishing good relations with the Russian, Ignatiev. When further attempts at a modus vivendi failed Russia declared war on Turkey in March 1877, ensuring Austria's neutrality with the promise of Bosnia and Herzegovina. For five months the Turks held back the Russians at Plevna, in Bulgaria; but they were finally routed and forced back almost to the gates of Constantinople before they agreed to an armistice. By the Treaty of San Stefano an enlarged Bulgaria became an autonomous state, and other concessions were made to Russia. Throughout the war the British Cabinet was badly divided, at one point, according to Disraeli's characteristic exaggeration, into seven camps. These ranged from the Foreign Secretary, Derby, who wanted to avoid war at all costs, to a war party urging immediate assistance to the Turks. Disraeli favored going to war to stop the Russians from entering Constantinople. The danger of war was greatly increased when the British fleet entered the Dardenelles and army reinforcements were ordered from India to Malta. Derby finally resigned later in the crisis and was succeeded by Salisbury, who was prepared to take a firmer line but was more realistic than Disraeli. Earlier he had sympathized with Derby's attempts to reach a settlement with the Russians, but after the Russian declaration of war he had agreed that Russia must not be allowed to retain Constantinople. He had no sympathy with the Turks, but was determined to modify the settlement of San Stefano imposed on them by the Russians. In a cogent circular to all the powers Salisbury suggested means of achieving this at the international Congress of Berlin, which he attended with Disraeli himself. The Russians were persuaded to accept a reduction in the size of the new state of Bulgaria and its division, with the southern part remaining under Turkish rule, but with administrative autonomy. The Austrians accepted a protectorate over Bosnia and Herzegovina and the British, by secret agreement with Turkey, acquired the island of Cyprus in return for a guarantee to defend Turkey's Asiatic empire. Disraeli returned to England jubilantly claiming "peace with honour." He was at the peak of his fame, for the anti-Turkish demonstrations of the previous year had given way to a jingoistic cry for war with Russia when the Russians had threatened to occupy Constantinople.

The Disraeli government's imperial adventures in Africa and Asia were less successful. In both cases the fatal decisions were made by men on the spot, although these had been sent out by the Government, which assumed responsibility for their actions. The breakaway South African Boer state, the republic of the Transvaal, threatened with bankruptcy and extermination by the warlike Zulus, called on the British for assistance. The Transvaal government secretly agreed to annexation, but publicly denounced the act when it was carried out. Sir Bartle Frere, the new British high commissioner in South Africa, then made war on the Zulus, whom he regarded as a danger to all whites in South Africa. The war began with the disaster of Isandhlwana, where the British camp was wiped out by the Zulus, but after reinforcements were sent out from England it ended with the subjugation of the Zulu tribe, which was permanently broken up. With the Zulu threat removed the Boers began once again to demand their independence. In this they received the sympathetic support of Gladstone, who roundly condemned both the annexation and the Zulu war.

In India the Government suffered more serious reverses. Lord Lytton, whom Disraeli had appointed viceroy despite his lack of qualifications, invaded Afghanistan on the pretext of forestalling the Russians. After a successful campaign the British imposed a British minister on Afghanistan's Amir, but a few months later he and his entire staff were massacred. The result was a second invasion of Afghanistan under General Roberts, which did not succeed until after Disraeli's government had fallen.

In 1879 Gladstone, now returned to active politics, had accepted the nomination for the constituency of Midlothian, in southern Scotland. Although the election had not yet been called he began an unprecedented campaign, addressing large audiences from Liverpool to Edinburgh and back again via Glasgow, all the while denouncing the scandal of what he called Beaconsfieldism—the unnecessary acquisition of Cyprus, the denial of self-government to the Boers, the wanton aggression against the Zulus and the Afghans. "Remember the rights of the savage, as we call him," he cried on one occasion. "Remember that the sanctity of life in the hill villages of Afghanistan, among the winter snows, is as inviolable in the eye of Almighty God as can be your own." Huge crowds applauded his oratory and millions more read accounts of the speeches in the national press. Early in 1880 when the general election was held, he renewed the campaign with equal vigor, and it undoubtedly contributed to the decisive defeat of the Conservative government. Disraeli, isolated in the Lords and close to the end of his life (he died in 1881), could offer no such leadership to his party. Times were bad— always an embarrassment to the party in power—and the Conservative electoral organization had gone to pieces. In the Liberal camp the powerful National Liberal Federation had come into being. It was a grass roots organization that had been started a few years earlier in Birmingham by Joseph Chamberlain, who in the next quarter-century was a formidable force in national politics. In the new Parliament the Liberals outnumbered the Conservatives by 349 to 243, but in addition there were 60 Irish Home Rulers. They were in the process of being organized by Charles Stuart Parnell, another formidable new figure who would play in the next decade a larger role in British politics than any Irish politician since O'Connell.

Chapter Seven
THE IMPERIAL CHALLENGE

The Irish Question and Party Politics, 1880–1895

The period 1865–1880, which witnessed the dramatic Gladstone-Disraeli confrontation, was one of transition after the long afternoon of the Whig ascendancy, still dominated by men who had begun their political careers in the days of Melbourne and Peel. The 1880s began a new era with new issues. At the center of the stage were new men speaking in harsher, more strident tones—men like Joseph Chamberlain, the Unitarian screw manufacturer from Birmingham; Lord Randolph Churchill, the *enfant terrible* of the aristocracy; Charles Stuart Parnell, the formidable leader of a new Irish nationalism; Charles Bradlaugh, the militant atheist; and, in the next decade, the dour figure of Keir Hardie, the man in the cloth cap.

Chamberlain (1836–1914) represented a new force in British politics. He was a self-made businessman, hard as Birmingham ironware, and a militant Nonconformist. He had begun his political career in municipal politics, where he had been a champion of compulsory, free, and nondenominational education and an early pioneer in slum clearance. He entered Parliament at a by-election in 1876 and quickly teamed up with Sir Charles Dilke (1843–1911), another new Radical from a more conventional background but whose advanced views extended even to republicanism. Unlike earlier Radicals who showed little desire or aptitude for ministerial appointments, Chamberlain and Dilke sought office as soon as possible in order to get things done. Their philosophy was interventionist, not laissez-faire. They wanted to extend democracy and use the powers of the state for social ends. They also had positive views about empire outlined in 1868 by Dilke in his book *Greater Britain* and later advanced by Chamberlain as the century's most forceful Colonial Secretary.

Despite their dissimilar origins Lord Randolph Churchill (1849–1894)—a younger son of the Duke of Marlborough, Disraeli's Lord Lieutenant in Ireland—had the same cataclysmic effect on the Conservative party that Chamberlain had among the Liberals. Both were fearless, determined, and outspoken and no respecters of rank or station; both in their different ways professed to speak for the people. Churchill was a brash young aristocrat with an obsession for hunting, but apparently without the education or experience necessary for early political leadership. Temporary social ostracism resulting from a family quarrel with the Prince of Wales seems to have turned him accidentally to a political career. He soon showed hidden qualities, a prodigious memory, a quick mind, and a surprising capacity for hard work. He developed great facility in debate, especially for finding Gladstone's weak spots and driving his rapier in deep. He could carry rudeness to heroic heights and on occasion was ruthless. In the Parliament of 1880 he found three kindred souls on the Tory benches: John Gorst, the disgruntled organizer of the Conservative electoral victory of 1874; Arthur Balfour (1848–1930), Lord Salisbury's brilliant young nephew, whose book *In Defence of Philosophic Doubt* challenged science, not religion; and Sir Henry Drummond Wolff (1830–1898), a retired diplomat reputed to be as cunning in politics as in diplomacy. The four formed an alliance, quickly dubbed "the Fourth party," in an effort to revitalize the anemic Conservative Opposition led by the ineffectual Sir Stafford Northcote, whom they irreverently nicknamed "the Goat." They also attempted to win the new working-class electorate to Conservatism with Tory Democracy, a vague doctrine incorporating some characteristics of the Young England movement of Disraeli's early days.

Yet the first issue they seized upon to embarrass the Government was straight Tory with no hint of democracy. They determined to prevent the atheist, Charles Bradlaugh (1833–1891), from taking his seat in the House of Commons, to which he had been elected for the first time. Bradlaugh claimed the right to affirm in lieu of taking the usual oath, but the Speaker weakly left the matter to the House to decide. The Fourth party took up the challenge and made it an issue that lasted the entire life of the Parliament. Although Gladstone supported Bradlaugh he could not control all his followers, and Bradlaugh was not allowed to take the oath even when he offered to do so. He did not enter the Commons until a new Speaker in the next Parliament made a different ruling in 1886.

The Fourth party's tactic, planned at convivial dinner parties, was obstruction. Their endless speeches and questions in the House were detrimental to the Government's legislative program, but Churchill appeared equally intent on undermining the leadership of Northcote and promoting his own claims in the party. He did this by getting himself elected president of the

National Union, a hitherto unimportant body coordinating the local Conservative associations, and by challenging the central office, which was directly responsible to the party leaders for the organization of the party. In 1885 the struggle finally ended in a compromise. Lord Randolph moved on to the Conservative front bench and became a candidate for high office, while the National Union sank back in oblivion and the Fourth party, having served its purpose, came to an end.

The Irishman, Charles Stuart Parnell (1846–1891), whose mother was an American, was a more alien figure than Chamberlain or Churchill. Although a Protestant landlord, he had thrown in his lot with the underdog because of his abiding hatred for England and her long mistreatment of Ireland. His fine appearance, dominant personality, magnetic platform presence, and quickly-acquired parliamentary expertise made him a superb leader. He also cultivated a reputation as a man of mystery, which excited the Irish imagination. In the 1874 election another Irish Protestant, the gentler and more moderate Isaac Butt (1813–1879) had persuaded fifty-nine successful Irish candidates, mostly Liberals, to adopt his platform of "Home Rule" for Ireland. In 1878 Parnell wrested control of the nascent Home Rule party from Butt and in the new Parliament of 1880 proceeded to organize it on a strong grass roots basis. The secret of Parnell's success was his ability to appeal to the diverse elements in the Irish community: to such extremists as the Fenians and the Irish Republican Brotherhood by his intemperate speeches; to the Land League by assuming its presidency; to the Church by systematically putting parish priests on constituency committees; and to the parliamentary party by securing pledges of loyalty from all members. He pushed the Whig element out of the party, recruited lower middle-class members by providing financial support, and built up the tightest extraparliamentary party organization in the history of the United Kingdom. By the election of 1885 it had become a formidable electoral machine. Meanwhile in the House of Commons he developed the art of parliamentary obstruction to a higher and more effective degree than the Fourth party because of his group's greater numbers. The Parliament of 1880 would have been difficult for any prime minister to have mastered.

The nominal leaders of the Liberal party in 1880 were Lord Granville in the Lords and in the Commons Lord Hartington (a courtesy title for the son of a duke); but neither could form a government, they told Queen Victoria, because in the popular view it was Gladstone, the retired leader, who had won the election. With great distaste—for Disraeli had poisoned her mind against his rival—the Queen called upon Gladstone to form his second ministry. It proved much more frustrating and less successful than the first. Part of the trouble was Gladstone's own doing. Although he owed his return to support from the Radical wing of the party, he underrepresented them in the Cabinet out of deference to the old Whig aristocracy whom he respected. He reluctantly took in Chamberlain as President of the Board of Trade, but he did not give Dilke a seat until several years later. The history of the ministry was largely one of a continuous struggle between Hartington, fighting a rear-guard battle, and Chamberlain, who was never allowed to move as quickly or as far as he wished.

The main achievement of the ministry, passage of a third installment of parliamentary reform, illustrated the Whig-Radical struggle. When in Opposition the Liberals, on Radical pressure, had committed themselves to extension of the franchise to the working class in the counties, although the issue had not been emphasized in the Liberal election platform of 1880. Neither was it pressed in the first session of the new Parliament, since its passage would have required another election. Over the next few years, however, some four hundred meetings favoring reform were organized throughout the country. In 1883 Chamberlain and Dilke began to press the matter publicly and in the Cabinet, in face of opposition from Hartington. Eventually Gladstone agreed to a bill and introduced it himself in 1884. It was to add up to two million voters to the registers by extending the household franchise to the counties in the whole United Kingdom. It was a straight franchise bill, avoiding redistribution of seats, which was to be dealt with separately at a later date. The Conservatives bitterly attacked the bill for its inclusion of Ireland and its omission of redistribution provisions, but the Liberal majority ensured its passage in the Commons. In the Lords, however, it was defeated by the Tory majority led by Lord Salisbury, who hoped to force a general election while the Liberal government's policy in Egypt and the Sudan was also being criticized. Instead, the Government prorogued Parliament for the summer, and to the Queen's indignation the issue was brought to the people at a thousand meetings, many of them addressed by Gladstone, Chamberlain, and other ministers. A second bill was introduced in a special autumn session and, like the first, it passed the Commons. By this time both the Queen and moderate Conservative peers were beginning to put pressure on Salisbury to compromise. In the end he reluctantly accepted a government proposal to introduce a wide-ranging redistribution bill on agreed principles prior to the final passage of the franchise bill in the Lords, which would then be passed. Negotiations with the Conservatives and pressure from the Radicals in the Cabinet led to a much wider redistribution bill than the government had originally intended. Boroughs with a population below 15,000 lost all representation, and those with less than 50,000 were reduced to one seat. This arrangement made available 140 seats and two additional seats were added. These seats were redistributed among the more populous cities and counties, which in most cases were now subdivided as single-member constituencies. In the old three-member boroughs the Liberals had been able to win all three seats because of their overall majority. The increase in representation in single member units ensured the Conservatives some suburban seats, which helped to reconcile them to the measure.

The Redistribution Act was significant for adopting the principle of equal electoral districts averaging 52,000 voters, although there were still some anomalies in its retention of boroughs of between 15,000 and 50,000 inhabitants. Moreover, for the first time counties received equal representation with the boroughs in proportion to their population. The Franchise Act gave the vote to many agricultural laborers and industrial workers living outside borough boundaries, especially in mining districts. Nevertheless, there remained a 40 percent residuum of adult males who did not get onto the electoral registers; and the entire female population was also excluded, since female suffrage amendments to the bill had, as usual, been defeated.

The Government passed a number of other useful measures, including the Burials Act, to settle an old Nonconformist grievance; the Ground Game Act, to meet a tenant farmer grievance; the Women's Property Act, to extend women's legal rights; and the Patent and Bankruptcy Acts, both important pieces of commercial legislation. In addition in 1883 a Corrupt Practices Act, the first really effective measure of its kind, provided for the curtailment of election expenditures. Other issues, however, dominated public attention and preoccupied the government during these years, most obviously the problems of Ireland and of the Empire overseas, and, below the surface, social problems that in the end led to more lasting political changes. After a prolonged and extraordinary economic expansion and prosperity, Britain was now entering a period of adversity. The last quarter of the nineteenth century was marked by three stretches of economic depression—1873–1879, 1882–1886, and 1890–1896—and it became clear that Britain's industrial predominance and ability to feed herself were seriously threatened.

Disestablishment largely settled Ireland's religious grievance, but the economic problem was intensified with the great agricultural depression of the 1870s, and the political issue throve with the growth of democracy and nationalism. The disastrous fall in grain prices in the late 1870s left the tenant farmers too poor to pay their rents, with the result that they were evicted in large numbers (over 2,000 families in 1880 alone) as landlords turned their land to grazing. Agrarian outrages such as rick burning, cattle maiming, assault, and sometimes murder—the distracted peasant's instinctive answer to the collapse of his world—increased at an even faster rate (2,590 incidents in 1880), which led inevitably to Coercion Acts to give the Irish authorities arbitrary police powers. A more constructive response was the formation in 1879 of the Irish Land League, the brainchild of Michael Davitt (1846–1906), whose history exemplified the sufferings of his fellow countrymen. After his family's eviction from their cabin in the mountains of Mayo, Davitt went to work while still a child in a Lancashire cotton mill and lost an arm. As a young man he was active in the Fenian movement, which led to a long prison sentence. He was released after seven years, but during his incarceration he pondered Ireland's woes and thought out a plan to enlist the support of those Irish who had been driven from their homes in other parts of the world. He toured the United States with great success and in 1879 returned to Ireland to organize the peasants against their landlords. The main object of his League was to reduce exorbitant rents and promote peasant ownership of the land. The moral force of an organized and united peasantry determined to resist evictions by every means possible could have a considerable effect on many landlords. A technique known as boycotting (because it was first used against a Captain Boycott, the agent of a large landowner) was devised, by which any person renting a farm from which the previous tenant had been evicted was to be socially ostracized. The Land League became a powerful body and its significance was quickly appreciated by Parnell, who assumed its presidency to coordinate it with the aims of his Nationalist (i.e. Home Rule) party.

Unlike in 1868, Gladstone came into office in 1880 without having formulated an Irish policy, for his main concern was the reversal of Disraeli's foreign and imperial policy. But the Irish situation was far more serious than it had been twelve years earlier. One hundred thousand tenant farmers were in arrears of their rent and liable to eviction. The Government introduced a temporary compensation bill, but it was thrown out by the Lords. Despite Davitt's earnest attempt to restrain it Irish violence increased. The mythical Captain Moonlight stalked the countryside, as Captain Swing had roamed rural England a half-century earlier. Gladstone had appointed a royal commission under Lord Bessborough, which early in 1881 reported the failure of Gladstone's first Land Act and recommended implementation of the three Fs demanded by the Irish: fair rent, fixity of tenure, and free sale. In the face of opposition from his own colleagues and, subsequently, from the House of Lords, Gladstone obtained the passage of his second Land Act meeting these three demands. It infringed on the traditional concept of private property, and the price was high. The Whigs insisted on a coercion bill to give the Irish administration increased police powers. This bitterly antagonized the Parnellites, who consequently showed no satisfaction with the Land Act. When Parnell made threatening speeches to arouse the rabid anti-British Irish Americans, the Government decided on his arrest. This suited him admirably since it made him a martyr in the eyes of his extremist supporters.

The situation worsened during the months of Parnell's imprisonment in Kilmainham jail, as they were marked by increased violence and the spread of secret societies, which Parnell opposed for their extremism. As Parnell had foreseen, the Land Act was running into difficulties because, as amended in the Lords, it made no provision for tenants already owing rent. Conditions were thus ripe for the Kilmainham pact between Parnell and the government. It was engineered by Joseph Chamberlain through a most unfortunate intermediary, Captain O'Shea, whose wife was Parnell's mistress. Parnell was released after promising to cooperate with the Government in restraining the Irish tenants in return for an Arrears bill to assist those tenants behind with their rent. The result was that the Land Act began to take effect, but much of the value of the understanding was lost as the result of a tragic incident that followed soon after in Phoenix Park, Dublin: the murder of Bourke, a hated official, and the accidental killing of Lord Frederick Cavendish, the new Irish Secretary, a younger brother of Lord Hartington and a man devoted to Gladstone. The assassins were extremists, not associated with Parnell, but the incident reinforced growing upper-class distaste for the Irish and their agitation. Unhappily the Arrears Act had to be coupled with a still more stringent Coercion Act.

In 1885 Gladstone and Chamberlain tried in vain to persuade the Cabinet to head off Parnell's demand for Home Rule by agreeing to a moderate measure of local government for Ireland. Parnell came to the conclusion that he would get no more out of the Liberals. Convinced by Churchill that the Conservatives would not renew the Coercion Act, he joined the Opposition to carry a vote against the Government. The abstention of many Liberals from the division indicated the party's weakness and Gladstone resigned office without going to the polls.

At first it seemed strange for Parnell to reject Gladstone, the English statesman who had shown most concern for Ireland, and to turn to Lord Salisbury, who, like Disraeli, had never indicated any interest in that country. But Gladstone was hamstrung by the Whig element in his Cabinet and some of Salisbury's colleagues did show signs of being ready to take a new approach, Churchill especially, who said the Conservatives would not renew coercion, and Carnarvon, whom Salisbury made Lord Lieutenant of Ireland. In Parnell's view he had nothing to lose and his action was a warning to the Liberals.

The Conservatives did drop coercion temporarily, and before the end of the session passed the Land Purchase Act, a scheme that Gladstone had wanted to tie to local government legislation. This was a generous measure and pointed to the eventual solution of the Irish land question. The government loaned the entire purchase price at 4 percent interest with repayment over forty-nine years, which made the annual payment less than the existing rent. Carnarvon went even further. He agreed to a secret meeting with Parnell in which they discussed the possibility of Home Rule, but the Cabinet refused to consider such a plan. Unaware of the negative attitude of the Cabinet, Parnell supported the Conservatives in the general election of December 1885. His backing probably gave them as many as twenty-five seats in English constituencies with large numbers of Irish voters. Gladstone had by this time come to the conclusion that Home Rule was the best solution to the Irish problem, but he dared not give a lead, knowing the Whig opposition and the difficulty he would have with the House of Lords. Consequently he was evasive when Parnell approached him on the matter through Mrs. O'Shea, a lady of good English family known to Gladstone, whose intimate relationship with Parnell was a poorly guarded secret. Privately Gladstone suggested to Arthur Balfour, Salisbury's nephew, that if the Conservatives brought in a Home Rule bill he would see it got support. He knew Salisbury could put it through the House of Lords and he could not, but Salisbury refused to play the role of Peel, who had been repudiated by his party when he repealed the Corn Laws.

Shortly after the election, in which the Liberals won 334 seats to the Conservatives' 250, and the Irish Nationalists held the balance with 86, Gladstone's son, Herbert, indiscreetly revealed his father's conversion to Home Rule. The news antagonized Gladstone's colleagues, who had not been informed, and, if possible, strengthened Salisbury's opposition to it. When Parliament met the Conservatives announced a return to coercion. The honeymoon with Parnell was over and the latter joined the Liberals to turn the Government out of office. When Gladstone was called upon to form a government he made it clear to those to whom he offered office that it would be on the basis of Home Rule, with the result that Hartington and other Whigs declined to join. Chamberlain, who was opposed to Home Rule because he did not trust the Irish, accepted with some hesitation. No minister had given Gladstone more support on his Irish policy in the previous administration, but he had been annoyed by the failure of the Cabinet majority and Parnell to accept his Irish local government scheme and had fought the election independently on an ultra-radical "unauthorized" program. Gladstone never felt close to Chamberlain and failed to see the importance of conciliating him and taking him into his confidence. He also snubbed Chamberlain in his choice of office and slighted one of Chamberlain's chief associates. When Gladstone finally introduced a Home Rule bill Chamberlain refused to support it and resigned with fatal consequences. The bill provided for a separate Irish legislature and an executive responsible to it. Key matters such as foreign policy, defense, customs, and excise were reserved to the Government at Westminster. In gaining their own legislature, however, the Irish lost representation in the imperial Parliament, and no special provision was made for the Protestants in Ulster. By later standards the measure was modest, but the Irish accepted it. Ninety-three Liberals, most of them Whigs, but also Chamberlain and some of his followers, joined the Conservatives to defeat the bill. Such a large Liberal defection was a bitter blow to Gladstone and led to his resignation. He was actually well rid of conservative Whigs of the Hartington variety who had been such a drag on his second ministry, but he could ill afford to lose Chamberlain and his followers from the Birmingham area.

Gladstone's motives in again taking up the Irish problem and in finally espousing Home Rule merit respect. His goals were statesmanlike, but his tactics showed poor political sense. He may be criticized for his slowness in apprehending the importance of Home Rule, for his failure to see the need for educating his followers, and especially for alienating Chamberlain. He should have retired at this point—he was too old to grasp new ideas and increasingly was out of touch with most of his colleagues. To his large following in the country he had become the Grand Old Man, and was affectionately referred to as the G.O.M. With the departure of Chamberlain and Hartington there was no obvious successor, and Gladstone, with the obstinacy of old age, was determined to remain and settle the Home Rule issue.

In the subsequent election English voters declared decisively against Home Rule, and Salisbury once more became Prime Minister. The Conservatives won 316 seats and were supported by 78 Liberal Unionists, most of them permanently estranged from the Liberal party. The Liberals won only 191 seats but henceforth they were closely allied with the 85 Irish Nationalists, and for the next five years Parnell was a welcome figure on Liberal platforms. The majority of the British bourgeoisie had always been separated from the Irish by religion. Now shocked by the threat to property in Ireland and the growth of agrarian crime, they transferred their allegiance from the Liberals to what became known as the Unionist party in 1895 when the Liberal Unionists permanently joined forces with the Conservatives. The result was that the Conservatives, or Unionists, to use the new term, remained in office for seventeen of the next twenty years.

Like Gladstone's, the second Salisbury administration was mainly preoccupied with Irish and imperial affairs and passed little domestic legislation of note other than some measures to assist farmers, a factory act, and the important Local Government Act, instituting elected county councils (which were not extended to Ireland until 1898). Tory democracy sputtered out with the resignation of Randolph Churchill, who, as Chancellor of the Exchequer, failed to bully his colleagues on the matter of economy. He never returned to office and died prematurely some years later. Arthur Balfour proved to be the strong man of the ministry and in 1892 assumed the party leadership in the House of Commons. He distinguished himself as Irish Secretary with a policy of coercion and conciliation. He arrived in office just after the inauguration of the "Plan of Campaign" in Ireland, a scheme concocted by some Irish M.P.s (without Parnell's approval), which organized tenants against their landlords to lower rents. This led to evictions on some estates, more violence, and, eventually, to a fracas with the police in Michelstown in which three civilians were killed. The Government's answer was another severe Coercion Act, which Balfour administered with determination. He nevertheless undertook some useful remedial measures, the construction of light railways in the west, the setting up of the Congested Districts Board and a second land purchase act. In Ireland he was known as "Bloody" Balfour, but in the eyes of the Conservative party the dilettante philosopher had become a strong man of affairs.

During these years Parnell became more moderate, working in close cooperation with the Liberal party. They stood by him in his hour of trial in 1887, when *The Times* published a letter attributed to him expressing sympathy with the Phoenix Park murders. Parnell demanded a select committee to clear his name. Instead, the Government, which from the beginning took its lead from *The Times*, appointed a special commission to inquire into various allegations against Irish members in what amounted to a state prosecution. John Morley (1838–1923), Gladstone's biographer and Irish Secretary in 1886, has with reason compared the affair to the Dreyfus case in France, but in the end the letter was proved a forgery, and Parnell's name was completely cleared when the commission reported in 1890. The incident led a number of Liberal Unionists to return to the Liberal party, and for a short time Parnell's popularity throughout the United Kingdom was at its peak. A few months later, however, the "uncrowned king of Ireland" was toppled from his throne when he was cited as correspondent in a divorce suit brought against Kitty O'Shea by her husband. The English Nonconformist conscience would not allow the Liberal alliance with a party led by a convicted adulterer, and Gladstone felt bound to tell this to Parnell. The Irish Catholic bishops were similarly convinced of Parnell's unsuitability, and the majority of Parnell's followers insisted he withdraw from Nationalist party leadership. His refusal resulted in a bitter split within his party that lasted a decade, although three months after his marriage to Kitty O'Shea in 1891, Parnell was dead of exposure following a speech at a political meeting in the rain.

England remained predominantly opposed to home rule, but the so-called Celtic fringe of Ireland, Scotland, and Wales gave the Liberals and their Irish Nationalist allies a small majority in the election of 1892 (Liberals 274, Irish Nationalists 85, Conservatives 268, and Liberal Unionists 47). The Liberal

Unionists had lost half their membership through retirements, defeats, and returns to the Liberal fold, and the group that was left in time merged with the Conservative party.

Gladstone, who had remained in public life with the sole intent of settling the Irish question, now formed his fourth ministry. In 1893 at the age of eighty-four he introduced his second home rule bill. It was patterned after the first, except that it gave the Irish some representation in the Westminster Parliament while continuing to neglect the problem of Ulster. Everyone marveled at the old man's skillful conduct of the bill through the House of Commons despite fierce opposition from Chamberlain and others. Inevitably, however, it was defeated in the House of Lords, and Gladstone's colleagues, most of them less committed than he to home rule, were unwilling to face another election. The next year he finally resigned in a huff over growing naval expenditures. He was succeeded by the youthful Lord Rosebery (1847–1929), a Liberal imperialist and one of the few aristocrats left in the party. Although possessed of considerable intellectual ability and social prestige, he was a failure as Prime Minister and unable to heal the growing rifts among his colleagues to which he himself contributed. The Liberals had been elected in 1892 on the radical Newcastle Program, but had been ineffective in their efforts to implement it. Most of the important measures they initiated were defeated in the House of Lords with the exception of a new and extended inheritance tax of great significance for the future and the passage of the Parish Councils Act, which extended popular local government to the parish level and gave women the vote and the right to be candidates. Finally, because of its internal weaknesses, the Government resigned after defeat on a casual vote in the House of Commons in June 1895.

Lord Salisbury formed his third administration, bringing in the Liberal Unionists and giving Chamberlain the Colonial Office at his own request. The Conservatives won the ensuing election decisively with 341 seats plus 71 Liberal Unionists, against 177 Liberals and 82 Irish Nationalist seats. The one concession of the new Government to Chamberlain's radical past was the Workman's Compensation Act, a new departure in social legislation, despite the fact that the Lords had killed a similar bill introduced by the Liberals a few years before. Old-age pension proposals for the needy were rejected despite Chamberlain's pressing. Actually the Government and Chamberlain himself were more involved with imperial affairs, to which we must now turn.

Imperial Expansion and Party Politics, 1880–1902

British imperial expansion in the last quarter of the nineteenth century was part of a world-wide phenomenon, as the western European powers partitioned Africa and competed with each other for concessions in China; as Japan attempted to expand onto the Asian mainland; and as the United States built the basis of a Pacific empire on the ruins of a Spanish one. There is no simple explanation for the extraordinary expansion of the great powers at the expense of weaker peoples, some of it for the good, but most of it not. Of the motivating factors, some were of a universal character, others peculiar to the British. The circumstances often seemed beyond the Government's control, no matter which party was in power. In discussing the matter in the House of Commons Gladstone once spoke of "that perhaps irresponsible tendency of British enterprise to carry our commerce and the range and area of our settlements beyond the limits of our sovereignty in those countries where civilization does not exist."

Economic determinism was one of the earliest and most popular explanations for imperial expansion. This thesis was developed in 1902 by the English economist, J. A. Hobson, in his book *Imperialism,* and it was quickly taken up by the Marxists. Imperialism was seen as essentially a search for new markets and sources of raw material, and as a means of investing surplus capital by those capitalist countries lacking further opportunities at home because of the maldistribution of wealth. Obviously there was an economic factor in expansion, but it was only one of many. In fact there seems to be a lack of correlation between territorial expansion and overseas investment. British commerce and investment were world-wide and by no means confined to areas where the Union Jack flew; indeed, during the period of great territorial acquisitions in Africa British commerce and investment in that continent were unimportant except for the diamond and gold mines of South Africa. Trade with and investment in South America and the United States was far greater. Victorian statesmen for the most part preferred informal ties to imperial control, which was expensive, and annexations, when they came, were generally the result of local pressures. As always they saw India as an exception, but, as we have noted, it paid its own way.

Foreign competition was probably the most important single spur to British imperial expansion in this period. For more than half a century Britain had ruled a world-wide empire that had no rivals. France had begun the conquest of Algeria in the 1830s, but this posed no real threat to British interests, and between Algeria and Cape Colony, Africa was virtually untouched save for the moribund Portuguese Colonies of Angola and Mozambique and the two little Boer republics that had broken off from Cape Colony. Russia had been looked upon as Britain's chief imperial rival, but Russia's expansion had been continental. She had reached the Bering Sea by the end of the seventeenth century and in the nineteenth century was pushing into the semi-vacuum of central Asia but the Himalayan massif conveniently

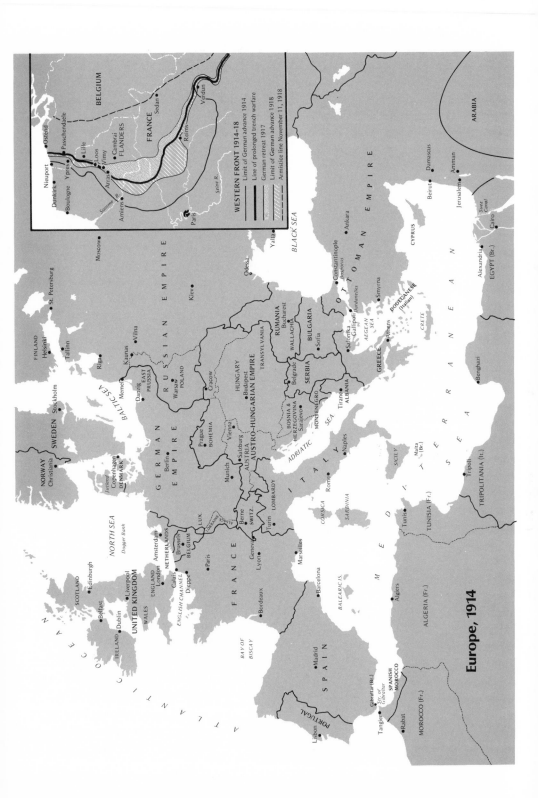

WESTERN FRONT 1914-18

Limit of German advance 1914
Line of prolonged trench warfare
German retreat 1917
Limit of German advance 1918
Armistice line November 11, 1918

Europe, 1914

separated Russia's Empire from India. Unification of Germany and Italy in the third quarter of the nineteenth century brought an era of intensified nationalism and territorial consolidation. These two powers were latecomers in the imperial contest; and France's defeat by Germany in 1870 led her also to salve her wounded pride in expansion elsewhere. Africa happily or unhappily was ripe for partition. In recent decades intrepid explorers had revealed the mysteries of the interior of the dark continent. Developments in transportation and tropical medicine made the continent more accessible to Europeans. When they saw other countries staking out claims to territory from which they would now be excluded, the British became apprehensive and more anxious to extend their own possessions. The other powers, while tending to be jealous of Britain's position, often seemed to prefer her to each other, perhaps because the British Empire did not surround itself by tariff barriers. In their book *Africa and the Victorians*, the English historians, Gallagher and Robinson, see British expansion in Africa in strategic terms as a defense of lifelines to the east, but also in the official mind as a reaction to challenges from new rivals.

The erroneous application to races and ethnic groups of the social Darwinian theory of the survival of the fittest was another contemporary explanation interpreted viciously by Karl Pearson, and more moderately in 1894 by Benjamin Kidd, a retired civil servant, in his book *Social Evolution*, which he later repudiated. Such theorists attributed British imperial success to the racial superiority of the Anglo-Saxon. This doctrine justified further British expansion as a civilizing mission, and there were many such as Joseph Chamberlain in his later career who believed in the idea of mission, or "white man's burden" as it was sometimes called, whether or not they subscribed to the full social Darwinian concept. They were easily convinced that the lot of uncivilized peoples could be improved through conquest mutually beneficial to the conquerors and the conquered. The Christian missionaries, who still played an important role in Africa, were precursors of the civilizing concept. David Livingstone, for instance, the most intrepid of African explorers, was a missionary, content to live and die among the people he was trying to convert.

The American historian, W. L. Langer, does not question the sincerity of British imperialists, but he recognizes their unconscious self-deception, explaining that "their huge Empire was a standing proof of their fitness to rule, consequently the extension of the Empire would be a boon to those people that were taken over even if they were brought in by force."[1] Such a man was Lord Curzon, who dedicated a book to "those who believe that the British Empire is under Providence the greatest instrument for good that the

[1] W. L. Langer, *Diplomacy of Imperialism, 1890–1902*, vol. I (New York: Knopf, 1935), p. 194.

world has seen. Another was Joseph Chamberlain, who declared his belief that the British race was "the greatest of governing races that the world has ever seen," and when he became Colonial Secretary in 1895 he was prepared to spend money on the social improvement of the tropical colonies. There was also Lord Rosebery, who once asserted: "The empire that is sacred to me is sacred for this reason, that I believe it to be the noblest example yet known to mankind of free adaptable just government."

The growth of interest and enthusiasm for empire was cumulative for, once it appeared, it was further stimulated by publicists on all levels. Sir John Seeley, Professor of Modern History at Cambridge, argued in his *Expansion of England* (1883) that English historians, in their preoccupation with constitutional development, had neglected the all-important theme in British history—the country's extraordinary imperial expansion. Dilke, in his *Greater Britain* (1868), and Froude, in *Oceana* (1885), struck a racist note in their emphasis on Anglo-Saxon superiority. Such novelists as H. Rider Haggard, Robert Louis Stevenson, and Rudyard Kipling found a wide audience for imperial themes, as did explorers, administrators, and soldiers—such as H. M. Stanley, Lord Milner, Lord Roberts, and the young Winston Churchill—for personal memoirs of their adventures. Popular weeklies like the *Illustrated London News* and such new cheap dailies as the *Daily Mail*, prototype of "yellow" journalism, played up stories of adventure and war in the interior of Africa and on the frontier of India. British governments often found themselves following rather than leading popular opinion in their development of imperial policy, for the emergence of a popular electorate was another influence on imperialism.

Attitudes towards imperial expansion cut across party lines. The jingoes, ready to fight at the slightest provocation, were a minority in the Tory party, as were the anti-imperialist Little England Radicals in the Liberal party. Modern historians divide both parties into two schools: the forward school, favoring continued imperial growth, and the consolidationists, generally hostile to further expansion but prepared to consolidate and develop what had already been acquired. Gladstone was a consolidationist, but in his Cabinets there was always a vocal forward element, led initially by Hartington and later by Rosebery. Salisbury was readier to accept the philosophy of the forward school, but some of his colleagues were more hostile, generally on grounds of cost. During his second administration Gladstone sometimes had to yield to the forward school to win their support of his Irish policies. Expansion continued under both parties. Ironically, it had begun on a large scale in the second Gladstone ministry, formed to reverse the policies of Beaconsfieldism.

It will be recalled that Gladstone had in particular denounced the invasion

of Afghanistan and the annexation of the Transvaal. Backed by the consolidationists in the Cabinet, Lord Ripon, the new Liberal viceroy, resolved to
evacuate Afghanistan despite General Roberts' military victory, but the new
amir installed by the British accepted British control of his foreign relations.
The Transvaal presented more of a problem, for on taking office the Liberals
discovered a plan for federation of the two Boer states with Cape Colony
and Natal. The Government decided to support this plan, but the Boers in
the Transvaal rebelled in disgust and early in 1881 defeated a small British
force at Majuba Hill. There was pressure on the Gladstone government to
avenge this defeat, but in view of the Boer attitude the consolidationists in
the Cabinet, led by Bright and, at this time, Chamberlain, got their way.
The independence of the Transvaal was recognized by the Pretoria Convention, subject to recognition of British suzerainty that was further modified in
1884. Thus after a faulty start the consolidationists won their second victory,
as might have been expected in a Gladstone Cabinet. Thereafter, however,
the tide went against them.

The financial affairs of the khedive of Egypt, who had been forced to sell
his Suez Canal shares to Britain in 1875, were in such a bad way by 1878 that
the British and French governments had intervened. Allegedly, it was a move
to protect the interests of the European bondholders to whom the khedive
was indebted, but Britain was motivated more by hope of retaining some
control over France than interest in the welfare of the bondholders. The result
had been the setting up of a Franco-British dual control of the khedive's
finances. This provoked a successful nationalist revolt in Egypt in 1881 under
Colonel Arabi Pasha. The Gladstone government was anxious for the combined intervention of the Concert of Europe (i.e., the Great Powers acting
jointly), but agreed to sign a joint note with France for fear of unilateral
French action. This only antagonized the nationalists, who imposed a new
constitution and a new ministry on the khedive. The British and French
governments then sent their fleets to Alexandria to protect their nationals
in case of disorder. Gladstone would have preferred Turkish intervention,
but a conference of the powers at Constantinople failed to produce any
solution. Riots ensued in Alexandria and fifty Europeans were killed.

These developments determined the British government, now concerned
also for the safety of the Suez Canal, to take a firmer stand. When Arabi
began fortifying Alexandria against the fleets, the British admiral was
authorized to issue an ultimatum but at this point the French fleet was withdrawn, since the weak French government could not depend on the support
of the French Chamber. Arabi ignored the order to stop building the
fortifications with the result that they were leveled in a ten-hour bombardment. The consequence was chaos in Egypt and the decision of the British

in favor of military intervention to restore the government of the khedive. For a variety of reasons the House of Commons supported the decision by a large majority, but the French Assembly turned down a similar request from the French government. General Wolseley, who in 1870 had suppressed the Riel rebellion in Western Canada and in 1874 had defeated the Ashanti tribe on Africa's Gold Coast, arrived in Egypt in less than four weeks with a small British army and quickly crushed Arabi at the Battle of Tel el Kabir. Gladstone had only intended to stay long enough to restore the power of the khedive, but it proved impossible to maintain the khedive without continued British support. The British consequently did not leave Egypt until after the Second World War. Another consequence of intervention in Egypt was the resignation of John Bright from the Cabinet.

Evelyn Baring (later Lord Cromer) was appointed British resident in Egypt and became the virtual ruler of the country until he left in 1907. He succeeded in putting Egyptian finances in order, improving the administration of justice, and introducing public works and social reforms, but his first priority was the protection of the interests of the bondholders rather than those of the poor Egyptian peasants. An early problem that faced Baring and the British government on assuming responsibility for Egypt was the Sudan, a rebellious Egyptian province on the upper Nile. An Egyptian army of 10,000 led by Hicks Pasha, a British officer in the Egyptian service, had been annihilated by rebels under a religious fanatic known as the Mahdi. The Egyptians wished to reconquer the Sudan, but the most the British would do was help them evacuate it. The Government commissioned the renowned general, Sir Charles Gordon (1833–1885), to execute this difficult task. Gordon had begun his military career with the British army in the Crimea, had served in the second war with China in 1860 and subsequently suppressed the Taiping rebellion on behalf of the Chinese government. After that he had gone into the service of the khedive of Egypt and played an effective role in suppressing the slave trade in the Sudan. R. K. Ensor has called him "perhaps the finest specimen of the heroic Victorian type—a Bible-taught evangelical, fearless, tireless, incorruptible." He was certainly a man who captured the public imagination, but he was an unwise choice for the evacuation of the Sudan, where the best years of his life had been spent creatively. He was so sure of himself he paid little attention to the orders of those to whom he was responsible.

Gordon's mission was ill-conceived and ill-executed. No realistic evacuation plan had been devised before he left Cairo, and precious months were lost after his arrival in Khartoum as he and the Cabinet in London, communicating via Baring in Cairo, bickered over to whom he would relinquish his authority on leaving. The ministers were exasperated by the bewildering and often bellicose communications with which he bombarded them, but failed to give him any firm lead. They were also alienated by his appeal to the public through an enterprising *Times* reporter, the only Englishman he found in Khartoum on his arrival. Gradually the hostile tribes closed in. The telegraph line was cut in mid-March, although indirect communication continued for some time longer. The Cabinet was slow to appreciate Gordon's danger and divided as to what should be done. The majority, led by Gladstone, were long reluctant to authorize a relief expedition, believing the cost in men and money unjustified in these circumstances. Should a whole army be risked to save two Englishmen and the Egyptian garrisons and officials for whom Britain had no responsibility? Eventually, however, in August, on pressure from the public and the forward party in the Cabinet, a relief expedition was authorized with General Wolseley in command. It was a more exacting task than the conquest of Egypt, for an army had to be transported up almost two thousand miles of river, and the upper reaches were blocked to steamers by great cataracts. Voyageurs were enlisted from Canada and special vessels constructed for the arduous journey. An army was quickly assembled and Khartoum was finally reached in January 1885, several days after its fall and Gordon's death. It was a magnificent effort, but it had failed, and the Queen, the Opposition, and the public condemned the Gladstone ministry, which fell a few months later.

In 1896 Egypt was flourishing after fourteen years of Lord Cromer's careful guidance. Lord Salisbury, now Prime Minister for the third time, decided to make use of the Italian-Ethiopian war to extend British strategic control up the Nile. Despite Cromer's reluctance an Anglo-Egyptian army was sent into the Sudan under Sir Herbert, later Lord, Kitchener. In 1898 the Mahdi and his dervishes were massacred by British machine guns in the battle of Omdurman, in which the young Winston Churchill participated as a cavalry subaltern and newspaper reporter. The Sudan was reconquered and an Anglo-Egyptian condominium set up, which lasted into the middle of the twentieth century. Kitchener then pressed on toward the headwaters of the Nile, having heard of a French expedition that had crossed the continent from French Congo and planted the flag of France at Fashoda. Major Marchand could only protest to Kitchener's superior force, and the conflicting claims were referred for solution to the home governments. Relations between the two countries were tense until France eventually accepted as a *fait accompli* the presence of the British on the Nile, which they had long resented. At no time during the partition of Africa had rupture between two European powers appeared more likely.

Throughout this period France remained jealous of Britain's occupation of Egypt, although she herself had seized Tunisia at about the same time. Britain was therefore made more dependent on the diplomatic support of

Germany, which was important in the subsequent division of Africa. Within a few years of her involvement in Egypt Britain began adding large territories in east and west Africa, partly on pressure from newly formed British companies, partly to prevent French or German occupation of these areas. The penetration of east Africa was also part of a general policy of maintaining routes to the East and controlling the headwaters of the Nile.

British interest in west Africa had long been confined to a few coastal possessions, Gambia, Sierra Leone, and the Gold Coast. More recently operations of the British antislavery squadron had led to acquisition of the island of Lagos, and activities of British traders had developed a British interest in the Niger River delta. Attacks by the Ashanti tribe had brought retaliation and defeat by General Wolseley in 1874 and consolidation of the British position on the Gold Coast. Following Britain's occupation of Egypt, France turned to the development of her position in west Africa and equatorial Africa, and French traders began to challenge British hegemony on the lower Niger. George (later Sir George) Taubman Goldie, an ex-army officer and, despite his eccentricity, a great empire builder of the period, united competing British traders in the area and bought out the French. The Liberal government had little appetite for assuming new responsibilities, but when France, Germany, and the King of the Belgians began carving up vast areas of equatorial Africa southward to the Congo basin, Britain authorized treaty negotiation with the various tribes along the lower Niger and proclaimed a protectorate over the region. The Berlin Conference, called by Bismarck in late 1884 to settle partition of the Congo basin, recognized Britain's position on the lower Niger.

The British government was relatively uninterested in West Africa, and in the next decade French expansion in the interior seemed likely to envelope all the British possessions and cut them off from further expansion. Goldie's company were nevertheless resourceful in combating French threats and, with help from Lord Salisbury, in pressing into the hinterland. Salisbury's concerns as an empire builder, however, were basically strategic and diplomatic. One of the first British statesmen to show an interest in empire for itself and to develop a positive imperial theory was Joseph Chamberlain, the ex-Radical who chose the Colonial office when he entered Salisbury's third ministry in 1895. It was late in the day, for by this time the partition of Africa was almost completed. Chamberlain threw his energies into the development of what is now Nigeria, investing capital in communications to stimulate the economy, creating a "West African Frontier Force," and in 1898 engaging France in tough negotiation over delimitation of the frontier. Within a few years administration of the country was taken over by the crown and the northern part pacified under the direction of Lord Lugard.

On the east coast of Africa Britain had long been dominant through activities in suppressing the slave trade and protecting the route to India. For decades the British consul had held a position of influence at the court of the sultan of Zanzibar, who exercised suzerain rights over much of the east African coast. But it was left to missionaries, explorers, and traders, of whom there were fewer than in west Africa, to open up the hinterland. When Germany showed signs of interest in the area in the mid-eighties the British could not afford to object because of their dependence on German diplomatic support in Egypt. In 1886 the Salisbury government signed an agreement with Germany, recognizing German control of the Dar-es-Salaam area in return for recognition of a British sphere farther north. In 1888 Salisbury granted a charter to William Mackinnon's Imperial British East Africa Company to develop what was to become the colony of Kenya and to push inland through Uganda, forestalling any French or German occupation of the headwaters of the Nile. It is interesting to note the resumption of the Tudor-Stuart practice of chartering commercial companies, to promote empire on the cheap. But as had often happened in the past, the imperial government was obliged within a few years to take full responsibility for the new territories in both east and west Africa.

In 1890 Salisbury negotiated a wide-ranging agreement with Bismarck. Although Germany had long coveted Zanzibar, she now recognized a British protectorate over that island, and the extension of British East Africa inland to the west bank of the Nile, thus giving Britain control of the strategically important area from Lake Victoria north to the Sudan. In return Salisbury abandoned the dream of a Cape-to-Cairo route by recognizing the extension of German East Africa westward to the Belgian Congo (but allowing Britain access to Lake Tanganyika from the south) and ceding to Germany the island of Heligoland off the German coast. It was said that Germany had given away a whole suit of clothes in Africa for a mere trouser button in the North Sea, but in 1914 it turned out to be a highly strategic button.

The fourth area of British expansion was in the south, and here again the instrument of the chartered company was used effectively in the early stages. The driving spirit behind British expansion in this area was a remarkable man, Cecil Rhodes (1853–1902), an extraordinary mixture of romantic dreamer and hard-headed businessman. After early success in the diamond fields of South Africa (whence he had emigrated a few years earlier on account of his health) he returned to Oxford in 1873. There he was inspired by the ideal of patriotic public service and imbued with the prevalent belief in Britain's destiny to rule. His idealism did not prevent him, however, from using ruthless business methods to achieve his goals. He returned to South Africa, where he amassed a tremendous fortune, consolidating his South African diamond mines and extending operations into the Transvaal. In 1885 he helped to promote the establishment of a protectorate over the vast but thinly settled area of Bechuanaland, ostensibly to defend the natives against the Boers in Transvaal, but also to prevent union of the Transvaal with the new colony of German Southwest Africa. In the same year part of the coast of Zululand north of Natal was annexed to prevent a German occupation, as the Germans had done in South West Africa the previous year. A few years later Tongaland, the gap between this area and Portuguese Mozambique was filled in by declaring it a British protectorate, thus barring the Transvaal from the sea.

In the meantime, Rhodes sent agents into Matabeleland to the north and made a nebulous pact with its chief, Logenbula. The following year, 1889, he obtained a charter for the British South Africa Company to open up the vast area that later became known as Rhodesia. When he brought in settlers contrary to his agreement with Logenbula the Matabeles rose against him in 1893, but were defeated by the superior weapons of the British. Although it lacked South Africa's great mineral wealth, the new colony prospered, having proved suitable for white settlement, and six years later its administration was taken over by the crown.

Rhodes' vision of painting the map red from the Cape to Cairo was foiled in 1890 by Britain's recognition of German East Africa, extending between the Belgian Congo and the Indian Ocean. In 1890 Rhodes became prime minister of Cape Colony, where at first he symbolized cooperation between British and Boer. This cordial relationship was ended by developments in the Transvaal, which had become overnight one of the world's wealthiest small states with the discovery of extensive gold fields. Its president, Paul Kruger, had led the fight for independence and was as determined in his own way as Rhodes, although in every other respect he represented the opposite extreme. The Transvaal was a small pastoral republic, peopled by stern Calvinist farmers. They had infrequent contact with the outside world and had changed little since their forefathers left Holland in the seventeenth century. They were uninterested in commerce or mining, but under Kruger's shrewd leadership they were ready to profit from the influx of gold-seeking "Uitlanders" by taxing them heavily. As the newcomers—mostly British from Cape Colony—grew in number they began to complain of unequal treatment in the courts and refusal to grant them the franchise. Rhodes, who had invested heavily in the Rand gold mines, conspired with the leading Uitlanders to overthrow the Kruger government. He sent his emissary, Dr. Jameson, across the border from Rhodesia with a small armed force. The internal uprising misfired, however, and Jameson's force was surrounded and captured.

The repercussions of the Jameson raid were widespread. The German kaiser sent Kruger a telegram congratulating him on dealing with the raiders "without appealing for the help of friendly powers," thus implying future German support against Britain. Though Chamberlain denounced the raid, he was suspected of complicity, despite exoneration by a select committee of inquiry. Jameson was turned over to the British authorities by Kruger. Even after his conviction a large segment of the British public still regarded him as a hero. Rhodes was censured by the select committee, although subsequently whitewashed by Chamberlain, but he was forced to step down as premier of Cape Colony since he had now lost the confidence of the Cape Boers, and also to resign temporarily from his chartered company. He devoted the few remaining years of his life to the development of Rhodesia and died in 1902, leaving his vast fortune to endow the scholarships that still bring students to Oxford from all over the Commonwealth and the United States.

The previously neutral Orange Free State now turned to the support of the Transvaal, where tension continued to grow over the next three years. Kruger began to spend a large proportion of his bouyant revenues on the import of arms against the coming struggle. The killing of a Briton by a Boer policeman further aroused the Uitlander and led to submission to Queen Victoria of a petition with over twenty thousand signatures. In the meantime the British government had appointed Sir Alfred (later Lord) Milner high commissioner in South Africa. He was an ardent imperialist, a man as proud and obstinate as Kruger himself and quite unprepared to temporize. Chamberlain urged Milner to come to terms, with Kruger and moderates on both sides offered a basis for settlement, but Milner rejected Kruger's proposals. Deciding that war was inevitable, Kruger took the initiative before Britain could bring in large reinforcements and declared war in October 1899.

Most of the male Boers were farmers who had been brought up to ride and shoot. They knew the country and were well armed, with the result that the war went their way in the early stages, to the consternation of British public opinion. The spectacle of this tiny community defying the mighty British Empire entertained the world and warmed the hearts of the Irish Nationalists. In the long run, however, the weight of numbers was decisive. The relief of Mafeking after a siege of 217 days was greeted with delirious joy in London. The Boers were forced thereafter to resort to guerilla tactics, at which they were skilled, and this prolonged the war for another year. Near the end Lord Kitchener (1850–1916), the British general who had succeeded Lord Roberts, resorted to interning women and children from Boer farmsteads in badly run concentration camps, where 20,000 died of disease. Nevertheless when the Boers finally surrendered, Kitchener gave them generous terms by the Peace of Vereeniging, signed in May 1902. By its terms the Boers had to accept British rule, but they were promised eventual self-government, and their language was retained in schools and courts. The British also paid £3,000,000 for rehabilitation. The war had cost Britain £222,000,000, and her casualties were 28,600, of which 5,774 were fatal, and 16,000 more died of disease. She had been forced to put almost half a million men in the field, including units from Canada, Australia, and New Zealand.

The Boer War was the only large-scale modern conflict to arouse fierce opposition in Britain throughout its course, much like the protest in the United States over American intervention in Vietnam. The Liberal party was badly divided—at one extreme stood the Liberal imperialist faction, who supported the war while criticizing the way it was conducted; at the other was the group known as pro-Boers, who had been against it from the beginning; in between were a varying number of moderates. The moderate leader of the party, Sir Henry Campbell-Bannerman, tried to bridge the gap, but later sided with the pro-Boers in denouncing the use of concentration camps as "methods of barbarism." One of the most vociferous pro-Boers was a young Welsh Radical, David Lloyd George, who was almost lynched when he tried to address a public meeting in Joseph Chamberlain's city of Birmingham. The government exploited the situation by holding (and winning) the "khaki election" in 1900, while the war was still on.

The length and the cost of the war thenceforth dampened imperialistic fervor. But the two preceding decades had already seen remarkable territorial expansion, and the spread had not been limited to Africa. The North Borneo Company had been chartered in 1882; in 1884 southern New Guinea had been occupied on pressure from the Australian colonies to anticipate a German occupation. Between 1885 and 1890 the conquest of North Burma was completed, a war precipitated by the excesses of a barbarous despot, but made more timely by a supposed French threat from Indochina. The expansion of British rule in the Malay Peninsula, largely by treaty, was continued until 1914. In the same period more than a hundred islands with a combined population of a third of a million were acquired in the Pacific, and leases to the ports of Kowloon and Weihaiwei were obtained from China.

The new imperialism was by no means confined to the tropical empire. Queen Victoria's golden jubilee, celebrated in 1887, was the occasion of the first Colonial Conference, the gathering of prime ministers from all the self-governing colonies, an early forerunner of the Commonwealth conferences. In 1894 a second conference met in Ottawa. A third was held in 1897 on Victoria's diamond jubilee, and at this Joseph Chamberlain was in the chair. He made proposals for imperial centralization, especially in matters of defense. English-speaking Canada, New Zealand, and the Australian colonies, which in 1900, were federated into a Commonwealth, took up the imperial idea with enthusiasm and sent 60,000 volunteers to support Britain in the Boer War. At the 1902 colonial conference Sir Wilfrid Laurier, Prime Minister of Canada, proposed a system of imperial preference that later captured Chamberlain's imagination with great consequences for the future. Pro-British sentiment in the dominions, as they were now called, had been stimulated by increased emigration from Britain and improved communications. But it was also part of a world-wide trend toward large power blocs in the decades preceding the First World War.

Chapter Eight
THE TURN
OF THE CENTURY

The end of the century coincided with the end of the long reign of Queen Victoria, who died in January 1901—22 days after the new century had begun. Gladstone had predeceased her by three years, and Lord Salisbury followed in 1903, thirteen months after turning over the premiership to his nephew Arthur Balfour, whose political career continued until 1929. Victoria's reign had encompassed several distinct political generations. She herself had become something of an institution, for at her death few of her subjects could remember a time when she was not Queen. National pride in her longevity and what she stood for had been demonstrated in golden and diamond jubilee celebrations. There was more than a grain of truth in the Irish quip that Edward VII would not "be the king his mother was." As Prince of Wales he was an active figure in the social world, although many questioned the company he kept; but he lacked his mother's interest in affairs of state. With the death of Queen Victoria the crown assumed more clearly the figurehead role assigned to it by Bagehot,[1] exercising decisive influence only in rare moments of political or constitutional crisis. Although Edward had been involved in several scandals, he was weak rather than vicious. If less intelligent than his mother, he was more openminded, an attitude that suited the age to which he gave his name. As the nineteenth century gave way to the twentieth, Edwardian England developed a flavor and character of its own.

The turn of the century is therefore a convenient point to examine the social, economic, and cultural conditions of Britain and to assess what progress or what changes had taken place since the days of the Great Exhibition of 1851. The population of the United Kingdom had grown from 27 million in 1851 to almost 42 million in 1901, but there had been a decline in the birth

---

[1] Walter Bagehot (1826–1877), editor of the weekly *Economist*, wrote a most perceptive book entitled *The English Constitution*, published in 1867.

rate of six per thousand from the high point of thirty-five per thousand in the early seventies. The population increase in the United States and Germany had been much more rapid. The former had outstripped the United Kingdom in 1851 and by 1911 had twice Britain's population. By the same year imperial Germany had 65 million to the United Kingdom's 45 million, although eighty years earlier the same territories had had equal populations.

British agriculture had held its own until 1870, after which date it declined rapidly through competition from newly opened lands in the Americas and Australia and drastic reductions in world freight rates arising from improvements in transportation. Wheat prices were halved in the period 1870–1900, and the amount of acreage under wheat cultivation was reduced correspondingly. By 1900 there was some recovery—at least, a leveling out—as agriculture adjusted to the new state of affairs, but it was never to regain its earlier importance in the national economy. In these same years, British industry also received its first serious challenge, primarily from the United States and Germany, although Britain remained a major industrial and trading power. Coal production continued to advance until 1914, but there was some decline in efficiency. Britain fell behind the United States in coal production in 1899 but kept a long lead over Germany. Progress in steel and iron production was slower, owing to failure to develop new techniques with the result that Britain was outstripped by the United States in 1890 and by Germany in 1896. Nevertheless, domestic demand was high and the industry throve as did the mechanical and electrical engineering industries that manufactured for markets abroad. Britain lagged, however, in the production of electrical equipment, chemicals, and, after 1900, motor cars in comparison with her chief rivals; textiles, however, having declined in the second half of the nineteenth century, improved again after 1900. Britain continued despite foreign competition to lead the world in shipbuilding, where there was more innovation, with the result that as late as 1914 three-fifths of the world's ships were British built.

In the half century prior to 1914 mechanization increasingly characterized British industry, and was one of the most important aspects of British industrial development. This in turn led to another important development: mechanized industry required greater capital, which in many cases led to the concentration of business in the hands of larger companies, as private firms and partnerships gave way to limited liability companies. Most of these were characterized by sale of stock to investors on the open market: some developed through the mergers of competing businesses. The large corporations that would dominate the twentieth century were already a familiar feature of the business scene by the end of the Victorian age.

The cause of Britain's industrial lag behind the United States and Germany is open to conjecture. Some successful British businessmen retired from active business on entering the aristocratic upper class, but more important was the fact that long-established businesses found it difficult to change their ways. They were noticeably disinclined to invest in new means of production when the old ones could be made to do. British industry was kept busy by the growing domestic market, the continued demand in tropical countries for British cottons, and the need for British machinery in developing countries, even though American and German industry were proving more productive.

British trade continued to flourish. Exports had doubled in the period 1855–1875. In the last quarter of the century, however, the increase in value was only 5.4 percent, because of a world-wide decline in prices, although increase in quantity was much greater. After 1900 the situation was reversed and by 1913 the value of annual exports had increased 90 percent over the last years of the nineteenth century, although owing to higher prices the increase in quantity rose less rapidly. Imports increased at an even faster rate, but were offset by "invisible" exports: returns on overseas investments and income from shipping, banking, and insurance services. British foreign investments, which in 1870 were about £700 million, had risen to £2,400 million in 1900 and were £4,000 million by 1914. The rapid growth of foreign investment in the decade before the war may have slowed the development of domestic industry, and, of course, such investments became precarious after 1914.

The last quarter of the nineteenth century has misleadingly been called the Great Depression. It was a period of falling prices and lagging foreign trade, but there were only a few years of real recession. Indeed, over the last four decades of the century the general standard of living had begun to rise dramatically as real income per capita increased by at least 17 percent per decade. Real wages rose some 70 percent in the period 1860–1900. After a century of rapid expansion in population and of plowing capital back into industry, the Industrial Revolution was at last beginning to pay off for the masses. With the railway network complete, the new ports built, the merchant ships nearly all steam and steel, the demand for capital investment was less pressing and a higher proportion of the national wealth could be spent on consumer goods. Lower foreign commodity prices further favored the British consumer, who was so dependent on imports. But as prices rose again after the turn of the century, there was a marked leveling off in the standard of living.

Statements about prosperity and living standards are, of course, relative, and the historian should make his comparisons with what preceded and not with what was to follow. The standard of living of late-Victorian Britain was far below what it is today, and within this general prosperity were large pockets of poverty. The first sociological studies of poverty were made in this period, and the results were a great shock to the public. The investigations of Charles Booth (1840–1916) in the years 1887–1892, published under the title *Life and Labour of the People of London* revealed that 30.7 percent of London's population was indigent. In 1901 B. Seebohm Rowntree (1871–1954), published a similar study for York showing 27.8 percent of the population lived below the subsistence level. Booth, a wealthy shipowner, had formerly been a laissez-faire Liberal, but he was so shocked at his own findings that he concluded society must take charge of the impoverished, who were clearly unable to help themselves. Consequently he became an early champion of old-age pensions since a large proportion of the needy were in this category.

Social critics pointed out the continued maldistribution of wealth. It was estimated in 1908 that some 3 percent of income-receivers enjoyed over one-third of the national income, and that 12 percent received half of it. A new plutocracy had come into being for the decline in agriculture made the landed aristocracy relatively less wealthy, although some recouped their losses by business investments and a few by marriages to American heiresses. The income of the middle classes did not rise quite as rapidly as that of the working classes in this period, but the number of persons with white-collar occupations increased.

One modern historian, Arthur Marwick, estimates that 80 percent of the population of Edwardian Britain were in the working class, but he includes small shopkeepers and elementary school teachers, who might better be considered lower middle class. He estimates the upper class, including landed aristocracy and leading businessmen and professionals to be 5 percent of the population and the middle classes 15 percent.[2] There were about 400,000 salaried men earning over £160 ($800) a year, 330,000 of them in the professions; there were 580,000 farmers, and 620,000 employers, mostly small businessmen. The sons of the upper class traditionally attended one of seven historic public schools, but middle-class social aspirations led to the establishment of other expensive boarding schools modeled on the same pattern. The determination of the British middle classes to educate their children privately and guarantee their economic and social future has endured since the late nineteenth century. Probably in no other Western country have class distinctions been determined so precisely by accent as in Britain during the past century, although such distinction is less marked in the north and in Scotland than in the Midlands and the south.

In the quarter-century before 1914 an extraordinary number of innovations—the electric-light bulb, the phonograph, the moving-picture pro-

[2] Arthur Marwick, *Britain in the Century of Total War* (London, 1968) pp. 38–40.

jector, the telephone, the wireless transmitter, the typewriter, and automobile —came into use. The airplane was in its experimental stages; indeed in 1909 Blériot, the pioneer French aviator, flew the English Channel. Great progress was made in medicine, sanitation, and public health. There was a notable reduction in infant mortality, and the death rate decreased from 22 per thousand in the early seventies to 14.2 per thousand in 1913. The effects on the pace and style of twentieth-century life were, of course, felt by the whole Western world; Britain was no longer a pacesetter in the development of new inventions. With the large concentration of population in London and other large cities, probably the most dramatic changes were in local transport. The motor car began to appear on the roads just at the turn of the century. Archaic restrictions on its use were withdrawn, and by 1910 some 100,000 motor vehicles were in use. In 1904 London had two motor taxis, but their number grew to 6,300 in six years. Motor buses in London increased from 20 to 3,000 in the period 1905–1913. Along with the tube and underground railway (subway) and later the deep tube as well as the new electric trams (streetcars), they revolutionized urban transport and contributed to the indefinite growth of London suburbs. Improved railway service also led to the growth of a commuting population living in "dormitory" towns in a fifty-mile radius of London.

The proportion of people who lived reasonably well was probably higher than ever, but the contrast between ostentatious wealth and abject poverty was as sharp as before. One had only to compare the bustle and glitter of London's West End with its fine buildings, broad, traffic-filled streets, expensive restaurants, and fashionable theaters and the squalor of an East End slum where one water tap and one toilet served twenty-five cold, dirty houses.

The end of the century saw the undermining of many Victorian verities. Not only was the social and political ascendancy of the British landed classes upset by the decline of agriculture and land values, but the industrial supremacy Britain had enjoyed for more than a century was now challenged by new, larger industrial powers. The Victorian's implicit faith in classical political economy and its core doctrine of laissez-faire was under attack from right-wing capitalists who said home industry needed protection and left-wing reformers who had become socialists. Belief in free trade and economy died hard but it was beginning to be questioned at the turn of the century. Nor was the concept of Pax Britannica still meaningful. The division of Europe into two armed camps and the development of Germany as a naval power forced Britain to concentrate most of her navy in home waters.

In no area was change more noticeable than in that of religion, which now played a reduced role in national life. Churches were still well attended, but religion was no longer the central, driving force it had been half a century earlier. Until the middle eighties the number of churchgoers rose with the population, but the subsequent decline began to be noticeable about 1900. Even in the high Victorian era a large segment of the urban masses was untouched by religion, despite efforts by the churches to reach them. Under Frederick Denison Maurice (1805–1872), some Anglican clergy, loosely termed Christian Socialists concerned themselves with social problems. A number of them, as well as some Anglo-Catholics, dedicated themselves to work in the slums. But the Roman Catholic and Primitive Methodists and some other dissenting churches drew more working-class congregations. Many working-class leaders of the time were active Nonconformists, and practicing Dissenters may have just outnumbered practicing Anglicans by the end of the century. But there was also some decline in the vitality of dissent, with the exception of the Salvation Army, founded by William Booth about 1878 to bring evangelical Christianity into the streets. The number of Roman Catholics in Great Britain more than doubled in the years 1840–1900, while the number of their priests trebled.

By the turn of the century the religious zeal of the middle and upper classes had obviously diminished, with church attendance and family prayers becoming far less frequent. In 1902 a London survey indicated that only two in eleven Londoners attended church on a particular Sunday, but this was undoubtedly below the national average. There was a similar decline in the number of both Anglican ordinations and positions in education requiring clerical qualifications. Decreased returns from land also considerably reduced the value of the "livings" of the Anglican clergy.

Apart from the Salvation Army, which was in a sense a protest against the multiplicity of sects, the most obvious vitality among the Christian churches in the United Kingdom at the turn of the century was to be found in the Roman Catholic Church and in the Anglo-Catholic wing of the Anglican Church. Despite prosecutions for departures from the official Prayer Book and the fulminations of ultra-Protestants, the ritualist movement in the High Anglican Church flourished. This was an effort to revive many Catholic practices—such as the use of candles, incense and vestments, auricular confession, and other Catholic rituals—that had been abandoned or altered at the time of the Reformation. A small but steady flow of "converts," mostly from the upper classes and the intelligentsia, continued to move from the Anglican to the Roman Catholic Church. It has been suggested that the Catholic form of Christianity, with its emphasis on tradition, ritual, and the sacraments, fared better than Protestant forms based solely on the Bible when challenged by science and so-called higher criticism. Biblical criticism and scientific knowledge may have helped to undermine the faith of the intelligentsia, but the general decline in the practice of religion was probably due more to the hedonism and materialism that permeated all classes. Among the upper classes the increasingly popular long weekend out of town was not conducive to Sunday observances and at another level the bawdy humor of the music halls reflected the more down-to-earth tastes of the age.

The Victorian press was solemn and factual, aimed mainly at the male middle and upper classes. In 1896, however, the established newspapers were challenged by the appearance of a new sort of paper, the *Daily Mail*, founded by Alfred Harmsworth (1865–1922), a half-educated adventurer. Taking the American yellow press as its model, the new paper edited the news to make it more interesting and cut it up to make it short and snappy. The paper sold for a halfpenny—half the usual price—and was aimed at the masses, who had not the time or inclination, or often the education, to read the old-fashioned type of newspaper. Circulation skyrocketed, advertisers shifted to the new media, old established papers went to the wall, and new rivals of the *Daily Mail* quickly appeared, papers which Lord Salisbury said were "written by office boys, for office boys." In 1908 Harmsworth, now Lord Northcliffe, bought *The Times*, long regarded as a national institution. Although he kept it on a higher level than his other papers, he aimed to make it more popular and to use it to promote his own political ends.

The new popular press was one of the less attractive indirect consequences of the Education Act of 1870. A higher proportion of the population was now literate, but most people did not go beyond elementary school. The 1870 system worked well within its limitations, but Britain still lagged behind her industrial competitors in secondary and technical education. In 1859 the Department of Science and Art had been set up at South Kensington as a national examining body, and in 1889 the Technical Instruction Act extended its powers and set up local authorities. The Manchester School of Technology was one of the more outstanding institutions to evolve from this legislation. Many school boards extended classes into the area of secondary education and initiated night classes at which a wide range of theoretical and practical subjects were taught. Secondary education nevertheless remained inadequate, and despite broader curricula, grammar and boarding schools were below the standards of their foreign counterparts. "It was no longer possible to discount the fact," wrote Elie Halévy, "that a young Englishman on leaving school was intellectually two years behind a German of the same age by the consoling reflection that he made up in character what he lacked in information, and that if more ignorant, he was better equipped for practical life."[3] Finally in 1902, as the result of the reports of the two royal commissions and the discovery that school boards had entered the secondary field illegally, the

[3] *Imperialism and the Rise of Labour, 1894–1905* (London, 1951 ed.), p. 159.

comprehensive Secondary Education Act was passed. The passage of this all important legislation was the work of Arthur Balfour, who became Prime Minister at the same time. To the chagrin of the Nonconformists the voluntary church schools were retained, but the old school boards were abolished and in counties and boroughs educational authorities were set up, to administer elementary and secondary as well as technical education, under the supervision of the Department of Education responsible to a Cabinet minister. The new system flourished at both levels, and between 1905 and 1914 the number of pupils in grant-aided secondary schools more than doubled. The curricula of Oxford and Cambridge were expanded and the standard of these two universities greatly improved in the second half of the nineteenth century. They continued as upper-class institutions, but offered extensive scholarships to bright grammar school students. The University of Durham, founded in 1832, remained a small institution, but in other provincial cities new colleges sprang up, which trained students to take examinations for University of London degrees. Colleges at Manchester, Liverpool, and Leeds joined in 1884 to form Victoria University, but shortly after 1900 each became an independent university. Universities were also founded in Birmingham in 1900, in Sheffield in 1905, and in Bristol in 1909.

The post-Victorians of Lytton Strachey's generation condemned Victorian architecture and design for its ugliness. In public buildings this has been blamed on the Gothic revival, but the depressing appearance of most nineteenth-century private houses was a matter of economy. Cheap processed materials such as brick and slate, which were aesthetically repulsive, replaced local materials which had blended in with the local environment in small communities. Equally unattractive interior furnishings with ornaments and overstuffed upholstery were mass-produced. But late in the century the poet, William Morris (1834–1896), led a successful crusade for improved design, the revival of craftsmanship and application of artistic criteria to every area of daily life. By the turn of the century there was also a return in public architecture to buildings more in the classical tradition. Clothing lost much of its stiffness and became more attractive and comfortable. The high Victorian era had been characterized by the top hat and frock coat of the gentleman and the crinoline, bustle, corset, and trailing dress of the fashionable lady. While older fashions survived for more formal occasions, by 1900 men were beginning to wear lounge suits, tweed jackets, flannel trousers, and derby and straw hats. Women's clothes grew less constricting and voluminous, except for absurd hats that were pinned onto masses of hair swept up in the French style. Skirt lengths actually rose above the ankle, giving more freedom to young ladies who took up cycling and tennis.

During the last quarter of the nineteenth century there was a notable increase in the number of novels published, but the only great English novelist of the period was Thomas Hardy (1840–1928), who broke from the moral and sentimental conventions of the earlier Victorian novelists. During these years there emerged a literary gulf between the general public, who continued to read novels by such popular authors as Dickens, Thackeray, and Trollope, and a younger generation of writers. The aesthetes of the eighties preached "art for art's sake," and the decadents of the nineties reflected a fatigue, ennui, and disenchantment; many of their leading lights died young, including Oscar Wilde (1856–1900), whose brief but brilliant career ended with his conviction on a morals charge. The outlook of the decadents contrasted sharply with the vigorous imperialism of writers such as Rudyard Kipling (1856–1936), whose forte was the short story. The decadents talked of *fin de siècle* but, according to the historian R. K. Ensor, the young men of 1900, "felt themselves at the beginning, not the end of an age."[4] The Edwardian Age was one of transition, but it belonged more to the twentieth century than to the nineteenth.

In the last two decades of the nineteenth century militancy grew among the working classes, and various forms of socialism emerged as workers became disillusioned at the neglect of their problems by older parties. W. C. Preston's popular *Bitter Cry of Outcast London*, published in 1893, helped to create a widespread feeling that something had to be done to combat the appalling poverty of London's East End. In 1886 rioting and looting after the breakup of a meeting of unemployed in Trafalgar Square created apprehension among the upper classes, who sought to buy off the threat to their security with higher contributions to the Lord Mayor's relief fund. A more genuine response was the slum settlement movement started by Samuel Barnett, an Anglican clergyman, with the foundation of Toynbee Hall in the East End slum of Whitechapel. Through this and similar projects university men who later became influential (such as Clement Attlee) came into direct contact with slum conditions.

In 1888 public sympathy was aroused by the strike of a relatively small but badly exploited group of girls employed in the London matchmaking industry, a strike that proved successful and an inspiration to others. The "new unionism" (as it was called to distinguish it from the craft unionism of earlier times) began with the formation by Will Thorne in 1889, of the National Union of Gas Workers and General Labourers. It won an eight-hour day for London members and soon boasted a national membership of 30,000. London dockworkers quickly followed suit headed by Ben Tillet, John Burns, and Tom Mann. In the London dock strike later that year the demands of these exploited workers for better hiring conditions and sixpence an hour pay

4 *England, 1870–1914*, p. 527.

quickly aroused public interest and sympathy, brought financial support from the public and from other unions as far away as Australia. One reason for the strikers' success was the organizing skill and inspiring leadership of John Burns (1858–1943), himself an engineer, who in no time could draw a crowd on a street corner with his foghorn voice. The strike was finally settled by mediation, in which the aged Cardinal Manning took a leading part. A few years later the new unionism suffered reverses as employers began to take countermeasures and advantage of the recession of 1893–1894. Some strikes were unsuccessful, including one in 1897 by the powerful Amalgamated Society of Engineers. By the end of the century, however, the number of trade unionists had increased to two million. The new unionism may have been a flash in the pan, but the old unions were stirred out of their torpor and ceased to be so exclusive. The new unions catered chiefly to lower paid workers and were not confined to particular trades. They relied on low fees, large membership, and aggressive tactics. They promoted local trade councils, favored political action on the municipal level, and began to permeate the staid old Trade Union Congress. Their leaders were generally young, aggressive, and socialist.

Karl Marx (1818–1883) and Fredrick Engels (1820–1895) based their social philosophy on a study of English industrial conditions. Marx, living in exile in England, produced his *Das Kapital* after years of research in the British Museum, but British socialism owes little to their inspiration. Its roots go back through Chartism and Owenism to the working-class radicalism of the Peterloo era and even derive some nourishment from Bentham and John Stuart Mill. While these influences were secular and rationalist there was also a distinct Christian element in late-nineteenth century British socialism. Many of its working-class leaders were from Nonconformists and brought to their new creed an evangelical enthusiasm. Marx's *Das Kapital*, the first volume of which was not published in an English translation until 1886, did not enjoy as wide a vogue as the work of the American, Henry George. His *Progress and Poverty*, published in 1879, advocated a direct tax on land as the solution to social ills.

One of the first Englishmen to read Marx (in a French edition) and be converted to his ideas was H. M. Hyndman (1842–1921), a well-to-do cosmopolite and ex-Tory Radical. With other middle-class converts to socialism, such as H. H. Champion, an ex-army officer, and the poet-artist, William Morris, he founded in 1881 a new organization, the Social Democratic Federation, which adopted a Marxist socialist program. As a political party its membership was never large, perhaps not more than a thousand, but in its early years it contained many future leaders of the Labour party. The SDF never succeeded in winning a parliamentary election, but it did stir popular opinion in the eighties by several giant protest meetings in Trafalgar Square. The first, a demonstration of the unemployed in 1886 (mentioned above), led to the arrest of four leaders, including Hyndman and Burns, who were acquitted by a sympathetic jury. In November 1887, a second meeting in defiance of police orders was later to become known as "bloody Sunday." Reinforced by cavalry, the police succeeded in clearing the square only after a pitched battle in which there were a hundred casualties, two of them fatal. Several leaders, among them John Burns, were sentenced to prison. The influence of the SDF soon waned, partly because of Hyndman's cantankerous personality and the consequent secession of other leaders, and partly because its brand of socialism had no sustained appeal for the working classes, although it did help to create a new mood of militancy among them.

The Fabian Society, founded in 1884, was of more lasting significance. It was not a mass movement, but a relatively small group of mostly middle-class intellectuals. Convinced that socialism would be achieved by gradual evolution, they banded together to educate and stimulate public opinion in that direction. They were a brilliant and fascinating group, including George Bernard Shaw (1856–1950), on the threshold of his career as the leading playwright of the early twentieth century; Graham Wallas (1858–1932), an early sociologist and later a lecturer at the Fabian-founded London School of Economics; and the Webbs—Sidney (1859–1947), a brilliant young civil servant of obscure origins, and his wife Beatrice (1858–1943), the emancipated daughter of a wealthy businessman. The Webbs were a dedicated couple, who over the years contributed much to the writing of English institutional history, which they saw as the basis of knowledge for social reform. The Fabians favored constitutionalism, rejecting the violent methods of the SDF. They were even reluctant to take separate political action at first. Their original policy was one of permeation of the existing political parties, especially the Liberals. But they became disillusioned in 1895 after the failure of the Rosebery administration. The home of the Webbs became the unofficial headquarters of the movement, and here they entertained many of the rising young men of both parties. These included six future prime ministers: Lord Rosebery, Sir Henry Campbell-Bannerman, Arthur Balfour, Herbert Asquith, Ramsay MacDonald and a little later, young Winston Churchill. However, the extent to which Fabian ideas influenced the guests is difficult to estimate.

The role of the Fabians was not unlike that of the Benthamites a few generations earlier. They were called in for advice by orthodox politicians who did not accept their philosophy but respected their knowledge. In the end the old parties disappointed the Fabians. The latter eventually accepted the institution of a third party, but in the meantime they were prepared to open all roads to the socialist utopia, as in their promotion of what was called "gas and water socialism" on the municipal front. They were particularly effective on the newly formed London County Council in the period 1892–1908.

The main thrust for independent political action on the national level came from the militant wing of the trade union movement, but it had to overcome a Liberal-Labour alliance that dated back to the election of 1868. Although the trade unions were temporarily disillusioned by the Liberal Criminal Law Amendment Act of 1871, two miners, Thomas Burt (1827–1932) and Alexander MacDonald (1821–1881), were elected to Parliament in 1874 with Liberal support. In the 1880 election the Liberals endorsed working-class candidates, known as Lib-Labs, in some constituencies, with the result that a third workingman, Henry Broadhurst (1840–1911), was elected, receiving office from Gladstone in 1886. The number of Lib-Labs was increased to twelve in 1885 and sixteen in 1892, but their influence on the Liberal party was minimal and many middle-class Liberals never warmed to the alliance. More militant trade unionists preferred independent action, but the Lib-Lab alliance, once formed, was not so easily set aside and was among the many obstacles to the formation of a Labour party.

One of the first trade unionists to break away from the old political system was James Keir Hardie (1856–1915), a Scottish miner who had started to work at the age of seven and personally suffered all the adversity arising from poverty and discrimination before becoming a successful trade union organizer. When he failed to get a Lib-Lab nomination for Lanark he stood as a miners' candidate at a by-election in 1888. Although defeated, he and his supporters set up a short-lived Scottish Labour party with a socialist program, but his socialism was influenced by Henry George and not by SDF, which he rejected. At the annual meeting of the Trades Union Congress in 1888 Hardie was defeated by Broadhurst, the old guard champion of the Lib-Lab alliance, when he advocated independent labor representation. Hardie and Burns, however, succeeded in getting elected to Parliament in 1892 as independent Labour members. In the same year independent labor parties were formed in a number of constituencies. In 1893 these met at a congress in Bradford with representatives from various socialist societies to form the Independent Labour Party. The party's ultimate objective was socialism, but its immediate task was to make workers realize the need for direct political action. For this reason it was deemed politic not to use the word "socialist" in the name of the party. The ILP appeal was highly emotional and reminiscent of the Methodist revival, a reminder of the influence of the Nonconformist tradition in the development of a native British socialism. "The Red Flag" became the hymn of the new religion and was sung at all meetings with evangelical fervor.

The new party won no seats in the election of 1895 (although the Lib-Labs, mostly miners in safe constituencies, retained twelve), but under Hardie's indomitable leadership they persevered. A proposal for fusion with the SDF came to nothing, for perceptive ILP leaders realized that the SDF was too doctrinaire and too insensitive to popular religious and moral beliefs ever to win mass support. On the other hand the Fabians, originally cool to the formation of a third party, assisted the ILP in its propaganda efforts; if the ILP was the soul of British socialism, in the view of one historian[5] the Fabian Society was its brain. Much of the vitality of British socialism at the turn of the century was reflected in the popular tracts of the Fabian Society, many written by Shaw, and in the socialist press, especially the lively *Clarion*. It was edited by Robert Blatchford (1851–1943), who wrote a popular series of articles, later published under the title *Merrie England*, which sketched for the common man a picture of what a happy land a socialist England might be.

The increased strength of the new unions in the Trades Union Congress and the growing sense of insecurity among unions generally, stimulated by the development of the Employers' Federation, finally in 1899 persuaded the TUC (by a small majority) to call a conference to promote improved labor representation in Parliament. Held in London in 1900, the conference was attended by representatives of the ILP, the SDF (who later withdrew), the Fabians, and the unions. The ILP proposals carried the day. The Labour Representation Committee was set up with Ramsay MacDonald, the ILP nominee, as its unpaid secretary. The purpose of the LRC was to promote the election to Parliament of a distinct labor group which would have its own whips but be prepared to cooperate with any party in the passage of labor legislation. Thus was born what in a few years was called the Labour party.

Little notice was taken of this momentous event for newspapers were preoccupied with the Boer War. Moreover, the trade union movement itself was still halfhearted, and initially a large number of unions refused to participate. Only fifteen candidates were nominated in the surprise "Khaki Election" of 1900, which was fought on a budget of £33, and only two were elected—Keir Hardie and a trade unionist, Richard Bell, who later defected. The future of the LRC looked bleak until it was suddenly presented with an issue that brought it much needed trade union support—the celebrated Taff Vale decision of the House of Lords. The very right to strike was called into question by this decision, which granted the Taff Vale Railway Company damages for losses resulting from a strike. The Conservative government refused to bring in any remedial legislation to meet the legitimate grievances of the unions. Consequently the latter were reluctantly driven to accept the logic of direct political action. The LRC membership (measured

[5] G. D. H. Cole, *A Short History of the British Working Class Movement*, vol. III (London, 1927), p. 23.

in the membership of affiliated unions and societies) jumped from 376,000 in 1901 to 861,000 in 1903, and three more LRC representatives were elected to Parliament at by-elections. This success was in part due to a secret electoral pact between Ramsay MacDonald and Herbert Gladstone, the Liberal whip, who agreed not to oppose each other's candidates in certain constituencies. At its annual conference in 1903 the LRC tightened its constitution and increased levies on constituent members to establish a fund to pay Labour members of Parliament.

It may seem paradoxical that the Unionist party was in office for sixteen of the twenty years after the passage of the Third Reform Act. This is explained not only by its superior financial resources and the internal divisions plaguing the Liberal party during this period, but also by the growing English dislike of Irish nationalism, and by the popularity of imperialism up to the end of the Boer War. When the war was over Balfour succeeded Salisbury as Prime Minister, and the political pendulum swung rapidly in the opposite direction despite some notable achievement of the new administration in foreign affairs and defense policy.

The heavy cost of the Boer War had dampened the appeal of imperialism, while the land purchase policy of successive Unionist governments reduced Irish tensions for the time. The Taff Vale decision and the Education Act of 1902 gave Liberals and Labourites two other live issues on which to attack the ministers. The Government's decision to allow importation of indentured Chinese labor into South Africa further alienated Labour and Nonconformist Liberals on both moral and economic grounds, since it precluded emigration of English workers to South Africa and exploited Chinese coolies. But the last straw was the issue of protection. It was raised by Joseph Chamberlain, who resigned from the Government to promote it. The Unionist party and the Cabinet were split three ways, for the ardent Freetraders also resigned, leaving Balfour stranded in the middle, vainly seeking some compromise. Eventually in December 1905, he gave up the task and resigned. The Indian summer of the old Tory aristocracy had ended.

Chapter Nine

THE NEW LIBERALISM

The resignation of the Balfour government resulted in the formation of the first Liberal administration in more than a decade. The Prime Minister was Sir Henry Campbell-Bannerman (1836–1908), an elderly Scottish businessman, well-to-do, well-liked, and politically moderate. The Liberals came into office because of divisions in the Unionist party rather than through their own efforts. As we have seen, the Boer War divided Liberals into pro-Boers or "Little Englanders" on the one hand and Liberal Imperialists or "Limps" on the other, although there were undoubtedly many members who fell between the two extremes. There was also a less clear division between the old nineteenth-century Gladstonian type of Liberal and the new collectivist Liberal, who was not wedded to the idea of laissez-faire. The Gladstonian Liberals—of whom John Morley, Gladstone's former colleague and biographer, was the best example—were concerned with such issues as free trade, Irish home rule, temperance, disestablishment, and secularization of state schools; most of them were Little Englanders. The Liberal Imperialists did not reject the Gladstonian type of reforms although some were lukewarm to home rule, but they put more emphasis on preservation of the empire, maintenance of the armed forces, and continuity in foreign policy. As imperialists they were prepared to accept state intervention, and as Liberals they were not averse, within limits, to treading on the toes of vested interests. But we cannot merely equate them with collectivist Liberals, since such pro-Boers as Lloyd George were also prepared to accept state intervention.

Although the strain of Gladstonian liberalism was still strong, it is clear that a new liberalism had evolved. Over the next half-dozen years the Liberals carried out policies that would have been inconceivable in Gladstone's time. This is not to say that they had come into office in 1905 with a strikingly new program, or even that there had been any very conscious reevaluation of the meaning of liberalism on the part of the mass of the party. The change was largely effected by the imagination of a few, pressure from the left, and a growing awareness that times had changed and government had to play a larger role. The nineteenth century Liberal party was drawn almost entirely from the land and from business, but of 400 Liberals elected in 1906 only 62 were landowners. There were still a considerable number of business men, but in addition there were many from a wide variety of other callings, including about 145 professional men, 44 authors and journalists, and some 26 working men (mostly "Lib-Labs").

Nineteenth-century liberalism was primarily concerned with securing liberty for the individual. It was naively supposed that if special privileges were taken from the old ruling class and every responsible person had equal rights, political and legal, he would best be able to look after his own interests without state intervention. The repeal of the Corn Laws is the classic example of nineteenth-century liberal reform, removing the special privilege that the landed classes had long enjoyed and thereby ensuring a fairer price of bread for the masses. Complete acceptance of the teachings of classical economists, which insisted that supply and demand, wages and prices, could only be regulated in the free market, inhibited the nineteenth-century Liberals from opposing state intervention in economic issues. Toward the end of the century, however, liberal intellectuals began belatedly to see the flaw in this argument. In the modern capitalist system the individual worker is powerless to govern the conditions of his employment or unemployment. The old idea that an able-bodied unemployed man should be despised if he appealed for public assistance under the Poor Law was becoming less credible. It was also perceived that something must be wrong with a system that permitted almost a third of the population to live at or under the poverty line in the wretched slums that existed in all the large cities at a time when the rest of the nation was prospering. The influential Oxford philosopher T. H. Green (1836–1882) provided Liberals with philosophic justification for a new approach to the state. There was a strong religious element in Green's political philosophy and he emphasized the high moral principles of the Gladstonian tradition, but he put greater emphasis on the state's role in securing freedom, arguing that the individual achieved "his highest self-realization in communal institutions." Although influenced by Hegel, he avoided deification of the state and urged autonomous groups to guard against tyranny by the majority. He believed in private property providing it was subject to state control to ensure the true freedom of the individual. Green's published writings were limited, but his influence as a teacher was great; Herbert Asquith, who presided over many of the Liberal reforms of the early twentieth century, was one of his pupils.

The best popular summary of the new Liberal thinking, however, is found in a little book entitled *Liberalism*, published in 1911. The author, L. T. Hobhouse (1864–1929), was an Oxford scholar who, after some years as an editorial writer on the *Manchester Guardian*, became the first professor of sociology at the University of London. Hobhouse recognized the achievement of older Liberals in the spheres of civil, fiscal, personal, and political liberty, and acknowledged the pioneer work of Gladstone in the fields of national and international liberty. But he saw they had largely ignored social and economic liberty. He argued that, since the workingman was not really a free agent in modern capitalist society with its economic depressions and constant undermining of old skills, the state must intervene to protect the disadvantaged by providing old-age pensions, unemployment insurance, medical services, etc. The old Liberals could not accept the cost of such reform. They said it was wrong arbitrarily to tax the rich for such purposes, since it violated the right of private property. Hobhouse argued that there was a social increment in the production of wealth, an increment that resulted from the contribution of society as a whole. Consequently, society through the auspices of the state, was justified in taking back its share of the wealth in the form of taxes. Thus the social increment could be used to pay for the services that must be provided in order to guarantee social and economic liberty for all. Not all Liberals accepted this reasoning, but it helps explain the party's gradual abandonment of laissez-faire.

With some difficulty Campbell-Bannerman succeeded in persuading the formidable trio of Liberal Imperialists—Grey, Asquith, and Haldane—to join him, but at the price of offering them three key offices. They had hoped to force him into the Lords as a nominal Prime Minister, but in this they failed. He proved an unusually effective leader in the Commons until a fatal illness forced his retirement early in 1908, and by the time Asquith succeeded to the premiership the divisions that rent the party at the turn of the century had largely disappeared. Campbell-Bannerman formed a strong government that was both broad-based and colorful. Sir Edward Grey (1862–1933), member of an historic landed family, motivated to public life by duty rather than ambition, was chosen for the Foreign Office, where he remained until 1916. Herbert Asquith (1852–1928), a middle class-Nonconformist, a distinguished Oxford scholarship student, and a successful barrister, became Chancellor of the Exchequer until he succeeded Campbell-Bannerman as Prime Minister in 1908. R. B. Haldane (1856–1928), another lawyer, a brilliant intellectual who had studied at Edinburgh and at Gottingen where he had imbibed the German idealist philosophy, became a great reforming Secretary of War and, in 1912, Lord Chancellor. John Morley, Herbert Gladstone, and Lord Ripon represented the old Gladstonians, but there were several less orthodox yet significant appointments. David Lloyd George (1863–1945), the fiery Welsh nationalist educated at a village school in Caernarvon and a solicitor's office, became President of the Board of Trade and in 1908 succeeded Asquith as Chancellor of the Exchequer. John Burns, the militant trade unionist jailed in the eighties for the Trafalgar Square riots became President of the Local Government Board, where unhappily he accomplished little. Winston Churchill (1874–1965), who was the son of the ill-fated Lord Randolph and the American heiress Jenny Jerome; who had gone to war as a soldier and a journalist with the British army in India, the Sudan, and South Africa, and as a neutral observer in Cuba; and who had more recently broken with the Conservatives on the free trade issue, accepted junior office and in 1908 succeeded Lloyd George at the Board of Trade.

The Liberals won a landslide victory in the subsequent election of January 1906 with a total of 400 seats, including 23 Lib-Labs. The new Labour party won 30 seats thanks to their electoral pact with the Liberals, the Irish Nationalists 83, and the Unionists only 157, despite having polled 43.6 percent of the vote to the Liberals' 49 percent. But the Unionists had a massive majority in the hereditary House of Lords, now that most of the Whigs had deserted the Liberal party, and it remained to be seen how the will of the democratically-elected lower house would be respected.

The Liberals' election platform looked backward to the sins of omission and commission of the late Unionist government and made no great promises of social reform. Most of the Ministers were primarily concerned with saving free trade and reversing Unionist policies on the issues of South Africa, education, and liquor licensing. In office they found South Africa's importation of Chinese labor a more complicated issue than it had seemed in Opposition, but it was eventually settled with some compromise. More important, self-government was granted almost immediately to the conquered Boer communities, and in 1909 the four colonies of Cape Colony, Natal, the Orange Free State, and the Transvaal were united in a new dominion, the Union of South Africa. Boer and Briton were legally equals, but not the Bantu. The Boers outnumbered the British, but the forgotten Bantu natives were still the vast majority. The South African settlement was matched by reforms in India, which took a step toward Indian self-government by introducing partially elective Indian Councils and appointing some Indians to the executive councils. The Liberals also went beyond the Unionist practice of holding regular colonial conferences, which Chamberlain had made very much his own, by transforming them into imperial conferences of premiers with the British Prime Minister replacing the Colonial Secretary in the chair.

Chamberlain's hopes of imperial tariff preferences were rejected, but there was continued centralization of imperial defense. At the War Office Haldane proved to be the greatest reforming secretary since Cardwell. In the Liberal tradition reorganization and reform were combined with retrenchment. Belatedly a general staff was created to plan future operations and an expeditionary force was organized in case of war on the Continent. Unionist plans for naval expansion of a new Dreadnought fleet were continued and expanded in the face of a growing threat from Germany. The Committee of Imperial Defence, instituted by Balfour in 1904, was also continued. It became important in the overall direction of defense policy, and Balfour himself remained a member.

The greatest achievements of the ministry, however, were in social reform. In the elections the Liberals had promised to remedy the situation produced by the Taff Vale decision by appropriate legislation to legalize picketing. But the Labour members were far from satisfied with the complicated lawyer's bill introduced early in 1906. Campbell-Bannerman surprised his colleagues by meeting these objections with the acceptance of a Labour amendment that greatly simplified the bill and gave the trade unions virtual legal immunity in civil cases, a peculiarly privileged position. Two Education Acts were passed in 1906 and 1907. The first, a result of Labour pressure, authorized school lunches for underfed children. The second provided for medical inspection in school. In the view of one modern social historian these "marked the beginning of the construction of the Welfare State,"[1] for both provided a social service without any deterrent clauses, such as were contained in the Poor Law. Further acts in 1908, 1909, and 1912 authorized medical treatment as well as inspection for schoolchildren and generally consolidated regulations protecting children's rights. These reforms were largely the work of Robert Morant (1863–1920), a civil servant who authored the Education Act of 1902. Morant included the medical inspection provision in a larger bill so that it passed almost unnoticed.

Far more attention was given to the question of old-age pensions, which had been publicly discussed for a decade, but which the Unionists had failed to introduce despite Chamberlain's advocacy. As soon as Parliament met Campbell-Bannerman and Asquith were under pressure from left-wing Liberals and Labour to introduce old-age pensions, and Haldane proposed an elaborate scheme suggested to him by the Webbs. Asquith was sympathetic, but saw no way to finance noncontributory, universal pensions. In 1908, however, he introduced a limited scheme providing 5 shillings a week for citizens over age seventy whose annual incomes were less than £21 and lesser amounts for those with incomes up to £31 10s. It was not

[1] Bentley B. Gilbert, *The Evolution of National Insurance in Great Britain* (London, 1966), p. 102.

very much, but it was a beginning. Old people were delighted to get what seemed an unbelievable windfall simply by going to the post office every Friday.

The two ministers whose interest and contributions to the extension of social welfare were greatest were Lloyd George, who took over Asquith's Pension Bill, and Winston Churchill. Both were adventuresome and imaginative opportunists, uninhibited by past conventions. The results were an act in 1907 setting up conciliation boards to avert strikes, an act in 1908 establishing an eight-hour day in the mines, an act in 1909 introducing labor exchanges. The Trades Boards Act, also in 1909, aimed at raising standards of pay in so-called sweated industries where wages were substandard. Churchill and Lloyd George saw old-age pensions and labor exchanges as merely the first steps in a comprehensive system of national insurance, and Lloyd George visited Germany in 1908 to study the German system. The legislation was delayed by the constitutional crisis of 1909–1911, but in 1911 Lloyd George introduced the momentous National Insurance Bill, providing health insurance for approximately one-third the population and unemployment insurance for selected industries employing over two million people. Trade unions and "friendly" (mutual insurance) societies were to be involved in its administration under the direction of the National Insurance Commission, to be headed by Sir Robert Morant. The system was to be financed by weekly contributions from the employee, the employer, and the state. It was a long step forward in provision of social services and went well beyond the German model, but it was criticized by the Labour party and the unions, who objected to contributions from the employees; by society ladies for the iniquitous requirements that they lick stamps to provide for their servants; by the medical profession who wanted permission for patients to choose their own doctors and a raise in the per capita allowance for doctors; and by friendly societies and insurance companies, who feared a loss of members or customers. Nevertheless, Lloyd George persisted. After laborious negotiations with these special-interest groups, he forced the bill through an autumn session of Parliament. Although it stirred up a remarkable amount of antagonism and was marred by too many concessions—resulting often in contradictory clauses—it nevertheless was a great personal accomplishment for Lloyd George and formed the basis of the modern British welfare state. Socialists may criticize its contributory principle and its concessions to private insurance companies, but it is unlikely any scheme of such magnitude could have passed the pre-war Parliament without such compromises. It could have been better, but it did bring medical services within reach of the working classes. Unfortunately, Lloyd George was forced by opposition from friendly societies and insurance companies to abandon his original plan to include benefits for widows and orphans.

The sum of the 1906–1914 social legislation of the Liberal government is impressive, but its passage was overshadowed by more dramatic and politically explosive events. To many Liberals the most important measures the new government initiated were the Education Bill of 1906 and the Licensing Bill of 1908. The former attempted to withdraw privileges given church schools in the Act of 1902, while the latter tried to meet temperance demands by gradual elimination of the existing licensing system and its replacement by local option. Both bills were defeated in the House of Lords or amended beyond recognition, as were ten other government bills in these three years. Lloyd George, in an attack on the upper house, called it "Mr. Balfour's poodle," since it did whatever the leader of the Unionist party told it to do. The same thing had happened during the Liberals' brief period in the nineties, and both Gladstone and Rosebery had spoken of doing something about the Lords' unscrupulous misuse of power. In 1907 Campbell-Bannerman introduced resolutions into the House of Commons to restrict the power of the Lords to hold up government legislation. He died before he could implement these proposals, and Asquith decided not to press the matter immediately.

In April 1909, Lloyd George, now Chancellor of the Exchequer, introduced the controversial "People's Budget," as it was called, which greatly increased taxation by some £14 million. It was to cover not only old-age pensions but also large naval expenditures demanded by the Opposition. In his peroration he called it a "War Budget—for raising money to fight implacable warfare against poverty and squalidness." The Unionists in both houses were especially angry at proposed taxes on the unearned increment the landlord enjoyed from the ownership of land and on land that was allowed to go undeveloped. These taxes represented a very small part of the budget increases, but they goaded the landed classes since they seemed to be a response to attacks on landed wealth in the writings of Henry George and Chiozza Money and in the tracts and speeches of Fabians and other socialists. Lloyd George probably saw them as future sources of greater revenue. But the 1909 budget's financing came chiefly from two areas. Direct taxation provided almost half the additional revenue. A graduated income tax was introduced, with a supertax on incomes over £5,000; death duties were increased; stamp duties were raised on Stock Exchange transactions. The balance came from new or higher taxes on licenses, beer, liquor, tobacco, petrol, and cars. This latter category drew strong criticism, especially in Ireland. The opposition was unprecedented as the proposals were hotly debated throughout the summer and autumn, often in all-night sittings. The Opposition forced 554 divisions before the budget finally passed the House of Commons in November, only to be defeated in the Lords. That conservative body had become revolutionary by ignoring the precedent of two centuries during which the upper house had never rejected a budget. It was a foolish action, for the government had been losing some of its popularity, and this issue gave them the opportunity to call—and win—an election. They would gain another five years or so of office and a chance to curtail the Lords' veto power.

The ministers, especially Lloyd George, made the most of the opportunity. Even before the summer was over the chancellor denounced the wealthy and indolent aristocracy at public meetings. The way he aroused class antagonisms shocked the king and angered the peers. In one speech he inveighed against the "scheme of things whereby one man is engaged through life in grinding labour to win a bare and precarious subsistence for himself . . . and another man who does not toil receives every hour of the day, every hour of the night, whilst he slumbers, more than his neighbours receive in a whole year of toil." In particular he excelled in ridicule. "A fully equipped Duke," he once told an audience, "costs as much to keep up as two Dreadnoughts". It would be unfair to say he introduced the budget to bring the conflict with the Lords to a head, but he certainly profited by the chance. "At last," he said on the day Parliament was prorogued, "the cause between the peers and the people has been set down for trial in the grand assize of the people, and the verdict will come soon." The public, however, did not rise in wrath as they had done in 1831. The constitutional question was not so obvious and the increased tax on beer gave the peers many allies. The government was returned in the subsequent election of January 1910, but the results were disappointing. The Liberal numbers fell to 275, the Unionists rose to 273, and the balance was held by 40 Labour and 82 Irish Nationalists.

When the new Parliament met the government promised to deal with the House of Lords, but it was determined first to pass the budget. The Irish Nationalists threatened to desert unless Lords' veto resolutions were passed ahead of the budget. On this point the Cabinet was divided on whether to reform the composition of the House of Lords or reduce its powers. Radicals preferred the latter, since restructuring the upper house might well increase its power. Although it refused to make any direct promises to the Irish, the government introduced resolutions and followed them with the Parliament Bill even before the budget had been finally passed. The resolutions and legislation called for removal of the Lords' final veto, their noninterference with finance bills, and reduction of the length of a parliament from seven to five years. But a preamble to the bill stipulated that these provisions were to be made pending the reform of the Lords. Resistance was expected from the existing House of Lords, but the sudden death in May 1910 of Edward VII temporarily postponed the crisis.

In private conduct and public service the new king, George V (1865–1936), set higher standards than his father. He had been educated as a naval officer, and became heir to the throne in his late twenties only as a result of the premature death of his older brother. Thus despite his strong sense of duty he was inadequately prepared for the serious constitutional problem that now faced him. Both parties were inclined to postpone the issue, and Balfour and Asquith therefore agreed to an attempt at compromise. A series of meetings between party leaders was held through the summer into the autumn. The meetings were undertaken with goodwill on both sides, but it was impossible to find a basis for agreement, since the Unionists would not consider any solution that might lead to unimpeded passage of an Irish home rule bill. During the course of the conference, with Asquith's permission Lloyd George broached the possibility of forming a coalition government to settle certain important questions. He received encouragement from some more adventuresome Unionists, but the proposal came to nothing. It was basically unrealistic for that time, but it revealed Lloyd George's detachment from the party system with all its traditions and foreshadowed his leadership of a wartime coalition that would be the ruin of the Liberal party.

When it became clear that the Unionists would effectively resist the Liberals' Parliament Bill in the House of Lords Asquith asked the King for a second dissolution and a commitment to create enough new peers to force such a bill through the new Parliament if necessary. Reluctantly the King consented. The alternative would have been Asquith's resignation, and had Balfour then tried to form a government it is unlikely he would have won an election. The King would have found himself in the same position as William IV in 1835.

The public was even more apathetic in the pre-Christmas election of December 1910 than it had been eleven months earlier. There was little change in party standing. The Unionists lost one seat and the Liberals three (although increasing their popular vote), while the Irish Nationalists and Labour each gained two. The government had a clear majority of 398 to 272 for the Parliament Bill, since both minority parties fully supported it on that issue. When the new Parliament met the government forced the Parliament Bill through the House of Commons, despite the tabling of 900 amendments. In the meantime the Unionist majority in the Lords had fruitlessly been discussing a bill to reform their own composition. When the Parliament Bill came before them they decided to turn it inside out with amendments in the committee stage. When the bill returned to the Commons at the King's request, Asquith was at first prevented from speaking by sustained Unionist heckling, which Churchill described as "a squalid, frigid, organized attempt to insult the Prime Minister." Some of the more reasonable amendments were accepted, but the more outrageous were rejected, and the bill returned to the Lords. It was now made clear that the government would resort to creation of a sufficient number of peers to ensure the Bill's passage through the House of Lords. By this time the Unionists had become divided and leaderless. A group known as the "last ditchers," led by the ancient Lord Halsbury (who was born nine years before the first Reform Act of 1832) and Lord Willoughby de Broke (heir of a Lancastrian peerage) were prepared to resist the bill to the very end. But moderate Unionists were now urging the abandonment of the struggle to avert an absurd increase of membership in the upper house that would further reduce its credibility. The final two-day debate in the House of Lords began on August 9 under dramatic circumstances. England was suffering from the severest heat wave in memory. On that day the thermometer reached the 100-degree mark, the highest reading ever recorded in Britain. The Liberals could only muster eighty-odd peers, but Lord Lansdowne and Lord Curzon had persuaded some two hundred or more Unionist peers to abstain. The House, however, was filled with "backwoodsmen"—peers who rarely or never appeared at Westminster— who had responded to the call of the militant "ditchers," and the issue remained in doubt until the vote was taken. It was clear that to pass the bill some Unionists would have to support it. In fact 37 did so and 13 bishops also approved. The bill was saved by a vote of 131 to 114.

The Parliament Act prohibited money bills (to be so defined by the Speaker) from being opposed by the Lords, other bills passed by the Commons in three successive sessions of the same parliament would become law over the opposition of the Lords. The life of a parliament was reduced from a maximum of seven to a maximum of five years, which ensured that the Parliament Act could be invoked only to enforce controversial legislation introduced in the first two or three years of the parliament's existence. The provision for forcing opposed bills through the Lords was a clumsy one, rarely used until it was amended in 1948. This was partly because most governments from 1915–1945 had a majority in the Lords and partly because the passage of the Parliament Act made the Lords more discreet, knowing the limitation of their powers. Nevertheless, the immediate political significance of the act— and the reason it was so strongly resisted—was the knowledge that it made possible passage of an Irish home rule bill.

Because of increased prosperity and the success of the Unionist land purchase policy, Ireland had been relatively quiet in the two decades following Parnell's death in 1890. A Liberal amendment in 1909 had helped to accelerate land purchase, and by 1914 two-thirds of the arable land had been sold to the tenants by the old landlords. During this period the Irish Nationalist party was less effective than it had been in Parnell's time in voicing Irish national feeling. The worst divisions within the party following

Parnell's downfall had been healed by 1900 with the election of John Redmond as leader of a reunited party. But the Irish members, long committed to the Liberal alliance, had become part of the Westminster establishment and were increasingly out of touch with their own constituencies. Redmond had inherited Parnell's nationalism, which was political, not cultural and could function within English political conventions. Redmond sought Irish self-government but not independence, for he fully accepted the British imperial concept. The new Irish nationalism expressed itself in a variety of ways and established new forms of identity outside the parliamentary party. The Gaelic Athletic Association to promote Irish games was formed in 1884 and the Gaelic League in 1893 to revive the use of Ireland's national language. In 1905 Arthur Griffiths founded the Sinn Fein (Ours Alone) Society, with both cultural and political objectives beyond those of the Nationalist party. The old Irish Republican Brotherhood, taking a new lease on life, revived their revolutionary demand for a republic. Under the leadership of James Larkin (1876–1947) and James Connolly the Irish labor movement became militant and nationalist. By 1912 Redmond's time was running out. His Liberal allies had been in office for six years and done little except promote land purchase and pass the 1908 Irish University Act. Besides other pressures on the Liberals there was the impasse in the House of Lords, where in 1907 the Irish Evicted Tenants Bill had been badly mangled. In the same year the Devolution Bill (for increased local government) had been rejected as inadequate by the Irish National Conventions. Having finally passed the Parliament Act in 1911 the Asquith government was bound to turn its attention to Ireland, and a Home Rule bill was introduced in the following session. It proposed a separate Irish legislature in Dublin with larger powers than in either of Gladstone's bills; but foreign and defense policy, religion, tariffs, coinage, land purchase and for the time being, taxation, the constabulary, and social services remained reserved to Westminster, where forty-two Irish members would continue to sit. The bill thus gave Ireland provincial rather than dominion status (similar to Ulster's position in the United Kingdom from 1921 to 1972). No special constitutional provision was made for Ulster, where four counties were predominantly Protestant.

Despite its limited scope the bill was welcomed by the Irish Nationalists and the public in the south of Ireland, but even before it was introduced the Protestants of Ulster had begun organizing resistance to home rule. They planned to set up a provisional government for Ulster the day a home rule bill became law, and they selected a leader to carry out this resolve. He was Sir Edward Carson (1854–1935), an eminent Protestant barrister from Dublin, a man of iron who, in the years that followed, showed leadership qualities of the Cromwellian variety. In seventeenth-century Puritan tradition thousands of Ulstermen signed a covenant promising "throughout this our time of threatened calamity to stand by one another in defending . . . our cherished position of equal citizenship in the United Kingdom and in using all means which may be found necessary to defeat the present conspiracy to set up a Home Rule Parliament in Ireland." Their intent was made clear with the formation in 1913 of the Ulster Volunteers, a private army that drilled and armed in defiance of the Government, with the secret connivance of at least one senior general in the War Office. One million pounds were raised by public subscription as a pension fund for voluteers who might fall in defense of Ulster, and in 1914 a large consignment of arms was smuggled in from Germany without any effort by the government to seize them. Nor were these warlike preparations repudiated by the Ulstermen's Unionist allies in Britain. After passage of the Parliamentary Act Balfour had resigned the leadership of the Unionist party and been succeeded by Andrew Bonar Law (1858–1923), a dour Glasgow businessman, son of an Ulsterman who had migrated to Canada, where the future British prime minister was born. The choice of Law reflected the direction in which the party was moving. Under his leadership the Unionist party gave full support to Carson and the Ulster Unionists. The bill was resisted fiercely in the House of Commons through endless stormy sittings that continued until January 1913. At a Unionist rally at Blenheim the new party leader went so far as to say that he "could imagine no length of resistance to which they [the Ulstermen] might go in which they would not be supported by the overwhelming majority of the British people." Worse still, the government, probably for the first time since 1688, could not rely on the loyalty of the army. In March 1914 sixty British officers at the Curragh barracks in Ireland indicated that they preferred dismissal to carrying out duties in Ulster. The Secretary for War made some unfortunate concessions that forced his resignation. Asquith himself temporarily took over the War Office, but a bad impression was left regarding the reliability of the army.

The opposition of the House of Lords automatically held up the Home Rule Bill until 1914, but with its third passage in the House of Commons it would then become law. A real crisis had been reached and the country was close to civil war for the first time since 1832. Ironically, this time it was "loyal" Ulster Unionists who proposed to fight the governments' enforcement of the law, and Catholic Southerners who offered the services of their Irish volunteers, a rival body that had emerged in the South, to help enforce it. In 1914 the government introduced an amending bill, allowing any county in Ulster to opt out temporarily, but even this did not satisfy the House of Lords. In July a conference of party leaders met unsuccessfully to seek a solution. Both North and South were opposed to partition, and in any event no agreement was in sight on the fate of the mixed counties of Tyrone and Fermanagh where Catholics and Protestants were fairly evenly divided. The government consequently decided on an amending bill without a time limit. The outbreak of war in Europe gave the government an excuse to postpone home rule until the war was over. Redmond, a firm believer in the justice of war with Germany, accepted the decision, even urging Ireland to join in the struggle against a foreign enemy. The last chance to settle peacefully the Irish question had been lost.

Ireland posed the most serious, but not the only challenge to the British government in the years just before the outbreak of war in 1914. Despite the relatively extensive social legislation of the Liberal government labor was becoming increasingly restive. The steady rise in real wages that characterized the last forty years of the nineteenth century had ceased, and prices were rising more rapidly than wages. Trade union leaders had grown more militant and were inclined to turn their backs on Parliament. Some, such as Tillet and Mann (returned from Australia) and, in Ireland, Larkin and Connolly, were infected by the syndicalist philosophy of French trade unionists, which urged attainment of socialism through direct action by unions culminating in a general strike. After initial success in a series of strikes in Dublin, Larkin was beaten by William Murphy, a tough Irish businessman whose Employers Federation successfully locked 25,000 workmen out of their jobs in 1913. Losing the support of the British trade union movement, Larkin and his followers became more nationalistic and revolutionary in their outlook. Meanwhile, in England the time lost through strikes was increasing. While President of the Board of Trade, Lloyd George had shown a flair for settling major trade disputes, especially in his averting of a railway strike in 1907. More and more labor disputes were being settled by conciliation boards, due in large part to Sir George Askwith, an extremely successful Board of Trade arbitrator. But in 1910 strikes and acts of violence were becoming more frequent. In the following year the country again faced the threat of a railway strike, which was averted once more by the intervention of Lloyd George. In 1912 a miners' strike put over two million men temporarily out of work, but eventually the government passed the Minimum Wage Act, which laid the basis for a settlement. In the two years before the war there was a move toward amalgamation of smaller unions into giant national bodies. A newly formed alliance of three of the largest unions—the General Transport Workers, the National Union of Railwaymen, and the Miners Federation—threatened the country with a general strike. By 1914 some four million workers were unionized. In July 1914 Lloyd George warned that the labor threat plus the danger of rebellion in Ireland could produce the gravest situation to face any government in centuries.

A third (if less terrifying) challenge to the established rule of law and order in these years was posed by the militant suffragette movement, and for this the government (especially Asquith) shared some of the responsibility. Unsuccessful attempts had been made to extend the franchise to women on passage of the second and third Reform Acts in 1867 and 1884. Nevertheless women property holders had received the right to vote in local government elections in 1869 and 1888; in 1907 they were permitted to sit on county and borough councils. In other areas women's rights had been extended in the second half of the nineteenth century by the Divorce Act in 1857, suspension of the Contagious Diseases Act of 1873 (discriminating against prostitutes), and various Women's Property Acts in 1870, 1874, and 1882. A statute of 1875 permitted the new universities to grant degrees to women, a right of which they gradually availed themselves in the following decades. Oxford and Cambridge admitted women in the 1880s, but did not yet grant them degrees. The Royal College of Surgeons was forbidden in 1875 to exclude women, and six years later 25 women had qualified as doctors, increasing to 477 by 1911. By the same year there were 51,000 women employed in the civil service or by local authorities.

With the twentieth century the movement for enfranchisement of women had strengthened, and four times before 1906 favorable motions were passed in the House of Commons. It was not a party issue; there were advocates and opponents in both major parties, and the movement had more support in the middle than in the working class. Two rival associations appeared: the National Union of Women's Suffrage Societies and the Women's Social and Political Union, the second founded in 1903 by the formidable Mrs. Emmaline Pankhurst (1857–1928) and her two daughters. The militant suffragettes, as the latter were known, abandoned the traditional means of lobbying and developed the technique of direct confrontation that has become so familiar half a century later. Public speakers were heckled, in and out of Parliament; politicians such as Asquith, Lloyd George, and Winston Churchill were physically attacked; property was damaged, in one case a young zealot leapt to her death under the hoofs of the King's horse at the Derby. When jailed the suffragettes went on hunger strikes, which led the government to introduce a bill known as the "cat and mouse act" providing for the release of prisoners on hunger strike and their rearrest when they had recovered. Numerous private bills to extend the franchise to women failed in the years 1908–1912, but in 1913 when the government introduced a bill extending the male franchise, it said it would accept a female suffrage amendment if it was passed on a free vote. Unfortunately the Speaker ruled the amendment out of order before it could be discussed, and the wrath of the suffragettes was increased. With the outbreak of war the movement evaporated as women became more and more involved in the war effort, and by 1918 their position in society was greatly transformed. The franchise was extended to women over thirty in the Reform Act of 1918 without any serious debate, and to all women over twenty-one in 1928.

The decade preceding 1914 was one of the strangest and most turbulent in the last century of British history. A Conservative and aristocratic government had given way to a Liberal democratic one, which had laid the foundations of the twentieth-century welfare state. Yet discontents mounted on all sides, real income ceased to rise, and the aspirations of the common people continued to be frustrated. The trade union movement became more militant and large-scale strikes more common. The suffragettes added to the tension with their persistent defiance of authority. Most serious was the challenge to law and the state itself by the unbending Ulster Unionists and their allies on the other side of the Irish Sea. On the eve of a world war the very loyalty of the army was in doubt, but the unexpected outbreak of war in 1914 demonstrated that the country was still capable of closing its ranks in the face of a threat from without.

Chapter Ten
THE END OF ISOLATION

In the last two decades of the nineteenth century the foreign and imperial policy of Britain became almost indistinguishable, since her significant foreign relations were largely with imperial powers and her differences with these powers were mainly over imperial issues in Africa, Asia, and the Near East. At the end of the century Joseph Chamberlain was probably the only Colonial Secretary in British history to have taken over for a time the direction of foreign policy. From 1885 to 1900, however, Britain generally followed the line set by Lord Salisbury, for during the few years the Liberals were in office in this period Lord Rosebery, the Foreign Secretary, ensured its continuity.

British foreign policy in the late nineteenth century has been described as "splendid isolation," but the phrase is open to question. It is true that Britain stood apart from the two military alliances that had come into being in Europe: the Triple Alliance, formed by the juncture in 1882 of Italy with Austria and Germany, and the more surprising Dual Alliance of France and Russia inaugurated in 1891. But over the century Britain had accepted diverse obligations under various international treaties, the continuing significance of which was a matter of speculation. In 1815 she had guaranteed the neutrality of Switzerland and in 1863 that of Luxembourg; in 1832 she had guaranteed the independence of Greece and in 1839 that of Belgium. By the Treaty of Paris in 1856 she became involved in various undertakings in the Black Sea area, and in 1878 she had given assurances to Turkey in the Cyprus Convention. The closest she had come to joining either of the armed camps emerging in Europe in the last quarter of the century was in the Mediterranean Agreement of 1887 with Austria and Italy, which sought to preserve the status quo in the eastern Mediterranean and Black Sea area. Russian pretensions in Bulgaria and France's continued hostility to the British occupation of Egypt help to explain Britain's rapprochement with the central powers,

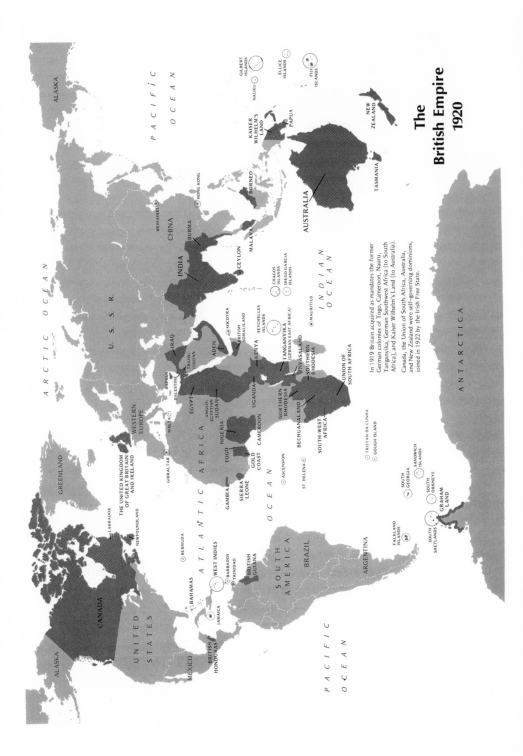

The
British Empire
1920

In 1919 Britain acquired as mandates the former German colonies of Togo, Cameroon, Nauru, Tanganyika, German Southwest Africa (to South Africa), and Kaiser Wilhelm's Land (to Australia). Canada, the Union of South Africa, Australia, and New Zealand were self-governing dominions, joined in 1922 by the Irish Free State.

for the Mediterranean Agreement was made with Bismarck's blessing. Salisbury would have liked to work out a detente with France, but the circumstances were not propitious and in the imperial sphere Germany was more accommodating. However, when Bismarck suggested in 1889 that Britain should join the Triple Alliance, Salisbury pleaded constitutional restrictions on commitments that would bind his successor should he be turned out of office.

With the dismissal of Bismarck in 1890 Anglo-German relations entered a difficult, unpredictable phase. The British government had little trust in the mercurial young Kaiser William II, who surrounded himself with Anglophobe advisers. When Rosebery took over the Foreign Office in 1892 he endeavored with little success to maintain friendly relations with Germany. Differences with France in Indochina were smoothed over, but Egypt remained a stumbling block. Despite Gladstone's misgivings Rosebery was determined to keep the British flag flying on the Nile. Disputes with Russia in central Asia were eased, but new grounds for discord arose in China and Turkey. Britain's position was more isolated when Salisbury returned to office in 1895, but he was unable to reach an understanding with the Triple Alliance. Turkish massacres of Christians, in Armenia in 1894 and in Constantinople in 1895, had outraged British opinion and finally persuaded Salisbury to abandon Disraeli's hope of shoring up the Ottoman Empire. Britain's role was then taken over by Germany, and before long there were plans for a Berlin-to-Baghdad railway. The Kruger telegram of 1896 underlined the deterioration of Anglo-German relations, although a few years later the German Kaiser became more friendly. In the meantime President Cleveland's sharp warning to Britain in the boundary dispute between Venezuela and British Guiana further emphasized Britain's growing isolation; this dispute, however, was settled by arbitration.

Britain's isolated position was the subject of general comment. Sir George Foster, a Canadian politician, called it "splendid," a term quickly picked up by Chamberlain and The Times. "Splendid Isolation" was more a description of Britain's actual situation in the world in the late nineties than of the policy her government pursued. Yet it is true that both a reluctance to make entangling commitments and a firm confidence in their island strength as center of a world-wide empire, made the phrase acceptable to many Britons. While anxious to eliminate differences with other powers, Salisbury was opposed to binding commitments. He is said to have believed in the Concert of Europe without sharing Gladstone's idealistic view of its purpose. By 1898, however, Salisbury's grasp was failing, and Chamberlain's influence was becoming the dominant one in his government.

In 1898 a rather hollow agreement with Germany over future disposition of the Portuguese colonies in Africa allowed Britain to fight the Boer War without German interference. Chamberlain went further and proposed an alliance with Germany, renewing the proposal the following year when Kaiser William visited England and a third time in 1901. But for a variety of reasons these overtures came to nothing. Public opinion was hostile in both countries; Germany was reluctant to antagonize Russia, while Salisbury was unwilling to support Germany against Russia or upset British relations with France. Probably the most serious obstacle to an Anglo-German settlement was the German Naval Law of 1898, designed to make Germany a sea power. The British saw German naval development as a direct threat, but the Germans saw it as necessary in maintaining a position of global (rather than European) power.

In seeking a German alliance one of Chamberlain's motives was the hope of thwarting Russian expansion in Manchuria, but Germany showed no interest in stopping this. Britain's sense of isolation was especially evident in the Far East, where the powers were beginning to seek spheres of influence and abandon in China the Open Door policy which free-trade Britain had cherished. Britain's world-wide interests were in part responsible for her disinclination to join a continental European alliance, but growing awareness of isolation made her uneasy about her ability to defend these interests— especially in the Far East—now that the need for naval strength in home waters was becoming more obvious. In 1902, when another attempt at detente with Russia failed, Britain turned as a last resort to a defensive alliance with Japan. Their pact provided that if either party was attacked by more than one power the other would come to its support. The British were not keen on the alliance, but they hoped it would enable them to reduce their naval commitments in the Pacific.

The British public was more anti-German than was the government. But after failing to establish close connections with Germany, Lansdowne, the new Foreign Secretary, turned his efforts toward improving relations elsewhere, with France and especially with Russia. Progress was made in the latter direction until Japan began to make an issue of Russia's failure to withdraw from Manchuria in 1903, as she had promised. In danger of having to defend Japan against Russia and possibly France, Britain now started in earnest to seek an entente with France. The climate was auspicious; a growing cordiality between the two countries had been emphasized by the success of King Edward VII's official visit to Paris. On the return visit of the French president and his foreign minister, Delcassé, the first serious talks between the two governments took place, and within a few months a wide-ranging agreement had been worked out despite the suspicion of the British military. France was anxious for British recognition of her aspirations in Morocco, agreeing in return to accept, without any further hostility, Britain's position in Egypt. In the pact that was signed in April 1904, the two countries promised each other diplomatic support to implement their agreement on Egypt and Morocco. Other disputes in Africa and Asia and a controversy over the Newfoundland fisheries were also settled. By now Britain's ally, Japan, had declared war on France's ally, Russia; but since France stood aloof Britain was able to remain neutral. A dangerous incident occurred when a Russian fleet passing through the North Sea on its way to the Pacific inexplicably fired on some British fishing boats. The danger of war was averted only when Russia apologized and promised compensation. To the surprise of most observers Japan won the war in the Far East, and Russia's weakness was exhibited to the world. The Japanese victory meant a great deal to Britain, for it not only transformed Britain's position in Asia and the Pacific, but the elimination of the Russian navy made the Royal Navy stronger than those of Germany, France, and Russia combined. As a result Britain was quite ready to renew the Japanese treaty on a broader basis.

The signing of the Anglo-French entente was an important turning point for both countries. They had been hostile neighbors during the greater part of their national history, for the Crimean alliance had not been a lasting one. Britain did not fully realize its significance at the time, for the immediate motivation was to avert danger from Russia, but in the years that followed Britain and France recognized a common threat from Germany. Ideologically France's rapport was stronger with Britain than with Russia, for France and Britain accepted the principle of political liberty based on representative government. Although the entente with France had not been made against Germany, it led to further cooling of Anglo-German relations. The press in the two countries became increasingly hostile. Lord Fisher (1841–1920), the eccentric First Sea Lord of the Admiralty, rashly recommended a "preventive" attack on the German navy, in the way the Danish fleet had been sunk at Copenhagen to prevent its joining Napoleon. Further expansion of the German navy was now inevitable.

Germany wasted no time in testing the Anglo-French entente. In March 1905 the kaiser precipitated the first Morocco crisis. He went to Tangier to visit the sultan of Morocco and demonstrate Germany's interest in the country France regarded as her special sphere of influence. Fearing that Germany planned to build a naval base in Morocco, Britain joined France in resisting German demands for a conference. But shortly afterward the French government lost its nerve. Delcassé, the chief architect of the entente, was forced to resign, and the German demand for a conference was accepted by France and Britain under certain conditions. Lansdowne and his colleagues remained cooler and more detached than either their anti-German advisers at the Foreign Office, or the public, which was becoming strongly pro-French. Lansdowne seemed more interested in renewing the Japanese alliance than in solving the Moroccan crisis. But the hope of peace in Europe darkened with the meeting at Björkö in the summer of 1905 of the German kaiser and the Russian czar.

There was no sharp break in the continuity of British foreign policy when Sir Edward Grey succeeded Lansdowne as Liberal Foreign Secretary in December 1905. Grey showed more commitment to the entente and more interest in European affairs than Lansdowne. With the agreement of the Prime Minister, but without consulting the Cabinet, he authorized the initiation of staff conversations with the French to clarify what steps should be taken in the event of France and Britain becoming allies in a war against Germany. Grey put loyalty to the entente ahead of his hope of conciliating Germany when he realized that the French would not compromise. At the Algeciras conference, which opened early in 1906, his diplomatic support helped sustain France's position in Morocco. The result was a serious diplomatic defeat for the Germans who found themselves in a minority at the conference.

The way was now clear for settlement of differences with France's ally, Russia, and the consequent creation of the Triple Entente despite the unpopularity of Czar Nicholas's autocratic government with the rank and file of the British Liberal party. Grey pursued this objective to create a counterpoise against German power in Europe, of which he was much more apprehensive than Lansdowne had been. The result was the Anglo-Russian entente of 1907, in which Russia recognized Britain's special interests in Afghanistan and southern Persia in return for British acceptance of the Russian sphere of interest in northern Persia.

In 1908 Europe was shaken by Austria's unilateral annexation of Bosnia and Herzegovina. The action was especially offensive to Serbia and to Russia, the self-appointed champion of Slavs in the Balkans. It was strongly opposed by Britain, but Germany backed Austria and the Russians were forced to swallow their pride and accept the *fait accompli*. The result was a general deterioration in the relations between the two camps; six years later a similar situation led to war. In 1911 Germany precipitated the second Morocco crisis by sending a gunboat to Agadir to protest continued French intervention in Moroccan affairs. The British Foreign Secretary reacted vigorously, and Lloyd George, hitherto identified with the pacific element in the Liberal government, made a notable public speech warning Germany that Britain would stand by France. Once again Germany backed down after receiving some compensation from France in the Congo area. But Europe had clearly come a step closer to war, and the question was how many such crises could be survived. The naval race between Britain and Germany had been stepped up with consequent deterioration in their relations. Between 1908 and 1914 the British government made almost annual attempts to work out a settlement with Germany to curtail their naval programs. In 1912 a special effort was made by Haldane, who had been educated in Germany and was friendly with Kaiser William II; it was no more successful than the three previous attempts. The Germans could not accept the British claim to superiority, and the British could not desert the entente by promising complete neutrality as the Germans demanded. The result was another German naval bill and an informal agreement between Britain and France to concentrate the French navy in the Mediterranean and the Royal Navy in the North Sea. It was followed in 1914 by a less important naval agreement between Britain and Russia.

The Balkan Wars of 1912 and 1913 further threatened the peace of Europe, but this situation saw Grey at his best, presiding successfully at an international conference in London. To the annoyance of his entente partners, he worked closely with the central powers for a peaceful settlement, but the effort was lost on Germany, who redoubled her preparations for war. Nevertheless, in 1913 and again in 1914 Britain renewed the attempt at a detente with Germany, and tentative agreement was reached on a number of outstanding questions in Africa and the Middle East. But the murder of Austria's Archduke Ferdinand at Sarajevo on June 28, 1914 precipitated one crisis too many. Austria was determined once and for ever to settle with Serbia, and Germany was ready to give her ally a blank check. On July 24, the day after the Austrian ultimatum to Serbia, Grey proposed mediation through an ambassador's conference, but Germany rejected the proposal. Austria declared war on Serbia on July 28, which prompted Russia to mobilize. The consequent German ultimatums to Russia and France made full-scale war a reality, and Britain was faced with the difficulty of deciding on a course of action. Grey and Asquith saw no alternative but to support Britain's entente partners, but the country and even the Cabinet was unprepared for such a decision. The German attack through Belgium settled the matter. Except for two ministers who resigned, the Cabinet unanimously agreed to resist this aggression, a decision that was supported by all opposition parties and the nation. Had it not been for the invasion of Belgium, there would have been no such unanimity and it would have been extremely difficult for the Government to have fulfilled what Grey felt to be its moral obligation.

How well prepared was Britain for war? Psychologically she was clearly unprepared. Almost to the last minute the great majority of her people and politicians had been preoccupied with internal matters that, as we have seen, seemed to undermine the national fabric. However, ranks closed to a surprising extent when the die was cast. At the time no one anticipated what the country would undergo in the next four years, but the morale of the people was high. Politically Britain was also at a disadvantage. It is true that a political truce put an immediate end to the current political squabbles, but the Liberals in office were not an ideal team to direct a vigorous war effort. The task cannot have been congenial to those with Gladstonian convictions, no matter how hard they tried. Their opposition to conscription and other forms of compulsion that had been anathema to nineteenth-century liberalism, illustrates the difficulty. The senior ministers in this government had been in office for nine tumultuous years. It should not be surprising that some showed signs of weariness and lacked the vigor and ruthless determination the situation demanded. This charge was directed in particular against Asquith. He had been a good peacetime Prime Minister—serene, confident, wise, capable on occasion of energetic action. He had also been an able peacetime chairman of the Cabinet, shrewdly assessing the political ramifications of the situations confronting him, and retaining an element of detachment that gave him resilience. But he lacked the dynamic qualities of a great war leader. He was too ready to sit problems out (a viable course in peacetime), too content to rely on old associates and old ways. He was committed to the cause for which Britain had gone to war, but not sufficiently engaged in its prosecution.

As in the Napoleonic wars, Britain's economic resources were considerable, although her industrial supremacy had now been seriously challenged. In the early stages (until she turned over the role to the United States) she resumed her role as paymaster, or rather banker, of the Allies. Her heavy industry would be of great value after its adaptation to the needs of war. But dependence on overseas sources for food and materials threatened to be her Achilles heel with the unforeseen appearance of the German submarine menace.

The Royal Navy was well prepared when war came in 1914. Despite the misgivings of the Little England wing of the Liberal party, the Liberal government had met the German naval challenge by a great shipbuilding program, and in terms of capital ships the navy was never stronger, although new weapons were to pose unforeseen threats. Winston Churchill had become First Lord of the Admiralty in 1911 and served with vigor and enthusiasm. On his own initiative he kept the fleet mobilized after its July maneuvers, and when war came he was able to report that the fleet was ready.

By European standards Britain was scarcely prepared for land warfare on a large scale, for she was the only major power without a conscript army. But thanks to the Haldane reforms—in particular the institution of a general staff—the British army was highly professional and in a state of readiness. A war book had been prepared, detailing the steps to be taken on the outbreak of war. When the Government decided after some hesitation to send its small expeditionary force of seven divisions to France, the operation was carried out with dispatch. Within three weeks of the British declaration of war this force, nicknamed "the Old Contemptibles," fought their first action with the advancing Germans at Mons on the left flank of the French.

Britain's overseas empire was also to some degree ready for war. Throughout the preceding decade the small military and naval forces of the self-governing dominions had maintained close contact with the defense forces of the mother country. Dominion forces were organized along British lines, used British types of equipment, and, perhaps most important, had sent their senior officers to Britain for staff training. Imperial defense policy had been worked out in a series of conferences. The British Empire was still a sovereign entity by international law, and the entire empire including the dominions and India were legally involved by the British declaration of war. The dominions were, however, free to decide whether and to what extent their forces would participate. Canada, Australia, New Zealand, and—with more hesitation—South Africa, decided on full participation. As a result of the prewar planning the military and naval forces of the dominions were quickly and efficiently integrated with those of the mother country, and contributed substantially to the overall British war effort.

The appointment as Secretary of War of Lord Kitchener, the national hero of the Sudanese and South African campaigns, drew universal acclaim but proved a mistake. Kitchener was greatly overrated by both the public and the politicians. Indeed, he was venerated as the Duke of Wellington once had been, but with less reason. He never understood the mechanics of cabinet government and took little part in ministerial deliberations. He failed to make proper use of the general staff Haldane had created, and abolished the territorials, a reserve force Haldane had set up as a source of wartime manpower. Kitchener's one great achievement was the successful institution of a large-scale recruiting campaign, for he foresaw the need for a large army in what he rightly considered would be a long war. A famous recruiting poster showed him full face, staring sternly at the viewer, his index finger outstretched, with the message YOUR COUNTRY NEEDS YOU in large block letters. The army grew rapidly; over twenty divisions were in the field by the end of 1915, and by 1918 there were sixty. In previous wars the British army had recruited for the most part from its trained reserves, the militia, and the unemployed or underemployed, especially in Ireland. For the first time a genuine citizen's army came into being, made up of men from all walks of life who volunteered from a sense of duty or social compulsion, or more likely a combination of the two.

The Great War, as it was called, of 1914–1918 had no historical parallel.

On both sides armies numbering millions were locked for more than four years in an uninterrupted death struggle, waging slaughter and destruction on a scale hitherto inconceivable. The Germans almost won in the opening weeks, as they had in the war of 1870, by a lightning stroke at Paris, this time through Belgium. At the last moment the Allied Armies, as yet predominantly French, succeeded in stemming the flood. The Germans withdrew to a long line running, roughly, from the Swiss border north to Verdun and thence north and west in an arc, reaching the coast just inside the Belgian border west of Ostend. Here the two sides dug in, developing an extensive and elaborate network of trenches from which they launched expensive and fruitless attacks for the next four years. Generally the Allies took the initiative—especially when British numbers began to swell—for until 1917 the Germans were also heavily involved with Russia in the east. The losses in these successive and senseless attacks were astronomical. The British alone suffered almost 60,000 casualties in April and May of 1915 in the second battle of Ypres (where for the first time the Germans used poison gas); 420,000 casualties in the battle of the Somme, which lasted from July to September 1916; 245,000 (a revised figure) at Passchendaele from August to November 1917; and 300,000 resisting the final German offensive in the spring of 1918. Even in quiet periods when not engaged in actual fighting the front-line troops lived in misery and squalor, as the flat plains of Flanders were turned into a quagmire by incessant shelling and endless rain. Early idealism gave way to grim fatalism, but the troops on both sides showed extraordinary stamina and on the whole morale was miraculously maintained. A camaraderie developed between those who shared the same dangers that could not be matched in peacetime experience. There was no love, however, for the generals (known as "red tabs") safe at base headquarters, who sent them into this senseless carnage, or for those at home who waxed fat from the profits of war. The British produced no great general, unless it was Allenby (1861–1936), who commanded comparatively small forces in the Middle East. General Sir Douglas Haig (1861–1928), who in 1915 succeeded Sir John French (1852–1925) as British Commander in Chief, was responsible for most of the costly mass offensives in which the British army was involved. Historians have judged him even more harshly than his contemporaries. Politicians had little faith in him, but he had friends in high places. Not even Lloyd George was able to get rid of him, and in fact, there was no obvious replacement.

Some more imaginative members of the British government—notably Lloyd George and Winston Churchill—urged the adoption of such new weapons as the light mortar and the tank, and the opening of alternative fronts in the east. When Turkey entered the war as an ally of Germany, cutting off access to Russia via the Black Sea, Churchill persuaded the Government to undertake the Gallipoli campaign. Its purpose was to gain the Dardenelles, to knock Turkey out of the war and reopen communications with Russia. It was a well-conceived but poorly executed plan, largely because of ineffective liaison between the army and the navy. In the end the landing force had to withdraw after suffering heavy casualties. The failure of the Dardenelles expedition raised a storm in England and clouded the reputation of the young First Lord of the Admiralty; Churchill had to wait another quarter of a century to show his prowess as a war minister. An Allied landing at Salonika in a vain effort to help Serbia immobilized large numbers of French and British troops to no purpose for the rest of the war. A substantial British force was also tied down in Egypt defending the Suez Canal, but farther afield the British were more successful in rolling back Turkey's imperial frontiers. T. E. Lawrence (1888–1935), one of the few legendary heroes of the war, raised some desert Arab tribes in revolt against Turkey. Early in 1917 British forces, from India, after initial reverses, captured Baghdad in Mesopotamia (now Iraq); Allenby, leading a British army from Egypt, captured Jerusalem later that year and Damascus the following year. With promises of territorial gain Italy was induced in 1915 to come into the war, but her entrance proved of little advantage. The battle of Caporetto in 1917 was one of the worst defeats suffered by the Allies.

The war at sea took a strange turn. The oceans of the world were cleared of German ships after some preliminary naval skirmishes in the Mediterranean and the South Atlantic. The German grand fleet, in which the kaiser and Admiral Tirpitz had made such a great investment, remained cooped up in port throughout the war except for one sally into the North Sea on May 31, 1916. This led to a brush with the British fleet at the Battle of Jutland, the only major naval battle of the war. Britain lost fourteen ships to Germany's eleven, but the Germans broke off the action and withdrew under cover of darkness, never to put to sea again until the war ended. Ignoring the 1909 Declaration of London, a tight British blockade effectively cut Germany off from the world overseas at the price of antagonizing neutrals, among them the United States. But the Germans, by utilizing the submarine—a new weapon—carrying torpedoes, responded with a counterblockade that brought Britain, dependent for her life on imports, to the verge of disaster. In 1915 German submarines sank over 700,000 tons of shipping, including the British passenger liner *Lusitania*, an act that shocked the world. Of more than 1,000 fatalities, 114 were Americans. President Wilson's protests brought temporary curtailment of German submarine warfare, but it was only the lull before the storm. In 1917 an enlarged German submarine fleet engaged in unrestricted warfare, sinking 866,610 tons in April that year alone.

Politically Germany's action boomeranged, for it brought the United States into the war against her. Under pressure from Lloyd George the conservative-minded Admiralty agreed reluctantly to adopt the convoy system, which reduced Britain's losses only just in time.

The invention of the airplane in 1903 opened a new dimension in warfare. By 1918 the newly established Royal Air Force had 22,000 planes, which at first were used primarily for reconnaissance by the army at the front. Most air engagements were plane-to-plane dogfights. It was a métier for individual heroes. Aces on both sides chalked up their counts of downed enemy planes; it was the only aspect of this dreadful war that had an element of romance, reminiscent of days when knights in armor met in single combat. A grimmer aspect of aerial war was introduced by the Germans with raids on cities by planes and airships (known as Zeppelins). The air raids caused 4,820 civilian casualties in Britain and led to retaliation in Germany by the RAF.

On the home front state controls were instituted on a scale unimaginable in prewar liberal England. The "new liberalism" had made inroads in the temple of laissez-faire, but now the whole structure was dismantled piece by piece. "Business as usual," a slogan thoughtlessly coined at the war's beginning, was discarded as incompatible with an all-out war effort. The Bank Act, which tied the pound to the gold standard, was suspended at the outset, and before long the Government assumed virtual control of the money market. Steep tariffs, called "McKenna duties" were placed on certain luxuries to conserve foreign exchange and raise revenue where it was spent. The income tax was raised eventually to an unprecedented six shillings on the pound (almost 30 percent) after exemptions; exemptions were lowered, thereby extending this tax to the working classes, and a stiff excess-profits tax was instituted. War loans increased the national debt from £625 million to £7,809 million by 1918. Under the energetic direction of Lloyd George, the Ministry of Munitions was set up in 1915, with power to requisition supplies as necessary and step up production of munitions on a scale undreamed of by the War Office. The government nationalized many mines and quarries, opened new munitions plants, and made arbitration mandatory in the 'munitions industry to prevent loss of time by strikes. The Government also took over operation of the railways, which were now run as a unified system, and made bulk purchases of sugar and wheat to ensure supply and control prices. The all-pervasive Defence of the Realm Act gave the Government unprecedented powers of control and supervision in these and many other areas, such as censorship. Conscription, which was introduced in 1916 over the objections of the trade unions and old-fashioned Liberals, was used to keep men in key industries such as mining as well as to provide reinforcements for the army. Alcoholic beverages were heavily taxed, their alcohol content was reduced, and restrictions were placed on hours of sale to combat drunkeness and ab-senteeism in war industry. Daylight saving time was introduced in the summer of 1916 to lengthen the workday; late in the war rents were controlled; to deal with shortages rationing was begun. Much emergency regulation was hit-and-miss and was quickly abandoned when the war was over, but there could never be a complete return to the prewar liberal economy.

In wartime Conservatives were readier than Liberals to adopt state inter-vention, and many of these innovations were due to pressure from the Oppo-sition and the Opposition press that eventually led to Coalition. From the beginning of the war the militant Unionists—the "patriotic" party—and their noisy newspaper allies could not abide the fact that the conduct of the war was in the hands of the Liberals, whom they regarded as pacifist and anti-military, although Asquith, Grey, and Haldane were long-time Liberal Im-perialists. Their most intense hatred was reserved for Haldane, despite his great reform achievements as Secretary for War, because of his prewar German connections. They drove him out of the Government by a campaign of abuse and vilification unparallelled in modern British history. Churchill was undeniably an energetic minister, but the Unionists found it hard to forgive his desertion in 1904. Lloyd George they had long regarded as a dangerous radical, but they recognized his energy and ability and eventually came to realize his lack of party inhibitions. The resignation of Admiral Fisher, the erratic First Sea Lord, because of disputes with Churchill, many years his junior but his political superior, precipitated a long-brewing Cabinet crisis, the first of the war. It enabled Asquith in May 1915 to form a coalition government of twelve Liberals, eight Unionists and one Labour member. Haldane was excluded and Churchill demoted, but other Liberals kept the key posts. The Unionists came into the ministry without enthusiasm, but it was politically impossible for them to refuse office under the circumstances. Lloyd George was transferred to the new Ministry of Munitions to remedy the serious shell shortage, which had been one of the factors leading to the crisis. Churchill was succeeded at the Admiralty by Balfour; Asquith much preferred the former Conservative leader to Bonar Law, on whom he looked with near contempt. Lloyd George, however, found Unionists like Law and Carson more congenial than his old Liberal colleagues, for he preferred businessmen to intellectuals. Indeed he made a great success of his new ministry by enlisting able businessmen and giving them free reign.

The prewar Liberal party was beginning to dissolve. Increased infringe-ments on personal liberty, especially the threat of conscription, were more than old Liberal back-benchers could swallow. Two ministers had resigned in 1914 and eight more were now pushed out. Churchill soon resigned because of his demotion, and a year later Sir John Simon left over conscription.

Lloyd George, who had never been a strong party man, was clearly slipping away. His aim in politics had always been to get things done. As a man of the people social reform had long been his main pre-occupation, and with his boundless energy and persistence combined with flexibility and personal magnetism he had achieved an amazing amount in the years 1906–14. In foreign policy he had been a Little Englander suspicious of Conservative aims to build up the armed services. But once Britain had become involved in a conflict he regarded as righteous he was eager to apply to winning the war the talents that he had exercised so successfully in peacetime. He was now the most able and energetic member of the Cabinet. Unfortunately, Winston Churchill was still too young and brash to suit his colleagues or the public. Lloyd George became increasingly depressed and frustrated about the conduct of the war; the lethargy of Asquith, who gave no leadership in the Cabinet; the obscurantism of Kitchener, who refused to take his civilian colleagues into his confidence; and the incapacity of the generals, whose blunders led to a succession of senseless bloodbaths. Much of the press— especially the sensational and unscrupulous Harmsworth papers—expressed the same views more harshly. Demand for conscription came to a head early in 1916. Lloyd George and a minority of Liberals became convinced of its necessity and sided with the Unionists. A compromise measure limiting conscription to single men satisfied no one; finally Asquith abandoned his former pledges and in May 1916 introduced a full-scale conscription bill, which was passed with only a handful of Liberal and Labour members opposing it.

Another crisis was precipitated in 1916 by the Easter Rebellion in Dublin. Only a fraction of the Irish Volunteers were involved, and their cause was hopeless from the beginning, since they had no widespread support. Yet when the rising was suppressed the British military executed all but one of the leaders after summary courts-martial. The exception was a young school-teacher named Eamon De Valera (1882–   ), whose life was saved because of the American citizenship of his father. The inept action of the military made martyrs of the rebel leaders and turned Sinn Fein overnight into a nationalist movement. After visiting Ireland Asquith asked Lloyd George to work out an Irish settlement. Incredibly, the latter managed to persuade Carson and Redmond to endorse a plan granting immediate home rule to Ireland with the exception of the six predominantly Protestant counties in the north. The proposals fell through, however, when some Unionist Cabinet members refused to accept them.

Lord Kitchener had been drowned when a German mine sank the ship bringing him to Russia. Having completed work at the Ministry of Munitions, Lloyd George agreed to take over Kitchener's former position at the War Office. There he suffered increasing frustration owing to lack of cooperation from the chief of staff, General Robertson. In the autumn of 1916 Lloyd George and Bonar Law demanded a reorganization of the Government, with a small war council to run the war. Asquith half agreed and then changed his mind when he read an attack on himself in *The Times*. He plainly thought it had been planted by Lloyd George, whereupon the latter resigned. Lloyd George's discontent with the Prime Minister's weak conduct of the war resembled Lord John Russell's in the Aberdeen coalition of sixty years earlier, but his resignation had different results. When the Unionist ministers made it clear to Asquith that the government could not go on he tendered his resignation to the King. At a hastily called conference at Buckingham Palace party leaders failed to persuade Asquith to be part of any new combination, and Bonar Law consequently gave up the attempt to form a government. The King then called on Lloyd George, who succeeded in doing so. Most Unionists did not trust Lloyd George, but they recognized his abilities and having no leader of their own, accepted office under him. From the beginning he was much dependent upon their support and gave them the most important appointments. Fourteen Cabinet offices went to Unionists and two to Labour. Liberals received only six Cabinet appointments, mostly of lesser importance; except for Lloyd George all Asquith's Liberal Cabinet colleagues remained outside. In forming the coalition the role of Max Aitken (1879–1964), the irrepressible young Canadian millionaire who had become a British M.P. and a friend of both Lloyd George and Bonar Law, is told in his fascinating book *Politicians and the War*. He received the title of Lord Beaverbrook in recognition, but had to wait until the Second World War before he played an important part in government.

The traditional Cabinet was scrapped for the duration of the war. In its place Lloyd George set up a War Cabinet of five, consisting of himself, Bonar Law, Arthur Henderson (1863–1935) of the Labour Party, and Lords Curzon and Milner, two Unionist peers distinguished as imperial proconsuls rather than parliamentarians. He also created new ministries to meet war needs in the areas of shipping, food, pensions, national service, labor, and aircraft and filled them with businessmen and others with no political experience. The War Cabinet was much more efficient than its predecessor. It met more frequently and had its own secretariat, with a most capable secretary, Colonel Hankey, who kept regular Cabinet minutes—an important innovation. Churchill was initially excluded by Tory prejudice, but returned in 1917 as Minister of Munitions. This was the team that led Britain to victory despite stresses and strains. Lloyd George also met the demands of the dominion prime ministers for a share in the direction of the war effort to which they were contributing so heavily by summoning them to an Imperial War Conference in 1917, which recognized their newly found autonomy, and by inviting them when in London to attend sessions of an Imperial War Cabinet.

While the war lasted and for several years afterward Lloyd George worked easily with his Unionist colleagues. In sparking the war effort he did the job they wanted, and was quite ready to use their talents and those of their friends. The government was now preponderantly Unionist led by an independent Liberal. The Unionists felt no remorse that the formation of the Lloyd George's coalition had split the Liberal party, although they did not necessarily realize that the blow was mortal. Asquith promised independent support for the Government, but he and his former colleagues out of office sat on the Opposition front bench. Only once did they vote as a bloc against the Government in 1918. Asquith demanded an inquiry into questions raised by General Maurice as to the veracity of official figures on the number of troops maintained in France. In the subsequent division 100 Liberals voted with Asquith, 71 with the Government. Clearly throughout the six years of his premiership, Lloyd George was completely dependent on the support of his Unionist allies.

Lloyd George's battle with the brass, as the senior military were known, continued. He managed to get rid of Robertson, the recalcitrant chief of staff, but could never dislodge Haig, the British commander in chief in France, on whom he blamed the unnecessarily high casualties of the western front. Before the war ended, however, he promoted a unified Allied command, placing Haig (much to his disgust) under France's Marshal Foch, although the latter's powers were limited. Lloyd George's contribution to victory lay in his energetic efforts to cooperate with the Allies, especially France; his clear enunciation of war aims; his advocacy of the convoy system, long opposed by the naval command; and most of all his indomitable courage and drive, which acted as a tonic on national morale. The middle and upper classes and the Liberal and Unionist parties generally gave wholehearted support to the war effort, but the working classes and the Labour party did so with reservations. Some Labour ministers remained in the coalition government until the end of the war, but Arthur Henderson, the most distinguished, resigned in 1917 to be free to explore peacetime objectives with socialists in Britain and abroad. The working classes and their trade union spokesmen were also unhappy about conscription, the soaring cost of living, and war profiteering scandals. When Churchill became Minister of Munitions in 1917 he dealt with many labor grievances in the Munitions of War Act. Government subsidies were introduced to keep down the price of bread, and the excess profits tax was increased to 80 percent.

Britain's part in the eventual victory was substantial. By 1918 her commitment on the western front equalled that of France, for Haig now had nearly two million men under his command. Outside factors, however, brought the war to its conclusion in the last months of 1918. The withdrawal of Russia in 1917 had been a severe blow to the Allies, since it had released many German troops for the western front. But it was more than compensated by American intervention, and in 1918 the arrival of American troops in large numbers promised an eventual Allied superiority. Germany, nearing exhaustion after four years of war on two fronts, planned a major offensive in the west in the spring of 1918. It almost succeeded as the Allied lines were pushed back many miles, but in the end they held. Lloyd George took charge of the War Office and quickly dispatched large British reinforcements to the front. He also persuaded President Wilson to send the American army under General Pershing into action earlier than had been intended.

With their superior manpower and sustained morale the Allies were ready to take the offensive in the late summer and autumn after the German offensive had collapsed. The Germans no longer had the strength or the will to resist. On November 11 they signed an armistice in the hope of a reasonable peace treaty based on President Wilson's Fourteen Points. It was in fact a military capitulation, resulting in Allied occupation of western Germany. Victory was won by Britain and her Allies despite their generals, as a result of the determination of their troops at the front and civilians at home, and of the final collapse of the enemy. The price in lives had been very high. Of 6,000,000 recruits to the armed forces in the United Kingdom there had been 2,500,000 casualties, including 750,000 fatalities. The empire had provided 2,500,000 of whom 200,000 had been killed. The term "lost generation" may have been an exaggeration, but psychologically it contained some truth. The economic and social costs of the war and their consequences are less easily determined and will be discussed in the next chapter.

Chapter Eleven
PARTY POLITICS BETWEEN THE WARS

The fighting was over but much remained to be done to clear up the mess and no one was readier than Lloyd George, the "Welsh Wizard," to apply himself to the task. But to do so he needed a political base, and the only one possible seemed to be the continuation of the coalition. His Unionist colleagues agreed, even before the armistice was signed, and the election was held four weeks after that date. It was called the "coupon election," a derisive term used by Asquith because all candidates, Unionist and Liberal, supporting the Coalition were given a joint letter of identification by Lloyd George and Bonar Law. Asquith had earlier rejected an offer of office and in effect led his followers to fight the election as Opposition candidates, although they did not claim to do so. The Coalition won an overwhelming victory with 474 seats, of which 136 went to Coalition Liberals. Asquithian Liberals won only 26 seats (with Asquith himself defeated), while the Labour party, which had withdrawn from the coalition, became the official Opposition with 59 seats. The new Sinn Fein party supplanted the Irish Nationalists by winning 73 seats in the south of Ireland, but they refused to go to Westminster.

With this tremendous victory and his position as Prime Minister secure for some time to come Lloyd George could turn his full attention to the peace settlement. He had ceased to be a conventional parliamentary prime minister, appearing infrequently in the House of Commons, which he left to Bonar Law to lead. The peacetime Cabinet was restored, but Lloyd George did not consult it in the traditional way and set up his own staff of private advisers in what was dubbed the "Garden Suburb" (because it was housed in St. James Park). His neglect of Parliament and Cabinet was unwise and led ultimately to his downfall, but for the time being he was all-powerful. He was now primarily concerned with his role on a world stage. With Wilson and Clemenceau he made major decisions that affected international affairs for the next twenty years. There was much wrangling between the major powers, but Lloyd George was usually the moderator between the extremism of Clemenceau and the idealism of Wilson. On the question of Germany's punishment he was readier to stand up to Clemenceau, for his own views were more reasonable than those of the British public, who demanded the head of the kaiser and full payment of war costs by Germany. During the election campaign Lloyd George had gone along with this hysteria, but although harsh, the final peace terms were not as vindictive as those demanded by Clemenceau and the extremists at home.

The Treaty of Versailles, signed less than eight months after hostilities had ceased, fixed on Germany responsibility for the war, returned to France the lost provinces of Alsace and Lorraine, turned over part of Silesia to the new state of Poland, placed German overseas colonies under mandatory control of Britain, France, Australia, and South Africa, provided for Germany's disarmament, and imposed continuing military occupation of the Rhineland. The amount of reparations to be paid by Germany remained unsettled. After years of arguing the unrealistic original figure of £24 billion was finally reduced to £2 billion, of which £1,000 million was paid to France and Belgium with the help of American loans. An important feature of the settlement was formation of the League of Nations. While this was a cardinal element in Wilson's Fourteen Points, the idea had been given a good deal of thought in England during the war under the impetus of the Union of Democratic Control, a group of liberal and socialist intellectuals demanding a new approach to foreign policy and abandonment of secret diplomacy. As a result the British government came to the peace conference with the most detailed proposals; they were more limited and down to earth than those Wilson had envisaged, but substantially formed the basis of the League Covenant that was approved. France was more interested in tangible pledges of security and was promised a treaty of guarantee that was never obtained after the League's rejection by the American Senate. Despite the hesitation of the other powers, the British dominions and India received separate representation in the League, and the dominion prime ministers, who attended the peace conference as part of the British Empire delegation, signed the Treaty of Versailles in their own right.

The unresolved issues of reparations and a treaty of guarantee led to a series of international conferences in the following decade. Other treaties provided for the partition of the Austro-Hungarian and Turkish empires in the name of self-determination, but Lloyd George showed more respect for the principle than Wilson when it came to defending the claims of Germany against Poland in Silesia. British occupation of Palestine allowed its establishment as a Jewish homeland to meet Zionist demands despite the vague and conflicting promises that had been made about the disposition of this former Turkish province. The obstacle was Palestine's overwhelmingly Arab population, and the commitment to the Zionists—first made in 1917 by Balfour as Foreign Secretary—was an unhappy one for the British. In later years Britain's effort to hold the balance between Arabs and Jews antagonized both. The settlement with Turkey caused more trouble, and eventually contributed to Lloyd George's downfall.

One of the stated objectives of the League of Nations was the promotion of world disarmament to remove what was thought to be one of the causes of war. Little progress was achieved, with the exception of the Washington Conference of 1922, one of the last international conferences in which Lloyd George played an effective role. At the preceding Imperial Conference he had agreed, on the advice of Canada's Prime Minister Arthur Meighen, to drop the Japanese alliance to avoid antagonizing the United States. Now—again on Canadian urging—he accepted an American proposal to limit the naval strength of the five major naval powers (the United Kingdom, the United States, Japan, France, and Italy) on a ratio of 5:5:3:1.7:1.7. It was proof of the importance Britain attached to good Anglo-American relations that her government was prepared to abandon its age-old formula of naval supremacy and accept parity with the United States. Japan was persuaded to sign the treaty by the inclusion of a clause prohibiting further fortifications on islands in the Pacific; this left Hong Kong in an exposed position. The ten-year naval building moratorium in the Washington agreements was a substantial achievement. It has been observed that the price Britain paid in her goodwill gesture to the United States was permanent weakening of her position in the Far East, but in the long run this would have been inevitable.

Britain was attempting with indifferent success to adjust to peacetime conditions. The cost of war had been far more than the ghastly totals of those killed and maimed. The cost to the exchequer was £9 billion, which rose to £12 billion during the period of winding up in the years 1919–20. The national debt had increased tenfold to £7 billion, of which over £1 billion had been borrowed from the United States. Almost £2 billion had been loaned to the Allies, most of it irrecoverable. Britain also had lost over seven million tons of shipping, although much of it had been replaced. About 10 percent of overseas investments had been liquidated during the war and another 5 percent confiscated. More serious was the 63 percent decline in exports between 1913 and 1918. The prewar level was never regained in the years before the next war. As her share in world exports dropped Britain's share in world trade fell from 13.1 percent in 1913 to 9.2 percent in 1932. Many of her old customers had learned to provide textiles and machinery for themselves in the war years when Britain had none to sell abroad. The strain of war had also taken its toll on housing and industrial facilities. Factories, mines, and railways had run down after four years of heavy use without normal maintenance and replacement, and more than 600,000 homes had not been built or had been destroyed by air raids. In the years 1919–20 there was a short postwar boom as plants were put to work to supply the old market. But when it was discovered they no longer existed or had greatly contracted, the boom was followed by a sharp depression. The parts of the country where textiles and the old heavy industries had flourished—especially Clyde-side, South Wales, and the north of England—became known as depressed areas, because of the long-term high unemployment that ensued. The Mid-lands and London area were less affected, because of the growth of new industries producing goods such as cars and electrical appliances. The sluggish-ness of the British economy in the postwar years may be explained by a combination of factors. Along with the loss of foreign markets was a certain lack of adaptability on the part of British business, and a reluctance of people with money to invest. Despite good intentions successive governments con-tributed to these difficulties by frantic efforts to cut expenditures and generally to pursue deflationary policies. When the gold standard was finally restored in 1925 the value of the pound was set too high, which had a further adverse effect on British exports.

With full employment, higher wages, controlled rents, and food subsidies, British labor had done relatively well during the war, and inevitably the dis-locations of the postwar period produced much labor unrest. There were numerous strikes in the years 1920–21 as the prewar labor militancy re-appeared, somewhat strengthened by the knowledge that a socialist revolu-tion had succeeded in Russia. By and large British labor did not approve of Russian Communism—a system clearly outside their democratic tradition—but they took grim satisfaction in the knowledge that in one part of the world the bosses had been put down. The conservative middle and upper classes, on the other hand, tended to equate trade union militancy with Communism and call active union leaders "Bolshies." Labor applauded the refusal of London dockers to load munitions to be used by the Poles against the Russians, but such gestures of sympathy did not mean they were planning a Bolshevik revolution in Britain. They may have believed in the class war, but they were content to use the traditional weapons of the strike and the ballot box. With the loss of foreign markets, the development of alternate power sources at home, and failure to modernize coal mining became one of the most depressed industries in these years and the miners the most restless group in the union movement. Trouble was postponed by the appointment of a coal commission, but the commissioners were divided in their recom-mendations. The Government rejected the joint proposal of Mr. Justice (later Lord) Sankey, the chairman, and the labor representatives for nationalization of the mines, but a miners' strike was temporarily warded off by a government-awarded wage increase. In 1921, however, the Government returned control of the mines to the owners, who promptly announced a cut in wages to make ends meet. The miners went on strike and appealed to the revived "Triple Alliance" of major unions for support. The government made overelaborate military arrangements; on "Black Friday" April 15, 1921, when the miners refused a proposed government compromise, the railwaymen and transport workers withdrew from the alliance. J. H. Thomas and Ernest Bevin, spokesmen for those two unions, represented a less militant type of unionism that preferred compromise and partnership to class war.

The Lloyd George Liberals were an ineffective political party, but like the Liberal Unionists in the late nineteenth century, they had some success in nudging their Conservative allies on social questions. In 1918, before the war was over, the coalition government introduced a franchise bill giving the vote to all men over the age of twenty-one with six months' residence at one address, and to women over thirty. The country was divided into 707 equal electoral districts of approximately 70,000 each (reduced in 1922 to 615 after the withdrawal of the southern Irish). The act of 1918 was the largest and least controversial reform act in British history. Women and working-class men still unenfranchised had proved their right to the suffrage by the part they played in the war. The results of the 1918 election showed the Conservatives they had little to fear; indeed, the female vote was apparently predominantly Conservative.

The Liberal Coalitionists also produced a reforming Minister of Education in the historian H. A. L. Fisher (1865–1940), whose Education Act of 1918 raised the school-leaving age to fourteen and provided continuation schools for pupils up to sixteen, although these suffered from later government economizing. Fisher also improved the teachers' salaries, provided a national system of pensions for teachers, and made available more free places for pupils in secondary schools.

The reform record of the Coalition after the election of 1918 was disappointing owing to the preoccupation with foreign affairs of its once-radical leader and to the increased strength of the Unionist element. It was responsible, however, for three important measures that substantially extended the base of the welfare state laid in the decade before the war. An act in 1919 set up the new Ministry of Health, which centralized the functions of a variety of departments and local authorities and assumed the regulation of housing. The first Minister of Health was the controversial Dr. Addison, a Liberal member of the government whose enthusiasm for social reform outweighed his ability as an administrator. Addison was responsible for the

Housing and Town Planning Act of 1919, which recognized state responsibility for development of a national housing policy. Local authorities were required to survey their housing needs and draw up plans for approval by the ministry, which provided building subsidies and controlled low rents. Some subsidy was also subsequently given for houses built by private enterprise. The Unemployment Insurance Act of 1920 extended the limited scope of the 1911 bill to most manual workers other than domestics and agricultural laborers. It was passed before the boom broke and without expectation of the prolonged unemployment crisis that followed. Over the years the government had to subsidize the scheme on an unanticipated scale to provide for extended payments. The centrally administered unemployment insurance was in many cases a welcome alternative to the old locally administered Poor Law. The system was further extended in 1921 by limited payments to wives and children of the unemployed, a further assumption of social responsibility by the central government.

The attitude of British business now largely dominating government, to state intervention and control was pragmatic. The laissez-faire of the Manchester school was a thing of the past. A large segment of the probusiness Conservative Unionist party now believed in protection, which entailed state intervention, on behalf of British industry. During the war they had accepted state controls and increased taxation, but as soon as the war was over demand for decontrol was strong. Dissolving many of the war ministeries and abolishing wartime controls was soon effected, but the experience of state intervention during the war made it easier to accept increased state responsibility for social welfare. Unfortunately, in 1922 the government's reaction to the unexpected slump was to inaugurate drastic budget cuts, nicknamed the "Geddes Ax" after Sir Eric Geddes, the author of the proposals. The limited social reforms of the Coalition were thus seriously curtailed. On the other hand, despite the misgivings of Coalition Liberals the government in 1921 took a long step toward protection with the continuation of the wartime McKenna Duties and passage of the Safeguarding of Industries Act to protect key industries or those threatened by the "dumping" of cheap foreign goods.

Of all the problems facing the postwar Coalition the most formidable was the smoldering Irish question, which had now burst into flame. Redmond and the Irish Nationalists had lost control of the situation because of mishandling by the Government and the military of the aftermath of the 1916 Easter Uprising and the 1918 conscription crisis, when plans for Irish conscription had been announced. Lloyd George had appeared to accomplish much on his mission to Ireland in 1916, but he had promised different things in Dublin and Belfast and so reduced his credibility. In any Irish settlement he now had to carry the Unionists with him, which greatly restricted his room for maneuver. After the passage of the peace treaties the Government was faced with the implementation of the Home Rule Act of 1914, but by that time the measure was no longer acceptable to the majority in southern Ireland. They had now turned from the Nationalist party to Sinn Fein, which had swept the board (outside of the six counties) in the election of 1918. Almost half these new Irish members—including Griffith, the founder of Sinn Fein, and De Valera, the hero of the 1916 uprising—were in prison, but the rump met in Dublin and proclaimed the Irish Republic. They committed themselves to a left-wing "Democratic Program," which proved, in the words of one historian, to be "a social revolution that never was."[1] They also made unsuccessful appeals for recognition to President Wilson and the Peace Conference in Paris. In the meantime, De Valera and others had escaped from prison and the government released the rest soon afterward. The expanded Dail, as this new Irish parliament called itself, then elected De Valera as Prime Minister, and he chose a Cabinet from among leaders of the movement. Although their operation was of necessity underground they had surprising success in raising revenues, setting up courts to supplant the British jurisdiction, and exercising a degree of control over local government. De Valera went on a long visit to the United States to seek American aid, and during his absence the situation deteriorated. The Irish Volunteers, now dominated by the Irish Republican Brotherhood, became the Irish Republican Army (IRA), but its forces were not easily controlled by the provisional government. Before long guerrilla warfare broke out between the IRA and the Royal Irish Constabulary (RIC), the police arm of Dublin Castle. This was waged on a small scale until the latter part of 1920 when the British government began to recruit a nondescript force of war veterans, mostly soldiers of fortune, to supplement the RIC. This force, which became known as the Black and Tans, was prepared to outdo the IRA in terrorism and to exact for every ambush reprisals that often involved civilian casualties. For instance, on "Bloody Sunday," November 21, 1920, when the IRA raided the homes of eleven British civilians suspected of being intelligence agents and killed them in cold blood, the Black and Tans retaliated that afternoon by breaking up a Gaelic football game, shooting indiscriminately at players and spectators, killing twelve and wounding sixty. A few weeks later, following a successful IRA ambush in which almost forty RIC Auxiliaries had been killed, the Black and Tans and the Auxiliaries raided Cork City, drinking, looting, burning, and leaving waste much of the city's center.

The excesses of the Black and Tans shocked a large segment of opinion in Britain and elsewhere. Criticism went well beyond party lines as the

---

[1] Quoted in F. S. L. Lyons, *Ireland since the Famine* (London, 1971), p. 401.

Northcliffe press led by *The Times*, the Archbishop of Canterbury, and several Conservative M.P.'s joined Liberal and Labour spokesmen in demanding that the Government put an end to these methods of barbarism. King George was equally upset and at the suggestion of General Smuts and the editor of *The Times* persuaded his ministers to allow him to appeal for peace on a visit to Belfast. The warm reception given this gesture led the Government abruptly to reverse its course and invite De Valera, now returned from the United States, to discuss peace terms. After months of protracted negotiation the Irish representatives signed a treaty in London early in December 1921. The Irish had to give up claims for a republic and a United Ireland, accept Britain's retention of naval bases, and take an oath of loyalty to the crown. In return they received dominion status similar to Canada's. The boundary with Ulster was to be settled by a commission. The Irish representatives were persuaded this would leave Ulster too small to be a threat; but on this point they were betrayed, for the commission never reported. With heavy hearts the Irish representatives signed for they were told by Lloyd George immediate resumption of the war was the alternative. The Dail was bitterly divided and after long debate ratified the treaty only by a narrow majority. De Valera opposed it and resigned as President. The result was a civil war that lasted until early 1923, but the new Irish Free State managed to survive. Lloyd George was thus the only British statesman who had succeeded in settling the Irish question, but the price was Ireland's partition. Half a century later it is still being paid for in Northern Ireland, where British troops are once more engaged with the gunmen of the IRA.

Nor did the Irish settlement, although approved by his Unionist colleagues, endear Lloyd George to the Unionist back-benchers on whose support his government relied. Shortly afterward the "Chanak incident" further undermined their confidence in the Prime Minister. When the revolutionary Turkish army defeated the Greeks at Smyrna and threatened to advance on the British position at Chanak in the neutral zone on the Dardanelles, the British government issued a warning to Mustapha Kemal and appealed to the dominions and Balkan allies for support. Lloyd George and Winston Churchill, now Colonial Secretary, issued a flamboyant communiqué. It was published before the dominion prime ministers had received the request, much to their annoyance and that of Curzon, the Foreign Secretary, who had not been consulted. The crisis passed when the Turks agreed not to enter the neutral zone, but the incident further alienated the Tory rank and file.

The Lloyd George coalition was doomed to collapse eventually, and the Chanak incident only helped to precipitate its dissolution. Most of Lloyd George's Unionist colleagues remained loyal—such was his charisma and their respect for his ability—but this loyalty was not shared by party organizers or back-benchers. Lloyd George's only hope of consolidating his position was to achieve a fusion of his followers with the Unionists, but neither group was willing. By themselves the Coalition Liberals ("Lloyd George's stage army" as they were dubbed by a cynical Conservative) were too weak to depend upon indefinitely for effective support. The 136 seats they had won in the 1918 election had been gained through the government's popularity at the hour of victory and lack of Unionist competition. There were able ministers among them—of whom two eventually resigned from the ministry when their plans were frustrated—but many of the back-benchers were inexperienced and undistinguished. Moreover, the Lloyd George Liberals had no real basis in the constituencies. Their electoral machinery was weak or nonexistent, and in the years 1919–22 they lost ten seats in by-elections. They had no sense of permanence, and when elected many had assumed they would eventually reunite with the Asquithian Liberals. At the time of the 1918 elections the relationship between the two groups was still fluid, and it had been suggested when Asquith lost his seat that Lloyd George might seek the leadership of a united Liberal party. He had refused to do so for fear of alienating his Unionist allies. After the election the Asquithian Liberals organized as an independent Liberal party nicknamed the "Wee Frees," and in 1920 Asquith returned via a by-election to lead them.

The one asset the Lloyd George Liberals enjoyed was money, for their leader sold titles in an unscrupulous manner reminiscent of eighteenth-century political practices. Although the proceeds of the sales were shared with the Unionists, the Prime Minister and his Coalition were further discredited. Many Unionists wished to put an end to the abuse. The crisis came in the autumn of 1922, when the Cabinet decided to hold an election without consulting the whips or the Unionist Central Office. Bonar Law regretfully came out of retirement to lead the Opposition at a party meeting at the Carlton Club. He was supported by Stanley Baldwin, who had just resigned office in disgust at Lloyd George's leadership and what it was doing to the Conservative party (as it was now called once again). As a result of their appeals a motion to fight the next election as an independent party and thus end the Coalition was passed by 187 to 87 votes. The spell of Lloyd George was broken and so was his political career, although he fought hard for years to make a comeback. He was one of the greatest war leaders in British history, and before that a great peacetime social reformer. No British prime minister before him had played a role in world affairs as important as his in the years 1917–1919, but his career since then had been mostly anticlimax. For all his ability and charisma he had two failings —one moral and the other political—that made his downfall inevitable. In his public and private life he was amoral and he laughed at such impeccable men as Austen Chamberlain, who, he said, "always played the game and always lost." More surprisingly he failed to see that ultimately political success in the parliamentary system had to be based on party. Some historians believe the British Liberal party was doomed anyway, but Lloyd George made that event more certain.

With the resignation of Lloyd George, Bonar Law formed an all-Conservative administration, but since most of the Conservative members of the previous Cabinet, with the exception of Curzon and Baldwin, refused to join, it was for the most part a ministry of nonentities like the "Who Who Ministry" of 1852. Nevertheless he won an overall majority in the subsequent election with 345 seats and 38.2 percent of the national vote. Labour remained the official Opposition with 142 seats elected by 29.5 percent of the national vote. The Lloyd George Liberals, who fought the election independently, dropped to 62 seats with only 11.6 percent of the vote, while the Asquithian Liberals increased their numbers to 54 with 17.5 percent of the vote.

Bonar Law's main accomplishment as Prime Minister was the reestablishment of Cabinet government. The Prime Minister's Garden Suburb was abolished, although the Cabinet secretariat was retained under the able direction of Sir Maurice Hankey, and the direction of foreign policy returned to the Foreign Secretary. Lord Curzon (1859–1925), who held that office, worked out a settlement with Turkey at the Conference of Lausanne, but relations with France deteriorated when Britain objected to their occupation of the Ruhr. Stanley Baldwin, the new Chancellor of the Exchequer, went to Washington where he agreed to a debt settlement that was criticized in England as too generous to the Americans, and which almost led Bonar Law to resign. A few months later, in May 1923, he was forced to do so when he discovered he was dying of throat cancer.

The King had to make the difficult choice of a successor between the veteran Lord Curzon and the inexperienced Stanley Baldwin (1867–1947). Law had made no recommendation, although his private secretary had emphatically let it be known that Law favored Baldwin. In terms of experience and ability, the obvious choice was Curzon, who had been a member of Lloyd George's War Cabinet and a former Viceroy of India. But he was one of the most unpopular men in public life. Baldwin, although as yet not well known, had the advantage of being in the House of Commons. In the view of Lord Balfour, who was consulted, this was decisive; it was probably the reason the King chose Baldwin—to the chagrin of Lord Curzon, who was confidently expecting the summons.

The first Baldwin ministry was short-lived. Attempts to win back the Coalition Unionist ministers failed, and the summer was spent largely on the endless problem of reparations and in efforts to restrain the harsh French policy of Poincaré toward Germany. In the autumn Baldwin proposed to resurrect the Conservative doctrine of protection, which had been shelved by Bonar Law. This meant calling an election. Labour and the Liberals rallied to the old cause of free trade, and the Conservatives were turned out of office. They had won 258 seats, but there was a combined free-trade majority against them, 191 Labour and 159 Liberals, temporarily reunited under Asquith. The Liberals were less than one percent behind Labour in the national vote, but it was the last time they were in the running. Since the election had been fought on the free trade issue, Asquith refused suggestions to unite with the Conservatives to keep out the Socialists, and his neutrality enabled Ramsay MacDonald to form the first Labour government. The King also resisted pressure to exclude the so-called "wild men," telling his mother "they ought to be given a chance and ought to be treated fairly." Since there were four ex-Liberals, including Lord Haldane, in the Cabinet and the government lacked a majority in the House of Commons, its enemies had little to worry about.

Some Labour supporters questioned the wisdom of accepting office under these circumstances, since it would be impossible to pass any socialist measures through Parliament. The one important measure to the new government's credit was Wheatley's Housing Act, which went further than the previous Conservative measure in providing housing for the working classes. At the Exchequer Philip Snowden introduced an orthodox free-trade budget, which abolished the McKenna duties and received the full support of the Liberals. The main significance of the short-lived Labour government of 1924 was that Labour showed the country it was capable of governing. In administration as opposed to legislation they showed a more distinctive approach, but the outbreak of a transport strike provided an embarrassment. MacDonald himself took the Foreign Office and in this field raised the Government's reputation. He settled, at least temporarily, the reparations question by persuading France and Germany to agree to the Dawes Plan, but his proposal of an elaborate security treaty known as the Geneva Protocol, which was to put teeth into the League of Nations, died with his ministry. The government's recognition of Soviet Russia and endeavor to arrange a Russian trade treaty, however, aroused the suspicion and hostility of the other parties. Consequently, when the Labour ministers showed signs of being soft on communism by withdrawing prosecution charges against a communist trade union official, the Opposition parties combined to defeat them by a vote demanding a commission of inquiry. The Conservatives tried to make the most of the anticommunist cry on the eve of the subsequent election by exploiting the publication of the "Zinoviev letter." This was an alleged attempt by the Russian government to persuade the British Communist party to stir up trouble in Britain among the unemployed. In any event the government was defeated and the Conservatives returned to office with 419 seats to 151 for Labour. The reunited Liberal party dropped to 40.

Thus, in the short space of one decade, a party in office with more than two centuries of political tradition behind it had ceased to have political credibility. We may ask how this could have happened. Some historians regard the Liberal party as a nineteenth-century phenomenon and see the split over Home Rule in 1886 as the beginning of the end. Undoubtedly nineteenth-century Liberalism had its own special characteristics, but it was by no means static, and the electoral success of 1906 suggests it was capable of adapting to the twentieth century. George Dangerfield, in *The Strange Death of Liberal England* (1935), argues that Liberalism was actually dying in its apparent heyday, 1906–1914. He defends this thesis by noting the decline or disappearance of old liberal values at various levels of society, citing the militancy of the new trade unionism with the General Strike as its ultimate weapon, the shrill ferocity of the suffragette movement, eager to break the law to attract attention to their cause, and the folly of the Unionist party, encouraging Ulster's armed resistance to Home Rule. The prewar Liberal government undoubtedly faced grave crises, but the way in which the country rallied in 1914 to present a solid front against external danger suggests Dangerfield's picture was exaggerated. At the beginning of the twentieth century Britain was in a state of transition, not disintegration. The same might have been true of the Liberal party, which still had the largest number of seats in 1910. Are we then to say that its demise was the result merely of the split between Asquith and Lloyd George? Both established parties had survived such divisions in the past—the Conservatives in 1846 and the Liberals in 1886. It has been pointed out by C. L. Mowat and others that after 1922 there was no longer a purpose for the Liberal party in Britain: the old issues dividing them from the Conservatives, especially home rule, had been resolved. This is not entirely true, since there was room for difference of opinion on free trade, approaches to social problems, particularly unemployment, and foreign policy. On the other hand, the Liberal party was caught between two ideological poles, the Labour party nominally converted to socialism, and the Conservative party championing the old Liberal cause of free enterprise. Whether this was sufficient to crush a great political party is debatable.

The truth lies somewhere in the middle. The split of 1886 had advantages as well as disadvantages. The loss of Joseph Chamberlain and his followers was an undoubted blow, but not a mortal one, as was proved in 1906; and the

Liberal's potential as a party of the left was strengthened by being purged of the Whigs. The party was not as strong as the 1906 election results suggested, but it did win two succeeding general elections (although without an overall majority), scarcely the sign of a dying party. Until 1914 Asquith had been an effective prime minister, but by then his best days were over and he was not the man to plot a new course for the party after the war. He seemed to be rather more concerned with his personal position than with the good of the party, although undoubtedly he and his family thought the two inseparable. Lloyd George, who was eleven years younger than Asquith, was at the height of his powers when the war ended, but he showed no concern over the future of the Liberal party. He was basically not a party man and cared nothing for the party's traditions. He was interested in getting things done, often worthwhile things, and maintaining his own position. He would have been glad to form a new center party at the expense of the old parties had their members allowed him to do so. Of the other eminent men in Asquith's Cabinet, Grey, too, had reached the end of the road and played little part in political affairs after 1916. Haldane was able but unpopular and lacked the temperament of a leader. Winston Churchill was the most brilliant of the younger men in the party, he probably held stronger convictions than Lloyd George, but he too lacked strong party feeling, which was not surprising given his Conservative origins.

The replacement of the Liberal by the Labour party in the twenties made sense, since differences in outlook between Conservatives and Labour were more marked than between the Liberals and either of the others. However, what seems logical or rational is not necessarily what happens. Left-wing third parties have not displaced either of the traditional parties on the national level in the United States or Canada, although from a socialist point of view there may not be much choice between either of the older parties. In a two-party system the traditional large parties are always favored. Many people never change their vote, and others feel that a vote for a third party is a vote thrown away. Thus the party in office and the largest party in opposition are likely to get the lion's share of the votes.

The Conservatives in the years after 1846 and the Liberals in the years after 1886 could afford their splits because there was no rival opposition party in a position to challenge them, but this was not the case in 1918. Had Lloyd George withdrawn from the Coalition in 1918—as did Labour under Attlee in 1945—and reunited the Liberal party, the Liberals would have won more seats and become the official Opposition, if not the Government party. But the temporary Liberal division was Labour's opportunity, since the Coalition Liberals were supporting the Government. Labour by default became the official Opposition, even though they had only 59 seats. Belief in the Liberals as a party that might form an alternative government had weakened, and henceforth both members and voters began looking right or left. Throughout the twenties the Liberals fought unsuccessfully to regain their credibility. The mutual distrust of Lloyd George and Asquith, even after their nominal reunion in 1923, helped to ensure the failure of the Liberals, but the main damage had already been done.

Once the Labour party had been recognized as the official Opposition, voters and candidates were readier to regard them as the alternative government. There was, of course, more to it than that. The Labour party had to show itself capable of rising to opportunities, and on the whole it did this. Before the war, there was nowhere for the Labour party to go as long as there was a strong reforming party on the left. Labour might criticize the shortcomings of Liberal reforms, but it had to support them. The party gave workers a voice in parliament, but its popularity soon reached a ceiling, as it failed to win as many as fifty seats in three successive elections. However, there were developments in its favor after 1914; in addition to the Liberal decline, the extension of the franchise among the poorer classes in 1918 seemed likely to benefit Labour. Moreover, the party's participation in the wartime Coalition showed its patriotism and the administrative ability of some of its leaders. It is true that Ramsay MacDonald had withdrawn as party leader on pacifist grounds, but after the war people respected him for this. In 1922 he was reelected to the post he had resigned in 1914. Despite his later failings MacDonald was a remarkable man, and in public estimation stood far above his colleagues. His credentials were impeccable. He had risen from poverty through his own ability (helped, it must be admitted, by a marriage that brought him some money). He had been an original member of the party—its first secretary—and before that a Fabian and a member of the ILP. He was an intellectual, although largely self-educated, and the author of books and essays on socialism and other topics. In appearance he was also one of the most striking members of the House of Commons and one of the best speakers. He was actually a moderate, but his fiery speeches won him the early support of the left.

Before the war the Labour party was little more than a loose alliance of trade unions and socialist organizations such as the ILP and the Fabians. In 1918, however, through the efforts of Sidney Webb and Arthur Henderson, the Labour party adopted a new constitution and approved a new policy statement. In *Labour and the New Social Order*, the policy statement drafted by Webb and Henderson, the party adopted a cautiously phrased set of non-Marxist socialist objectives that were the blueprint for the next half-century. The constitution provided for formation in the constituencies of local party organizations largely superceding the trade councils and the ILP. It was now possible to join the party as an individual instead of through a union or socialist group. But at the same time the trade unions were required to make larger contributions and were ensured a major role on the party executive. Even with better organization the Labour party remained an awkward alliance of unions and left-wing intellectuals, mostly from the Fabian Society and the ILP. Local party associations, however, permitted direct recruitment from both working and middle classes; and in 1929 cooperative societies entered a loose electoral alliance with the Labour party that was developed further after the Second World War.

The Conservatives proved the dominant political party in the interwar period. Given their record in the years 1900–1914 this requires almost as much explanation as does the downfall of the Liberal party. Clearly the accident of the Liberal split and Lloyd George's dependence on his Unionist or Conservative allies facilitated the Conservative recovery. So, too, did the circumstances of the war, for as the "patriotic" party the Conservatives were more in their element in a war situation and more in tune with the popular mood. But in the years immediately following the war the Conservatives were in an awkward situation. Most of their leaders continued loyal to Lloyd George, while the rank and file grew increasingly restive. When the break came it brought to the top the businessman, Stanley Baldwin. His right-hand man from the beginning was another businessman, Neville Chamberlain (1869–1940), a younger son of Joseph Chamberlain. The day of the aristocratic control of the Cecils and the Stanleys was over, although members of those families remained active in Conservative politics. (In the period 1886–1916 55 percent of Conservative Cabinet ministers were of aristocratic background, but the percentage fell to 30 in the next forty years.) The attitude and outlook of the party had shifted. Although it still had a diehard wing, Baldwin realistically accepted Labour and developed a working relationship with the Labour party that gained him general respect. Neville Chamberlain was less accommodating, but he was an activist. As Minister of Health, 1924–1929, he carried on his father's tradition with a program of constructive measures. The party was antisocialist, but it was also paternalistic, and not blind to the need for social legislation. The Conservative party had finally accepted the twentieth century, and was flexible enough to capitalize on the inexperience of the Labour party and the collapse of the Liberals, from whom it won many voters. Conservative ascendancy in the interwar years was thus not surprising.

Stanley Baldwin came to the top by accident and yet he gave his name to the years 1923–1937 in which he led the Conservative party. Few men who have played such an important role in public affairs made their name so late in life. Baldwin was a Worcestershire ironmaster who in 1908 inherited both the family business and the seat his father had held in parliament. His scholastic career at Harrow and Cambridge was undistinguished, but he had a love of books and music and of the English countryside. For nine years he was an obscure back-bencher, but in 1917 the Coalition brought him minor office. He had only been a Cabinet minister for two years before he became Prime Minister. He was a heavy, square-faced man, unambitious, phlegmatic, and inclined to indolence, although capable when necessary of sustained effort. He was a moderate and humane person, a more attractive human being than most of his associates. With his pipe, pleasant manner, and John Bullish build he became a familiar figure to British newspaper readers. He was the first British politician to master the art of speaking on the "wireless," which after becoming Prime Minister he did often and well, cultivating the atmosphere of the "fireside chat" before Roosevelt. His radio speeches reflected his wide reading and love of country. He was naturally conservative, with great integrity and strong religious convictions uncommon in politicians of this period. His secret donation after the war of a fifth of his personal fortune to reduce the national debt illustrates his view of patriotism and duty. In an anonymous letter to *The Times* he suggested that other wealthy men might similarly help the country's financial problem by doing the same thing, but he had few imitators. He was a good mixer and helped to improve the atmosphere of the House of Commons by the good-natured way in which he dealt with the Labour party.

His tendency was to ride out the storm with a wait-and-see policy more appropriate to quieter times. He appeared easygoing, but in crises he showed a will of iron. This was demonstrated in his courageous and successful resistance to the ceaseless attacks of the press barons, Beaverbrook and Rothermere. On one famous occasion he accused them of seeking "power without responsibility—the prerogative of the harlot throughout the ages." Their tireless efforts to unseat him as party leader never succeeded.

In 1924 Baldwin returned to office with a large overall majority. He strengthened his party and the government by bringing into the Cabinet three leading members of the former Coalition, Lord Birkenhead (1874–1930), Austen Chamberlain, and Winston Churchill. Churchill, back in the Conservative fold, was Chancellor of the Exchequer in his father's tradition, trimming naval estimates with the same gusto that he had built battleships when at the Admiralty. In debates on these cuts he said he did not see the slightest chance of war with Japan in his lifetime. He satisfied orthodox economists, but not J. M. Keynes, by restoring the gold standard and unfortunately the prewar value of the pound. This was done to reestablish London's old role in international finance, but it had a deflationary effect that retarded expansion of British exports, since by ignoring Keynes's advice the pound was overvalued in relation to the dollar. At the Foreign Office Austen Chamberlain (1863–1937), a half-brother of Neville's, abandoned Mac-Donald's elaborate plans for the Geneva Protocol, but at the Locarno Conference of 1925 he agreed to a more limited security treaty with France, Belgium, Italy, and Germany. Although reparations, disarmament, and Rhineland demilitarization were not directly covered, Germany was brought back into the comity of nations, signing as an equal partner with Britain and France a treaty guaranteeing the mutual frontiers of Germany, France, and Belgium. This was followed by Germany's entry into the League of Nations and eventual Allied withdrawal from the Rhineland. The conference seemed a logical step toward the League's goal of collective security, but it failed to cover Eastern Europe where most of the problems lay; in fact the Locarno system failed to work when put to the test in the thirties.

The most substantive achievements of Baldwin's second ministry were in social reform. As Minister of Health, Neville Chamberlain took office with a program of twenty-five measures, of which twenty-three were enacted with the cooperation of Churchill at the Exchequer. Both followed the tradition of their fathers with the support of Baldwin, who was a more genuine disciple of Tory Democracy than Disraeli. National health insurance was extended to include pensions for widows and orphans and also workers and their wives at age sixty-five (apart from noncontributory old-age pensions payable at age seventy). A more controversial act extended unemployment compensation payments indefinitely (the "dole"), but with reductions in both contributions and benefits. Most sweeping was the Local Government Act of 1929, which abolished the old Poor Law unions and transferred their responsibilities to the counties and county boroughs. Local rates were reduced and replaced by block grants from the central government. The result was a sensible streamlining of local government, but the local authorities still exercised greater control than in most European countries. In public housing the Government continued to administer the Wheatley Act, which produced nearly 100,000 houses a year. Education allocations were increased even though the budget was being pared, and the income tax was reduced. Two other measures typified Baldwin's empirical attitude to state intervention. The Electricity Act of 1926 set up a Central Electricity Board responsible to the Ministry of Transport to rationalize distribution of power. Its success was a long step toward nationalization. Also in 1926 another act gave a public charter to the British Broadcasting Corporation, an independent, publicly owned body, which had a monopoly on wireless (i.e., radio) broadcasting. Its first director, Sir John Reith, imposed high but austere standards that contrasted greatly with North American broadcasting. Finally we may note that the Baldwin government was responsible for the last substantial extension of the franchise by reducing the voting age of women to twenty-one.

The most dramatic event of the Baldwin years, which unhappily over-shadowed these achievements, was the suppression of the General Strike of 1926. The failure of the first Labour government had pushed the labor movement further to the left. Economic conditions had improved to some extent since 1922, but coal mining remained a badly depressed industry. In 1925 the owners again sought to ease their situation by announcing wage reductions, without any corresponding effort to undertake the badly needed reorganization of the industry. The government intervened, to the annoyance of its right-wing supporters, and averted a strike by instituting another in-quiry, temporarily subsidizing the owners to maintain wage level. The com-mission was chaired by the Liberal, Sir Herbert Samuel (1870–1963), who had been Home Secretary in the 1916 Coalition and more recently British High Commissioner in Palestine. It recommended thorough reorganization, including nationalization of royalties, but agreed to the necessity of some wage reductions, to be mitigated by subsistance allowances. Miners and owners were equally obstinate in opposing recommendations with which they did not agree. Baldwin attempted unsuccessfully to mediate, but when typesetters in the *Daily Mail* composing room refused to print an antistrike editorial, the Government abandoned negotiations. The general council of the Trades Union Congress had intervened in 1925, hoping to influence the Government with threats to support the miners. Now that attempts at a solution had failed, the TUC were faced with the necessity of backing the miners by calling a general sympathy strike to begin on May 4, 1926. Despite their talk the responsible leaders of the trade union movement had not really been anxious to implement the threat and perhaps had not taken all the con-sequences of its implementation into consideration. The Government, on the other hand, had carefully planned for the maintenance of essential services and the provision of special constables to supplement the police. The union movement was angered by the Government's handling of the situation and responded to the strike call en masse. The middle and upper classes responded with enthusiasm to the government's appeal. There was violence (resulting in some 3,000 prosecutions) as government forces overplayed their hand. The King cautioned against unnecessary provocation and protested against the wording of instructions to the armed forces. When Samuel proposed a compromise settlement, the general council of the TUC seized on it as an opportunity to call off the general strike, to the relief of the nation. The miners refused Samuel's suggestions (as did the mineowners) and continued their strike for another six months to no avail.

Since formation of the prewar trade union "triple alliance" British labor had discussed the general strike as a means of winning what it wanted and believed it deserved. A revolutionary strike of that sort, however, was not in the British tradition, and the general strike of 1926 was really no more than a massive sympathy strike without any clear political objective. The uncertainty of union leaders and the resoluteness of the government helped to ensure its failure. On the whole the middle classes reacted strongly against the striking workers, and volunteered with enthusiasm for the special services set up by the government. Many of them treated the whole affair as something of a lark, but one unfortunate consequence of the strike was the inevitable accentuation of class differences.

Baldwin insisted that there be no retaliation against the strikers, but he was finally forced to accept legislation prohibiting unions from levying dues in support of the Labour party, except where a member had previously signified his willingness to have the deduction made. (Previous legislation had merely allowed individual members to opt out.) The 1927 Trades Dispute Act incorporating this provision also outlawed general strikes and forbade civil servants to affiliate with the TUC. There was a decline in union membership over the next few years, but indirectly the strike may have done some good as a warning to employers, for in no other major industry were wage cuts as drastic as in mining. There was a decrease in strikes in the years 1926–29, but also a decrease in the cost of living. During these years there was some effort by such enlightened industrialists as Sir Alfred Mond, head of Imperial Chemicals, and such moderate union leaders as Ernest Bevin (1881–1951), Secretary of the Transport and General Workers' Union, to increase production through labor-management collaboration.

Although they obtained a slightly higher popular vote the Conservatives only won 260 seats in the 1929 election to Labour's 288; the Liberals, with almost a quarter of the popular vote, won only 59 seats. MacDonald once more formed a minority Labour government, relinquishing the Foreign Office to Arthur Henderson, who acquired a reputation at the League of Nations as an internationalist, and was elected president of the long-prepared but ill-fated disarmament conference of 1932. On the domestic front the second Labour government produced little except the Coal Mines Act and extension of housing subsidies. The formation of the government was followed by the stock market crash of 1929 and a consequent massive increase in unemployment. MacDonald and his colleagues had no solutions, partly because of Snowden's fanatical adherence to orthodox economic principles. Two committees appointed in 1931 to advise on how to cope with the steadily deteriorating situation recommended orthodox measures of stringent economizing to balance the budget and meet international payment deficits. The politicians were not yet prepared to listen to John Maynard Keynes

(1883–1946), the foremost economist of the day, who advocated government monetary intervention to spur a flagging economy.

In August 1931 after a monetary crisis in Austria there was a run on the pound; but official opinion was adamant against devaluation. New York bankers, probably influenced by the bad advice of the May Committee on National Expenditures, refused to grant the short-term loans necessary to save the pound without assurances that the Government intended to balance its budget by reducing expenditures. This would have involved salary cuts for civil servants and schoolteachers and reduction in unemployment benefits. Nine members of the Cabinet were opposed, causing MacDonald to tender the Government's resignation. At the suggestion of Samuel, acting leader of the Liberals, and with the concurrence of Baldwin, the King persuaded MacDonald to form the National Government—a "Government of individuals," MacDonald called it—with the sole purpose of settling the crisis and saving the pound. The Liberals and Conservatives felt it important to include MacDonald, whose influence as a Labour leader could persuade the public to accept the unpopular economies they considered necessary. After some hesitation, but without consulting his colleagues, MacDonald agreed—out of a sense of duty in the view of his admirers, out of ambition in the opinion of his critics. The fact was that for some time he had been out of touch with his party, seduced, according to his critics, by the high society in which he mixed as Prime Minister. There is no doubt that he and the three colleagues who joined him were convinced of the situation's gravity and the need for the proposed action, but the party in general repudiated him, and in time he came to be regarded as its betrayer.

The new government made the necessary budget cuts, but this led to a minor naval mutiny and a renewed run on the pound, which was no longer viable. As a result the National Government, formed to save the pound, went off the gold standard within six weeks of its formation and the value of the pound fell from $4.86 to $3.40. Despite dire forebodings the overall effect proved beneficial, since devaluation was a stimulus to British exports. It was ironic that the left-wing Labour government fell because it dared not invite economic disaster by taking the country off the gold standard, while its right-wing successor did so with no ill effects. Yet a Labour government might not have been so successful because of lack of confidence in them by bankers.

The National Government had been intended to remain only until settlement of the financial crisis, but it stayed together indefinitely until replaced by a real coalition in 1940. After some Liberals withdrew in 1932, most of the remaining Liberal and Labour elements were simply absorbed into the Conservative party. The Liberal party, however, now broken into three parts, was fractured beyond recovery. Ramsay MacDonald and his few followers were repudiated by the Labour party and had nowhere else to go. The Conservative party under Baldwin was content to accept the facade of a National Government under MacDonald, but it was in fact the party in power. MacDonald remained Prime Minister until 1935, when Baldwin succeeded him, but during his last few years he was failing badly, and Baldwin was leader of the Government in all but name. He was the sort of man who was content to accept such a situation, for few modern Prime Ministers have had less ambition.

The National Government greatly strengthened their position by holding an early election in the autumn of 1931, "agreeing to disagree" on the subject of tariffs. They won an overwhelming victory, with 554 seats, of which 473 were Conservative. The Liberals won 72 seats, but were unable to exploit their apparent advantage over Labour since they were divided into three groups; those under Sir Herbert Samuel, who opposed protection and finally withdrew in 1932; those under Sir John Simon, who accepted protection and stayed in the Government; and Lloyd George, with three members of his family, who remained independent. The Labour party won only 52 seats, and all but one of the ex-ministers were defeated. Their situation was as bad as that of the Liberals in 1918, except that they had no competition for the role of official Opposition. The real nature of the Government was seen in the substitution of Neville Chamberlain for Snowden at the Exchequer, and the adoption of protection.

As Chancellor of the Exchequer Neville Chamberlain was responsible for three innovations in policy: protection, a managed currency, and low interest rates; the first two have lasted until now and the third for two decades. The Import Duties Act of 1932 extended protective tariffs beyond the existing safeguarding duties to cover three-quarters of Britain's imports. It was followed in the same year by the Commonwealth Economic Conference at Ottawa, where a series of bilateral trade treaties were signed between Britain and the dominions, in which, by the principle of imperial preference, a proportion of British trade was diverted from foreign to imperial markets. Also in 1932 Chamberlain set up the Exchange Equalization Fund, allowing the government to intervene in the market to maintain the value of the pound at its new level, another step away from nineteenth-century economic ideas. In June 1932 the bank rate was reduced to 2 percent, marking further encroachment by the Treasury on what had been the preserve of the Bank of England. This bold action enabled Chamberlain to refund the national debt over the next four years, i.e., to float new loans at lower rates to pay off the old ones, at an annual saving of £55.5 million to the British Exchequer.

The major social legislation of the National Government was Chamberlain's Unemployment Act of 1934 which endeavored to take unemployment assistance out of range of politics and local authorities by assigning it to the new, independent Unemployment Assistance Board. The National Government also made empirical use of state intervention by setting up two public bodies—the British Overseas Airways Corporation and the London Passenger Transport Board—to take over regulation of transport in two important areas formerly under private control. Other examples of state intervention and the consequences of the cheap-money policy we will examine in the next chapter.

The interwar period had seen important developments in the evolution of the Commonwealth. Centripetal forces seemed to govern Commonwealth affairs during the last years of World War I, and the first years of the peace when the dominion prime ministers had participated in the Imperial War Cabinet and the Imperial Peace Delegation. Thereafter, the Dominion prime ministers became absorbed with domestic problems and had little time for imperial affairs. There was some criticism from Canada and South Africa of the plan to have an imperial delegation at the Washington Naval Conference of 1922, and a direct rebuff from those dominions to Britain's call for support at Chanak. As a result of the attitudes of Canada, where Mackenzie King had succeeded Meighen; South Africa, where Hertzog had succeeded Smuts; and Ireland, where Cosgrave, a one-time rebel, was prime minister from 1922 to 1931, the Commonwealth developed in a centrifugal direction. The Imperial Conference of 1926 adopted the famous Balfour Declaration, which stated that Britain and the dominions were "autonomous Communities within the British Empire, equal in status, in no way subordinates one to the other . . . , though united by a common allegiance to the Crown, and freely associated as members of the British Commonwealth of Nations." Some of the dominions had already begun to implement this view by appointing their own diplomatic representatives abroad (Ireland took the lead by appointing an ambassador to the United States in 1924) and by signing treaties independently. The legal implications of the Balfour Declaration were spelled out in the Statute of Westminster of 1931, which defined the crown as the symbol of the free association and asserted that no British law would be binding on a dominion without its own consent.

In 1931 De Valera returned to active politics and to office in Ireland and carried Irish independence a step further by abolishing the oath of allegiance, downgrading the office of governor-general, and establishing separate Irish citizenship. He also refused to pay the land annuities arising from the Land Purchase Acts of a bygone era, on the ground that there was no reason why the Irish should have to buy back their own land from the British. This last action led to a trade war between Britain and Ireland, to their mutual disadvantage, which was finally ended in 1938 when Chamberlain's government came to a settlement with De Valera, accepting a small lump sum payment in lieu of the annuities. Chamberlain also voluntarily abandoned the naval bases Britain had maintained in Ireland since the 1921 treaty, to the great indignation of Churchill, who saw them as essential for the wartime protection of Britain. By this time De Valera had introduced a new constitution asserting Ireland's full sovereignty, but recognizing a vague external association with the Commonwealth. The remaining unresolved difference between Britain and Ireland was partition, to which the Irish Free State—or Eire, as it now called itself—was never reconciled.

India had by now replaced Ireland as the insoluble question in British politics. British rule of India was an anomaly not easily defended in the postwar world. Indians educated in the tradition of Burke and Mill were bound to demand the same freedom and political rights the British cherished, and since early in the century the Indian Congress party had been making this demand. A uniquely Indian character was given the movement by Mahatma Ghandi. This leader rejected force, to which the Irish had resorted, but preached an effective doctrine of civil disobedience. Baldwin, who, in his sympathy with Indian aspirations, was ahead of his party, had appointed the equally sympathetic Lord Irwin (later Lord Halifax) governor-general of India in 1926, and a nonpartisan commission under Sir John Simon to make recommendations on Indian government in 1927. Despite the misgivings of some of his colleagues Baldwin supported the Labour government's Round Table Conference in 1930. The Simon report proposals and two more Round Table Conferences led to the Government of India Act of 1935, the joint work of MacDonald and Baldwin. It introduced virtual responsible government in the provinces but left the federal government, where disputes between Moslems and Hindus were greatest, under British control. The bill was strongly opposed by Winston Churchill, whose differences with Baldwin on the subject had kept him out of the National Government in 1931. He could not forget the "great" days of the British Raj, when he had been a subaltern in the Indian army; but his obscurantism in this respect kept him isolated from the main body of the Conservative party throughout the thirties.

King George V celebrated his silver jubilee in 1935 amid much public rejoicing. He was a popular king, who in his later years had made himself known to his subjects in his successful radio broadcasts. As a young prince he had studied Walter Bagehot's *English Constitution*, and he played to perfection the role of monarch as Bagehot had envisaged it. Although old-fashioned and retiring, he impressed people by his sense of fair play; in the successive political and constitutional crises of the reign, 1911, 1914, 1916, 1921, 1926, and 1931 he always seemed to act with moderation and common sense. When he died in 1936 he was succeeded by his son, Edward VIII (1894–1972), who as Prince of Wales had been popular for quite different reasons. He was more active socially than his father and readier to accept "modern times." He had traveled widely as a royal ambassador and won a world-wide reputation for his geniality and lack of pretension.

In 1935 Baldwin had succeeded MacDonald as Prime Minister and gone to the polls a few months later. The Labour party had recovered slowly since its 1931 setback. The pacifist George Lansbury (1859–1943) had been ineffective as leader of the party in this period of mounting international tension. He was succeeded on the eve of the election by the unpretentious Clement Attlee (1883–1967), a former social worker and wartime army major who had held only a junior office in the second MacDonald government. The left-wing ILP had withdrawn from the party in 1932, politically cutting their own throats. But in the tradition of the Left they had been succeeded by another ginger group, that included such left-wing intellectuals as Stafford Cripps and Harold Laski. Labour improved its position by winning 154 seats in the 1935 election, not counting 4 won by the ILP. But the National Government still had an overwhelming majority with 432 seats, of which 387 were Conservative.

Baldwin's third term was an unhappy one, dominated by the deterioration of international relations, which we will consider in a later chapter. His best known achievement in his last term as Prime Minister was his arranging of the abdication of Edward VIII, who was determined to marry an American divorcée, Mrs. Wallis Simpson. In the government's view the proposed marriage was unacceptable, and public opinion in Britain and the Commonwealth seemed generally to support their attitude. Churchill and Beaverbrook vainly took up the King's cause. The popular young prince of yesteryear gave up his throne to marry the woman he loved, as he told the nation in a touching farewell radio address. As a result his less well-known brother, the Duke of York, succeeded to the throne as George VI (1855–1952). He had served in the navy at the battle of Jutland, and was a king in his father's tradition—a quiet family man with a strong sense of public duty.

In May 1938, following the coronation of George VI, Baldwin retired and was succeeded by his less congenial but more formidable colleague, Neville Chamberlain, who was almost completely preoccupied with foreign affairs and defense for the three long years of his inglorious premiership. Before turning to those somber developments, however, we may consider the condition of Britain in the interwar years.

Chapter Twelve
BRITAIN IN THE INTERWAR YEARS

Britain seemed in the interwar years to drift with no clear sense of direction. The leaders of the two major parties after 1922 showed little imagination and obviously lacked solutions for the problems that faced them. This lack of direction was also characteristic of the country's economy and of its spiritual life. Not until the late thirties is there evidence of the strong sense of values that brought the country into war in 1939 even more united—and certainly more sure of what it was fighting for—than in 1914. The prevailing attitudes during most of this period, however, were disillusionment, discontent, apathy, or an "eat, drink, and be merry, for tomorrow we die" philosophy.

Symbolically the rate of population increase slackened noticeably. The population of Great Britain (excluding Ireland) was 42,769,000 in 1921 and 46,560,000 in 1939, a rate of growth less than half what it had been seventy years earlier. The annual birth rate, which was 35.5 per thousand in 1870–2, had fallen to 15.1 in 1938. But people were living longer; life expectancy, which in 1871 had been forty-one years for men and forty-five for women, had risen in 1937 to sixty-one years for men and sixty-six for women. Child mortality rates had declined dramatically from 140 per thousand in 1900 to 50 per thousand in 1939, but there was a differential of more than two to one between the top and bottom levels of society. Nevertheless, demographers in the thirties worried that Britain's population might decrease rapidly and be halved by the end of the century. This was typical of the pessimism of the period.

Britain's economic position in the years between the wars was paradoxical. The country never seemed to recover fully its pre-1914 economic tempo, but living standards generally improved. Most of the old basic industries— textiles, coalmining, shipbuilding, and, to a lesser extent, production of iron and steel—floundered, exports fell, and the country experienced a high rate of unemployment for the longest period in its history. Unemployment never fell below the million mark between 1921 and 1939. During the years 1921–38 the unemployment rate among insured workers was 14.4 percent compared to a 4.8 percent rate for trade unionists in the period 1883–1914. By 1932 unemployment had increased to almost 3 million, over 22 percent of the work force. From this point there was gradual improvement until the third quarter of 1937, when it was down to 1.4 million, 9.1 percent of the insured population, but the average for the years 1934–9 was 13.3 percent. But it should be noted that because the birth rate had dropped, the ratio of adults to the total population and consequently the size of the prospective work force— increased during these years. Thus in the years 1921–1938 the available work force rose from 45.3 to 47.3 percent of the population, while the percentage actually employed climbed from 41.2 to 43.4 percent.

During the 1920s economic recovery proceeded more slowly in Britain than in any other Western countries. This may have been due to overvaluation of the pound and payment of higher wages than elsewhere in western Europe, but the basic trouble lay in the old export industries. The fall of foreign demand for textiles, coal, steel, and shipping was hastened by Britain's inability to maintain supply during the war; customers inevitably developed their own industrial capacity. Sooner or later British industry had to make the necessary adjustments, and this is just what it was trying to do in the interwar years. The economic trouble spots during this period were the so-called "depressed" areas—South Wales, Clydeside, Tyneside, and other parts of northern England—where the old industries that had been large employers of labor once flourished. Elsewhere new industries were developed to produce consumer goods, mainly for the home market: motor vehicles, radios, electrical appliances, new fabrics, and other items. Indeed Britain's business recovery in the thirties was due largely to this domestic consumer demand. The Midlands and the London area, where the new industries took root, never suffered severely. The industries were profitable, but they did not expand sufficiently to compensate for unemployment in the depressed areas or maintain Britain's prewar proportion of exports. The ratio of exports to national production fell from 33 percent in 1907 to 15 percent in 1938. In 1913 British exports were 13.11 percent of the world's total, but by 1937 had fallen to 9.87 percent. In volume, Britain's exports on the eve of the Second World War were only 67 percent of what they had been on the eve of the first.

There was also a reduction in income from "invisible" exports, such as returns on foreign investment, shipping, and other services. The loss of foreign investments during the war was more than replaced in the years 1919–29, but after that the trend was reversed. By 1938 total overseas investment was down to £3.7 billion, which yielded a £185 million annual return, both figures slightly lower than in 1913. Britain remained the leading shipping nation in the world, but she only just managed to maintain her prewar level of earnings, and her share of the world's carrying trade was reduced. London continued to be an important international financial center, but never regained prewar eminence; and earnings in this area dropped considerably in the 1930s.

Despite the fall in visible and invisible exports Britain maintained a higher volume of imports than before 1914. This was in large part made possible by the fortunate fall in world commodity prices, which meant that it took a smaller quantity of British exports to buy the same amount of imports as before the war. The most significant change, however, was that the ratio of Britain's exports and imports to the national income was halved since 1914, for despite stagnation in exports and chronic unemployment in the depressed areas, it was calculated that Britain's national income in constant prices increased 40 percent between 1914 and 1939. Real wages also rose, although not as rapidly as national income, the 44- to 48-hour week was now the norm, and by 1939 more than half the lower salaried labor force received paid holidays. The interwar years were not bad for those in employment and even those out of work were better off financially than the poorer-paid workers before 1914. It was reckoned that by 1937 between 5 and 6 percent of the national income had been redistributed from rich to poor through taxation. By 1939 an annual amount of £10 a head was being spent on social services, including education.

The heaviest burden of unemployment was psychological. The dole kept body and soul together, but at a lower standard than the rest of the nation; and the "means test" subjected people to the harassment of petty officials. Moreover, in the depressed areas unemployment was long-term. In 1936, for instance, 52,900 men had been out of work for more than five years, 205,000, for two years or more. In some parts of the country many young people had never worked. In 1934 67.8 percent of the insured workers were unemployed in Jarrow and 61.9 percent in Merthyr, whereas in Greater London the figure was only 8.6 percent and in Birmingham, 6.4 percent. In 1937, a year when the recovery suffered some recession, the unemployment rate as a percentage of insured workers was 23.6 percent in Northern Ireland; 22.3 percent in Wales; 13.8 percent in Northern England. In the Midlands and the south of England it only ranged from 6 to 8.2 percent.

There was still much poverty in Britain, but sociological studies in York and London in the 1930s, when compared with results of surveys at the turn of the century, indicated that the proportion of the population below the poverty line had been reduced by a third or more. But B. Seebohm Rowantree, who had conducted both the York surveys, argued that since the standard of living of the community as a whole had risen significantly in the intervening third of a century that in fact the proportion of the population living below a meaningful poverty line was really greater.

A dietary survey of the population conducted in the thirties by Sir John Boyd Orr found that 10 percent (20 percent of the children) in England were badly fed and that half were underfed. This was due in part to unwise spending. When life was drab it was always a temptation to splurge on chips and ice cream instead of buying less tasty but more nourishing foods. The plight of the depressed areas in those sad years, however, is better described in contemporary literature than in statistics. It was vividly portrayed by such authors as W. Greenwood in *Love on the Dole* (1933), J. B. Priestley— a latter-day Defoe or Cobbett— in *English Journey* (1933), and George Orwell in *The Road to Wigan Pier* (1937).

There is no single or simple explanation for Britain's economic recovery in the 1930s. The ideas of the economist J. M. Keynes were being discussed, but his definitive treatise, *The General Theory of Employment, Interest, and Money*, was not published until 1936. Some of the actions of the National government accidentally coincided with his theories, but insofar as they followed any policy it was a more old-fashioned and orthodox one of budget-balancing. The lowering of the bank rate was helpful, but it was done to facilitate debt conversion; economic historians do not regard it as a major factor in recovery. For instance H. W. Richardson writes: "Recovery began under its own momentum; cheap money merely helped it run smoothly."[1] Devaluation in 1931 gave British exports a temporary advantage until the dollar was devalued two years later. More significantly, abandonment of the gold standard led to new ways of maintaining exchange stability and removed the necessity for high interest rates to protect exchange reserves. Nor do economic historians consider that the new protective tariff much affected recovery. Most of the new industries were already protected by the earlier safeguarding duties. The tariff may have encouraged the iron and steel industry, but any gain there was balanced by a corresponding loss to the industries it supplied. They therefore conclude that the influence of the new tariff was marginal, except that it diverted some of Britain's trade into Commonwealth channels.

The Keynesian prescription for recovery included heavy government expenditure on public works, but the National government made no attempt to embark on a large-scale program, as Lloyd George had been prepared to do in 1929. The railways and London Transport received some assistance and a loan was made to the Cunard Line for completion of the *Queen Mary*,

[1] *Economic Recovery in Britain, 1932–1939* (London, 1967), p. 206.

to retrieve the North Atlantic blue ribbon for Britain. The government tried with limited success to persuade industries to move into the depressed areas. Official encouragement was given to construction of new steel mills, one of which was built at the government's urging in depression-ridden Ebbw Vale. In an effort to encourage agriculture, marketing boards were set up, farmers subsidized and quotas imposed on foreign imports, the result was some increase in production in the thirties, although agricultural employment continued to fall. The government was criticized for spending money to bolster agriculture when the world was overstocked with cheap food. But the policy paid unexpected dividends in the next decade when German submarines again threatened the country with starvation. The government had no master plan, but was becoming ipso facto more involved in the economy. Planning indeed was in the air and by no means confined to the Socialists. In 1931 an anonymous group of academics, professionals, and businessmen formed a body called Political and Economic Planning, which published a book called *The Next Five Years: An Essay in Political Agreement.* Young Conservatives such as Harold Macmillan (1894–), author of *Reconstruction: A Plea for a National Policy* (1933) and *The Middle Way* (1938), sought to persuade their party to use the power of the state to help capital and labor work together to promote production.

By 1939 Britain had emerged from the depression—although with a higher unemployment rate than in prewar years—but it could not be said that the government was primarily responsible for recovery.

Economists see recovery in Britain primarily as a concomitant of the business cycle, although its speed and direction may have been governed by a variety of factors, accidental and otherwise. "Rising real incomes for those in work, gains from the terms of trade, the stabilizing effects of government transfer payments, and the effects of taxation raised the share of disposable income in GNP," says Richardson. "Other factors such as shifts in the distribution of incomes, the behavior of consumers in response to falling incomes, and the introduction of new goods influenced the propensity to consume."

The 1930s housing boom is recognized as the greatest spur to economic recovery. Demands for housing was not an effect of low interest rates (although cheap money undoubtedly helped), since it had begun before rates were reduced. Lower construction costs, the rise of real income of those who were employed, and extension to the working class of building-society funds were among the causes of the boom that in turn stimulated the rest of the economy. Most of the construction was unsubsidized residential housing, but slum clearance and housing projects undertaken by local authorities under various acts were also continued. Almost 4 million houses were built in England and Wales during the interwar years. Of these 111,700 were built by local authorities, with the result that some slums were eliminated.

Finally rearmament played an important part in stimulating the economy, with government expenditure rising some £200 million in real terms in the years 1935–38. Had it not been for this increased expenditure the recession that began in late 1937 would undoubtedly have been more severe.

National boundaries make sense in political history where we deal with sovereign entities, but when we come to consider how people lived, their ideas and values, such distinctions are less relevant, especially in modern times. Generalizations about the style of life in the Western world in the twentieth century in terms of national entities are of doubtful significance since changes vary only in detail and degree. The influence of Einstein, Edison, Marconi, and Ford (and with some qualification, of Marx and Freud) have not been interrupted by national frontiers. When we discuss the effect of modern inventions and ideas on everyday life in Britain, the United States, or France, we are speaking about the same phenomena, operating with local variations at varying rates of change.

A major characteristic of the recent history of the western world is the acceleration of the rate of change. Within his lifetime a modern man's world becomes a completely different place. But probably no generation in the last two centuries saw greater change than the one which reached maturity at the end of Queen Victoria's reign. It had been born into a world that knew nothing of motor cars or airplanes, telephones or typewriters, electric light or power, radios, or moving pictures. Yet all these and many other inventions became commonplace throughout the western world in the interwar years, and before they died, members of that generation had come to terms with plastics, television, jet propulsion, computers, atomic power, and the hydrogen bomb. On the other hand if they survived the horrors of two world wars, their lives were prolonged by insulin, penicillin, and numerous other wonder drugs.

There were fewer appliances, telephones, radios, and cars in Britain than in North America in the interwar years, but they were becoming norms by which the new standard of living was measured. With these material changes came a marked change in values and a new informality in dress and conduct that in part sprung from the traumatic experience of the 1914–18 war. Men wore softer collars, softer hats, brighter ties and sweaters, and baggier trousers. Women's hemlines soared in less than a decade from the ankle to above the knee (soon to fall again to an unlovely halfway position). Bathing suits revealed more of the human body than had hitherto been seen outside of the bedroom or the burlesque show. In the twenties women cut their hair short in what was called a boy's bob, threw away their corsets, and wore straight low-waisted dresses and snugly fitting cloche hats that did little to enhance feminine beauty. Many of them smoked and drank in public without any embarrassment and went everywhere unaccompanied, for the war had ended the institution of the chaperone. People talked and wrote of sex with less inhibition as the work of Freud and Havelock Ellis became well known. Contraception became widely accepted (except in the Catholic Church) and smaller families were the norm. In 1937 divorce was finally made a little easier by A. P. Herbert's Divorce Act, which extended grounds for divorce from adultery to desertion and insanity, but divorce was still less common than in the United States.

The twenties were a decade of feverish search for something new and exciting. The demand was stimulated further by the popular press, which was always ready to play up new fashions or trends. Fads swept the country. Among them were Couéism (tell yourself you are better and you will be better), Pelmanism (character reading from handwriting), nudism, horoscope reading, and health and diet cults, some of which have survived or have been revived in our own time. A variety of crazes infected the public, particularly the middle classes, in their search for ways to fill their leisure. Bridge, mah jongg, monopoly, crossword puzzles, and other games were taken up with varying degrees of enthusiasm, and in some cases have remained popular.

The twenties was known as the Jazz Age. The fox trot and the Charleston replaced the old-fashioned waltz that had been considered daring half a century earlier. With the disappearance of chaperones public dance halls became popular, especially in Scotland, but they competed with many other forms of entertainment. The "cinema" theatre became universal at the expense of vaudeville and the legitimate stage, and in the late thirties was grossing £40 million a year. Spectator sports became more popular. Greyhound racing was the new rage, which led cynics to say that England was going to the dogs. Betting became the national vice, especially among the working classes, with £30 million a year being sunk into football pools alone by 1936. The pub remained popular as a typically British social institution, but consumption of beer and spirits declined over prewar years partly because of high excise taxes. Heavy taxation had less influence on smoking. Consumption amounted in 1938 to 189 million pounds of tobacco a year (compared to 92 million pounds in 1913).

British radio was unique in having instituted the government-regulated British Broadcasting Corporation. The first director of the public corporation and of the private company that had briefly preceded it was Sir John Reith, who imposed his powerful personality on it for many years to come.

Reith was a Scottish Presbyterian with a strong sense of mission who saw the new medium's potential for good or evil. He was determined to make it an instrument for good as he saw it. No breath of scandal was to touch its employees. The accents of its announcers would be impeccable. Its news service would be fair, authoritative, and devoid of sensationalism. The public was to be given what was good for it rather than what it wanted, and as long as Reith ruled Sunday programs had a distinctly Sabbatarian atmosphere. With Reith's departure on the eve of the war the BBC became less puritanical and more diversified, but the BBC accent gained worldwide recognition with the wartime overseas newscasts.

In terms of circulation the popular press flourished during these years. The Harmsworth brothers, who had pioneered the cheap sensational press before the war, had been rewarded for their accomplishments with the titles of Lord Northcliffe and Lord Rothermere. Northcliffe, the elder, died in 1922, but was succeeded by Rothermere as owner of the *Daily Mail* and other papers. He and Max Aitken (Lord Beaverbrook), owner of the *Daily Express*, made a sort of alliance to buy up many provincial papers. Some were sold to the Berry brothers, who became owners of the *Daily Sketch* and the *Daily Telegraph* and in return received titles as Lords Camrose and Kemsley. J. S. Elias (Lord Southwood), who made Odhams Press another giant of the industry, bought the *Daily Herald*, the Labour party's paper, when it was in difficulties, but agreed to let it remain Labour-oriented. In the 1930s the popular papers began an absurd and costly competition to bribe readers to boost their circulation (and consequently their advertising revenues), which led the *Herald* and the *Express* across the 2 million mark. The way politicians handed out titles to the irresponsible press barons who owned these popular papers—none of whom, except Lord Beaverbrook in his old age, did anything noteworthy for his country—attests unpleasantly to the influence with which they were credited.

Most of the Liberal papers went to the wall in those days with the exception of the *News Chronicle*, an amalgamation of two Liberal papers, and the *Manchester Guardian*, one of the few provincial papers with a national readership. *The Times* was rescued from the Northcliffe estate and regained its independence under the editorship of the controversial Geoffrey Dawson, who in the 1930s became the archpriest of appeasement.

In contrast to the mass press, which aimed at entertaining rather than informing its readers, *The Times*, *Telegraph*, and *Guardian* remained serious daily newspapers. There was also a select group of informed journals of opinion, some of them with long histories, which catered to a more discriminating readership, weeklies such as the *Economist*, *Spectator*, *New Statesman*, *Observer*, and *Times Literary Supplement*, as well as many smaller and more specialized periodicals.

There was no decline in intellectual creativity in the interwar years. The leading name in science was that of Ernest Rutherford (1871–1937), a poor New Zealand boy who had come to the chair of physics at Cambridge via McGill and Manchester universities, but he was only one of the pioneers in atomic physics at the Cavendish Laboratory in Cambridge. Sir James Jeans and Sir Arthur Eddington popularized astronomy and incidentally disputed the supposed incompatibility of science and religion. Julian Huxley and J. B. S. Haldane wrote about biology for educated readers. The most distinguished philosophers were Bertrand Russell (1872–1970), who applied mathematical principles to that discipline, and Ludwig Wittgenstein (1889–1951), who studied the philosophical implications of language; while, as we have seen, the most imaginative economist—in an age when the dismal science flourished—was J. M. Keynes. Awards of peerages were not confined to press barons and successful businessmen, and the work of Rutherford and Keynes was recognized by the granting of titles, but Russell disdained the one he had inherited from his grandfather, the nineteenth-century prime minister

Many leading prewar literary figures, such as George Bernard Shaw, Thomas Hardy (1840–1928), H. G. Wells (1866–1946), John Galsworthy (1867–1933), and Arnold Bennett (1867–1931), survived into the twenties; others, who had begun to write just before the war, such as E. M. Forster (1879–1970), D. H. Lawrence, and Aldous Huxley, now reached their prime.

The Edwardian novelists had enjoyed a freedom unknown to the Victorians but D. H. Lawrence (1885–1930) and James Joyce (1882–1941), went further in treating sex with a frankness that in Lawrence's *Lady Chatterley's Lover* (1928) and Joyce's *Ulysses* (1917) required first publication in Florence and Paris respectively. The general tone of postwar literature was a questioning of old values and a defiance of old conventions. This was the attitude of writers associated with Bloomsbury, such as Virginia and Leonard Woolf (1882–1941 and 1880–1969), and Lytton Strachey (1880–1932), the popular satirizer of the Victorians. The American-born T. S. Eliot (1888–1965) became the leading poet of the era with *The Waste Land* (1922) and other poems. He was also a critic of the age in which he lived, but one who turned to religion for inspiration. The wittiest commentator on upper-class society was the Catholic novelist Evelyn Waugh, whose *Vile Bodies* (1929) was first in a series of devastating social satires. J. B. Priestley's *Good Companions* (1929) and *Angel Pavement* (1930) were popular novels in the Dickensian tradition. Somerset Maugham's early work caught the disillusionment of the twenties. The list of successful British novelists of this period is seemingly endless.

Although nominally still a Christian country, England was predominantly secular in outlook and only a minority of the English were churchgoers. Three-quarters of the population had been baptized in the Church of England, but less than 3 million in England and Wales were communicants in the early twenties. Nearly 2 million were enrolled in free nonconformist churches, while the number of Roman Catholics in Great Britain was estimated at 2.5 million.

Although the Anglican Church remained the established church of England and continued to show signs of vitality, it was disestablished in Wales. The nonconformist churches had suffered most in vitality and membership, but the three largest Methodist churches in England reunited in 1932, while the bitter divisions among Scottish Presbyterians were happily brought to an end in 1929 by reunion of the Free Church with the Church of Scotland. The Roman Catholic Church was the only one to grow in numbers, with continued conversions from Anglicanism and immigration from Ireland. Ultra-Protestant tradition sprang to life to defeat an Anglican attempt in 1927–28 to reform the official Prayer Book of the Church of England in a Catholic direction, probably the last occasion on which Parliament settled a purely religious question. With such exceptions as Archbishop Temple (1881–1944) Anglican leaders were concerned primarily with keeping their church running smoothly. But a militant minority sought without altogether happy results to develop its sense of social responsibility at the time of the general strike, when Church support did little to help the miners. The churches had difficult adjustments to make in these years, but it would be a mistake to think that religion was stagnant or dying out.

The Jewish population in the early twenties was about a quarter of a million. Some British Jews migrated to Palestine, but in the thirties German Jews, including many distinguished scholars and artists, fled to England. Reaction to the barbarous treatment of Jews by the Nazis undoubtedly reduced the latent anti-Semitism that had continued to exist in England, and their presence helped remind the British public of Nazi iniquities.

High hopes for improved public education, stimulated by Fisher's Education Act of 1918 and the Hadow Report of 1926, were partly frustrated by budget cuts in 1921 and 1931, and enforcement plans for compulsory school attendance up to age fifteen failed to materialize. In the early twenties less than 13 percent of the children continued school on a full-time basis beyond the elementary level, and less than 5 percent of those leaving secondary schools went to the university. A sharp division remained between private schools (the most famous of which as we have noted were called "public schools") patronized by the upper and upper middle classes and state-financed schools serving the mass population, and thus the difference in accent between classes was in large part preserved. Nevertheless educational facilities continued to expand. The number of secondary schools rose by 50 percent in the years 1920–31, and the number of free places in these schools was increased.

New university colleges were founded at Swansea (1920), Leicester (1921), Exeter (1922), and Hull (1928), and additional state university scholarships were created to enable poorer students to attend a university. Perhaps the most significant development in English education in this period was reorganization of the state system to divide elementary from secondary schooling when students reached age eleven. "Modern schools" were created for children who did not want or were not qualified to go to grammar or technical schools.

As with any historical period generalizations about the interwar years are dangerous and open to dispute. But there were notable differences between the twenties, a decade of disillusionment and cynicism, and the thirties, when idealism returned. Along with widespread concern in the thirties with domestic social problems came a wave of pacifism, to be replaced by an equally strong wave of revulsion at Fascist excesses that in 1939 led Britain into another war.

Chapter Thirteen
THE PATH TO ARMAGEDDON

On the surface Britain's position in the world after 1918 was strong. With the new mandated territories in Africa and the Middle East, the British Empire and Commonwealth had reached its territorial maximum. Maps of the world were dominated by the British Empire, colored in red. Few people in those years could have imagined how transitory all this was to be, for it was an empire on a shoestring, and once the string snapped it would quickly break up. There were plenty of international difficulties and differences to be ironed out, but compared to the decade before 1914 (or that prior to 1939) there was little foreign menace to Britain in the twenties. The German navy was scuttled at Scapa Flow, the German army reduced to 100,000 men, and the German economy temporarily in chaos. Italy, a former ally, seemed to be busy putting her own house in order under a young dictator, Benito Mussolini (1883–1945), Britain so far regarded with indulgence. Soviet Russia it is true, was viewed with some suspicion because of the Comintern's avowed support of international revolution, but as yet that country was clearly preoccupied with colossal internal problems. The United States and Japan were the only naval powers capable of challenging Britain. But both had been allies, and war with the former was inconceivable. The latter was remote and could attack Britain only on the other side of the world. The Washington Treaties of 1922 seemed to settle problems in this area. In the twenties Britain had more differences with France, her chief ally, than any other country—over some of the peace terms, over reparations and war debts, over Turkey in 1922 and French occupation of the Ruhr in 1923—but their basic entente was never repudiated.

The future threat of air power to Britain's insular position was not yet apparent in the twenties. Apart from the interminable problem of reparations, diplomatic talk was mostly about new instruments for security to bolster the League Covenant and ways and means of reducing armaments. Public

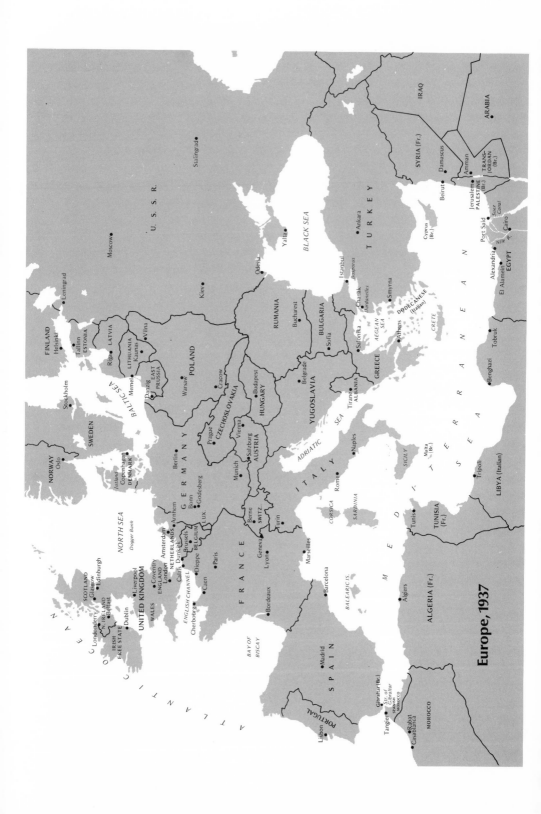

Europe, 1937

opinion tended to regard the League of Nations as a guarantee of peace, without reflecting that the League could stop an aggressor only by the threat of military intervention. Moreover, all the great powers were never in the League at once. Germany was in it only from 1925 to 1933; Russia did not enter until 1934; the United States did not join at all. The League had no serious testing in the twenties, and some diplomats evidently did not take seriously its clumsy machinery for preventing conflicts.

The World Disarmament Conference that opened in Geneva in 1932 had been seven years in the planning stage. By the time it opened it was clearly doomed to failure, although it continued to meet for some months after Germany's withdrawal in late 1933. By this time the world outlook had been completely transformed from what it had been in the twenties. Up until 1931 there was a natural tendency to look back to 1918–19, but from 1933 onward men began to look forward pessimistically to the date as yet unknown of the new Armageddon.

In the autumn of 1931 the Japanese invasion of Manchuria posed what in retrospect is often considered the first serious challenge to the League of Nations and the first step down the slippery incline that led to war in 1939. This view may be an exaggeration, but 1931 was certainly a turning point in the international climate, which from that time on grew progressively stormier. The new Nationalist government of Chiang Kai-shek had been recognized by Britain in 1927, but in 1931 it had antagonized all the treaty powers by unilateral abrogation of extraterritorial privileges of foreigners while negotiations on the matter were still in progress. Not unnaturally, Chinese nationals resented the privileged position of foreigners, and the Japanese in particular came under attack. Incidents in Manchuria gave the Japanese military an opportunity to seize the initiative from the pacific civilian element who had directed Japanese affairs in the twenties. The result was Japanese occupation of Manchuria, where they set up a puppet govern-ment.

China appealed to the League of Nations, which with the United States sought to settle the matter on a friendly basis. At this stage there was still a certain sympathy for Japan in Britain and the United States and a hope that differences between China and Japan might be settled amicably. Neither Britain nor France, the only strong nations in the League with interests and naval power in the Pacific, had any intention of using force to settle the dis-pute. The United States was equally anxious for a settlement, but Stimson, the American Secretary of State, and Simon, the British Foreign Secretary, acted at cross purposes and misunderstood each other's position. Simon was a cold man who alienated most of his own countrymen and could scarcely be expected to win the confidence of foreigners. The League of Nations delayed having to act by appointing a commission of inquiry under the chairmanship of Lord Lytton, which did not report until a year later. Japan had meanwhile compounded her first offense by an attack on Shanghai, and the bombardment of Nanking. On the basis of the Lytton report the League of Nations condemned the Japanese invasion of Manchuria, but took no steps to implement sanctions. Britain's inaction during the crisis was unheroic but not surprising in view of economic difficulties at home, lack of concern on the part of other nations, the geographical remoteness of the war, and Japan's naval superiority in the Pacific. In the eyes of the world, however, the League had suffered its first serious setback.

Nevertheless, Britain had long-standing economic ties with China and was unwilling to be shut out by Japan. As a result British relations with Japan remained tense throughout the decade. A special British mission to the Far East in 1935 helped China reorganize her currency, but failed to make any impact in Tokyo or Washington. The military and pro-Fascist elements in Japan were in the ascendant and showed their attitude in 1936 by denouncing the Washington naval agreement and signing the Anti-Comintern Pact with Nazi Germany. The situation further deteriorated with renewed Japanese aggression against China in 1937, and it preoccupied the British government more than the press or the public. The completion of the major naval base at Singapore (construction of which had been suspended in 1929 by the Labour government) attested to Britain's determination to remain a power in the Far East. Despite Japanese threats Britain allowed Hong Kong to become the main military supply route to China and supplemented it in 1938 with the opening of the famous Burma Road. Japanese harassment in 1939 of the British concession at Tientsin, in northern China forced the British to make some local concessions, but the signing of the Soviet-German pact in August of the same year reconciled the Japanese to accepting the British blockade of Germany when war broke out. Until 1939, and even after the outbreak of war, British Far Eastern policy has been described as "a holding operation, a policy of refusing to surrender vital interests but not to the point of war, of attempting to support China in an unspectacular way, and of showing readiness to negotiate with Japan over marginal points of friction."[1] Attempts to enlist American support or cooperation were generally unsuccessful. Britain's efforts to maintain a position in the Far East should be kept in mind when assessing her foreign policy in Europe during these years.

Early in 1933 trouble appeared much closer to home. Adolf Hitler (1889–1945) and his Nazi party, with their racism, ultranationalism, and glorification of militarism and war, came to power in Germany. Hitler's *Mein Kampf* might have been dismissed as the ravings of a madman, but there he

[1] W. N. Medlicott, *British Foreign Policy Since Versailles*, 1919–1963 (London 1968,), p. 164.

was: leader of potentially the strongest nation in Europe. He very quickly consolidated himself as absolute dictator with most of his opponents in prison or exile. Hitler kept his promise to repudiate the Treaty of Versailles, eliminate the Jews, and pull Germany out of the depression by putting her back to work. At first he took a soft line in foreign affairs, saying all he wanted was peace and equality. Italy, France, and England sought to conciliate him with the apparently innocuous Four-Power Pact that promised some reconsideration of the peace treaties, but it was looked upon with suspicion in Eastern Europe.

England was confused. The very people who were most likely to be revolted by Hitler's barbarous political philosophy were most conscious of the justice of some of Germany's grievances. On the other hand those who in 1918 would probably have been rapidly anti-German were now apt to see Germany as a protection against the Communist menace. It took time for both elements to realize that Nazi Germany was a direct threat to Britain. For the time being the Left tended to remain pacifist and insisted on disarmament in the face of growing dangers. In an overpublicized undergraduate debate the Oxford Union passed by a large majority a resolution that under no circumstances would they fight for king and country. A Conservative seat was lost in a by-election in East Fulham by a candidate who advocated rearmament. Beverley Nichols' best-selling *Cry Havoc* (1933) persuaded readers that war was stirred up by armament manufacturers. Antiwar novels and plays such as *All Quiet on the Western Front* and *Journey's End* (both published in 1929) were in vogue. But at the same time a pathetic faith was put in the League of Nations, as if it could prevent war without having the military resources to do so. The government gradually and reluctantly began to recognize the necessity of rearming, and in 1934 the first tentative steps were taken. The Labour party continued its contradictory policy of supporting the League while opposing rearmament, arguing that it would not trust arms in the hands of its political opponents.

In 1934 the French Foreign Minister Barthou traveled extensively in Eastern Europe in search of an Eastern Locarno. In October he and King Alexander of Yugoslavia were assassinated, an event that made people uneasily recall 1914. Nazi intrigues in Austria led to the murder of Chancellor Dollfuss, but a premeditated Nazi coup was foiled as Mussolini massed troops on the Austrian frontier.

Early in 1935 the British government issued a white paper on the need for increased arms expenditure in the light of Germany's illegal rearmament. Hitler now openly repudiated the armament restrictions of the Versailles Treaty and announced the existence of a new German air force and the adoption of military conscription. Britain, France, and Italy met at Stresa to condemn Germany's unilateral action, but a few months later Britain and Germany signed a surprising naval treaty in which Germany accepted a limitation of 35 percent of Britain's naval strength but was allowed equality in submarines. The French, who had taken the opposite line by concluding a mutual-assistance pact with Russia, were shocked at the step taken by their old ally behind their backs. The British ministers argued that it was better to know where they stood vis-à-vis German naval power and described the treaty as "a realistic contribution to peace."

In the summer of 1935, with a crisis in Abyssinia well above the horizon, the League of Nations Society circulated what they called a "Peace Ballot," which received an astonishing eleven and a half million responses. Eleven million supported British membership in the League, ten million approved use of economic sanctions against an aggressor, and 6.7 million favored military sanctions. Five weeks later Sir Samuel Hoare, the new Foreign Secretary, told the House of Commons that if necessary Britain would support collective League action against Italy if she invaded Abyssinia (now officially known as Ethiopia), and in September he reiterated this policy at Geneva. Italy, a latecomer in the race for empire in Africa, had long been interested in Abyssinia, which was bordered by two Italian colonies. Mussolini now made a border incident the occasion for declaring war and invading Abyssinia in October. Opinion in Britain and indeed in the government was divided. There were those who wanted to use the League machinery of collective security against Mussolini and those who felt Europe was more important, that it would be foolish to break up the Stresa front and drive Mussolini into the arms of Hitler. Moreover, Laval, the French Foreign Minister, had been making approaches to Mussolini in the spring. Britain and France vacillated between two extremes. They first threatened Mussolini by agreeing to a League imposition of economic sanctions and then tried to buy him off by a secret deal at the partial expense of Abyssinia. This was the infamous Hoare-Laval plan of December, which, when leaked to the press, was loudly repudiated by the public. The uproar led to the enforced resignation of Hoare. Italy was antagonized, but not stopped, by ineffective economic sanctions. Eden, the new Foreign Secretary, was prepared to include oil sanctions, but the French stalled; the failure of the President of the United States to do more than make moral appeals to the American oil companies made the success of oil sanctions unlikely. The final outcome was a complete Italian victory in Abyssinia, the general discrediting of the League of Nations and the emergence of the Rome-Berlin Axis.

The preoccupation of Britain, France, and the League of Nations with the Italo-Abyssinian war led to German reoccupation of the Rhineland, in defiance of the treaties of Versailles and Locarno, a year earlier than Hitler had intended. France and Belgium demanded sanctions against Germany, but Britain declined to take such a strong line, knowing the public—and the Labour party—would be opposed and that the French were divided over their government's position. Hitler was not yet ready for war, and in retrospect, it is easy to say this would have been the best moment to topple him. But it was not an issue on which to rally the people, who were inclined, like Eden's taxi driver, to think that Jerry might do what he wanted "in his own back garden."

Within three months of Italy's conquest of Abyssinia civil war broke out in Spain. Germany and Italy immediately came to the support of Generalissimo Francisco Franco, the right-wing rebel leader, while Soviet Russia gave assistance to the left-wing government. Britain persuaded France to help promote a policy of nonintervention to which the other powers paid lip service; but foreign aid continued despite Anglo-French efforts. There were long, drawn-out negotiations with Italy, leading eventually to the Anglo-Italian Agreement of April, 1938. Britain agreed to recognize Italy's position in Abyssinia, and Italy undertook to withdraw her "volunteers" from Spain, but this did not take place until the following year, by which time Franco was victorious.

The Abyssinian war and, even more, the Spanish civil war, changed the attitude of the British Left to foreign affairs. At the Labour party's annual conference in 1935, a resolution in favor of sanctions against Italy was carried on pressure from the outspoken union leader, Ernest Bevin, over the protests of the party's pacifist leader, George Lansbury, who then resigned. The parliamentary party, however, perversely continued to oppose the government's rearmament program until 1937, when they merely abstained from voting. The Spanish civil war was probably the chief cause of the Left's new militancy. It proved to them that Fascism could be defeated only by force, but they had no faith in the government's ability or willingness to follow this course. Many Labour supporters, however, joined the International Brigade in Spain.

In the spring of 1937 the ailing Baldwin finally retired. His record in foreign affairs was uninspiring, but he was less guilty than some of his critics claim. He was concerned about rearmament, but he failed to give strong enough leadership or alert the country sufficiently to the crisis it faced. As far back as 1933 the National government had recognized Germany and Japan as major threats, but until 1935 they failed to give the country a proper lead on the need for rearmament. Even then, Baldwin had to promise that it would not be very large and that there would be no conscription. Since the Labour party opposed even this limited armament program the only added pressure came from Winston Churchill and a few independent Conservatives.

Churchill also urged appointments of ministers of supply and defense, but in 1936 the government agreed only to appoint a minister of defense coordination. Chamberlain vetoed the appointment of Churchill, the obvious choice, fearing he would antagonize Hitler (not to mention his prospective Cabinet colleagues). In 1936 Britain was still spending only half as much on armaments as Germany, and too much of the aircraft appropriation was spent on bombers instead of fighter planes. But the invention of radar in 1935 by R. Watson Watt, a British scientist, and the development of an improved fighter plane, the Spitfire, revolutionized air defense and made it possible to protect Britain when war came. In 1937 Chamberlain introduced a special tax on armament profits and began to borrow money for additional armament expenditures. In the following year the government set out to direct industry and labor into armaments production.

Baldwin's successor was Neville Chamberlain, the last of the three members of his family, whose name had been famous for half a century, but the only one to become Prime Minister. Joseph, his father, might have succeeded Gladstone in 1894 had he remained loyal to his leader; Austen, his half-brother, would have succeeded Lloyd George in 1922 had he *not* remained loyal to the little Welshman. Although only a few years younger than Baldwin, Neville Chamberlain was more sure where he was going, but it turned out to be in the wrong direction. He was businesslike in promoting rearmament, but he was not prepared, as Hitler was, to sacrifice butter for guns. He anticipated that Britain's basic rearmament would be completed by 1939, but time was not entirely on his side. In the meantime his policy was appeasement. He made every reasonable concession, hoping the dictators would prove to be reasonable men. This policy was inherited, not new, but Chamberlain pursued it more vigorously. When an initial overture to Germany failed he turned to Italy, but the price of the Anglo-Italian agreement of 1938 was the resignation of Anthony Eden as Foreign Secretary. Eden had no faith in the Italians after his experiences with them in the Spanish Civil War. Moreover, he was annoyed at Chamberlain's refusal to agree with him on the importance of wooing the Americans. His successor, Lord Halifax, distinguished in India for appeasement in the best sense of the word, was more accommodating.

The year 1938 was the beginning of the end. The German occupation of Austria in the spring of that year was a severe blow, but no great surprise. There was little Chamberlain could do except protest, as he did in Parliament. Hitler's annexation of Austria left Czechoslovakia to be crushed between the German pincers. The Nazis immediately started to apply pressure with a propaganda campaign alleging Czech mistreatment of their German-Sudeten minority. The Sudetens had lived just inside the Bohemian frontier for six centuries. They had never been ruled from Berlin, and they were as well treated as any minority in Europe. In a speech in March in the House of Commons Chamberlain announced that Britain would not promise to help France fulfil her obligations to Czechoslovakia. But he added that if war broke out Britain was bound to defend France and Belgium, should they be invaded. In an April speech at Carlsbad, Henlein, the Sudeten Nazi leader, made several extreme demands at Hitler's behest. These included autonomy for the Sudetens and their recognition as Germans. On hearing rumors of a German mobilization in May the French government warned Hitler that France would not desert Czechoslovakia; the British government emphasized that Germany could not rely on Britain's neutrality if there should be a war. For the moment France and Britain appeared to have stopped Germany by their surprisingly resolute action. But Hitler was furious and ordered his generals to prepare for the early destruction of Czechoslovakia.

Despite his show of boldness Chamberlain was unhappy at the risks he had been forced to take in the spring of 1938. He and the French agreed to put pressure on the Czechs to be accommodating. During the summer he proposed that Lord Runciman (1870–1949), a former Cabinet minister, should act as an independent mediator. His choice offered no reassurance to friends of Czechoslovakia. The more Runciman pressed the Czechs, the more the Sudetens, under orders from Germany, raised their terms and Western appeasers began to advise turning over to Germany the Sudeten areas where Germans were in a majority. In fact Hitler had already set October 1 as the date his armies would enter the Sudetenland, and in the meantime Joseph Goebbels' propaganda ministry was manufacturing stories of oppression to justify it. On September 12 Hitler worked his fanatical followers into a frenzy at a giant rally in Nuremberg, and the world waited for the denouement. Hoping to make Hitler see reason, Chamberlain at age sixty-nine braved his first airplane journey for a personal meeting with the dictator at his Alpine retreat in Berchtesgaden. Chamberlain deprecated Hitler's threat of force, but promised to put concrete proposals before his colleagues and the French for a peaceful solution based on Sudeten self-determination. With a good deal of misgiving the Cabinet and the French ministers recommended to the Czechs the transfer to Germany of Sudeten territories where the majority of inhabitants were German, pledging to guarantee what remained of Czechoslovakia. The Czech government was dismayed, but accepted under pressure. Chamberlain flew back to Germany on September 22 to meet Hitler for a second time at Godesberg to give him the news. He was astonished to find that Hitler had raised his demands. He now insisted upon occupying between September 26 and 28 Czechoslovakian territories claimed by Germany, promising a plebiscite afterward.

The five days following Chamberlain's return were without parallel in British diplomatic history. The British and French cabinets were divided, and neither Chamberlain nor Bonnet—France's Foreign Minister and leading appeaser—could persuade his colleagues to accept the Godesberg terms. The decision to refuse was courageous, but as soon as it was made the appeasers attempted to undermine it. After consulting with the French Chamberlain sent Sir Horace Wilson (1882–   ), his personal envoy to Berlin on September 26. Wilson made a final appeal to Hitler for a peaceful settlement, with a warning that Britain would support France in the event of war. Hitler's immediate reaction was negative. At the Sportplatz in Berlin that night he delivered one of his most brutal speeches, with the result that on the following day a state of emergency was declared in Britain and the fleet mobilized. Air raid precautions (ARP) had already been set in motion. Gas masks were being issued, children evacuated from London, and slit trenches dug in the parks. On September 27, ignoring mounting antagonism in the House of Commons, Chamberlain attempted to persuade the Cabinet to put pressure on Czechoslovakia to accept the Godesberg plan, but, led by Halifax, his colleagues resisted despite the warning of the War Office that Britain needed six months to prepare for full-scale war.

That evening Chamberlain made a moving but defeatist broadcast to the public, conveying his deep hatred of war and his readiness to do anything to prevent it. He said he found it "horrible, fantastic, and incredible" that they might have to face war "because of a quarrel in a faraway country between people of whom we know nothing." That same night, however, there were indications that Hitler might be ready to talk, and the next morning the British and French ambassadors in Berlin were on his doorstep. Hitler saw that the game was his, for clearly the British and the French were grasping at straws. On September 28 he invited Chamberlain, Daladier, and Mussolini to meet him in Munich. Chamberlain was giving a despondent account to the House of Commons of all that had happened in the previous week when Hitler's invitation was handed to him. He read it aloud and the House went delirious with relief, except for a few worthy members who sat in silence and consternation.

The following day, September 29, the leaders of the four powers met in Munich—Soviet Russia and Czechoslovakia had been ignored. Under the circumstances it was inevitable the conference would be a sellout, a mere papering over of the Godesberg demands that a few days before had been rejected as unacceptable. The German takeover of the Sudeten territory was to be extended over ten days (October 1 to 10) instead of two. It was to be supervised by an international commission, with representatives of the four powers and Czechoslovakia, which would be responsible for delimiting the territory still in doubt and determining where plebiscites needed to be held. Four major areas, however, were designated for immediate takeover on an agreed schedule. The British and French leaders made it clear to the Czechs that there was no choice and that they were expected to accept, which they did. Perhaps the most bizarre part of the whole proceeding was Hitler's agreement to sign a piece of paper that Chamberlain (without consulting the French) put before him. It stated a mutual desire for closer Anglo-German relations and a determination never to go to war. Chamberlain had been under great pressure and endured exhausting physical strain for a man his age. But critics find it hard to forgive his smug elation on arriving in London, where he told welcoming crowds that he had brought back not only "peace with honor" (as Disraeli had claimed on returning from Berlin), but also "peace in our time." He seemed to forget the fate of Czechoslovakia, which he had sealed. That country had lost 11 million square miles of territory; a population of 3.6 million, of whom 800,000 were Czechs; most of her fortifications; and a large percentage of her basic industries. It may be noted that the British Cabinet, which had thwarted Chamberlain in his pursuit of appeasement in the days after Godesberg, had played no part in the final Munich settlement.

In the view of one British historian "Munich was the greatest moral defeat suffered by Britain in this century." Yet at the time it was welcomed in Britain and the Commonwealth as an escape from a war nobody wanted. The Munich settlement has been defended on the grounds that it would have been wrong to oppose the principles of self-determination upheld by the Allies after the last war; that public opinion in the country and in the Commonwealth would have been divided; and that there would have been insufficient support for fighting on such grounds. It was further argued that Britain and France were not ready for war and that another year was needed to complete Britain's air defenses. There were equally compelling political, moral, and military arguments against the capitulation at Munich—that it had undermined the credibility of the democratic powers and that it was a betrayal of Czechoslovakia, which had been created a sovereign nation by the Allied powers in 1919 and guaranteed by France and Russia. It was also claimed that Hitler was not ready for war in 1938, that his generals were very nervous, and that the extra year allowed him to complete his western defenses known as the Siegfried line and enlarge the German army, which would have to fight on two fronts. Moreover, Czechoslovakia, although a small country, was well armed, highly industrialized, and not easy of access. The major criticism of Chamberlain is not so much that he sought to avoid war by compromise as that he so palpably deceived himself about Hitler. It should have been obvious, had he taken better advice, that Hitler was completely untrustworthy and that all Britain and France had bought at Munich was time, at the terrible price of surrendering the Czechs. Chamberlain's lack of sympathy for Hitler's victims and his self-satisfaction on returning to London after Munich remain as a blemish on his reputation.

The moral argument for Munich is easily disposed of. The Sudeten Germans had for centuries lived within the natural boundaries of old Bohemia (the nucleus of modern Czechoslovakia). Even if there had been a case for their withdrawal from the Czechoslovakian state—which is doubtful—there could be no case for Czechoslovakia's surrender to the unscrupulous bullying of Nazi Germany. Nor could there be any moral justification for turning over Jews, Czechs, and other anti-Nazis living in the Sudeten area to the horrors of a Nazi police state. The political and military arguments were more valid. There is little doubt that in 1938 Britain and the Commonwealth were psychologically less ready for war than they were a year later. Whether a military advantage was gained by the delay remains a matter of speculation. Winston Churchill, among others, was certain no purpose had been served by postponing war; nor did Chamberlain appear to sign the Munich agreement in the belief that he was merely buying a year's time. It is true that British air defenses were improved in this extra year, but six months was lost before essential decisions were taken to increase the strength of the army.

The international commission set up by the Munich agreement proved to be a travesty, for the Germans got their way with everything. Other parts of Czechoslovakia were awarded to Poland and Hungary without consultation with (or protest from) Britain and France; the guarantees in the agreement proved meaningless. Six months later, on March 15, 1939, Hitler occupied Prague and annexed what was left of Czechoslovakia, allowing Hungary to take Ruthenia. In Britain the initial reaction of the government was mild, but indignation in the press and Parliament convinced Chamberlain he must take another course. On March 31 Britain and France dramatically announced a new policy guaranteeing the independence of Poland. This policy was subsequently extended to Rumania, Greece, and Turkey and followed by formal agreements with these countries. Britain and France were at last convinced that Hitler was not to be trusted, that his ambitions were apparently insatiable, and that unless a line was drawn quickly all Europe would soon be under his sway. Alone no state could now resist Germany, not even France, but an alliance of nations still had a chance of success. Had Britain and France realized earlier what they would have to deal with they might have stopped Hitler when he started to rearm, or even as late as 1936 when he reoccupied the Rhineland, but only Winston Churchill and a few other independents had recognized the danger and public opinion was not then prepared to support a policy of preventive force. Now Hitler's perfidy was unmistakable and his terrible persecution of Jews in Germany fully confirmed, as if such confirmation were necessary, the infamy of Nazism. The thought of war after the experience of the last had been so appalling that Britain had been willing to go to extraordinary lengths to avoid it. Now, however, the real significance of Munich was finally clear and for the first time since the advent of Hitler the British government and public opinion were ready to face the future and accept the consequences of resolute action. Indeed from this point to the outbreak of war in September 1939, the main concern of public opinion and of the Labour Opposition was whether the government would stick by its new policy. If any further confirmation were necessary of the aggressiveness of the dictators, they provided it almost immediately with the German seizure on March 23 of Memel, a former German Baltic port, from Lithuania and the Italian occupation of Albania in the week of April 6.

Germany now turned her attention to Poland, demanding the reincorporation into the Reich of the Free City of Danzig and a corridor across the Polish Corridor to link East Prussia with the rest of Germany. Hitherto German-Polish relations had not been bad; after Munich, Germany had even honored a Polish claim against Czechoslovakia. But when the Poles resisted these demands Goebells's propaganda machine began manufacturing evidence of Polish atrocities against Germans to rouse German nationalism and justify new aggression. When Poland showed signs of resisting Germany's demands she then began to receive the full treatment from Germany that Czechoslovakia had endured the previous summer. The British government again sought to avert the coming crisis by urging negotiation. But an air of unreality marked the diplomacy of the summer of 1939, and the British and French fatalistically awaited the inevitable. The Opposition pressed for closer relations with Soviet Russia and the two Western powers made some attempt to do this but the stumbling blocks were mutual distrust and the very real apprehension of Poland and other Baltic countries over allowing Russian troops to cross their frontiers to protect them against Germany. Russia proposed a defensive alliance with military guarantees to designated smaller nations whether they agreed or not. Britain sent a senior Foreign Office official, not a minister, to negotiate, but balked at adopting Russia's suggestion and the talks made little headway. On pressure from the French and in view of the worsening diplomatic situation, the British finally agreed to military conversations with the Russians. On August 21, before any progress had been made, the world was stunned by the announcement of the Soviet-German Nonaggression Pact, which left Poland and her Western allies in a precarious position.

Hitler was ready for war and was determined to destroy Poland. Chamberlain's last-minute attempts to appeal to him were of no avail, but worried those in Britain who feared another Munich. Chamberlain's confidence in Sir Horace Wilson, a treasury official with no diplomatic experience except his role in the Munich debacle, and in the British ambassador in Berlin, Sir Neville Henderson (1882–1942), an arch appeaser inclined to play down any hardening of the British position, gave them good cause for alarm. Hitler was indeed confident that these men, so easily browbeaten the previous year, would again give in, and he was taken aback when on August 23 Henderson flew to Salzburg to deliver a personal letter from Chamberlain warning that Britain would stand by Poland. He rejected British proposals for a truce, but on the 25th of August made counterproposals that Henderson brought back to London.

In the meantime the British Cabinet had taken preliminary measures for mobilization and summoned Parliament to meet on August 24 to pass the Emergency Powers Defense Bill. With the French they had cautioned the Polish government to avoid fresh cause for provocation. On August 28 Henderson returned to Berlin with proposals for British mediation of the differences between Germany and Poland. Germany accepted, but the terms made success unlikely, since the Poles were not given time to send an envoy. At the same time the Germans continued to fabricate atrocity stories. When the Polish envoy failed to arrive by midnight on August 29 Ribbentrop, the German Foreign Minister, declared that he considered Germany's proposals, which he then presented for the first time, to have been rejected. On August 22 Hitler had informed his generals of his decision to fight, although on the 25th he temporarily postponed the date of invasion. By August 28 it was set for September 1, and Britain's eleventh-hour mediation efforts in the final days of August were no more than shadowboxing. Even after the Germans had invaded Poland Britain and France still tried to secure their withdrawal through the intercession of Italy, to the indignation of the House of Commons, where there was much uneasiness at the failure of the government to declare war immediately. On Sunday, September 3, an ultimatum was finally sent which expired at 11 A.M. To the sound of air raid sirens Chamberlain thereupon announced to the House of Commons that Britain was at war. Significantly the French declaration followed several hours later.

The invasion of Poland was the occasion, but not the cause, of the outbreak of the Second World War. There had been much more sympathy for Czechoslovakia, a Western type of democracy, than for Poland, which had a less popular and more autocratic regime. Both the Corridor and the Free City of Danzig were creations of the Versailles settlement that might legitimately have been reviewed; Danzig was a predominantly German city, and the Polish Corridor did cut East Prussia off from the rest of Germany. There had been good reason for setting them up after the German defeat in 1918, but there was also a case for reconsidering them. The Second World War was not fought because Danzig and the Corridor were regarded as sacrosanct, but because the Western powers had come to the conclusion that Hitler could not be trusted, that he was bent on the domination of Europe and had to be stopped. The British people accepted this verdict and remained committed to the destruction of Hitler and Nazism until the task was accomplished.

Chapter Fourteen
THEIR FINEST HOUR

Britain went to war in 1939 in a different frame of mind from that of 1914. On the first occasion war had come almost as a surprise, but the country had faced it with confidence and a sense of exhilaration. In 1939 war was accepted with little fuss and even some relief, after having been so long expected. In 1914 Britain could look back on a century of unprecedented economic expansion and more than half a century of peace with all European powers. In 1939 the horrors of the First World War were still vivid memories, and Britain's economy had never fully recovered from the shock. In 1914 British naval power was at its zenith, and the army had never been as ready to fight a land war. In the interwar years Britain's naval strength had been allowed to decline (although admittedly the threat to her supremacy was less obvious); the army, while much the same size as in 1914 was relatively less well-equipped to fight a modern war. The air force was a new element, whose strength remained to be tested. In 1914 Britain had joined France and Russia after the war had already begun; in 1939 the British declared war ahead of the more hesitant French, while Russia was hostile. Basically, Germany was weaker than in 1914 but her greater preparedness and her superiority in such new weapons as dive bombers and tanks at first tilted the scales in her favor.

To older Britons, like the journalist Sir Philip Gibbs, whose reports were reproduced in the *New York Times*, the early days of the war had a strange, dreamlike quality. A small British expeditionary force crossed the Channel, just as it had done twenty-five years earlier, to take its place on the left flank of the French army. Here the similarity ended, for there was no fighting on the western front during the eight months of the so-called "phony war." The Allies remained passive while the Germans quickly conquered Poland in an alarming demonstration of the new blitzkrieg method of warfare. The subsequent partition of Poland between Russia and Germany and the Russian occupation of the Baltic countries confirmed the fact that Russia was in the enemy camp. When Russia invaded Finland in December Britain and France, having failed the Poles, began to concoct mad schemes to rescue the Finns; but the Finns, despite their heroic resistance, were forced to make peace before any assistance reached them. Lightning German attacks on Denmark and Norway came in April. Norway's resistance provided a chance for the superior Allied naval forces to intervene. But the landing at Narvik was a failure because of German air supremacy. The world was also disturbed by the appearance of a sinister German ally, "the Fifth Column," in this case a band of Norwegian traitors led by Vidkun Quisling, who betrayed the country from within.

The Norwegian disaster was a great shock to the British people, who had been puzzled at the government's failure to help Poland and had seen the opening of the Norwegian theater as the ideal opportunity to strike effectively at Germany. The helplessness of Allied military and sea power in the face of German air supremacy was disillusioning. The government was attacked vehemently in the House of Commons by the Opposition and by Conservative dissentients, led by Leopold Amery, an old Tory imperialist. Amery concluded a biting speech with the words which Cromwell had used to dismiss the Long Parliament: "You have sat too long here for any good you have been doing. Depart, I say, and let us have done with you. In the name of God, go!" The white-haired Lloyd George added his voice to the cry for Chamberlain's resignation, and in the subsequent vote the Government majority was so reduced by Conservative dissentients that the Prime Minister bowed before the storm.

Winston Churchill was now the only man capable of forming a genuinely national government, for Lord Halifax wisely refused to attempt the task. Despite their former hostility to his position on the General Strike of 1926 and the India Act of 1935, the Labour party accepted office under Churchill, whose determination to fight on and will to win was an inspiration for all. He in turn treated them with characteristic magnaminity, giving their leaders important places in the new administration, which enabled them to play important roles in the conduct of the war. These included Ernest Bevin, the hard-headed trade union leader, as Minister of Labour, Herbert Morrison, the irrepressible Cockney, at the Home Office and elsewhere, and Clement Attlee, the dour pipe-smoking "Major," who became deputy Prime Minister. Another newcomer was the dynamic, if unorthodox, Lord Beaverbrook, who, by breaking all the rules and upsetting many of his colleagues, managed to raise the production of aircraft to unprecedented heights. A few months later Eden returned to the Foreign Office, while Lord Halifax, prince of appeasers, meekly went off to be an excellent ambassador in Washington.

Chamberlain accepted office under Churchill, but died some months later. Clearly Churchill's Coalition was formed much more easily and with more good will than Lloyd George's Coalition which Asquith refused to join in 1916. As a result it was a more effective and more united wartime government and Churchill's position as Prime Minister was much stronger than Lloyd George's had been. Churchill set up a small War Cabinet, which included Attlee, Bevin, and Sir John Anderson, a former civil servant, from 1940 and Eden from 1941 to the end of the war, but it never played a major role. Ministers exerted pressure within their spheres, but Churchill virtually ran the war in close consultation with his chiefs of staff and other military and technical advisers, exerting powers similar to those of an American president.

Churchill was sixty-five years old when he assumed office and his past career was not entirely reassuring. He had often been accused of errors in judgement and had not infrequently suffered from his own impetuosity. Nevertheless he immediately proved himself to be just the leader the country was looking for and most doubts quickly evaporated. Despite his age he showed amazing energy throughout the war, keeping a sharp eye on every detail but never loosing sight of the whole picture. His extraordinarily innovative mind was always planning how to beat the enemy, whether it was by the promotion of some new instrument of war, the improvement of efficiency, or the development of grand strategy. A constant flow of queries and orders poured from his office praising, chiding, exhorting, and questioning all those in positions of responsibility in the government or in the forces. Nothing relevant to the waging of the war was beyond his interest, from egg production to the intervention of the atomic bomb. He never allowed anyone to rest, but he inspired great devotion and loyalty in those who worked with him and for him, even though he often drove them up the wrong paths. Never since Chatham had a British statesman shown such a flare for war leadership. Considering his background Lloyd George's achievement may have been the more remarkable, but Churchill, who had a life-long interest in military and naval affairs, took the helm with surer grip. His military experience went back to active service in the Northwest Frontier of India and in the Sudan in the 1890s, but, unlike many soldiers, his mind was always open to new ideas. He had no illusions about the glory of war, which he recognized as a grim necessity and not as something to be welcomed for its own sake, and he was determined to avoid the useless bloodbaths that had characterized the western front in the war of 1914–18.

Churchill's greatest achievement, however, was the moral leadership that he gave to the British people throughout the six long years of his wartime ministry. In innumerable great speeches in the House of Commons and in broadcasts to the country at large and to Britain's friends overseas, he constantly voiced defiance, determination, and hope. The oratory may have been old-fashioned, but it hit the right note; it was noble and inspiring and at the same time down-to-earth. In his first speech after taking office he told the Commons: "I have nothing to offer but blood, toil, tears and sweat." As A. J. P. Taylor has said, this was just what the appeasers feared, but it was what most of his countrymen wanted to hear, and they never looked back.

For a long time, however, the prospects were grim. The very day Churchill assumed office Hitler unleashed his attack on Holland and Belgium, which were quickly overrun. The French Maginot Line was turned and the British army driven back to the sea at Dunkirk. Miraculously the great majority escaped, thanks to the protection of the Royal Air Force, the Royal Navy, and a providential calm in the English Channel. The evacuation of Dunkirk was a masterpiece of improvisation as every available ship and boat in south-eastern England was pressed into service, but Britain's only army lost almost all its equipment. At the end of May the 51st Highland Division and the 1st Canadian Divisions nevertheless were the only fully-equipped divisions left in the country. They were promptly sent to France, but to no avail. On the fall of France in June the British forces had to endure a second if more orderly evacuation, and further loss of precious equipment. The British were accompanied by 20,000 Polish troops and a handful of French who had left on their own despite the surrender of the French government, which had turned down Churchill's offer of a union of the two countries.

The odds were formidable against Britain, her Commonwealth allies, and the Allied governments in exile (of Belgium, the Netherlands, Norway, and Poland) that had joined her with the remnants of their armed forces. Indeed the Allied position looked hopeless. Hitler now controlled all western Europe and his Luftwaffe appeared invincible. The battle for Norway had shown the vulnerability of the navy against land based air power in narrow waters, so a German invasion of England seemed inevitable. Even if, miraculously, it were resisted, what chance would there ever be of toppling Hitler from his commanding position on the European mainland? Russia was still Hitler's ally, and the United States remained wedded to a policy of isolation even though American sympathy and admiration for England were growing. Yet never for a moment did Churchill contemplate suing for peace. In his most famous speech, shortly after Dunkirk, he promised:

"We shall fight on the beaches, we shall fight on the landing grounds, we shall fight in the fields and in the streets, we shall fight in the hills; we shall never surrender, and even if, which I do not for a moment believe, this island or a large part of it were subjugated and starving, then our Empire beyond the seas, armed and guarded by the British fleet, would carry on the struggle, until, in God's good time, the new world with all its power and might, steps forth to the rescue and liberation of the old."

For Britain the supreme test of the war came in the late summer and early autumn of 1940 when Hitler launched an all-out air attack, preliminary to an intended invasion. He failed in his efforts to wipe out British fighter bases in the southeast of England, for the RAF Fighter Command under Air Marshal Dowding was stronger than he anticipated. In the Battle of Britain the RAF destroyed 1733 German planes, mostly bombers. The RAF lost 915 planes, but they were quickly replaced and the majority of the pilots survived, since they came down on English soil. Nevertheless it was a question of how long Britain's small fighter force could keep up the ceaseless battle. In mid-September Hitler gave up the attempt and turned the Luftwaffe instead to night raids on London and other cities that lasted into the spring of 1941. The invasion plans were at first postponed and in October cancelled for the winter, but the British army, supported by a recently recruited Home Guard remained on the alert for many months. The successful outcome of the Battle of Britain guaranteed Britain against invasion for the rest of the war, but the losses and devastation suffered from air raids that winter were very heavy. Of 60,000 fatal civilian casualties suffered during the war one half occurred during the period forever after known as the "Blitz." As $3\frac{1}{2}$ million houses were damaged or destroyed many more civilians were made homeless.

Nevertheless the morale of the people remained amazingly high and their confidence was bolstered by news of surprising victories in the Middle East. Britain still had military forces in Egypt (to protect the Suez Canal), in the protectorates of Palestine and Iraq, and in the East African colonies. These were reinforced by land and air forces under the command of General Wavell. In the course of war five African divisions were also raised in British East and West Africa that contributed to Britain's overall military power. Churchill showed his determination to maintain Britain's position in the Middle East by dispatching an armored brigade from England to Egypt in the summer of 1940. It seemed a foolhardy decision with the threat of the invasion at home, but it paid off: North Africa proved to be a theater where, despite their weakness in numbers, the British and their Commonwealth allies were able to meet the Axis forces with some hope of success.

Having foreseen the fall of France, Italy had declared war in June 1940, and now, with six times as many troops in Libya as the British had in Egypt, she decided to seize the latter. The small British army, however, quickly routed the Italians and chased them hundreds of miles back into Libya as far as the port of Benghazi. Over 100,000 Italian prisoners were taken, with fewer than 500 British and Australian soldiers killed. This reverse forced the Germans to come to the rescue of their Axis partner early in 1941, but at the same time they extended the war into Yugoslavia and Greece (where the Italians had earlier made an unsuccessful attack). The British government made the quixotic decision to send a force of 60,000 men from the Middle East to Greece, but the situation was hopeless. The British were forced to withdraw first from the Greek mainland and later from Crete, with heavy losses. Moreover, this dispersion of their limited forces led to an early reversal when the Germans reached Libya and forced the British to retreat, leaving a beleaguered garrison in Tobruk.

Churchill, whose mother was an American, looked from the beginning to the United States for support and to the day on which that country would ultimately become involved in the war. His strong historical sense made him realize in 1940, when the prospects looked so black, that Britain's hope lay in unforeseen events that might drive the Americans from their chosen path of isolation. He already had the sympathy and moral support of his old acquaintance President Roosevelt, with whom he developed a warm friendship in the course of the war. Although they differed in many respects, each instinctively recognized and appreciated the other's Olympian qualities. In the autumn of 1939 Roosevelt had managed to obtain the amendment of the American neutrality acts to permit British purchase of war supplies; orders were placed on a large scale but with little effect until late 1941, since the American economy was not yet geared to war production. In the summer of 1940 Roosevelt initiated a policy of American aid "short of war" by releasing to Britain half a million surplus rifles for the Home Guard and, a little later, fifty out-of-commission First World War destroyers for the Royal Navy in return for British bases in Newfoundland and the West Indies. Probably more important than the equipment was the precedent, for it indicated the direction in which Roosevelt was moving. In the winter following his re-election, he initiated the much more significant Lend-Lease program. The United States undertook to provide the supplies that were needed for the duration of the war in return for certain restrictions on British exports, which would benefit American competitors. Lend-Lease did not become fully effective until 1942, by which time almost all of Britain's dollar resources had been exhausted, but for three and a half years after that it proved to be an invaluable contribution to Britain's war effort. It was matched by a gift from Canada of one billion dollars plus mutual aid, which on a per capita basis was an even greater contribution than that of the United States.

In the summer of 1941, foiled in his intended invasion of England, Hitler, like Napoleon, turned east and invaded Russia. Churchill, putting aside his long hostility to the Soviets, immediately promised cooperation and aid in fighting the common enemy. Shortly afterward Churchill and Roosevelt held the first of their seven wartime meetings on a warship off the coast of Newfoundland. They agreed on the terms of the Atlantic Charter, a declaration of the principles of international relations on which they hoped to build in the future. More important for the moment, the United States agreed to take over convoy duties in the western Atlantic. In December the Japanese made the war world-wide with their dual attack on Britain and the United States in the Pacific. When Hitler came to his ally's support with a declaration of war on the United States Churchill's dream was realized. From that day he was confident that in the long run victory could be achieved. Immediately, however, the reverses were staggering. While American sea power was decimated by the attack on Pearl Harbor, which was followed by the loss of the Philippines, Britain suffered the losses of Hong Kong, and the Malay States, and the invasion of Burma, which remained a battlefield for the rest of the war.

The Japanese tidal wave was finally brought to a stop with the American naval victories in the Coral Sea and off Midway Island in May and June of 1942, but on other fronts the strategic picture remained black for some months more. With the help of South African and Indian troops the Italian front in East Africa had been routed in the spring of 1941, and the Emperor of Ethiopia returned to his throne. Nevertheless a renewed British offensive in Libya failed, the beleaguered fortress of Tobruk was captured with its garrison, and the German General, Erwin Rommel (1891–1944) pressed into Egypt and by July 1942 had reached El Alamein, sixty miles from Alexandria. In Russia the Germans had surrounded the bastion of Stalingrad and plunged into the Caucasus. The Russians were crying loudly for a second front, but the bloody reverses suffered in a predominantly Canadian probing of Hitler's west wall at the French seaside town of Dieppe in August 1942 proved the time was not yet ripe for an invasion of France. The pendulum of war still had a long way to swing back in the autumn of 1942.

The war at sea remained in doubt to 1943. Until then the submarine menace was a constant threat to Britain's survival. Shipping losses from submarines, surface raiders, mines, and air attack reached an alarming height in the early months of 1941, and imports were reduced to a dangerously low level. The situation became even worse after the entry of the United States into the war as the U-boats extended their operations into the western Atlantic and the Caribbean. Losses reached their peak of 700,000 tons in March of 1943. Then the situation improved as more American and Canadian warships became available and more effective antisubmarine measures were developed. German surface raiders caused some havoc, but the pocket battleship *Graf Spee* had been cornered and scuttled at Montevideo in the early months of the war, and the battleship *Bismarck* was destroyed in May 1941 by planes from a British aircraft carrier after she had sunk the British battle cruiser *Hood*. In 1943 Germany's remaining battleship, the *Tirpitz*, was put out of action by British midget submarines and her remaining battle cruiser, the *Scharnhorst*, was sunk by a British battleship. The Italian navy was crippled by a raid on Taranto harbor in 1940 and in the battle of Matapan in 1941, but British losses in the narrow confines of the Mediterranean were very heavy, and the retention of the island of Malta was something of a miracle. The sinking in December 1941 of a battleship and a battle cruiser by Japanese air power in the Pacific was a further blow to British naval strength and to morale.

It is not surprising that, given her insular position and the obvious obstacles precluding any early return to the mainland of Europe, Britain long pinned her hopes on bombing. Berlin was bombed as early as August 1940, during the Battle of Britain; and in May 1942, under Air Marshal "Bomber" Harris, Bomber Command launched a thousand-plane raid on Cologne, part of an ever-increasing aerial attack designed to bring Germany to a standstill. With the arrival of the U.S. Air Force, around-the-clock bombing of Germany and of German-occupied Europe commenced, but this tremendous effort was both callous and misdirected. Allied losses were very heavy, yet German war production was not seriously interfered with until late in the war. At the time, the British government and undoubtedly most of the people took heart in this bombing offensive as a demonstration that the tide had turned and that Germany, once thought to be supreme in the air, was receiving a richly deserved punishment. After the war, however, it was slowly realized that there had been little justification for the wanton destruction of German cities and their inhabitants. The gigantic production efforts that went into the bombing offensive reduced resources available for the more important production of ships, landing craft, tanks and other equipment needed for the eventual invasion of Europe, and left Britain and her allies with the moral responsibility for having adopted needlessly barbarous methods of warfare.

One of the most striking features of the Second World War after the entry of the United States was the close cooperation between that country and Britain, thanks largely to the understanding between Churchill and Roosevelt and their mutual determination to work together despite real national differences in interests and temperament. Immediately after Pearl Harbor Churchill, with his chief staff officers, set off for Washington to consult Roosevelt about the future direction of the war. A joint strategy of war was initiated, with Germany designated as the primary enemy, and a Joint Chiefs of Staff was set up in Washington. The American army and air force began their great build-up in Britain, which soon assumed the role of a giant aircraft carrier off the coast of Nazi-dominated Europe. There were many differences, but in the end they were generally reconciled. The Americans were anxious to respond to Russian demands for a Second Front, first in 1942 and then in 1943, but Churchill was certain that they did not yet have the resources, and eventually persuaded Roosevelt to undertake a campaign to clear the Axis forces out of North Africa. As a result a combined Anglo-American force under an American commander, General Dwight D. Eisenhower, landed in Morocco and Algeria in November 1942. A previous expedition of British and Free French forces under General Charles de Gaulle had failed in 1940 to win over the Vichy French garrison at Dakar; but now the Vichy French Admiral, Darlan, sensed the way the war was going and ordered the garrison to abandon resistance. Shortly afterward he was shot by an assassin, and eventually De Gaulle emerged as undisputed French leader in the Allied camp. The Germans put up stiff resistance in North Africa, and the Allied army made slow progress into Tunisia. Farther east the British Eighth Army under General Sir Bernard L. Montgomery (1887–), the most distinguished British general to emerge during the war, had routed the Germans under Rommel at El Alamein (October 23–November 4) and chased them back to Tunisia. In the spring of 1943 Allied armies from the east and from the west joined hands and pushed the Germans right out of North Africa. The tide also had turned on the Russian front with the Germans defeat in February at Stalingrad. By early 1943 the Germans had lost the war, but it took them two more years to acknowledge the fact.

Churchill and Roosevelt met in Casablanca in December of 1942 to plan the next stage of the war, the invasion of Sicily, which was successfully accomplished in the summer of 1943. It was followed by the invasion of southern Italy and the surrender of the Italian government. After withdrawing from the toe of the Italian peninsula, the Germans resisted bitterly all the way up the long backbone of the Apennines, and the Allies did not enter Rome until June 1944. Eleven more months of hard fighting awaited them in Italy, but by this time the center of interest had shifted. At the end of November 1943 Churchill, Roosevelt, and Stalin had met in Tehran in Persia. The Western Allies promised a spring invasion of France (Operation Overlord), and Churchill agreed to a scaling down of operations in the Mediterranean. Stalin planned an offensive to be coordinated with the Allied landings and also committed Russia to enter the war against Japan when Germany was defeated.

By this time probably no other country was as fully mobilized as Britain. As A. J. P. Taylor has observed,[1] capital and labor voluntarily accepted a form of war socialism for the duration of the struggle. The overall organization of the home front and the working out of an elaborate manpower budget were accomplished primarily by Sir John Anderson (1882–1958), a former civil servant, who exercised authority second only to Churchill's. As minister

[1] *English History 1914–1945* (New York and Oxford, 1965), p. 507.

of labor, Ernest Bevin effectively protected working-class interests, but persuaded working men and women to accept conscription in the form of job allocation when necessary.

As a result of all this planning the British war effort reached its peak about the end of 1943. Production of planes and ships had approximately tripled since 1939. The working population had reached its maximum of over 22 million, and by 1945 the armed forces had passed the 5 million mark. There was less labor strife than in the First World War and although there was some wasteful overproduction of shells there were no munitions scandals. Despite achievements in production, however, more than a quarter of Britain's military requirements in the last two years of the war were obtained on lend-lease from the United States. Without such aid from the United States and Canada the British war effort could not have been sustained.

Through the influence of the ubiquitous Keynes, the financing of the war was carried out more efficiently than in 1914–1918. A higher proportion of the cost came from taxes and most of the balance from forced and voluntary savings that helped to curb inflation, while rigid exchange controls prevented the flight of capital. As a result of full employment and a fairly effective program of rationing and price control (especially rent control), many of the working classes were better off than before 1939. Average weekly earnings rose by 80 percent between 1938 and 1945. Prices rose only 31 percent in the same period, thanks to increased productivity and government food subsidies. In comparison the standard of living of the upper and middle classes was more drastically affected. A steeply graduated income tax put a ceiling on income, and a 100 percent excess-profits tax largely eliminated war profiteering.

At no time in British history have all classes worked and lived so closely together or shared such a sense of national identity as in these years, but it was a situation that could scarcely outlast the war. There was no class discrimination in air raids, and strangers talked easily to each other as never before about their common experiences. Food supplies remained adequate throughout the war despite the submarine threat until 1943, but meat and dairy supplies were limited and strictly rationed, as were clothes. Queues were a part of everyday life, demonstrating the general belief in fair shares for all and everyone taking his turn. Many consumer goods became very scarce or nonexistent as their production was cut almost in half, and rigid petrol (gas) rationing put an end to private driving. But the government realized the importance of keeping up the public's morale. Adequate supplies of beer, tobacco, and sweets were maintained and the entertainment industries were permitted to remain active. Cinema attendance increased; pubs were fuller than ever, their clientele augmented by thousands of uniformed visitors from overseas, and horse racing survived. Special efforts were made to cultivate the arts as part of the war effort by government subsidies to symphony orchestras and repertory theaters. The BBC catered to millions both on the home front and by short wave to the forces overseas, with a wide variety of programs ranging from Tommy Handley's *Music Hall* to *The Brains Trust*, starring Julian Huxley, the scientist, and C. E. M. Joad, the popular philosopher. The whole world listened to the BBC news and the voice of Winston Churchill in his numerous broadcast reports on the course of the war.

General satisfaction with these arrangements and confidence in the Churchill government's direction of the war kept civilian morale high to the end; strangely enough for many the war was the most exhilarating experience of their lives. The morale of Londoners, however, was seriously tested in 1944 with the appearance of Hitler's secret weapons, the *V-1* flying bomb and the *V2* rocket. The former, a robot plane, was easily identified by the eerie, high-pitched beat of its motor. Its potential victims could hear it coming and knew, when the motor cut out it was about to dive. The *V2* was even more terrifying, for it came so quickly that the first sound survivors heard was its earsplitting explosion, and the only evidence of its arrival was half an acre of smoking rubble. Fortunately, the dislodging of the Germans from France and Belgium greatly reduced the threat from these devilish weapons. Had they appeared earlier, morale might have been seriously affected and the government might have been forced to evacuate the capital.

The social policy of the government was also conducive to the boosting of public morale. Despite hesitations and differences of opinion, planning for the future was more effective than after 1918. Both political parties began to draft postwar social programs, and in 1941 an indepedent committee of business executives and professionals initiated a public discussion of social planning. The government commissioned the veteran social planner, Sir William Beveridge (1879–1963), who had helped draft the 1911 National Insurance Act, to report what social services would be required after the war. The report went further than anticipated, but was based on the Liberal premises of individual contributions and maintenance of a subsistence minimum. It proposed extension of social security, children's allowances up to about age sixteen, development of a comprehensive health and rehabilitation service, and state action to prevent mass unemployment.

Although some Conservatives were frightened by the plan's implications, some Socialists believed it did not go far enough. But the report was generally well received and given a great deal of publicity. No matter which party was in power after the war its implementation was virtually assured, and some steps were taken immediately. Under Lord Woolton (1883–1964), a nonparty businessman who had been a successful minister of food, the Ministry of

Reconstruction was set up in 1943. This was followed in 1944 by a Town and Country Planning Act and a Housing Act, which provided building funds for temporary housing. More important was the passage in 1944 of R. A. Butler's Education Act, which centralized the system and made universal secondary education a reality by raising the school leaving age. It made a break between elementary and secondary education at the age of "eleven plus," which resulted in the brighter children being directed into grammar schools following their eleventh birthday, and the rest into secondary modern schools, which were of a mixed quality and did not prepare students to enter a university. Just before the coalition broke up in 1945 measures were passed for family allowances of 5 shillings a week per child after the first, continuance of school meals, and special assistance to depressed areas.

On D-Day, June 6, 1944 a combined American, Canadian and British force carried out "Operation Overlord," landing three airborne and six infantry divisions on the coast of Normandy between the mouth of the Seine and the Cotentin peninsula. The invasion fleet of several thousand ships, including British and American battleships that provided heavy covering fire, was supported by an Allied air force of 5,800 bombers and 4,900 fighters that flew some 14,000 sorties in the first twenty-four hours. It was an even larger operation than the Allied landing in Sicily the previous summer, and it was much more hazardous because of strong German defenses and unfavorable weather in the English Channel. The overall operation was under the supreme command of General Eisenhower, as the head of SHAEF (Supreme Head-quarters Allied Expeditionary Force), while the landing operations and early stages of the campaign (during which period the British component approximated that of the Americans) were under the direct tactical command of the experienced but controversial General Montgomery. The landing was met with bitter German resistance, which took two months to overcome; it was particularly strong on the eastern end of the front between Caen and Falaise, where the Canadians and British were committed. The original nine divisions were, however, rapidly augmented with the expansion of the bridgehead; and early in August the Americans broke through in the west, executing a great wheeling movement, with General Patton's U.S. Third Army in the vanguard on the right flank. The Germans were caught in a pincers between the Americans advancing on Falaise from the south and the Canadians and British pressing down from the north; those who escaped were forced to withdraw eastward across the Seine with heavy losses. A long pursuit followed while a secondary Allied invasion on the French Riviera in August quickly drove the Germans out of southern France. By early autumn almost all of France and Belgium had been liberated by Allied forces now numbering fifty-eight divisions.

A heroic attempt by the British 1st Airborne Division to capture the bridges crossing the Rhine at Arnhem in an air drop on September 17 failed, but Americans landing further to the south at Nijmegen held out until contact was made with land forces coming from the south. Extended Allied supply lines and increased resistance as the Germans fell back on their own borders finally brought the Allied advance to a standstill for the time being. In December a surprise German counteroffensive in the Ardennes temporarily threatened the whole Allied position in northeastern France. The crisis passed despite heavy American casualties, and in the spring the Allied offensive was renewed. The Rhine was crossed in March and Germany was rapidly overrun as the Russians pressed around Berlin from the east. Allied bombing of Germany continued to the end. It was devastating in terms of casualties and damage, but not decisive, and Germany was defeated essentially by the Russian and Western Allied armies on the ground. After Hitler's suicide in his Berlin bunker Germany finally surrendered on May 7, 1945.

The Anglo-American war alliance had been very closely integrated despite serious differences of opinion on a number of important matters such as the Riviera landings. In the end, these were surmounted, more often than not by Churchill realistically recognizing the necessity of deferring to the greater power of the United States, although in the final stages he did so with a heavy heart as he saw the balance of power in Europe slipping towards Russia. Eisenhower in northwest Europe, and Alexander, his British successor in Italy, believed firmly in submerging national differences; but such colorful subordinates as Generals Montgomery and Patton, who had little love for each other, sometimes found it hard to practice this injunction. Churchill and Roosevelt and their staffs had continued their close liaison in two summer conferences in Quebec in 1943 and 1944. At the first, final decisions were made regarding "Operation Overlord," while the second was devoted to plans for the war against Japan following the defeat of Germany.

Britain's relations with Russia were never as close, although in 1942 the two countries signed a twenty-year mutual assistance pact after Anthony Eden's Moscow visit. Despite the dispatch of large quantities of war supplies sent over the dangerous Arctic route to Murmansk, at a great cost in men and ships, the Russians remained suspicious of the Allies. In the autumn of 1944, shortly after the second Quebec conference, Churchill visited Moscow. He reached an understanding with Stalin regarding spheres of influence in the Balkans by a formula reminiscent of the Anglo-Russian entente of 1907 (when Persia was divided into three spheres). Stalin recognized Britain's preponderant interest in Greece in return for Britain's recognition of Russia's preponderant interest in Rumania and Bulgaria, while they tentatively agreed to be involved on an equal basis in Yugoslavia, where the Allies were helping Tito, the partisan leader. By this time the Germans were withdrawing from Greece, but when the royal government returned from exile, it was confronted by a Greek Communist underground movement. The monarchy was sustained by 60,000 British troops and the intervention of Churchill who flew to Athens on Christmas day of 1944. Stalin stood by his bargain and did not interfere when the revolt was supressed. Churchill's remarkable activity in this crisis suggested that the spirit of Chanak was not yet dead.

In February 1945 Churchill, Roosevelt, and Stalin met again in Yalta, on the Black Sea. Stalin promised to join the war against Japan, but Roosevelt had to yield in matters affecting Eastern Europe, especially the future of Poland. Stalin also agreed to participate in the founding of the United Nations, which took place the following June at a conference in San Francisco. In July the Big Three met at Potsdam to discuss military government of Germany, define the new frontiers of Poland, and arrange for the coming peace treaties. By this time, however, Roosevelt had been replaced by Truman, and Churchill was accompanied by Attlee, who succeeded him as Prime Minister before the conference concluded. With the end of the war in Europe the Labour party had withdrawn from the coalition government, despite Churchill's urging that they remain until Japan's defeat. The resulting summer election brought an unexpected and decisive Labour victory. By this time the war with Japan was nearly over. The British had virtually completed the reconquest of Burma with the capture of Rangoon in May. The Americans had secured naval supremacy in the Pacific, recovered the Philippines, landed on the Japanese islands of Iwo Jima and Okinowa, and begun the all-out air assault of Japan. The dropping of the atomic bombs on Nagasaki and Hiroshima on August 6 and 9 led to the surrender of Japan on August 14 which brought the war to an end. In the early years of the war scientists in Britain had worked out a method of applying the new knowledge about nuclear fission to the production of an atomic bomb, but after the entry of the United States into the war the two countries agreed to cooperate and British scientists joined their American colleagues in the Manhattan project, as the atomic bomb program was called.

It had been a long and exhausting struggle for Britain. Her economic resources had been gravely dissipated, as we shall see in the next chapter. She had suffered almost 400,000 fatal casualties, 60,000 civilian, 35,000 in the merchant navy, and 300,000 in the armed forces. By the end of the war military personnel numbered more than 5 million but they were distributed among the three services and spread around the world. In addition to being active in operations in Europe large forces remained tied down in the Middle East, that vast area extending from Iraq to Libya and from Syria to Kenya, all of which had been saved or recovered from the Axis by British and

Commonwealth troops. At the end of the war there were also six British and Commonwealth divisions actively engaged in Burma, with lines of communication back into India.

In North Africa, Sicily, and Normandy Britain's military role had been roughly equal to that of her American ally, but with the last of these operations she had reached the end of her manpower resources. War production required more workers than in the previous war, and Britain's labor supply was extended to the utmost. The air force, navy, and merchant marine were so short of men that it had been necessary to place a ceiling of 2 million on the army. Thus while the United States could pour a stream of new divisions into Europe after D-Day, Britain had come to the bottom of the barrel, and in the final Allied order of battle in northwest Europe there were only thirteen British divisions to sixty American, ten French, five Canadian, and one Polish. Added to these were divisions in Italy, the Middle East, India, and Burma, totaling thirty British divisions on active service at the end of the war, plus various brigade groups and numerous lines of communications and headquarters troops. The 5 million men and women in the British armed services at the end of the war comprised more than 10 percent of the entire population.

Although Britain's manpower in the final stages of the war was less than that of the USSR and the United States, her role in the defeat of Hitler was immeasurable. Her most important contribution was in the middle years of the war; if Britain had not held out after the fall of France, supported by Commonwealth partners and governments in exile, the history of the war and indeed of the world might have been very different. Britain really did not have the resources to play the world role to which Churchill aspired. But the moral and political leadership he gave the western world in the dark days and his part in forging the grand alliance that defeated the Axis earned him and his country a position that after 1945 could not be sustained. Churchill constantly demanded the impossible of his service chiefs, his colleagues, and his countrymen. But unlike Hitler, as Professor Medlicott has pointed out, he always accepted political realities, and his constant prodding did produce something of a miracle in the British war effort. To Churchill and his admirers around the world his electoral defeat in the summer of 1945 seemed a poor return for all he had done. His work was complete, however, and he was not the man to take on the task of reconstruction or even of reshaping of the postwar world. In fact it was not Churchill, but the party he had accidentally come to lead that was rejected at the polls. Britain wanted different direction than it had had after the previous war.

Chapter Fifteen
NATO AND THE WELFARE STATE

A historical perspective on the years since 1945 is difficult, since many events are within the memory of this writer. Some sources documenting the postwar era are not yet available, and research is still needed in those that are. Thus, no definitive account of these years has yet been written and any survey must be tentative in its conclusions. With this qualification it may be suggested that 1945 began a new era, which future historians may see as ending with Britain's entry in 1973 into the Common Market. For Britain the formative years of the postwar era were 1945–50. In those years Britain painfully began to adjust to the fact that she was no longer a great imperial world power; that she was living in a two-power world; that the days of the British Empire were numbered and the significance of the new Commonwealth was uncertain. During these years the structure of the welfare state was completed and the role of government in the national economy established. Conservative capitalists became resigned to a degree of socialism that would have been anathema before 1939, while many socialists began to realize the practical difficulties in achieving the millenium they had long sought. These years also posed problems of economic viability—the maintenance of the balance of payments and of the credibility of the pound sterling —that were to perplex all postwar governments. Decisions about relations with Europe, the sterling area[1] and the United States shaped Britain's course for the next quarter-century.

Since Churchill was determined to have an early election after the conclusion of the war in Europe, the Labour party withdrew from the coalition despite his protests. With only 47.8 percent of the total votes they won a landslide victory, securing 393 seats to 213 for the Conservatives, who polled 39.8 percent of the votes. The Liberals, with 9 percent, won only twelve

[1] This is a reference to all those countries with currencies tied to the pound sterling, and includes all Commonwealth countries except Canada.

seats, while 2.8 percent of the voters managed to elect twenty-two other candidates representing various splinter groups. The results were a surprise to many, especially to observers outside Britain who assumed Churchill would be swept back into office in recognition of his achievements in leading the country to victory. But British voters cast ballots for candidates in their own constituencies and not directly for the party leader, although the latter's appeal may influence them. The electoral pendulum was bound to swing against the Conservative party, which was identified with the failures of the interwar years, depression, unemployment, and appeasement; and Churchill, as Conservative leader, could not shake off this image. He also stepped off his pedestal by indulging in election smears against his former Labour colleagues. These may have been the fault of bad judgment rather than bad faith, but they backfired. The Labour party, on the other hand, had raised its stature as a result of the war, for its leaders had held key positions in the war-time government and had shown their ability to govern. Clement Attlee, Ernest Bevin, Herbert Morrison, Sir Stafford Cripps, and others were now trusted national figures who could be depended upon to do things "in the British way." The Labour electoral program also carried more conviction and was closer to the aspirations of the war-weary masses. In the constituencies the Labour electoral machine was in better condition; and, significantly, in the armed forces (whose members were given a mail ballot) the majority were for Labour.

Clement Attlee (1883–1966) was a taciturn man of unimpressive appearance but with great integrity and unsuspected ability. He was an upper middle class intellectual who, after graduating from Oxford, turned to social work and became an active socialist in the Fabian Society and the ILP. He served in the army throughout the First World War and rose to the rank of major, by which title he was known in the interwar years. In 1919 he was elected mayor of Stepney, an East End London borough, and in 1922 he entered Parliament. He held junior office in the second MacDonald ministry and, as we have seen, became leader of the party in 1935 almost accidentally. In the wartime coalition he proved an effective second-in-command to Churchill, especially in chairing Cabinet meetings in Churchill's absence. As Prime Minister he was remarkably good at keeping his difficult team of colleagues together and getting things done. His approach was matter-of-fact and realistic, as is his brief and unexciting autobiography, characteristically titled *As It Happened*. Churchill, who wrote many volumes about himself, once unfairly described Attlee as a modest little man who had much to be modest about. He may have lacked color, but few members of his generation had as solid a record of achievement.

Attlee's senior colleagues were Hugh Dalton (1887–1962) and Sir Stafford

Cripps (1889–1952), also upper middle class intellectuals, and Herbert Morrison (1885–1965) and Ernest Bevin (1881–1951), both representing the masses in speech and appearance. Dalton was more colorful but less dependable than Attlee, as may be seen in the three readable and informative volumes of his *Memoirs*, but in 1947 he was forced to resign from the Exchequer as the result of an accidental indiscretion about the contents of his Budget. He was succeeded by Cripps, the austere puritan socialist, who more than any other minister shaped the economic policy of the Labour government. Herbert Morrison, who, had he not lost his seat in the 1931 election, might have been leader of the party, as Lord President of the Council conducted much of the government's social legislation through the House. Perhaps the most striking and successful appointment was that of Ernest Bevin to the Foreign Office, normally an aristocratic preserve. The orphan who had gone to work at age thirteen and had risen in the hard school of the trade union movement proved extremely popular with the professionals in the Foreign Office. His long experience as a union leader and negotiator seemed to qualify him for postwar diplomacy, and he stood up to the Russians perhaps more stiffly than an aristocratic Conservative might have done. His special talent was getting to the heart of a matter and taking practical steps to achieve a solution.

In 1945 the Labour party had an ambitious electoral program titled *Let Us Face the Future*, which with some refinements and modifications, was based on their prewar platform, itself stemming from the manifesto of 1918, *Labour and the New Social Order*. It proposed to complete the framework of the welfare state with social legislation, to nationalize key industries, and to maintain full employment. In five years the Labour party succeeded in accomplishing almost all they had set out to do, but not always with the results anticipated.

The situation facing the Labour government when it took office in the summer of 1945 was a formidable one. For four years the country had spent more than half the national income on the war. In addition to the grievous human casualties already mentioned the economic toll had been heavy. Half a million homes had been destroyed and another 4 million severely damaged. Many industrial plants were run down and 18 million tons of merchant shipping had been destroyed, of which only two-thirds had been replaced. Britain's overseas investments had been reduced by more than £1,000 million; the returns from these investments, so important for Britain's balance of trade, were cut in half, while external indebtedness had been increased by over £3,000 million. Volume of exports had been halved. To accentuate these difficulties lend-lease, on which the country had become so dependent for necessary imports, was cut off as soon as the war was over with no period of adjustment. The government might have been tempted to abandon its great plans and confine itself to the problem of economic survival, but from the beginning it attempted to do both.

Economic dislocation produced by the war resulted in a long period of austerity and continued rationing punctuated by periodic financial crises. The most pressing needs were to reabsorb the millions of service personnel into the civilian work force, to replace "blitzed" homes and rundown plants, and to increase exports, which were essential to pay for the needed imports of food and raw materials. The situation was aggravated by a severe winter that led to a fuel shortage early in 1947, with a resultant temporary fall in production and employment as well as widespread hardship from cold and darkness owing to power cuts. It was a serious setback that enlarged the trade deficit and led to a run on gold, forcing Britain to abandon the attempt at convertibility undertaken at the Bretton Woods Conference of 1945. Henceforth rigid controls had to be imposed to prevent the transfer of funds from sterling area. British hopes for interest-free credits to meet the crisis following termination of lend-lease in 1945 were not realized, but long-term loans were negotiated with the United States and Canada. These tided the country over only until 1947, but in that year the American secretary of state, George Marshall, made his famous proposal for a long-term plan whereby the United States would help to set Britain and other European countries on their feet economically. The challenge was accepted by Bevin, who took the initiative in obtaining a European response. The result was the setting up of the Organization for European Economic Recovery and development of the Marshall plan, through which the United States pumped sufficient funds into western Europe to rebuild its economy. It was a shrewd but most generous and farsighted action and its execution was a significant achievement in international cooperation in which Bevin played a major role.

British economic recovery in the five or six years after 1945, though slow and painful, was substantial. A conscious decision was made to retain wartime controls to avoid a 1919 type of short-lived postwar boom, but the problem of inflation was not foreseen. Exports increased 77 percent in real terms between 1946 and 1960, but most important in social terms was the maintenance of almost full employment in contrast to the severe underemployment of the interwar years. In the immediate postwar years industrial production rose steadily at 8 percent per year, and between 1945 and 1950 the volume of British exports rose by 175 percent. At the same time strenuous efforts were made to curtail imports in order to maintain the balance of payments; but there was always a dollar shortage, which in 1949 became so severe that the pound sterling was belatedly reduced to $2.80, a devaluation of 30.5 percent. By 1950 the situation was greatly improved, but by that time Cripps, the main architect of recovery, was forced to retire, owing to ill health.

When the Labour government came into office it possessed greater economic powers than any previous peacetime government as a result of the extraordinary economic developments of the war—in 1946 the government controlled 37.7 percent of the gross national product. Plans for nationalization pointed to a further increase of government control, but socialist economists began gradually to recognize that fiscal control was more important than physical planning, i.e. the direction of men and materials, which was as objectionable to unions as to employers. Consequently after 1947 there was a gradual shift to fiscal control and despite left-wing emphasis on regulation of resources and production, physical planning gradually withered away. The government was fairly successful nevertheless in inducing management and labor to exercise restraint in determining wages and profits, and with improved conditions in 1948 there was a considerable reduction in rationing and other controls.

Despite overwhelming economic problems resulting from the war, the Labour ministers were determined to implement their plans for nationalization from the moment they took office. The principle had long ago been adopted, and the sectors of the economy to be dealt with first had been determined; but there was a surprising lack of blueprints, and the measures that were enacted were drawn up with very little prior preparation. These included nationalization of the Bank of England, the railways, air and road transport, coal mines, electricity and gas, and, eventually, iron and steel. It was a substantial amount of nationalization, but a nondoctrinaire argument could be made in each case except that of iron and steel. Other nonsocialist countries had national banks, nationalized railways, and nationalized electrical power, while the case for nationalizing the inefficient British coal industry had been widely accepted even before the Second World War. Moreover, stockholders in these industries were compensated at current market prices. The management of the nationalized industries was placed in the hands of public boards ultimately responsible to the government. Vesting day, as the ownership transfer date was called, was looked upon as a great occasion by the coal miners, but it passed with little notice in other industries. The new employers did not differ much from the old. Nationalization was not disastrous, as many capitalists expected, nor did it bring the changes that workers had anticipated. The one controversial step was nationalization of the iron and steel industry, which was held up until 1950 and required an amendment of the Parliament Act to prevent the House of Lords delaying its passage for more than two sessions. It was still in the process of implementation when the Labour government fell in 1951, and it was the single major measure the Conservatives reversed when they came into office. British Railways is now taken as much for granted as the British Broadcasting

Corporation, and the old names—Southern Railway, Great Western, London Midland and Southern, and London Northeastern—are nostalgic memories. Nationalization has allowed for some rationalization, but railway workers are just as inclined to strike against the new management as against the old. Unfortunately, despite the size of the system, British Railways was subordinated—along with Road Transport, Inland Waterways, and London Transport—to the centralized British Transport Commission. Capital was not provided for needed renovations after the war and the railways suffered in competition with other forms of transport, although probably not as much as in some other parts of the world. For fifteen years British Railways lost money. In 1962 a Conservative government abolished the British Transport Commission and set up the new British Railways Board. It was headed by Dr. Beeching, a director of Imperial Chemical Industries on loan to the government, who planned wholesale curtailment of services, to the annoyance of an aroused public. When Labour returned to office they set up the Transport Advisory Council under a special advisor to coordinate all forms of transport, and Dr. Beeching went back to private enterprise. The new Labour plan of 1966 sounded like a return to the principles of the Nationalization of Transport Bill of 1946.

The nationalization of coal has probably been more successful despite serious problems facing the industry ever since the end of the war. Recent competition from other forms of power has forced some cutback in coal production and the closing of less efficient mines, but working conditions and efficiency have been improved, a high degree of mechanization introduced, and productivity increased. The working and living conditions of British miners have much improved since George Orwell described them in *The Road to Wigan Pier*, but their wages have lagged compared with other industries. Nationalized electricity has also succeeded, although in 1957 the original Electricity Authority was replaced by the Central Electrical Generating Board, which generates and distributes power to area electricity boards, and the Electricity Council, responsible for general policy. Since 1947 there has been a great increase in industrial and domestic power consumption. Several nuclear power stations have been built, but coal remains the chief source of energy for developing electrical power.

The two most important measures passed by the Labour government were the National Insurance and the National Health Services acts of 1946, which implemented the main proposals of the Beveridge report. Since the Coalition government had supported the general principles on which these acts were based the Conservatives confined their opposition to detail. The National Insurance Act rounded out the welfare system begun in 1908 by Asquith's Old Age Pension Bill. It was designed to "establish an extended system of national insurance providing pecuniary payments by way of unemployment benefit, sickness benefit, maternity benefit, retirement pension, widow's benefits; guardian's allowance, and death grant." The measure included everyone from school-leaving age to retirement except married women and certain self-employed individuals earning less than a minimum amount. For those not covered under the Insurance Act relief was administered by the reorganized National Assistance Board, and care for homeless children was provided for in the 1948 Children's Act.

The National Health Act, a very large and complicated measure, was introduced by the fiery left-wing Welshman Aneuran Bevan (1897–1960), who had been an independent critic of the Coalition government during the war. It provided free medical, dental, and hospital services to everyone, going far beyond the earlier health insurance, which had only applied to lower-income wage earners, excluded their dependents and self-employed persons, and made no provisions for dental care, hospitalization, and drug prescriptions. Initially doctors strongly opposed some features of the act, especially those governing pay rates, but at the last moment they accepted some minor compromises. The new system became operative in July 1948 and by 1950 88 percent of the nation's doctors were participating. Succeeding Conservative governments have made only minor changes, such as authorizing small charges for prescriptions and false teeth. The middle classes profited most from the measure, since they had received nothing from the earlier Health Insurance; but the whole country benefited greatly, although the inevitable price was paid in bureaucratization. The national health system came at a good time, after several decades of war and depression when many doctors welcomed a guaranteed income. In a period of affluence the concept would have been difficult to introduce.

Other legislation passed by the Labour government included two housing acts that led to construction of 806,000 new homes and renovation of 330,000 old ones; the Town and Country Planning Act and the New Towns Act, encouraging large-scale urban planning and even formation of entire new towns, to relieve existing congested areas; and various other measures for promotion of the arts. In education the government limited itself mainly to implementation of the Butler Act of 1944.

In foreign policy there were no major differences between Government and Opposition. Indeed there was a remarkable continuity in foreign policy in the forties and fifties in contrast to the thirties, when Labour leaders had postulated a distinctive socialist foreign policy. Attlee, Bevin, and the others abandoned this idea as a result of their wartime experiences. In his memoirs Eden said that in foreign policy he had agreed with Bevin's aims and most of his actions, but had refrained from making this too clear in his speeches to avoid embarrassing Bevin. The left wing of the Labour party had misgivings, for Bevin's policy was to maintain the American alliance and stand up to Russia. Bevin did not reject such old ideals as collective security and the rule of the law, but he was much more a realist than Labour leaders in the interwar years in his method of pursuing these ideals.

From the beginning the Western Allies and Russia had serious differences over Germany. The Russians were intent on seizing immediate reparations, but the Western Allies objected to a hasty stripping of Germany's remaining resources in view of the Russian refusal to help feed the Germans in their industrialized occupation zones in the west with produce from the Russian-dominated eastern zone. No peace treaty was ever worked out for Germany, but the Western Allies agreed eventually to the union of the British, French, and American zones to form what became in 1955 the Federal Republic of West Germany. In the meantime the Western Allies insisted on maintaining their share of control in Berlin, which was also divided into four zones, although surrounded by the Russian-occupied East German zone (which became the German Democratic Republic in 1949). When the Russians sought to counter the establishment of the West German Republic by cutting off land communications between it and Berlin, Britain and the United States responded with the Berlin Airlift which successfully kept West Berlin supplied until the Russian blockade was abandoned in May 1949. Peace treaties were signed in 1947 dealing with Hungary, Rumania, Bulgaria, and Finland—countries that were henceforth dominated by Russia. Poland and Czechoslovakia were likewise sucked into the Soviet System, the former when the Russians installed a communist government in 1945, the latter as a result of a Communist coup d'état in 1948. In Greece and Turkey right-wing anti-Communist governments were maintained with British support, but the great power role that Britain was playing in occupied Germany, in the Berlin airlift, and in the Mediterranean was beyond her resources. In 1947 the United States took over Britain's supporting role vis-à-vis Greece and Turkey with the announcement of the so-called Truman Doctrine.

The fact was that in the two years following the end of the war there was a semivacuum in western Europe. The United States had withdrawn most of its troops as rapidly as it could. In standing up to the Communist challenge in Berlin and in the Eastern Mediterranean Britain had attempted to maintain her wartime equal partnership with the U.S.A., but she no longer had the power to do so. All western Europe was floundering economically, and if Russia had had the predatory designs with which some credited her, she could have moved her legions westward with little opposition. Communist coups—or even election victories—in both Italy and France were well within the realm of possibility in the summer of 1947. It was at this point that Marshall made his dramatic offer. This led to the organization of the Committee of European Recovery representing sixteen European nations and the working out of a European Recovery Program, founded by Marshall Aid, which was approved by the American Senate in April 1948.

Meanwhile, in 1947 Bevin had signed a fifty-year treaty of alliance with France, thus going further than any previous peacetime government in committing Britain to a French alliance. This was followed in 1948, again at Bevin's instigation, by the Brussels Conference which brought Britain and France together with Belgium, the Netherlands, and Luxembourg, the so-called Benelux nations. The resulting Brussels Treaty promised military, economic, and social cooperation between the signatories and the setting up of a Council of Europe. This was expanded a year later with the formation of the North Atlantic Treaty Organization (NATO), in which the U.S., Canada, Iceland, Denmark, Norway, and Portugal joined the Brussels Treaty countries with a Supreme Headquarters of the Allied Powers in Europe (SHAPE) under General Eisenhower. This was primarily a military alliance (later embracing West Germany, Greece, and Turkey) designed to defend western Europe against the threat of Russian aggression. After the experience of the thirties and Russian intransigence in the late forties this threat seemed real enough, but in retrospect it may appear to have been exaggerated. Russia's complete domination of all countries east of "the Iron Curtain" (Winston Churchill's phrase in a 1946 speech in Fulton, Missouri) seemed sufficient warning to the western European countries, all very much aware of their own military weaknesses and glad to welcome the return of American troops as part of a protective shield east of the Rhine. NATO was never able to assemble anything like the military land power of Russia and her satellite allies of the Warsaw Pact, the Soviet counterpart to NATO, but for the time being the American monopoly of the atomic bomb gave the West some false sense of security.

Palestine was another heavy responsibility for Britain in the immediate postwar years. The Zionists demanded that more Jewish refugees should be allowed into the country, which was still a British mandate, and that an independent Jewish state should come into being, while the Arabs urged resistance to these proposals. Both demands were the legacy of conflicting promises made in the First World War. The cost of maintaining troops in Palestine was too heavy and British public opinion was appalled by the killing of British soldiers by Jewish terrorists. Consequently, seeing no solution to the irreconcilable demands of Arabs and Jews, the British government abandoned its mandate in 1948 and withdrew its troops. The state of Israel that was immediately established in the western part of Palestine has so far survived, despite the hostility of neighboring Arab countries and of the Palestinian Arab refugees who fled eastward across the Jordan.

When the Korean war broke out on the other side of the world in 1950,

Britain gave the United States limited support by sending a strong naval component and some troops as part of the United Nations force. The invasion of South Korea was seen as part of the world-wide Communist threat rather than an attempt by the North Koreans to unite the divided country. The fact that it was supported by Communist China, which had been recognized by Britain but not by the United States, seemed to underline the danger, but the British were fearful that the Americans might go too far and use the atomic bomb against the Chinese.

The Labour government also faced the most momentous decisions of the century in the field of Commonwealth and imperial affairs. Indian nationalists had been pressing for self-government for more than half a century and had not been satisfied with the India Act of 1935. At the time Churchill had strongly opposed the amount of self-government in that measure, but his wartime government had promised that Indian demands would be met after the war. The Labour party was committed to this pledge and, in any event, had always been sympathetic to Indian aspirations. The difficulty lay with the division of opinion in India between the Hindu Congress party led by Nehru and Jinnah's Moslem League. The Moslems were demanding a separate state of Pakistan, although they were concentrated in two geographically remote regions, the northwest and the Indus valley in eastern Bengal. The Attlee government appointed the King's cousin Lord Mountbatten (1900–   ), wartime Supreme Commander in Southeast Asia, as the last British Viceroy of India. When the rival factions continued to differ they were finally given an ultimatum, and in the summer of 1947 an act was passed in the imperial Parliament providing for the division of the subcontinent, in the following year, into the two independent states of India and Pakistan. Lord Mountbatten executed his difficult commission with great skill, retaining the respect of both Moslems and Indians, and at the request of the Indian leaders he became the first Governor General of India for a transition period, in order to facilitate the transition. India and Pakistan both decided to remain within the Commonwealth (the word "British" was dropped about this time), but to meet Indian susceptibilities Commonwealth members were allowed to choose a republican form of government, merely recognizing the crown as the link between members, and the old imperial conference became a more informal conference of prime ministers. (De Valera had proposed such a relationship in the thirties, but he was a decade ahead of his time. Ironically, during a brief period when he was out of office after the war, the Irish government of John Costello withdrew Ireland from the Commonwealth just on the eve of its transformation.) India soon adopted the republican form of government, but Pakistan retained the dominion system with a governor general until 1956. Burma and Ceylon were also given their independence, the former electing to leave the Commonwealth and the latter to remain a member.

Commonwealth countries were now completely independent, although most still accepted the King as head of state, nominating their own governors general to represent him. Some, such as Canada, continued to use the imperial Parliament for certain constitutional changes, largely for domestic political reasons, and a few retained the Privy Council as a final court of appeal. Henceforth, however, the Commonwealth was simply an association of states sharing some common heritage in institutions, law, and, to a certain extent, language and culture. English remained a working language in the new Asian Commonwealth states, and much of the English educational system was continued. English universities and Inns of Court (where British lawyers are trained) continued to draw students from these countries. The military system in all Commonwealth countries was likewise modeled on the British and the staff colleges of the various members have continued to exchange officers. Imperial communications, and membership, except for Canada, in the sterling area continued to provide tangible bonds between Britain and the Commonwealth members.

Few administrations have achieved as much in terms of legislation and of new departures in the field of foreign and imperial policy as the postwar Labour government, but these had not been easy years for Britain. Some wartime controls remained, including some food rationing, and it was still difficult to convert sterling into dollars; nor had the experiments in nationalization brought about the millennium. The country's foreign and imperial commitments still pressed heavily on British taxpayers, and now they were involved in a remote and unpopular war. Consequently, it was not surprising that the electoral pendulum swung away from Labour in the election of 1950, reducing that party's overall majority to ten. Ill health forced Bevin and Cripps to retire and both of them died soon afterwards; other senior ministers were weary after ten strenuous years in office. As a result the second Attlee administration faltered and was forced to the polls again in 1951. This time the Conservatives won 321 seats to 295 for Labour, with the Liberals reduced to 6.

The Korean War had pressed hard on the delicate British economy, causing a sharp rise in Britain's already swollen defense expenditures and a painful increase in world commodity prices that upset the British balance of payments. Hugh Gaitskell (1906–1963), Cripps' successor as Chancellor of the Exchequer, had been forced to meet these contingencies with measures that alienated the left wing of the party and contributed to the collapse of the Government. A few months before the election of October 1951, however, the fighting in Korea had virtually come to an end and, consequently, soon after the Conservatives came into office the harsh economic climate abated. A period of comparative affluence ensued and the Conservatives remained in power for a surprising thirteen years.

Total production, measured in constant prices, rose 40 percent in the years 1951–1964. The consumption of durable consumer goods increased by leaps and bounds. The number of private cars, for instance, went up from $2\frac{1}{4}$ to 8 million, and there were similar increases in the purchase of refrigerators, television sets, and washing machines. The number of telephones in use doubled, and millions of people began to take holidays abroad as exchange regulations were gradually relaxed. Compared with the 8.5 percent rise in population between 1950 and 1965, the percentage increase in expenditure on food was 25.7, on alcohol and tobacco 29.8, on clothing 35.4, on housing and maintenance 37.3, on furniture and household goods, 42.4, on electrical equipment 181.4, and on motor vehicles and fuel 594.1 percent. The unemployment rate did not go over 2.6 percent in any year in this period and remained under 2 percent during most of them. As Harold Macmillan crudely put it in 1957, the British people had "never had it so good." There was only one fly in the ointment; most other countries in Western Europe were doing considerably better. In the decade 1950–1960 the British gross national product increased at an annual rate of 2 percent compared to percentages of 7.2 for West Germany, 6.3 for Italy, and 4.4 for France. The same was true for exports, which Britain increased by 29 percent between 1951 and 1962, while France's increased 86, West Germany's 247, and Japan's 378 percent. Of course, both in production and in exports these countries started from a much worse position than Britain and, consequently, in the early stages of recovery it was to be expected that the percentages would be more dramatic. But the hard fact was that the countries that had started from the bottom caught up to Britain and passed her at least in terms of production.

The Conservative return to office in 1951 was not entirely the result of Labour collapse. The Conservative party was also divided between a right wing that wanted to turn the clock back and a left wing that realized that this was unrealistic and that accommodations must be made in the postwar world. R. A. Butler (1902–   ), a former university don who had been an undersecretary in the Chamberlain administration, took the lead in preparing the party for the future. Realizing that in 1945 they had failed to show there was a Conservative alternative to socialism, he called in the following year for "a total reorganization of the social structure" on which the party rested, "an acceptance of redistributive taxation to reduce the extremes of poverty and wealth, and repudiation of laissez-faire economics in favor of a system in which the State acted as a "trustee for the interests of the community and balancing force between different interests." The right wing called this pink socialism, but Butler saw himself in the tradition of Bolingbroke and Disraeli. In his view, Conservative principles in the postwar world should lead to "humanized capitalism." As a result of his prodding, the party set up a Conservative Political Centre and Research Bureau on the Fabian model. Butler himself chaired an Industrial Policy Committee, which included Harold Macmillan (1894–   ), a left-wing antiappeaser in the thirties. They drafted the Industrial Charter of 1947, which may be compared to the Tamworth Manifesto of a century earlier. "We were out-Peeling Peel in giving the Party a painless but permanent facelift," Butler wrote later in his memoirs. Accepting the main principles of Keynsian economics the Charter promised, in Butler's words, "that, in the interests of efficiency, full employment and social security, modern Conservatism would maintain strong central guidance over the operation of the economy." The worker was to be assured steady employment, but at the same time the businessman was to get a reduction in government controls and in taxes. In the election of 1951 the Conservatives promised to set the people free, but also to build them 300,000 houses a year.

Less than four months after the formation of the last Churchill government, George VI died prematurely. He had been a king very much in the tradition of his father, although more informal (as befitted the age), and he had strengthened the monarchy by the example he had set during the war. He was succeeded by his daughter, Elizabeth II (b. 1926), whose coronation a year later was a glamorous affair conducted with all the traditional pomp and ceremony and filmed in technicolor for the world to see. Since times were clearly improving people began talking hopefully of a new Elizabethan age. The parallels have not been particularly obvious.

Although primarily interested in foreign affairs, Churchill was determined that his new government would not be regarded as reactionary in its domestic policy. He was prepared to follow a policy of industrial appeasement despite its inflationary cost, and to implement the election promise about housing he appointed Harold Macmillan as the minister in charge, with orders to reach the target. The Labour government had been unable to reach the 200,000 mark because of its many other commitments, especially in starting the National Health Service and in rearmament. The improved international climate made it possible for the Conservatives to direct more resources into housing, and as a result of prodigious efforts, Macmillan reached his goal in 1953; furthermore, that rate was maintained for years to come. The Labour government had favored the erection of Council Houses, built and owned by the local authorities, but the Conservatives gave much more encouragement to the building of private houses, partly to meet the demands of the middle classes and partly because philosophically they favored private home ownership. As the better off workingmen became homeowners their attitude was expected to become more conservative. A total of 249,000 local authority houses were built in 1954, but from then on the number fell sharply, while the number of private houses built increased rapidly from a mere 25,000 in 1951 to 200,000 a year in the mid-1960s. The Conservative achievement in housing is impressive, but it was said afterward that they put too high a proportion of the country's resources in this sector. The expanded program increased the demand for imported raw materials and reduced the available funds for investment in the export industries, thus contributing to the perennial balance-of-payments problem.

In the direction of the economy, a major role of government in the Keynesian scheme of things, the Conservatives did not do a very good job, but they did not upset the mixed economy and the welfare state that Labour had created. Iron and steel and road transport were the only industries that were denationalized, and nationalization of the former had only just been completed. On the other hand, not all the road transporters wanted to buy their businesses back and so the nationalized Road Services remained in business. As the gross national product grew the Conservatives increased expenditures on the health services in the same proportion, and were able to employ 18 percent more doctors and 30 percent more nurses. There were similar increases in expenditures on education and other social services between 1950 and 1965. The purchasing power of old age pensions went up by fifty percent during the Conservative stay in office. Indeed, there is a certain irony in the fact that during the period the Conservatives were in office, defense expenditures dropped from 8.6 to 6.8 percent of the gross national product, while expenditures on social services rose from 12.5 to 16.1 percent. The continuity in domestic policy as well as in foreign policy between Labour and Conservative administrations is quite striking in view of their mutual low opinion of each other, but of course they were both influenced by public opinion as expressed in the opinion polls and the ballot box.

One might have expected the party of business to have been more successful in the direction of the economy. Butler was no economist, as Gaitskell had been, but Churchill told him (just as a century earlier Derby had assured Disraeli) this did not matter—he would get good advice. His objective was expansion. He reduced taxes and food subsidies and in 1954 finally abandoned rationing, but he raised old age and widows' pensions. For several years all went well, but in 1955, despite signs of inflation, he brought in an election budget with further tax cuts that fanned the inflation and led to belated emergency measures in that autumn after the election was won.

In defense and foreign affairs Eden continued Bevin's policy of supporting NATO but opposing closer European union, which in opposition Churchill had seemed to favor. Bevin had shown little enthusiasm for the Council of Europe, and the Labour government had refused to join the European Coal and Steel Community when it was formed in 1951. The Conservative government followed suit when it refused to participate directly in the Messina Conference of 1955 which led to the Treaty of Rome in 1958 and the creation of the European Economic Community, or Common Market. In 1951 the French government had proposed the formation of a European Defense Community of the western European powers as a means of rearming Germany without allowing the German government full control of their armed forces. Eden approved the plan in principle, as had his predecessors, but declined to sanction British participation. The French Assembly then turned down the treaty that had been negotiated by the six west European partners. Eden, nevertheless, was anxious to find some substitute solution to the West German problem, which would help guarantee the security of western Europe. With the support of the American government he therefore called a conference in London in September 1954, at which he proposed to expand the Brussels Treaty of 1948 by bringing in Germany and Italy to form a Western European Union. WEU was to differ from ECD in that it could not be supranational. The proposals were accepted on Eden's promise that Britain would continue to maintain the four divisions and tactical air force that she then had on the Continent. The occupation of West Germany was ended and the Western European Union merged with NATO, which Germany now joined. It was probably Eden's greatest success as Foreign Secretary and had been achieved through strenuous preliminary preparation. In 1954 Eden also committed Britain to the American-sponsored Southeast Asia Treaty Organization (SEATO), a somewhat looser complement to NATO in the Pacific.

SEATO was the sequel to the Geneva Conference of 1954, which brought the long drawn-out war in French Indochina to an end. The conference was chaired jointly by Molotov and Eden, who cooperated closely to make it a success, but its outcome did not entirely satisfy the American secretary of state, John Foster Dulles. The United States had wanted to intervene on behalf of the French at the time of the fall of Dien Bien Phu, but had been restrained by Britain's opposition to such intervention.

Churchill's last ministry was rather a pathetic one in that the old man yearned to resume his wartime role in the direction of world affairs. In particular he was anxious to renew the close Anglo-American relationship of the war years—especially after his old colleague General Eisenhower became President in 1953—and through this connection to promote a summit meeting of the heads of the great powers. Eisenhower was friendly but elusive, tending to leave foreign policy to his less cooperative Secretary of State, Dulles. As a result the long-heralded summit meeting between the USSR, the United States, France, and Britain was not held until 1955, by which time Eden had succeeded Churchill as Prime Minister. The Geneva Conference did little except demonstrate that the new Russian leader, Nikita Khrushchev, was not as remote as Stalin had been. Churchill suffered a stroke in 1953, but Eden was too ill to succeed him, so the old man remained another two years, resigning shortly after his eightieth birthday. His was one of the most colorful careers in modern British history, but, like Gladstone, he hung on too long.

Sir Anthony Eden had been Churchill's logical successor for fifteen years. He had a distinguished record as Foreign Secretary in war and peace and was among the few Conservative ministers of the thirties to survive with an untarnished reputation. As a Prime Minister, however, he was a failure, and his term of office was brief. Having lived so long in Churchill's shadow, he may have lacked self-assurance on his own, for he seemed to have lost the poise and good sense for which he had been known. He made a good start by deciding on an early election, which was held a few months after he took office, before the honeymoon was over. Thanks to his previous reputation, the prosperity of the four preceding years, tax cuts in the preelection budget, and divisions in the Labour party, the Conservatives increased their majority from 17 to 60 (345 seats to 285 for Labour). But after the election everything went wrong. The economy began to get out of hand, necessitating an autumn budget and new anti-inflationary taxes to restrict purchasing power. This and a reshuffling of the Cabinet, in which Butler was replaced at the exchequer by Macmillan and the little-known Selwyn Lloyd (b. 1904), was appointed to the Foreign Office, brought loud criticism from the press and denials from Eden that he intended to resign.

Eden was inexperienced in handling domestic affairs but his greatest failure was in foreign policy, his own field. As Churchill's Foreign Secretary, he had negotiated a settlement with Egypt in 1954, after prolonged terrorist activity against British troops in the Canal Zone. The treaty provided for British withdrawal from the Canal Zone, ending the temporary occupation begun by Gladstone in 1882. Under existing international agreements, the Suez Canal Company was to continue to run the canal, which was to remain an international waterway. This final settlement was concluded with the revolutionary government of the new Egyptian nationalist leader, Colonel Nasser. The United States and Britain had arranged to finance a giant project to dam the upper Nile at Aswan, but both countries had second thoughts when Nasser began to flirt with Moscow. In the summer of 1956, Dulles withdrew the American offer without consulting the British. Nasser's response was to nationalize the Suez Canal with provision for compensation, although in 1954 he had recognized the rights of the Canal Company, which ran to 1968. It was a high-handed and illegal act, but with nationalist feeling running high in former colonial countries of Africa and Asia, it was hardly a surprising one.

Reaction in Britain, part owner and major user of the Canal since the 1870s, was strong and bitter. Even Gaitskell, leader of the Labour Opposition, compared Nasser's ambitions to those of Hitler and Mussolini. Eden was furious and denounced Nasser in such strong language that future negotiations were made more difficult. The Egyptian President declined to attend a London meeting to discuss the situation with the chief users of the canal. Eighteen of the twenty-two powers at the conference consented to recognize Egyptian sovereignty over the canal, in return for a new convention based on the principle of international control. Robert Menzies, the Prime Minister of Australia, presented the proposals to Nasser with no success, although he warned the Egyptian president that the alternative might be the use of force. Britain and France were already collecting the necessary armed forces for such an eventuality but, confident that the Americans would do nothing, Nasser stood pat. Britain was now prepared to bring the matter to the Security Council of the United Nations, but Dulles strongly objected and persuaded Britain and France to embark on a fruitless experiment known as the Suez Canal Users' Association. This was an attempt to organize the chief canal users to send their ships through the canal in convoy, holding back the dues. It was a stalling device on Dulles' part for he seems to have had no intention of making it operative. His concern was to postpone any crisis until the American election was over. Late in September Britain and France finally appealed to the Security Council. Agreement was reached on six principles, but on October 13 Russia vetoed the steps proposed to implement them.

The patience of the British and French governments was now exhausted. Indeed, from the very beginning they had been making plans for armed intervention, should negotiations fail, and gathering the necessary military forces in the Mediterranean. A plan, "Operation Musketeer," had been approved by Eden and the French Minister, Mollet, in mid-August; this involved the assembling of a large invasion of 100,000 British and 30,000 French troops, supported by 100 British and 30 French warships, 36 squadrons of the Royal Air Force, and 7 squadrons of the French Air Force. The French were more anxious for early action, because Nasser was supporting the rebels in Algeria, but since the British were providing the bulk of the forces they had agreed to the fruitless appeal to the United Nations, on pressure from the British Foreign Secretary, Selwyn Lloyd. Meanwhile, the French government had informally made a proposal for an Israeli attack on Egypt, which the Israeli government had accepted. The British government took no part in these negotiations but was ready to agree, should Israel invade Egypt, to launch Operation Musketeer on the excuse of separating the contestants. Actually, it appears the Israeli invasion was largely dependent on Allied air support, which was promised by the French. But to avoid any appearance of collusion, the British refused to let their forces leave Malta before the Israeli attack began on the night of October 29. On the following day, on the pretext that the Canal was endangered, the British and French governments issued ultimatums to Egypt and Israel requiring them to withdraw ten miles from either side of the Canal. When the Egyptians refused the Allied air forces proceeded to bomb the Egyptian airfields and other special targets, but several days had to pass before their invasion fleet could reach Port Said.

The Anglo-French intervention brought a shocked reaction from a large segment of the British public and from friendly countries overseas. The American government was naturally upset that its chief allies had acted so inconsiderately and without warning on the eve of the American election. Actually, Dulles had been warned in general terms for some time that Britain and France might be driven to resort to force over the Canal, but he seems to have thought that he had satisfied them with the S.C.U.A. plan. On October 30 the United States introduced a resolution in the United Nations Assembly calling on all parties engaged in hostilities to agree to a ceasefire and to halt the movement of armaments into the area. In the course of the debate Lester Pearson, the Canadian Minister for External Affairs, urged the creation of a United Nations peacekeeping force, a suggestion made by Eden in a speech the previous day. The American motion was passed by a vote of 64 to 5. Australia and New Zealand were the only countries to support Britain, France, and Israel.

In the House of Commons and in a public broadcast Gaitskell emotionally denounced the government, appealing to peace-loving Conservatives to overthrow it. Aneurin Bevan, now the Labour party's spokesman on foreign affairs, was more moderate in addressing a vast peace meeting in Trafalgar Square. Public opinion was divided as deeply as it had been in the Eastern crisis of the 1870s and basically between the same schools of opinion—one favoring a foreign policy based on morality and international understanding and one concerned with national interest and prestige. Many Conservatives were clearly embarrassed, including R. A. Butler, who had not originally been consulted, but who had accepted the decision made in his absence by an inner group in the Cabinet; two junior ministers resigned. The strongest protests came from the middle and upper classes, especially the intelligentsia, but the rank and file of working-class Labour supporters did not respond to the indignation of their leaders. Opinion polls showed more support for the Government than the Opposition.

Despite the outcry in Britain and the United Nations resolution, the Government decided to continue the operation. Paratroops were dropped near Port Said on the night of November 5; seaborne troops landed the next morning, took the town, and proceeded south toward Suez at the other end of the canal. The next day the General Assembly accepted Pearson's proposal for immediate establishment of a United Nations police force. At this point Eden capitulated, and with the reluctant agreement of the French (who had no alternative, since the expedition was under British command), promised to withdraw in favor of the United Nations. Churchill, watching restlessly on the sidelines, is reported to have said to Eden, "I am not sure that I should have dared to start, but I am sure that I should not have dared to stop." Eden's motives are a matter of conjecture. He claims (unconvincingly) that, with formation of a United Nations police force to keep the belligerents separated, the British-French objective had been accomplished. But Nasser was still in control of the canal, and it remained for the United Nations, not Britain and France, to clear it of blockade ships and arrange for resumption of traffic with payment of dues to Egypt. The decision of the British government was influenced by other considerations. On November 5 they received a most menacing message from the Russian government threatening intervention and the use of rocket missiles against Britain; in addition, a heavy run on sterling had endangered the value of the pound; and finally, there was the grim realization that in this rash enterprise Britain and France had no friends in the rest of the world, with the exception of Israel, Australia, and New Zealand.

The strain was too much for Eden, whose health collapsed. Butler, as acting Prime Minister, had to work out the details of a settlement with the United Nations, which were scarcely satisfactory from the British point of view, and the following January, continued ill health forced Eden finally to resign. It was a sad end to a long and honorable career. Eden had been a competent lieutenant to Churchill, but he was not cut out for first place. For Macmillan, his successor, the reverse was true.

Chapter Sixteen
BRITAIN SINCE SUEZ

Eden's obvious successor was R. A. Butler, chief architect of the Conservative electoral recovery of 1950–51, workhorse of the Churchill and, Eden administrations, and acting Prime Minister during Eden's illness. Butler, however, was suspect for his lack of enthusiasm in the Suez venture and, consequently, was *persona non grata* to the right wing of the party. The Queen consulted Churchill and Lord Salisbury (b.1893), a senior Cabinet member and die-hard Tory; both recommended Harold Macmillan (b. 1894), who had been a firm supporter of the Suez venture. Salisbury and the Lord Chancellor had consulted the chief whip and others and had polled the Cabinet. As each minister came into the room, Salisbury demanded, with his well-known lall: "Well, which is it? Wab or Hawold?" There was no question that Macmillan was the favorite, and he was duly summoned by the Queen.

With the exception of Churchill, the survivor of an earlier age, Macmillan was the most colorful postwar prime minister. He was the son of a successful Victorian publisher and an American mother, a strong-minded woman who greatly influenced him. He had an upper-class education, with scholarships to Eton and Balliol College, Oxford, where he took a first-class degree. He joined the army in 1914, fought with a famous Guards regiment, and was badly wounded in 1916. As a young man he had been a rather shy, aloof intellectual, "I learnt books before I learnt people," he said, years later. But the camaraderie of army life broadened him and was an important ingredient in his future political career. After the war he went into the family business and in 1924 entered parliament at the age of thirty. In the thirties he rebelled against the stuffy Conservative leadership, but during the Second World War he played an important role as British minister at Allied Force Headquarters in the Mediterranean, where he worked closely with General Eisenhower. The early postwar years were frustrating, except for his successful term at the Ministry of Housing, where he had a free hand; Macmillan was a "loner," who did not work easily under someone else's direction. As Prime Minister he came into his own and developed an inimitable style that caught the public imagination. His hooded eyebrows, drooping moustache, and generally shaggy appearance suggested an elegant walrus, but there was a glint in his eye and a sharp undertone to his nonchalant drawl that reflected inner vitality and toughness.

Prime Minister Macmillan's chief interest was foreign affairs, especially renewed cordial relations with the United States. As a realist he accepted the lesson of Suez, but he still believed Britain had an important world role to play, similar to that of the Greeks in the Roman Empire. As the son of an American he did not resent (as perhaps Eden may have done) the major influence of the United States in international affairs, and he continued to have faith in Britain's special relationship with that country. He agreed with Churchill in regarding this as the first of three spheres in which Britain must concentrate her efforts; the other two were the Commonwealth and Europe. Macmillan's ambition was to mediate between East and West and bring about the longed-for detente. Like Churchill, he constantly pinned his hopes on a summit conference, looking back, perhaps nostalgically, to his wartime experiences. Peacetime problems were more intractable and not easily solved in short meetings between the men at the top, but Macmillan was tireless in promoting these conferences in his frequent journeys to Paris, Bonn, Moscow, Washington, and other capitals, and on his visits to Commonwealth countries around the world. His first important achievement was the healing of the rift with the United States and here the American President, his old wartime friend "Ike," met him halfway, conferring with him in Bermuda in March 1957. In February 1959, after many false starts towards a summit conference, Macmillan agreed to visit Russia despite, or perhaps because of, a crisis that was looming over Berlin, which the Russians wished to incorporate into East Germany. Macmillan had a mixed reception, for Khrushchev was a temperamental host, but the visit ended on a positive note as the Russians agreed to consider British proposals for the abolition of nuclear tests. From Moscow Macmillan went to Bonn, Paris, and Washington; he was received with varying degrees of skepticism, although Eisenhower, as usual, was friendly. Eventually agreement was reached on a summit meeting in Paris in May 1960. Unfortunately on the eve of the meeting the Russians discovered that high flying American reconnaissance planes were spying on Russia, after actually shooting one of them down. Eisenhower handled the incident ineptly and Khrushchev made it the occasion of breaking off the conference. That autumn, however, Macmillan and Khrushchev both attended the United Nations meeting in New York at which Macmillan made a statesmanlike speech that contrasted favorably with Khrushchev's bombast. The two leaders had some useful talks in private. Despite their differences in age Macmillan established a close relationship with John F. Kennedy when the latter succeeded Eisenhower as President; they kept in close touch during the Cuba missile crisis of October 1962, but there was little that Macmillan could do beyond promising Britain's support at the United Nations. He also took that opportunity to appeal to Khrushchev again for a nuclear test ban treaty, and the following year, shortly before leaving office, he had the gratification of seeing this achieved. In Commonwealth affairs the Churchill and Eden ministries had marked time after the great changes that had taken place during the Attlee administration. As we have seen, the relationship of the members had been redefined, but for the time being there were no further additions. During the Macmillan years the process of decolonization was greatly speeded up. In the dozen years following the war, the Colonial Office had been reorganized and had continued to flourish. It administered a large part of Africa and many island colonies and protectorates in the Caribbean Sea, and the Pacific and Indian Oceans.

Nationalist movements, however, were developing in most of the African colonies, and by the late fifties the will to resist them was ebbing. Kenya was the one African colony in which there was a period of prolonged guerrilla warfare before independence was granted. The stamping out of the Mau Mau movement was a costly and bloody operation, involving the imprisonment of Jomo Kenyatta, the most distinguished nationalist leader in Kenya, who eventually became its president after independence. The first African colony to receive its independence with dominion status in the Commonwealth in 1957 was Ghana, the former Gold Coast in West Africa. Ghana became a republic in 1960 under the presidency of the British- and American-educated Dr. Kwame Nkrumah, a pioneer African nationalist. In 1957 the Federation of Malaya also became independent, an event that had been postponed by a long, drawn out struggle with Chinese Communist guerrillas which British troops had eventually brought to a successful conclusion. In 1963 British Borneo joined the Federation that became known as Malaysia, but in 1965 Singapore withdrew to become a separate member of the Commonwealth. Nigeria, Britain's largest and most advanced African colony, became an independent dominion in 1960 and a republic in 1962, but before long it was torn by a long and bitter civil war. Sierra Leone and Tanganyika became independent in 1961, the latter becoming Tanzania on its union with Zanzibar in 1964; Uganda in 1962 (as well as Jamaica, Trinidad and Tobago in the West Indies); and Kenya in 1963. The Rhodesians presented the most difficult problem. Southern Rhodesia's white population numbered 180,000 in 1951 among 2 million blacks. For thirty years, the whites had enjoyed a substantial

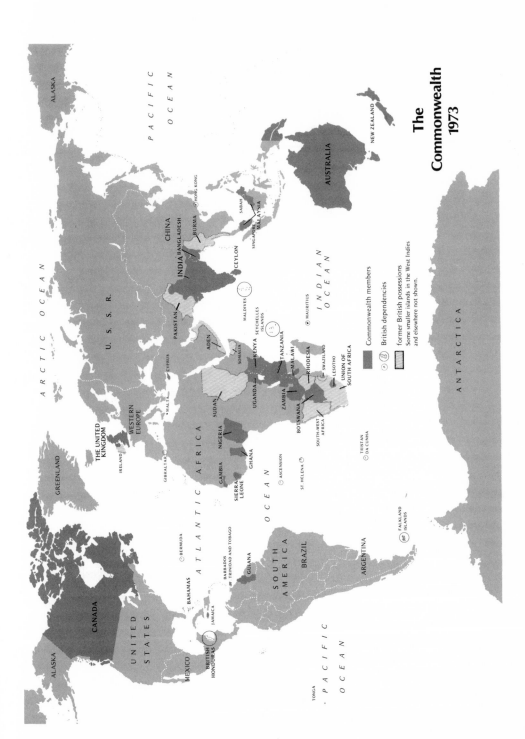

ALASKA

PACIFIC
OCEAN

ARCTIC OCEAN

U. S. S. R.

CHINA

BURMA

INDIA BANGLADESH

PAKISTAN

CEYLON

MALDIVES

HONG KONG

SABAH

SINGAPORE
MALAYSIA

NEW ZEALAND

AUSTRALIA

INDIAN
OCEAN

MAURITIUS

SEYCHELLES
ISLANDS

ADEN

SOMALIA

KENYA

TANZANIA

UGANDA

MALTA

CYPRUS

WESTERN
EUROPE

THE UNITED
KINGDOM

IRELAND

GREENLAND

ALASKA

GIBRALTAR

BERMUDA

ATLANTIC

OCEAN

AFRICA

SUDAN

NIGERIA

GAMBIA

SIERRA
LEONE

GHANA

ASCENSION

ST HELENA

ZAMBIA

MALAWI

RHODESIA

BOTSWANA

SWAZILAND

LESOTHO

SOUTH-WEST
AFRICA

UNION OF
SOUTH AFRICA

TRISTAN
DA CUNHA

ANTARCTICA

CANADA

UNITED
STATES

MEXICO

BRITISH
HONDURAS

BAHAMAS

JAMAICA

BARBADOS
TRINIDAD AND TOBAGO

GUIANA

SOUTH
AMERICA

BRAZIL

ARGENTINA

FALKLAND
ISLANDS

PACIFIC
OCEAN

TONGA

PACIFIC

OCEAN

The
Commonwealth
1973

Commonwealth members

British dependencies

former British possessions
Some smaller islands in the West Indies
and elsewhere not shown.

amount of self-government, under the supervision of Westminster. Northern Rhodesia and Nyasaland, with smaller white populations, had been administered directly by the Colonial Office. The Churchill ministry had sought to solve the problem of government in the whole area by creating, over native protests, a federation dominated by white Rhodesians. The experiment failed, and after visits from Macmillan and Butler and investigation by a Royal commission, it was abandoned, to the disgust of Sir Roy Welensky, Rhodesia's white Prime Minister. Zambia (formerly Northern Rhodesia) and Malawi (formerly Nyasaland) as indicated, became independent black states in 1964, while Southern Rhodesia, the Ulster of British Africa, remained in a state of suspension until its white supremacist government unilaterally declared independence in 1965. Rhodesia has remained a thorn in Britain's side, since no British government can condone Rhodesia's harsh treatment of the black majority, who have always been excluded from any meaningful participation in Rhodesian affairs.

Nationalist movements also developed in the Mediterranean islands of Malta and Cyprus. Malta eventually became an independent dominion in 1964, but the Cyprus problem was more difficult: the Greek majority wanted union with Greece, and the Turkish minority looked to Britain for protection. The British tried to stamp out the guerrilla movement by force, as they had done successfully in Malaya. But the situation in Cyprus was different, because the movement had popular support. The failure of the Suez operation had proved the uselessness of Cyprus as a military base, and in 1957, on prodding from Eisenhower, Macmillan allowed the exiled Cypriot leader, Archbishop Makarios, to return. In 1960 the island became an independent republic within the Commonwealth, under the Archbishop's leadership. With the withdrawal of British troops, however, rioting broke out between the Greeks and Turks, and the United Nations was called upon to maintain the peace.

Macmillan did not confine himself to foreign affairs. In 1957 he made an unprecedented tour of Asian and Pacific Commonwealth countries—India, Pakistan, Ceylon, Australia, and New Zealand—that proved a great success. He followed it in 1960 with an African tour, visiting Ghana, Nigeria, Rhodesia, and the Union of South Africa, where he lectured the South Africans frankly but unsuccessfully on the "winds of change" blowing through the Dark Continent. He was anxious to keep South Africa in the Commonwealth, but when the Union became a republic, the new members and Canada refused at the Commonwealth Conference of 1960 to accept South Africa as a continuing member as long as the policy of apartheid was continued. Consequently South Africa left the Commonwealth that Hertzog and Smuts had played an important part in shaping in happier times.

The dissolution of empire was not a congenial task for Macmillan, who was by temperament an old-fashioned imperialist, but he was also a realist, and he saw what had to be done under the circumstances. Moreover in Ian Macleod (1913–1970) he chose a colonial minister from the progressive wing of the party who firmly believed in the policy he was carrying out. This was not true of the right wing under Lord Salisbury, the man most responsible for Macmillan's succession, who resigned in protest after the decision to allow Markarios to return to Cyprus.

Throughout the fifties the British armed forces had been kept busy around the world, maintaining the imperial position in Malaya, Kenya, Aden, Cyprus, and British Guiana (where the Marxist, Cheddi Jagan, an East Indian, was removed from office with the support of the Negro section of the population). In addition Britain maintained more than four divisions in Germany, and until 1954 a large force had been kept in the Suez Canal Zone. All these activities were a severe strain on the frail British economy, enhancing the balance-of-payments problem and contributing to various sterling crises.

No British statesman was more anxious than Macmillan to see Britain continue to play a leading role in world affairs. But having been chancellor of the exchequer at the time of Suez he was aware that limitations on military expenditures were necessary. Even before Suez, Eden's government had been planning to reduce conventional military appropriations, while continuing to develop the country's nuclear potential. Macmillan implemented this policy with the appointment of a powerful minister of defense to whom the service ministers and all three military services were responsible. Duncan Sandys (b. 1908) was responsible for the 1957 White Paper on Defense, which proposed abolition of conscription by 1960 and sharp reductions in British defense establishments and the number of British troops in Germany. Britain had just successfully tested her own hydrogen bomb and expected by the following year to equip her most modern bombers with these deadly weapons. By this time, however, ballistic missiles were beginning to replace airplanes as vehicles for carrying nuclear weapons in the tactical planning of nuclear powers. At the first Bermuda conference Eisenhower agreed to provide Britain with missiles until Britain's own "Blue Streak" missile was developed, but some years later Blue Streak was abandoned because of its cost. The Americans had also abandoned the Skybolt missile, on which the British had been relying, but at a meeting in Nassau with Macmillan in January 1963 President Kennedy promised Britain Polaris missiles for launching nuclear warheads from submarines.

The decision to put more emphasis on nuclear power and to cut back on conventional forces was made partly for economy, and partly to maintain

Britain's position as a world power. Although Britain's nuclear weapons would be put in the service of NATO it was thought they would also give her greater independence vis-à-vis other nuclear powers. Had she had a nuclear striking capacity at the time of Suez, it was argued, the danger of a Russian missile attack would have been reduced. There was an element of self-delusion in this thinking, however, for Britain remained dependent for missiles on the United States and experience since 1945 has proved that non-nuclear weapons are more likely to be needed in the sort of armed conflicts that break out in the modern world.

The Labour party was put in a difficult position by the Conservative government's nuclear policy, since it was merely a development of an earlier decision by the Attlee administration. Gaitskell and most of his senior colleagues were loath to attack the policy, knowing that in the near future they might have to take responsibility for the country's defense; but a large segment of rank-and-file members and a vocal segment of the public reacted strongly. The campaign for nuclear disarmament, which began in 1958, was a widespread moral outburst similar to the Bulgarian-atrocities agitation of the 1870s. It was led by the same sort of people, whom Disraeli had dismissed contemptuously as "priests, poets, and historians." Its chief priest was Canon John Collins of St. Paul's cathedral, the campaign Chairman, its prose poet, J. B. Priestley, who had started the agitation with an article in the *New Statesman*; and its leading historian, A. J. P. Taylor, one of its most popular speakers. But its high prophet was the ancient Bertrand Russell, leading his next-to-last crusade in his middle eighties. The CND organized an Easter protest march—from Trafalgar Square to the atomic research establishment at Aldermaston, fifty miles from London—that was repeated annually for a number of years. The movement infiltrated the Labour party and at the annual conference of 1960 won a small majority against Gaitskell, the party leader, in support of unilateral repudiation of nuclear weapons. Gaitskell fought the decision, however, and obtained a reversal of the vote in the following year. As often happens with movements of the Left, it began to splinter; and by the time Gaitskell was succeeded by Harold Wilson in 1963 its force was spent.

The British economy picked up quickly after Suez, and Macmillan rode the crest of prosperity, winning another election in 1959 against a divided Labour party. His dramatic interventions abroad and the better times for which he was credited won him the happy nicknames "Macwonder" and "Supermac." In 1961, as inflation and another sterling crisis threatened the new prosperity, the tide began to turn. Selwyn Lloyd, who had left the Foreign Office for the Treasury, overreacted in the deflationary measures he instituted. The economy slowed down for two years and unemployment increased. Macmillan panicked, as by-elections began to turn against the Government, and in one of the most drastic purges in modern British history, he dismissed Lloyd and six other Cabinet ministers. Other posts were re-shuffled, and seven new men came into the Cabinet. The epithet "Mac-wonder" gave way to "Mac the Knife."

Britain had stood aloof from the Common Market since its formation, although she had participated in setting up the less important European Free Trade Association, comprising most of the western European countries out-side the six in the Common Market. As economic clouds began to gather again in the early sixties, and it became apparent that the Common Market countries were outstripping Britain in industrial production and in their rate of growth, Macmillan and his colleagues began to have second thoughts. Gaitskell, speaking for Labour, opposed entry with a Tory-sounding appeal to a "thousand years of history." Butler gave the avant-garde reply on behalf of the Conservatives: "For them, a thousand years of history books. For us, the future."

After preliminary inquiries, Britain made formal application for member-ship in 1963, but Britain's entry was vetoed by De Gaulle, who feared it would upset the balance against France. De Gaulle also resented the special relation-ship between Britain and the United States seen in the Nassau agreement about Polaris missiles. De Gaulle's action was callous, in view of what Britain had done for him during the war, but it was in keeping with his intense and narrow national views. Although they resented the snub, many in both Britain's political parties were relieved, for there was a continuing insular suspicion that closer relations with Europe might threaten British sovereignty. It was also feared that membership in the Common Market might adversely affect Britain's relations with the Commonwealth. Had Britain been in the Market from the beginning, she would have been in a much better position to resist France's demands for agricultural protection; coming in late meant she would have to accept tariffs on agricultural products that would raise the cost of food in Britain and reduce agricultural imports from the Common-wealth. Unless special concessions could be obtained, this would be a par-ticularly hard blow to New Zealand, whose economy was dependent on exporting food products to Britain.

The last year of the Macmillan ministry was marred by scandals and rumors of scandal. In the Vassall spy case, the press made insinuations against two members of the government, one of whom resigned. A commission of inquiry exonerated both ministers, but several journalists were imprisoned for contempt of court when they refused to reveal their sources of information, and the government's unpopularity with the press increased. More serious was the case of another minister, John Profumo, who first denied and then was forced to admit a liaison with a call girl, known also to have had a relationship with a Soviet embassy official. Profumo was forced to resign when it was revealed he had deceived the House of Commons in his earlier statement, but the incident strengthened charges in the press that the government was lax in security matters. Macmillan in particular was criticized for his failure to learn the facts sooner and take the necessary action. Despite his earlier success, many members of his party were becoming impatient with his leadership, as charges of arrogance, indifference, aloofness, and complacency were leveled against him. There was no obvious successor, however, and by the summer of 1963 Macmillan seemed to have recovered his position. Then, in October, just before the annual conference of the Conservative party, he became ill and was forced to resign his office. Nevertheless, from his sickbed he took an active part in choosing his successor. He interviewed each member of the Cabinet individually and also polled party members in both Houses and in the constituencies. The obvious choice again was R. A. Butler, who on different occasions had been acting Prime Minister for Churchill, Eden, and Macmillan. But Butler was never very popular with the party or the public, perhaps because he refused to court them. His chief opponent was Lord Hailsham, the former Quintin Hogg (b. 1907), a more colorful personality, ebullient and outspoken, who overplayed his hand. The majority apparently favored a quiet, dark horse candidate, Lord Home (b. 1903), who had succeeded Selwyn Lloyd as Foreign Secretary. It appears that Home was Macmillan's own preference, and the outgoing Prime Minister lost no time in proposing the Foreign Secretary as his successor while tendering his formal resignation. Despite some last-minute attempts by senior Cabinet ministers to stop his appointment, Home became the first peer to be appointed prime minister in the twentieth century. Taking advantage of recent legislation permitting resignation of a peerage, he gave up his peerage the following year to be a candidate in the general election of 1964, as Sir Alec Douglas-Home, but to no avail. The Conservatives were defeated after thirteen years in office.

During their years in Opposition the Labour party had been wracked by divisions. The right wing paid lip service to nationalization, but urged consolidation of what had been achieved. The left wing demanded faster nationalization and more control by workers, but their plans were rather vague. They tended to take a more independent line in foreign policy, criticizing nuclear weapons, German rearmament, and British support of the United States. The 1955 election had discredited the old right-wing leadership, but Attlee's successor, Hugh Gaitskell, belonged to a third group, the revisionists, who argued that Labour must rethink its policy of socialization and not allow itself to be tied down to forty-year-old shibboleths. When Gaitskell tried to amend Clause 4 (the nationalization clause of the party's constitution), he was rebuffed by the majority at the annual Labour party conference of 1959. Gaitskell died prematurely in 1963, and his successor, Harold Wilson, avoided the mistake of touching the party's sacred cows. Instead, he took the line that the Conservatives were clumsy amateurs who had let the country drift, and the socialists were the practical men who would set it on its course again. In particular he argued that modern government must be science-conscious, and that the socialists were the ones to promote scientific revolution.

The Labour party won the election of 1964 by the narrow margin of 317 seats to 304 for the Conservatives and 9 for the Liberals, giving Labour an overall majority of only 4 seats. As a result, for two years Labour ministers had to be within reach of the House of Commons, when Parliament was sitting, to take part in all important divisions, which was a particularly onerous task for ministers with heavy department duties. Of the twenty-three new Cabinet members only three had held Cabinet office before, which allowed Wilson, one of the few survivors of the Attlee administration, to keep a firm control over them from the beginning.

Harold Wilson (b. 1916), came from a lower-middle-class Yorkshire family, but he went to Oxford on a scholarship, where he studied economics and remained briefly as a teaching fellow before going into the wartime civil service. He was elected to parliament and received a junior appointment in the Attlee administration in 1945, and entered the Cabinet in 1947. With Bevan, he resigned in 1951 in protest against introduction of charges for prescriptions into the free National Health Service and thus made himself popular with the Left. In the years that followed he took an independent course, challenged Gaitskell's leadership in 1960, and impressed the Left by his rhetoric, as Ramsay MacDonald had once done. As Prime Minister, Wilson proved himself a pragmatist, but also a tough, articulate, partisan politician. He was an excellent debater in the House of Commons, where his command of facts, biting wit, and quick turn of phrase delighted his supporters and terrorized his opponents. With his pipe and his soft Yorkshire accent he assumed a more urbane role on television, outshining his opponent, Sir Alec Douglas-Home.

From the beginning Wilson made himself master of his Cabinet (only two other members were survivors of the Attlee Cabinet), establishing business-like rules of procedure and taking an active interest in all the major business of the administration. In his memoirs, he expresses the view that a modern prime minister must be a "director general" as well as a chairman and that he must make his own speeches on major policy matters. Wilson was particularly active in foreign and Commonwealth affairs and probably no prime minister, not even Macmillan, traveled as much. There were frequent visits to various European capitals, including two to Moscow; several to African capitals; and annual trips to Washington, with side visits to Ottawa.

Wilson's chief rival—and, until he resigned in 1968, the second most important member of the Cabinet—was George Brown (b. 1914). Brown was Wilson's opposite in almost every respect. His father was a London truck driver and trade unionist, and Brown, despite his high intelligence, had to leave school at fifteen to earn a living. After working in a London department store, he became a union organizer and was elected to parliament in 1945. He was hotheaded, warmhearted, and ebullient, with a knack of getting along well with all sorts of people. He had tremendous energy, a wide range of interests and knowledge, and a remarkable ability to get things done. Unfortunately, he lacked discretion. Wilson put Brown in charge of the new Department of Economic Affairs, a task he took up with great gusto, although many of the problems facing the ministry proved insoluble. In 1966 he went to the Foreign Office, where, except for his belief in the European Common Market, he followed in the footsteps of his old mentor, Ernest Bevin.

The Wilson ministry is difficult to assess. It faced many problems—the balance of payments, inflation, Rhodesia, Vietnam, Ulster, and the Common Market. For its first two years, moreover, it was hampered by a precarious majority, but this was increased substantially in the election of 1966. The day it took office in 1964 the Labour government was confronted with a sterling deficit of over £7,000 million. Although this was reduced, the adverse balance of payments was to haunt the ministry for five of its six years in office. In retrospect it is clear that the pound should have been immediately devalued or let float in the international money market, but there seemed to be strong arguments against such a course. Labour had devalued the pound in 1949, and the party feared it would be accused of indifference in maintaining the soundness of sterling. The pound sterling was an important international currency, used in a large part of the world, and it was vital that no British government appear to break faith with foreign creditors who kept sterling balances in London. It is true that devaluation would, at least temporarily, have encouraged British exports; but prices would have been driven up at home. Rather than risk a politically unpopular move, the new government took other measures. Temporary surcharges were placed on imports, some rebates were given to exporters, and a large loan was negotiated with the International Monetary Fund. Wilson refused at this stage to take any deflationary measures that might increase unemployment. In November 1967, however, devaluation became unavoidable. The pound was reduced in value from $2.80 to $2.40, but not before heavy losses of sterling balances had been suffered. Nor were the results of devaluation as effective as they would have been earlier. The pressure on sterling continued for another two years, and the government was forced to combat it with traditional measures —higher taxes, higher interest rates, and reduced expenditures—that led to increased unemployment.

The Labour government took office in 1964 with the conviction that, under their rational direction, the economy could be revitalized, the gross national product increased, and the national income redistributed more fairly. It is true that Macmillan had already embarked on indicative planning two years earlier, when he set up the National Economic Development Council (NEDC), but Wilson went well beyond this. He created two new ministries —the Department of Economic Affairs (which absorbed NEDC), under a first secretary of state, and the Ministry of Technology. Although the less important, "Mintech" proved the more successful, first under union leader Frank Cousins (b. 1904), and, after his resignation in 1966, under the colorful and dynamic A. Wedgewood Benn (b. 1925). Britain lagged far behind the United States in industrial research and the new ministry strove to close the gap by active government intervention. British scientific research had until then been spread too thin, and returns in terms of industrial development had been disappointing. Mintech's aim was, in Wilson's words, to "drag firms kicking and screaming into the twentieth century." It proceeded directly or through the Industrial Reorganization Corporation, an instrument of DEA, to intervene in industry on a large scale. It was particularly interested in developing industries to supply goods hitherto imported, to the detriment of Britain's balance of payments. Mergers were encouraged to improve efficiency in the face of foreign competition, and new processes were developed. Huge aluminum smelters were built, with government support, to reduce reliance on imported aluminum. Development of natural gas and oil from newly discovered deposits under the North Sea was promoted. A special accomplishment of the ministry was its promotion of a computer industry capable of competing with that of the United States. The ministry was also responsible for diverting research funds from military to civil purposes and channeling resources from production of military to civil aircraft. In 1967 the Labour government, for political and ideological reasons, fulfilled its pledge to renationalize the steel industry, but the issue was by then less controversial than in 1950–51. It is too soon to assess the value of these developments, most of which were continued by the Conservatives after 1970. But many basic problems remained to be solved.

The Department of Economic Affairs was made responsible for long-range economic planning and coordination and development of a prices and incomes policy, while short-term responsibilities were left to the chancellor of the exchequer. In 1965 the new department produced a pretentious national plan setting growth objectives that were never reached. The plan did not fail through lack of effort by the dynamic minister, George Brown, who claims the failure was due to the government's refusal to give it priority and the Treasury's pursuit of diametrically opposite goals. The Department was also saddled with the apparently impossible task of developing a prices and incomes policy. Initially Brown had considerable success in getting cooperation from both industry and trade unions. In 1966, despite union reluctance and his own misgivings, he gained acceptance for the controversial Prices and Incomes Act, which provided for an initial period of wage freezes, followed by a second period of severe restraints, and then a final period of limited ceilings on wages and prices. A second act was passed in 1967, but plans for a third had to be abandoned in 1968 in the face of increased trade union opposition.

There was a widening rift between the government and the trade union movement in the last years of the ministry. Wilson and his minister of labor, Barbara Castle, were forced to back down in their efforts to impose some controls over trade unions, especially in their ill-fated Industrial Relations Bill of 1959, with respect to wildcat strikes; but they did secure a promise from the Trade Union Congress to set its own house in order. Ignoring the government's calls for deflationary wage restraint, the militant trade union movement had been negotiating higher wage settlements than government guidelines permitted. The result was a slowing down of the rate of industrial growth and an increase in the amount of unemployment, and by 1970 the benefits that had been won were eaten up by the rapid rise in prices. In the view of most economic historians, the overall record of the Labour government was, to say the least, disappointing.

Rhodesia was another problem that plagued the Labour government throughout its six years and absorbed a tremendous amount of time. Rhodesia's unilateral declaration of independence was made only some months after Wilson took office. He made valiant efforts to forestall it, including a visit to Rhodesia's capital, Salisbury. Rhodesia's landlocked position, flanked by the Union of South Africa and the Portuguese-run colonies of Angola and Mozambique, which were all sympathetic to the white Rhodesians, prevented any use of force by the British government. The latter did, however, institute sanctions against the rebel administration. At the same time a continual effort was made to get the Rhodesian Prime Minister, Ian Smith, and his colleagues to abandon their position and return to colonial status until a new constitution was worked out, which would recognize the political rights of the black majority. Wilson met Smith twice on board British battleships—in 1966, on H.M.S. *Tiger*, and in 1968, on H.M.S. *Fearless*, at Gibraltar—and got his agreement to a set of basic principles, but these were always repudiated by Smith's more extreme colleagues. Britain was under unremitting pressure from African and Asian Commonwealth members to take a stronger line. At a tempestuous Commonwealth meeting in London in 1966 Wilson agreed, should Smith turn down a last compromise offer from Britain, to accept the Commonwealth formula (no independence without majority rule) and ask the United Nations for international sanctions against Rhodesia. When the *Tiger* talks failed, sanctions were invoked, but were ineffective because of noncompliance by the Union of South Africa and Portugal. The problem was still unresolved when Labour left office in 1970.

Another African problem arose in Nigeria. A prolonged civil war had resulted from efforts of the large Ibo tribe in the south to set up the independent state of Biafra. The Biafrans excited much sympathy in Britain and internationally partly because a large number were Christian, while the government was predominantly Moslem, partly because the latter were suspected of carrying out a policy of genocide against the Biafrans. But the British government was adamant in honoring its commitments to the official Nigerian government. It was a relief when the war finally came to an end in 1970 and Britain could provide relief assistance to wartorn Biafra.

The war in Vietnam did not directly concern Great Britain, but it was a constant source of embarrassment to a socialist government. The left wing of the party repeatedly urged Wilson to denounce American aggression in that country, but Wilson placed the Anglo-American connection first and refused to make any public break. He did, however, put constant private pressure on the American government. At times these efforts annoyed President Lyndon Johnson, who had taken office in 1963, after the assassination of President Kennedy. During one hot-line telephone conversation in 1965, Wilson was told to look after his own affairs in Malaysia and let the United States look after its affairs in Vietnam without interference. Johnson did encourage Wilson in 1967 to discuss peace overtures to Hanoi with Soviet Premier Alexei Kosygin, and after close consultation with a presidential representative in London, they worked out a formula. It might have led to a ceasefire, but at the last minute, "hawks" in Washington persuaded the President to raise his terms, and the effort failed.

Northern Ireland was a problem that erupted in the last years of the Wilson administration, although it had been simmering for half a century. Ever since partition of Ireland in 1922, the six counties of Northern Ireland, which were self-governing for local purposes, remained an enclave in the United Kingdom, where the Roman Catholic minority (who numbered a third of the population) were deprived of basic civil rights. Many were denied the right to vote in local government elections; constituencies were gerrymandered to perpetuate the Protestant ascendancy; and no Catholic ever participated in the government, which over the years remained solidly Protestant and Unionist. Catholics were also discriminated against on the job market and in public housing. In many ways they were as badly treated as blacks in the most backward southern states of the United States before the civil rights movement of the 1960s. Not surprisingly, the success of such movements in the United States and elsewhere led to similar demands in Northern Ireland in 1967. Under pressure from the Wilson government, the moderate Northern Ireland prime minister, Terence O'Neill, tried to introduce limited reforms, but he met severe resistance from the Unionist right wing and finally resigned in April 1969. His successor did no better, and in August, renewed violence resulted in the summoning of British troops to maintain law and order. The Home Secretary, James Callaghan (b. 1912) visited Ulster and took charge of the situation with a firmness that impressed the British public and the moderates in Northern Ireland. But it was too late for successful British intervention, and in 1970 extremists on both sides took over. When Labour went out of office Callaghan handed over an intractable situation to his successor.

Immigration and the assimilation of immigrants were other issues inherited by the Labour government from its predecessors in 1964 and handed back to them in 1970 far from solved. In the fifties and sixties there was a sudden unprecedented influx of nonwhites from the West Indies, Africa, and Asia, who, as members of the Commonwealth and Empire, had long enjoyed the rights of British subjects, including free entry into the "mother country." By 1961 the net inflow was 125,400, and the total for the years 1953–61 inclusive reached 377,650. Most newcomers found jobs, but on the already crowded island of Britain, it was more difficult to provide them with adequate housing and social services. Moreover, their tendency to congregate in areas where living conditions were already poor added to existing social tensions. Race riots occurred in some cities. In 1961 the Conservative government, under strong pressure from its right wing, passed the Commonwealth Immigration Act, which restricted the flow of such immigrants. This policy was criticized by the Labour Opposition, but continued by them when they came into office; indeed, when Kenya passed legislation designed to drive 150,000 Asian residents out of that country, the Labour government quickly passed another immigration act, restricting the number of Asians who could be admitted annually. On the other hand the same government passed two race relations acts to protect nonwhite immigrants against racial discrimination. Meanwhile, the right wing of the Conservative party, led by Enoch Powell (b. 1912), began taking a belligerently racist line against these immigrants and demanded their repatriation. Although repudiated by the party leadership in the election of 1970, Powell unfortunately had a good deal of popular support.

Gaitskell had opposed British entry into the Common Market, but there were some leading members of the Wilson government who strongly favored membership, notably George Brown, who in 1966 became Foreign Secretary. Wilson was converted to the idea, providing the terms were right, and he persuaded the Cabinet to allow him and Brown to visit the six member nations to sound them out. The arguments for British entry were strong. Britain was no longer a world imperial power, and Commonwealth connections were not growing stronger, while the special relationship with the United States was perhaps illusory. As an industrial power, Britain could not afford to be left outside a tariff barrier that shut her out of most of Western Europe. In his annual Guildhall speech to an audience of London businessmen, Wilson emphasized that Britain could make important techno- logical contributions to the Market. There was a growing feeling that Britain could not afford to stay outside, and also that Western Europe needed a closer union to balance between the giant powers that dominated the world because of their size. If Britain and her EFTA partners were to join the Euro- pean Economic Community, the combined free trade area would include 300 million people. When the proposal was put before Parliament in 1967, Wilson managed to win the support of his party, despite the hostility of seven Cabinet ministers, but thirty-five Labour M.P.'s voted against the Government proposal and another fifty abstained. The Conservative Oppo- sition under Heath gave its support. Unfortunately, De Gaulle again vetoed Britain's application.

Many people are prone to self-deception, but politicians suffer from this failing to a marked degree. Conservatives deceive themselves into thinking things are not as bad as they seem, and reformers, especially out of office, persuade themselves that, if given the chance, they could right all the wrongs they detect. The Wilson administration is an example of how reforming politicians, with the best will in the world, can become the victims of cir- cumstance and see most of their fine plans thwarted. Wilson's *Personal Account* of Labour's six years in office makes it clear how he and his colleagues spent most of their energies in reacting to crises and keeping the Government afloat, leaving them little time to carry out long-range plans. This is not to say that they had no successes. They may have failed to steer the ship of state into a safe harbor, but at least they kept it off the rocks. Professor Beckerman, a severe critic of this government's economic record, makes the point that this failure was "in striking contrast to Labour's outstandingly civilized and enlightened record in many areas of social and educational policy."[1]

[1] *The Labour Government's Economic Record, 1964–1970* (London: Duckworth, 1972), pp. 67–68.

The social legislation of the Attlee ministry was largely the enactment of the wartime Beveridge plan, and as such was accepted by the Conservatives and continued by them during their years in office. This program had sought to protect everybody without discrimination under a national social insurance system covering unemployment, ill health, accident, old age, and death. There were separate benefits to cover these various eventualities and National Assistance payments, later called supplementary benefits, to fill any gaps in the system that might occur. The reformers of the forties were particularly anxious, where possible, to get away from the "means test" mentality of the thirties. By the sixties, however, it was recognized that despite these provisions, people at the bottom of the economic scale were not receiving adequate benefits, and that social welfare payments would have to be made on a more selective basis. In 1966 the new Ministry of Social Security was made responsible for payment of both pensions and supplementary benefits, in an effort to encourage those who needed the extra assistance to claim it. Increasingly, means tests were used to provide larger benefits for poorer families (in the matter of drug prescriptions, for instance). The family allowance system was also redesigned in favor of poorer families. The Conservatives had abandoned wartime rent controls, which undeniably had imposed hardships on many landlords and slowed down renovations, but before long there were many stories of pitiless exploitation of poor tenants by slum landlords. To meet this situation the Labour government introduced the new Rent Control Act and endeavored to keep at least 50 percent of new construction under the control of local authorities. Private house building, however, continued to escalate throughout the sixties. In 1962 Enoch Powell, as minister of national health in the Macmillan ministry, had inaugurated a new plan to improve hospital facilities, which Richard Crossman (b. 1907), his Labour successor, continued and enlarged. Capital expenditures were more than tripled, and the system of health centers for general practitioners was greatly expanded. Serious shortages in accommodation and manpower, however, continued to hamper smooth operation of the National Health Service.

There was also a degree of continuity in education when Anthony Crosland (b. 1918) replaced Sir Edward Boyle (b. 1923), one of the most progressive members of the Macmillan-Home government, as minister of education. Government spending on education at all levels rose rapidly throughout the decade until it reached 6 percent of the gross national product, more than was spent on defense. The number of students in universities, technical colleges, and teachers' colleges doubled, and at last the demand for universal secondary education was met. The placement of children into two separate academic programs at the age of eleven-plus was generally abandoned with the development of comprehensive schools, although their proliferation was slowed down when the Conservatives returned to office in 1970. The sixties were a decade of lively educational debate, and four major reports were published, examining all levels of the national educational system. But although more people may now be reaching the top without the traditional upper-class education, the select minority who attend "public" schools and go on to Oxford or Cambridge still have the best chance of success in later life.

During the Labour administration, laws on divorce, homosexuality, and abortion were liberalized, as in 1960, under the Conservatives, the law controlling gambling had been relaxed, and censorship of the theater was abandoned. In 1966 Wilson redeemed an election promise by appointing a parliamentary commissioner to act as an ombudsman in all cases of citizens' complaints referred through M.P.'s. In 1969, after a trial period of four years, capital punishment was finally abolished on a free vote in both houses.

Continuity in foreign and defense policy was maintained in the sixties, and objections expressed by individual Labour members during their years in Opposition were forgotten. Like Macmillan, Wilson was anxious for Britain to play her accustomed role in world affairs, and despite the cost, he and George Brown, Foreign Secretary from 1966–68, refused to abandon Britain's military commitment "east of Suez" until the devaluation crisis of 1967 forced them to do so. The Labour government did not abandon nuclear weapons, but according to Wilson they did reject the concept of an independent nuclear deterrent. They continued to rely on the Polaris arrangement negotiated by Macmillan at Nassau (which they had denounced when in Opposition), but refused to consider an American proposal for a multilateral nuclear force. Labour in Opposition had laid great stress on working for peace through the United Nations, but in office they soon learned how frustrating and hopeless a task this could be. George Brown was an energetic and well-meaning Foreign Secretary, but his efforts to solve the problems of the Middle East failed, and at the outbreak of the six-day Arab-Israeli war in 1967 Britain looked on, helpless to influence events in spite of her long commitment in the area and her dependence on both the Suez Canal and Middle Eastern oil. In 1968 Brown resigned over a personal disagreement with Wilson and shortly afterward went to the House of Lords as one of the small band of Labour peers.

The record of Wilson's Labour administration was less dramatic than that of Attlee's, and in the later sixties the polls and by-elections went against his administration. When the trend was reversed in 1970 Wilson called an election, but was narrowly defeated, as the Conservatives won 330 seats to Labour's 287. The Conservatives had denounced the Labour government's handling of economic and other problems facing the country and had promised (as Labour had done in 1964) a more professional management of the nation's affairs. The Conservatives had found a new type of leader in Edward Heath (b. 1916), who came from the same lower-middle-class background as Wilson and had earned a similar reputation as a tough, efficient, professional politician. They had both managed to get to Oxford, where Heath had gone in for debating and politics and acquired an upper-class accent, while Wilson had stuck to his books and his Yorkshire brogue and won a fellowship on graduation. Heath had joined the artillery in 1940 and risen to the rank of major. He entered parliament at a by-election in 1947, became a party whip in 1951, and chief whip in 1955, entering Macmillan's Cabinet in 1959. In 1962 he was the Conservative minister entrusted with the Common Market negotiations and he remained a convinced "European."

When the Conservatives came into office Heath determined to lift the economic controls imposed by the Labour government, but with galloping inflation and continued unemployment he was compelled within a year to abandon his hands-off policy. Most of the other problems he inherited seemed equally unmanageable. In Africa, Heath antagonized black members of the Commonwealth by taking a soft line toward South Africa and Rhodesia, but came no nearer to breaking the Rhodesian deadlock. The situation in Ulster grew more serious, and he was forced to suspend the Northern Ireland constitution, sending one of his best ministers William Whitelaw (b. 1918), to take over local administration from the defunct Stormont government. Despite Whitelaw's valiant efforts to woo the Catholic minority the situation went from bad to worse when British soldiers overreacted to a tense situation in Londonderry and killed thirteen civilians. In turn Protestant extremists began to arm and to vie with the IRA in a reign of terror that caught the British soldiers in the middle, hated by both sides and anxious to get out of an impossible situation.

The one area in which Heath succeeded where his predecessors had failed was in bringing Britain into the Common Market. This was made possible by the retirement of De Gaulle, and Heath took steps to ensure the support of De Gaulle's successor, Georges Pompidou. Most of the difficulties this time were domestic, for British enthusiasm had waned, even in Heath's own party. Wilson, seeing the way the wind was blowing—especially in Labour ranks—objected to Britain's entry on the grounds that the Conservative government had not negotiated acceptable terms, but a sizable minority in his own party, under the leadership of Roy Jenkins (b. 1920) repudiated his lead and supported the crucial second reading of the act of parliament required to authorize British entry. Labour support was all-important in giving Heath a respectable majority of 356 to 244, for some Conservatives had refused to support the government. In later stages it was touch and go, but the act was finally passed with small majorities for such momentous legislation. British industry gained entry into the European Economic Community, but it remained to be seen how well it could compete with European industrial powers whose economies had outstripped Britain's in the preceding decade. Moreover, membership seemed to mean a loosening of the Commonwealth connection and unwelcome price increases on food to protect French agriculture, although the latter could also be attributed to rising world prices. Experts were divided on the wisdom of the decision, but the triumphant promarketeers were convinced that Britain could not survive outside the new Europe. The die was cast, and in 1973 Britain entered a new era in her long history.

The postwar British historian can recount the political and economic changes that have taken place since 1945 and speculate on their causes and significance. It is more difficult to give any accurate description of the changes that have taken place in British society, much less to identify the social revolution that some pundits believe has occurred. The perspective is too short to make any meaningful generalizations for social change is not easily measured and the close observer is prone to exaggeration.

For almost a decade after 1945, wartime values seemed to hold. People were concerned with rebuilding and recovering the good things sacrificed during the war. The first signs of rebellion came in the middle fifties, at two different levels. These years saw the appearance of a generation of "angry young men," who scoffed at old values, particularly the materialism they identified with the new prosperity. Their prototype was John Osborne (b. 1929), whose play *Look Back in Anger* first appeared in 1956 to open a new chapter in the history of English theater. John Braine's best-selling novel *Room at the Top* (1957), which was later filmed, underlined this theme with more cynicism and less anger. In Kingsley Amis's *Lucky Jim* (1954) the tone was sardonic humor rather than anger, but again the central figure was an anti-hero and the message was social satire.

The "angry young men" were a relatively small group of young, avant garde intellectuals, but the same period witnessed the emergence of youth power on a much broader stage. The phenomenon spread through the Western world and beyond, but in some ways Britain led the "pop" revolution. Youth began to dictate tastes and fashions to a degree quickly appreciated by politicians and producers of consumer goods. The "Teddy boy" phenomenon of the middle fifties was something of an aberration, for it was confined to a hoodlum element of working-class youth with new money in their pockets, who tried to assert their egos by wearing extravagant Edwardian clothes, indulging in gang warfare, and leading the first race riots in the Notting Hill area of London. They marched to the beat of rock music and tore up cinema theaters with abandon, but the rock-and-roll movement had a wider appeal. Teddy boys were only the vanguard of a larger army of youth who dictated style in popular culture and broke through old class barriers. This was part of an international movement, but the sartorial style of Carnaby Street in London, the emergence of the Beatles, four young Liverpool singers with their new sort of pop music, and the proliferation of boutiques, discotheques, and night clubs made London the "swinging capital of the world." Pop art flourished in psychedelic posters and blow-up photography. Exports of hit records and "mod" clothes favorably affected the British balance of trade, and in 1965 the grateful Queen made the Beatles members of the Order of the British Empire on the advice of her Labour prime minister.

Pop culture emphasized the absurd, the bizarre, the erotic, and the unconventional. It invaded television with programs such as *That Was the Week That Was, Ready, Steady, Go,* and *Top of the Pops,* and films with *A Hard Day's Night* and all the other Beatle movies; but other films such as *Darling* and *Blow-Up* stressed the emptiness of the movement. Pop culture was essentially anti-intellectual and consequently had less to say in print. "Pop" in the words of the pop artist, Richard Hamilton, was "popular, transient, expendable, low cost, mass produced, young, witty, sexy, gimmicky, glamorous, and last, but not least, Big Business."[2] Here was an England that Matthew Arnold, W. E. Gladstone, and Queen Victoria could not have conceived or appreciated, but it is too soon to say whether its significance was more than temporary. Before long, much of the movement's apparent spontaneity was in fact engineered by the media, and as soon as they discovered this many young rebels abandoned it. Youth heroes and youth leaders age quickly and in the seventies the movement is showing signs of disintegration. In entertainment, youth "never had it so good" as in the "swinging sixties." But few outside the universities showed any political interest, and the nation's leaders have not been dislodged, although they may have made some changes in course to avoid unnecessary collisions. The "pop" revolution may be no more than an historical bubble, with as little importance as the South Sea Bubble that seemed at first to overwhelm early eighteenth-century society.

The historian is concerned with the past and should eschew the role of prophet. In looking at the present, however, he may discern much that is familiar as the bequest of past generations to the world in which he lives. The historian has a sense of man's reluctance to abandon this heritage and his efforts to adapt and preserve it. A few years ago, a distinguished American

[2] George Melly, *Revolt into Style: The Pop Arts in Britain* (London: Allen Lane, 1970), p. 143.

observer made this shrewd appraisal of Britain's liberation from empire and the probable consequences:

> . . . . There will be no more Kiplingesque poetry about valorous deeds in India and the Sudan, no more Palmerstonian rhetoric about Englishmen striding the world like Roman citizens of antiquity. The romance of world empire and of the Grand Fleet is at an end. It is understandable, probably inevitable, that the loss is saddening and disruptive. That it is deeply damaging as well, condemning the British people to neurotic despondency or mediocrity, I very much doubt.

> I doubt it because the passing of imperial primacy is a liberation as well as a loss. . . . Deprived of empire but not of the soil in which British greatness took root and grew, Britain is free, as she has not been for centuries, to devote her major energies to the recultivation of that fertile soil. The source of British greatness is and always has been Britain. It was not in the Empire or even in the seas, but rather in the life and history of the United Kingdom that British people created a great literature, spawned the industrial revolution, and developed their extraordinary talent for government.

> Britain has bequeathed a great legacy to much of the world, the legacy of her own experience in constitutional government, peaceful evolution, and the orderly accommodation of diverse interests within a society. . . .

> Empires come and go, but Britain's profound political impact on the world remains. It is a lasting heritage of which the British people have every reason to be proud. When the fleets and bases have been dismantled there will remain—east of Suez and north and south and west of it as well—something much more valuable and much more endurable; the legacy of British ideas which other nations have found worthy of imitation.[3]

The British imperial experience has come to an end, but it was only a short chapter in the country's history, and its passing is no proof that all the other traditions and institutions of the past are doomed.

Britons may take pride in the American senator's generous and moving tribute, but even, which is unlikely, should Scotland, Wales, and the six counties of Ireland follow the example of the departed colonies, we may recall the line in a popular ballad sung by millions in the darkest days of the Second World War:

> There will always be an England.

---

[3] Senator J. William Fulbright, "Liberation from Empire," *Manchester Guardian Weekly*, March 21, 1968, p. 10.

$\mathcal{A}ppendix$
A NOTE ON THE BRITISH
PARLIAMENTARY SYSTEM OF GOVERNMENT

Parliament consists of two chambers: the House of Lords and the House of Commons. Adult English male peers (dukes, marquises, earls, viscounts and barons, but not baronets who are merely hereditary knights) have always been entitled to seats in the House of Lords. Since 1963, peeresses in their own right have been entitled to sit, and heirs have been entitled to decline taking up a title passing to them.

Until 1963 the Scottish peers elected sixteen of their number at the beginning of each parliament to sit in the House of Lords, but since that date heirs of all the surviving Scottish peerages have been given seats. From 1801 to 1922 the Irish peers elected twenty-eight of their number to lifetime seats in the House of Lords, but none have been elected since the setting up of the Irish Free State. Irish peers, such as Lord Palmerston, who were not elected as representative peers were entitled to election to the House of Commons. Some sons of peers have the right to be called "Lord" as a courtesy title, but, as they do not sit in the House of Lords, they are eligible for election to the House of Commons until, in some cases, they succeed to their hereditary titles or until they are created peers in their own right. For instance, Lord John Russell, a younger son of the sixth Duke of Bedford, sat in the Commons until 1861, when he was created Earl Russell and consequently moved to the House of Lords. Although the House of Lords is traditionally a hereditary institution, life peers and peeresses have been appointed since 1958 with the right to seats in the House of Lords. The Archbishops of Canterbury and York and twenty-four other bishops of the established Church of England also have seats in the Lords.

The House of Commons consists of 635 members (658 in 1815) elected to represent county or borough (town) constituencies. A Parliament is elected for not more than five years (prior to 1911 for not more than seven), but it may be dissolved by the Crown on the advice of the prime minister at any time and a new election held. The Prime Minister holds his office because he commands a majority in the House of Commons (in some cases with the tacit support of minority groups, as in 1974). If he loses his majority either at a general election or because he no longer commands the confidence of his supporters, he has to resign.

All ministers are appointed by the crown on the advice of the prime minister, who normally chooses them from his followers in the two houses of Parliament. Senior ministers designated by the prime minister form the cabinet, which only consisted of fourteen members in 1815, but which numbers twenty-one in 1974.

The majority of the ministers sit on the front bench in the House of Commons, where the debates are generally longer and more significant, but prior to 1911 government legislation was often blocked in the House of Lords. Bills must pass three readings—the first a formal permission to introduce the bill, the second providing a debate on the principle, and the third to consider amendments in detail that have been introduced at an informal committee stage—in both houses and be approved by the crown before they become law. Private members, known as backbenchers (since they sit behind the ministers), are entitled to introduce private bills, but such bills have less chance of passing than government bills introduced by ministers, because of the pressure of time. At the beginning of each session the King's (or Queen's) Speech, prepared by the ministers, indicates the main government legislation proposed for the session. When the business of the parliamentary year is completed Parliament is prorogued by the crown on the advice of the prime minister and a new session is begun with new business, for bills cannot be carried over from one session to another. Today the new session normally begins in November but it used to begin in the New Year. Formal votes, or divisions, are taken by having members walk into the Government or Opposition lobbies, where they are counted by two tellers as they enter. When members of opposite parties make private arrangements to be absent at the same time and, consequently, not affect the results of a division, they are said to "pair."

One of the main differences between the parliamentary and the congressional systems of government is that the prime minister and his colleagues can and must attend parliament to answer questions and defend their policies. Parties opposed to the government are organized to resist legislation and to search for weak points in its policies. The head of the largest party opposed to the government holds the official position, now a salaried one, of leader of the Opposition. Some major debates are held, not on bills, but on resolutions upholding or condemning the government's policies. A government's defeat on a matter of confidence normally leads to its resignation or to the dissolution of Parliament and a general election.

The crown, i.e. the king or queen as the case may be, is the nominal head of the executive government and commander-in-chief of the armed forces, and acts of state are done in the royal name. The powers of the crown have decreased considerably since 1815, but its wearer continues to be charged with the important duty of finding a new prime minister when the incumbent resigns office. Normally the choice is obvious, since the successor must be able to command a majority in the House of Commons, but occasionally there may be some uncertainty on this point.

Select Bibliography

R. K. Webb, *Modern England from the Eighteenth Century to the Present* (New York, 1968) is an excellent general work covering the period from the 1760s to the mid-1960s in one large volume of more than a quarter of a million words, with greatest emphasis on the nineteenth century. There are three volumes (Woodward, Ensor, and Taylor, listed separately in the following sections) in the fifteen-volume *Oxford History of England*, covering the period 1815 to 1945. Elie Halévy's magisterial *History of the English People, 1815–1914* (tr. E. I. Watkin) was never completed, but the six volumes (listed below) that were published remain basic reading for the period they cover. D. L. Keir, *Constitutional History of Modern Britain* (London, 8th ed., 1966) remains a standard survey of modern constitutional history. J. P. Mackintosh, *The British Cabinet* (London, 1962) provides a historical approach to the subject, as do the older volumes by W. Ivor Jennings, *Cabinet Government* and *Parliament* (Cambridge, 1936 and 1940) and Robert Blake, *The Conservative Party from Peel to Churchill* (New York, 1971) covers a century of Conservative party history briefly but perceptively. W. C. Costin and Steven Watson (eds.) *The Law and Working of the Constitution*, vol. II (London, 1952), provides a useful collection of constitutional documents. J. H. Clapham, *An Economic History of Modern Britain*, 3 vols. (Cambridge, 1927, 1934, 1938; 2nd ed., 1950–52) remains the standard detailed economic history for the years 1820–1929. W. H. Court, *Concise Economic History of Britain since 1750 to Recent Times* (Cambridge, 1954) is a useful economic survey, while Peter Mathias, *The First Industrial Nation* (London, 1969), provides a more detailed analysis up to 1914, and Eric J. Hobsbawm, *Industry and Empire: an Economic*

Because of the necessary restrictions on the scope of this bibliography, many books of equal merit to others that have been included have unavoidably been omitted. Titles are included in what seem to be the most appropriate sections, but not repeated in subsequent sections where they may also be relevant.

History of Britain (London, 1968), gives a highly readable Marxist interpretation. Judith Ryder and H. Silver, *Modern English Society, History and Structure, 1850–1970* (London, 1970) is a useful sociological study with some interesting charts and tables. G. D. H. Cole, *Short History of the British Working Class Movement, 1789–1925*, 3 vols. (London, rev. ed., 1927), is one of many books by the same author in the Fabian tradition. E. J. Hobsbawm, *Labouring Men: Studies in the History of Labour* (London, 1964) is a collection of essays covering the period since 1834.

J. A. Williamson, *A Short History of British Expansion* (Volume II), *The Modern Empire and Commonwealth* (London, 4th rev. ed., 1953), although first published in 1922, remains a standard reference. A. L. Burt, *The Evolution of the British Empire and Commonwealth from the American Revolution* (Boston, 1956) and P. Knaplund, *The British Empire, 1815–1939* (New York, 1941) provide more recent surveys of imperial history. A. P. Thornton, *The Imperial Idea and its Enemies* (London, 1959), is a brilliant piece of interpretative writing, tracing the conflicting views of empire from its Victorian high noon to mid-twentieth century decline. There is a lack of general surveys of British foreign policy since 1815, but Lord Strang, *Britain in World Affairs* (London, 1961), is a readable, brief survey from the sixteenth century by a perceptive retired British diplomat who himself played a small role as Britain's envoy to Moscow in 1939. Modern Irish History is well and thoroughly covered in F. S. L. Lyons, *Ireland Since the Famine* (London, 1971), while more briefly, Lawrence McCaffrey, *The Irish Question 1800–1922* (Lexington, Kentucky, 1968), looks back to the Act of Union.

There is no major bibliography covering the whole period of this book. A. Taylor Milne (ed.), *Writings on British History*, 8 vols. (London, 1937–1960), covers books and articles published from 1934 to 1945. Two further volumes in this series compiled by D. J. Munro covering the years 1946–48 and 1949–51 have been published by the Institute of Historical Research, University of London, in 1973 and 1974. G. R. Elton, *Modern Historians on British History 1485–1945* (London, 1970) is a select critical bibliography of 1,351 books and articles published between 1945 and 1959, one-third of which deal with British history since 1815. B. R. Mitchell and Phyllis M. Deane (eds.), *Abstracts of British Historical Statistics* (Cambridge, 1962), and W. A. Cole, *Economic Growth 1688–1959: Trends and Structure* (Cambridge, 2nd ed., 1967), provide valuable statistical tables and information regarding economic growth from the beginning of the eighteenth century.

The Nineteenth Century

G. M. Young, *Victorian England—Portrait of an Age* (Oxford, 1936), is "an essay in interpretation" and already a classic in its own right. Donald

Southgate, *The Passing of the Whigs, 1832–1886* (London, 1962), surveys a big subject, but more detailed work needs to be done on party history. Joseph Altholz's bibliographic handbook, *Victorian England, 1837–1901* (Cambridge, 1970), is conveniently divided into fourteen sections, most of them subdivided into subsections on printed sources, surveys, monographs, biographies, and articles.

Walter Bagehot, *The English Constitution*, first published in 1867 on the eve of the second Reform Act, came out in a second edition in 1872 with an Introduction commenting critically on that act. It is the classic contemporary interpretation of the Victorian constitution and one of the most readable constitutional works ever written. Charles Seymour, *Electoral Reform in England and Wales: the Development and Operation of the Parliamentary Franchise* (New Haven, 1915, reprinted 1970), remains the best account of the subject covering the three Reform Acts of the nineteenth century. J. B. Conacher (ed.), *The Emergence of British Parliamentary Democracy in the Nineteenth Century: The Passing of the Reform Acts of 1832, 1867 and 1884–1885* (New York, 1970), contains readings from contemporary and secondary sources about the three acts. Henry Parris, *Constitutional Bureaucracy: The Development of British Central Administration since the Eighteenth Century* (London, 1969), is a useful introduction to a very large subject. David Roberts, *Victorian Origins of the British Welfare State* (New Haven, 1960), is a pioneer study on one aspect of the same subject. S. G. Checkland, *The Rise of Industrial Society in England, 1815–1885* (London, 1964), emphasizes the social aspects of economic history. W. W. Rostow, *The British Economy of the Nineteenth Century* (Oxford, 1948), is an important if controversial essay. F. M. L. Thompson, *English Landed Society in the Nineteenth Century* (London, 1963), and Harold Perkin, *The Origins of Modern English Society, 1780–1880*, in the same series (London, 1969) are valuable studies in social history, as is Brian Harrison, *Drink and the Victorians* (London, 1971). Asa Briggs, *Victorian People* and *Victorian Cities* (London, 1954 and 1963) are individual and corporate case studies in social history. J. W. Adamson, *English Education, 1789–1902* (Cambridge, 1930), remains a useful survey, while Mary Sturt, *The Education of the People: A History of Primary Education in England and Wales in the Nineteenth Century* (London, 1967), is a more recent study of elementary education in the nineteenth century. Lady Longford, *Queen Victoria: Born to Succeed* (London, 1964), is probably the best biography of the Queen, but there is still room for improvement. R. W. Seton Watson, *Britain in Europe, 1789–1914* (Cambridge, 2nd ed. 1955), is the best detailed survey of foreign policy. Kenneth Bourne, *The Foreign Policy of Victorian England* (Oxford, 1970), provides a selection of documents with useful introductions. Crane Brinton, *English Political Thought in the Nineteenth Century* (Cambridge, Mass., 1939, 2nd ed. 1949), is an early but useful volume by a versatile historian. D. C. Somervel, *English Thought in the Nineteenth Century* (London, 1929), is very summary but a useful introduction. Owen Chadwick, *The Victorian Church*, 2 vols. (London, 1966, 1970) is the best introduction to Victorian religion.

R. K. Webb, *English History, 1815–1914* (Service Centre for Teachers of History, No. 64, Washington, 1967), provides a short select bibliography for the nineteenth century. An annual bibliography of books and articles on Victorian England published in the preceding year has appeared in the journal *Victorian Studies* (University of Indiana) since 1958.

1850–1865

Elie Halévy's *England in 1815*, vol. I of Halévy's great *History*, translated by Edward I. Watkin (first published in French in 1912; 2nd English edition, 1924), is a brilliant and scholarly overview of the state of England at the beginning of the nineteenth century. The next three volumes, II, *The Liberal Awakening, 1815–1830* (rev. ed., London, 1949), III, *The Triumph of Reform, 1830–1841* (rev. ed., London, 1950), and IV, *The Age of Peel and Cobden, 1841–1852* (rev. ed., London, 1951), carry the story forward in great detail to midcentury, but Halévy died before the last volume was completed and the revised edition has appeared with a concluding essay by R. B. McCallum under the title *Victorian Years*. An older and still more detailed, but less analytical, history of these years is Spencer Walpole, *A History of England from the Conclusion of the Great War in 1815* in 6 vols. (London, new ed. 1890). A sequel, *The History of Twenty-five Years* in four vols. (London, 1904–8), covers the years 1856–80. Asa Briggs, *The Age of Improvement* (London, 1959), republished in the United States in paperback under the main title, *The Making of Modern England, 1784–1867* (New York, 1959), is an excellent volume in the Longmans *History of England* (in ten volumes edited by W. N. Medlicott), with the emphasis on social history. E. L. Woodward, *The Age of Reform, 1815–1870* (2nd ed., Oxford, 1962), covers the period for the *Oxford History of England*. The organization is awkward, but it has good chapters on foreign policy. Dereck Beales, *From Castlereagh to Gladstone, 1815–1880* (London and New York, 1969), is a briefer and more recent account of the period. The half century is partly covered by two volumes in the *English Historical Documents* series edited by D. C. Douglas, *Vol. XI, 1783–1832*, edited by A. Aspinall (London, 1959), and *Vol. XII (1), 1833–1874*, edited by G. M. Young and W. D. Handcock (London, 1956). The latter, divided into twelve parts, contains over a thousand pages of introductions, select bibliographies, and documents covering a wide range of topics. G. M. Young (ed.), *Early Victorian England*, 2 vols. (Oxford, 1934), contains a wide range of articles on social history and many illustrations. J. F. C. Harrison, *Early Victorian Britain, 1830–1850* (London, 1971), and Geoffrey Best, *Mid-Victorian Britain* (London, 1971), both companion volumes and well illustrated, offer more modern interpretations of the social history of the period. G. Kitson Clark, *The Making of Victorian England* (London, 1962), contains nine interpretative essays by a leading historian of the period. R. Robson (ed.), *Ideas and Institutions of Victorian England: Essays in Honour of George Kitson Clark* (London, 1967), is an important collection by some of Kitson Clark's former students and colleagues. W. L. Burn, *The Age of Equipoise: A Study of the Mid-Victorian Generation* (London, 1964), is an idiosyncratic but original contribution to Victorian social history.

E. P. Thompson in his monumental *The Making of the English Working Class* (London, 1963) develops the thesis that a revolutionary working class tradition ripened in the half century before 1832, in contrast to earlier liberal historians, such as Barbara and J. L. Hammond who, in a series of books published forty or fifty years ago, argued that the working class were downtrodden but law-abiding. A briefer and more conventional approach to the period is to be found in R. J. White, *Waterloo to Peterloo* (London, 1957). W. R. Brock, *Lord Liverpool and Liberal Toryism* (London, 1941), and Austin Mitchell, *The Whigs in Opposition* (Oxford, 1967), provide two excellent studies of party politics of the period, while G. I. T. Machin, *The Catholic Question in English Politics, 1820–1830* (Oxford, 1964), deals with the most important political question preceding Reform. G. S. Veitch, *The Genesis of Reform* (London, 1913), traces the demand for reform back to the 1770s. J. R. M. Butler, *The Passing of the Great Reform Bill* (London, 1914), remains the standard narrative account. Michael Brock, *The Great Reform Act* (London, 1973), provides a briefer but more recent treatment. J. Hamburger, *James Mill and the Art of Revolution* (New Haven: 1963), analyzes the role of the extraparliamentary Radicals in the passing of the Reform Bill. Norman Gash, *Politics in the Age of Peel* (London, 1953), provides an excellent analysis of the Reform Act, the debate over it, and its consequences, especially in the constituencies. His *Reaction and Reconstruction in English Politics, 1832–1852* (Oxford, 1965) contains six valuable essays on the state of the constitution and of political parties in the period. Geoffrey Finlayson, *England in the Eighteen-Thirties: Decade of Reform* (London, 1969), is a slighter and more general book. J. Hamburger, *Intellectuals in Politics: John Stuart Mill and the Philosophical Radicals* (New Haven, 1965), and Norman McCord, *The Anti-Corn Law League, 1838–1846* (London, 1958), deal with separate but related radical movements of the period. Robert Stewart, *The Politics of Protection: Lord Derby and the Protectionist Party, 1841–1852* (Cambridge, 1971), J. B. Conacher, *The Peelites and the Party System, 1846–1852* (Newton Abbot, 1972) and *The Aberdeen Coalition, 1852–1855* (Cambridge, 1968), and J. R. Vincent, *The Foundation of the Liberal Party, 1857–1868* (London, 1966), are four monographs dealing with various aspects of party politics in the mid-nineteenth century. C. A. Bodelson, *Studies in Mid-Victorian Imperialism* (Copenhagen, 1924, London, 1966), and R. L. Schuyler, *The Fall of the Old Colonial System* (London, 1945), are important studies of mid-Victorian imperial policy. There are many books on various aspects of Chartism, but Mark Hovell, *The Chartist Movement* (Manchester, 1918), remains the standard general work. Asa Briggs (ed.), *Chartist Studies* (London, 1959), is a valuable collection of essays stressing the regional aspects of Chartism. For the impact of Darwin see Gertrude Himmelfarb, *Darwin and the Darwinian Revolution* (New York, 1959) and Alvar Ellegard, *Darwin and the General Readers: the Reception of Darwin's Theory of Evolution in the British Periodical* Press (Goteborg, 1958).

The two- or three-volume official biographies of most leading Victorian statesmen are useful mainly for the private correspondence they publish, but there are some more modern interpretations. Norman Gash's *Mr. Secretary Peel* and *Sir Robert Peel* (London, 1961 and 1972) and Robert Blake's *Disraeli* (London, 1966) are outstanding. Other good biographies include John Prest, *Lord John Russell* (London, 1972), G. M. Trevelyan, *Lord Grey of the Reform Bill* (London, 1920) and *The Life of John Bright* (London, 1913), J. L. and Barbara Hammond, *Lord Shaftesbury* (London, rev. ed. 1936), and Geoffrey Best's briefer and more recent *Shaftesbury* (London, 1964), Donald Read, *Cobden and Bright: a Victorian Political Partnership* (London, 1967), and Angus Macintyre, *The Liberator: Daniel O'Connell and the Irish Party, 1830–1847* (London, 1965). Jaspar Ridley's *Lord Palmerston* (London, 1971) is readable and informative but has not superceded Herbert Bell's *Lord Palmerston*, 2 vols. (London, 1936). John Morley, *Life of William Ewart Gladstone*, vol. I of the official biography (London, 1903), covers this period.

1865–1914

Although dated, R. K. Ensor's volume, *England, 1870–1914* (Oxford, 1936) in the *Oxford History of England* covers this period very well, except that it awkwardly begins in 1870 in the middle of the Gladstone ministry, scarcely a turning point in British history. Much of the period is covered in detail in Herbert Paul's old-fashioned but informative *A History of Modern England*, 5 vols. (London, 1904–6), which covers the period from 1848 to 1895. Elie Halévy jumped ahead to write the *Epilogue* of his *History* in two volumes: *Imperialism and the Rise of Labour, 1895–1905* (London, 1929) and *The Rule of Democracy, 1905–1914* (London, 1934; divided into two parts in the 1952 edition) still present a perceptive, detailed account of the last twenty years of this period. W. Ashworth, *An Economic History of England, 1870–1939* (London, 1960), is a valuable survey of the subject.

F. B. Smith, *The Making of the Second Reform Bill* (Cambridge, 1966), is a sound, straightforward account of the Reform issue in 1866–67. Maurice Cowling, *1867: Disraeli, Gladstone and Revolution* (Cambridge, 1967), is even more detailed but unnecessarily involved. H. J. Hanham, *Elections and Party Management: Politics in the Time of Disraeli and Gladstone* (London, 1959), deals with the consequences of the 1867 Reform Act as Gash did with the 1832 act, but rather differently. Paul Smith, *Disraelian Conservatism and Social Reform* (London, 1967), a very thorough examination of the topic, indicates that the Disraeli Government of 1874–80 followed a Peelite tradition. R. W. Seton-Watson, *Disraeli, Gladstone and the Eastern Question: A Study in Diplomacy and Party Politics* (London, 1935), is a very detailed study, rather more partial to Gladstone than to Disraeli. R. T. Shannon, *Gladstone and the Bulgarian Atrocities, 1876* (Edinburgh, 1963), argues that Gladstone responded to, rather than led, public opinion on this occasion. Walter L. Arnstein, *The Bradlaugh Case* (Oxford, 1965), is a model study of an important issue. Peter Stansky, *Ambitions and Strategies: the Struggle for the Leadership of the Liberal Party in the 1890s* (Oxford, 1964), tells an intriguing inside story. A. M. McBriar, *Fabian Socialism in British Politics, 1884–1918* (Cambridge, 1962), is probably the best of many books on the Fabians, because it is more objective than most of them. Henry Pelling, *The Origins of the Labour Party, 1880–1900* (London, 1954), and J. H. Stewart Reid, *The Origins of the British Labour Party* (Minneapolis, 1955), treat the same topic differently. Pelling emphasizes the intellectual roots of the party, while Reid gives a more factual political account and brings the story up to 1914. Phillip P. Poirier, *The Advent of the British Labour Party, 1900–1906* (London, 1958), shows how the new party took root and made an electoral alliance with the Liberals. George Dangerfield, *The Strange Death of Liberal England* (New York, 1936), is an overly sensational book, exaggerating the thesis of Liberal decline. L. T. Hobhouse, *Liberalism* (London, 1911), presents a rationale for the new Liberalism and relates it to the older Liberalism of the nineteenth century. Donald Read, *Edwardian England 1901–1915* (London, 1972), is a critical and well illustrated survey of the period. Peter Rowland, *The Last Liberal Governments*, 2 vols. (London, 1968 and 1971), is a fairly factual detailed account of the subject. Neal Blewett, *The Peers, the Parties and the People: The General Elections of 1910* (London, 1972), rejects the Dangerfield thesis. Bentley B. Gilbert, *The Evolution of National Insurance in Great Britain: the Origins of the Welfare State* (London, 1966), while somewhat critical of the Liberal Government, throws much light on its social legislation.

Kenneth O. Morgan, *The Age of Lloyd George: The Liberal Party and British Politics, 1890–1929* (London, 1971), has a useful introduction and an interesting collection of documentary readings.

The Cambridge History of the British Empire, vol. III (Cambridge, 1959) contains several important articles on imperial policy in the last quarter of the nineteenth century. Ronald E. Robinson and John Gallagher, *Africa and the Victorians: the Official Mind of Imperialism* (London, 1961), is an important if controversial study emphasizing how strategic and political considerations were affected by the official mind. John A. S. Grenville, *Lord Salisbury and Foreign Policy: the Close of the Nineteenth Century* (London, 1964), and G. W. Monger, *The End of Isolation: British Foreign Policy 1900–1907* (Edinburgh, 1963), are two important recent monographs in this area. C. J. Lowe, *The Reluctant Imperialists: British Foreign Policy 1878–1902*, 2 vols. (London, 1967), is a more general account, the second volume containing illustrative documents. C. J. Lowe and M. L. Dockrill, *The Mirage of Power*, vol. I, *British Foreign Policy, 1902–1914* (London, 1972), carries the story forward to the First World War. C. C. O'Brien, *Parnell and his Party* (Oxford, 1957), is probably the best book on the subject, although J. L. Hammond, *Gladstone and the Irish Nation* (London, 1938) remains very readable and informative. L. P. Curtis, *Coercion and Conciliation, 1880–1892* (Princeton, 1963), is a scholarly treatment of Conservative policy towards Ireland.

John Morley, *The Life of William Ewart Gladstone*, 3 vols. (London, 1903), although written by a close associate within five years of Gladstone's death, remains the most important book on Gladstone. Philip Magnus, *Gladstone* (London, 1954), adds some details about Gladstone's private life. P. T. Marsh, *The Victorian Church in Decline: Archbishop Tait and the Church of England, 1868–1882* (London, 1969), is an important study of a key churchman of the period. There is no definitive biography of Salisbury, although the incomplete four-volume *Life* by his daughter, Lady Gwendolyn Cecil (London, 1921–32), is useful as far as it goes. Likewise Kenneth Young, *Arthur James Balfour: the Happy Life of the Politician, Prime Minister, Statesman and Philosopher, 1848–1930* (London, 1963), must do until a more definitive biographer appears. Roy Jenkins, *Asquith* (London, 1964), is better than the official biography by J. A. Spender and Cyril Asquith for the pre-1916 period. Randolph S. Churchill, *Winston Churchill*, vol. I (1874–1900) and vol. II (1900–1914) (London, 1966, 1967), cover Churchill's early life in great detail with three supporting volumes of documents. Robert Blake, *The Unknown Prime Minister: The Life and Times of Robert Bonar Law, 1895–1923* (London, 1955), is an excellent biography giving sympathetic treatment to an outwardly unattractive figure.

The Twentieth Century since 1914

Five books may be mentioned covering the major part of the period since 1914. A. F. Havighurst, *Twentieth Century Britain* (2nd ed., New York, 1966), the first major survey, is a well-informed and well-balanced textbook; W. N. Medlicott, *Contemporary England, 1914–1964* (London, 1967), the final volume in Longman's *History of England*, is a solid, if sometimes elusive, general narrative; T. O. Lloyd, *Empire to Welfare State—English History 1906–1967* (Oxford, 1970), is a sophisticated, informative, and highly readable general account of these years; David Thompson, *England in the Twentieth Century* (London, 1965), is a briefer and more general survey in the *Pelican History of England*; and Arthur Marwick, *Britain in a Century of Total War—War, Peace and Social Change 1900–1967* (London, 1970), is a most readable and thought-provoking social history, written from a left wing point of view. D. E. Butler and Jennie Freeman, *British Political Facts 1900–1967* (London, 2nd ed., 1968), is a mine of information regarding elections, changes in administrations, officeholders, etc., and also contains some social and economic statistics. D. E. Butler, *The Electoral System in Britain since 1918* (Oxford, 2nd ed., 1963), is a useful summary of electoral changes that have occurred during the period. Robert T. MacKenzie, *British Political Parties* (London, 2nd ed., 1963), provides a lucid account of the organization of the major political parties and how they work. Sidney Pollard, *The Development of the British Economy 1914–1950* (London, 1962), and A. Youngson, *The British Economy 1920–1957* (London, 1960), are useful economic surveys of much of the period. Henry Pelling, *A Short History of the Labour Party* (London, 1962), provides a short sketch down to 1960. W. N. Medlicott, *British Foreign Policy since Versailles 1919–1963* (London, 2nd ed., 1968), is a useful extension of an earlier survey by an able diplomatic historian.

1914–1945

A. J. P. Taylor, *English History, 1914–1945* (New York and Oxford, 1965), is perhaps the most readable and most controversial volume in the *Oxford History of England*. Despite gaps and clearly expressed prejudices, it is both witty, informative, and thought-provoking, and has an excellent annotated bibliography. C. L. Mowat, *Britain between the Wars, 1918–1940* (London, 1955), the first thorough study of the interwar period, is a masterpiece of its kind, weaving together the political, social, and intellectual history of the period with consummate skill. G. D. H. Cole, *History of the Labour Party from 1914* (London, 1948), is a detailed and informative history of the party from the inside, covering the period. Trevor Wilson, *The Downfall of the*

Liberal Party, 1914–1935 (London, 1966), is a thorough and sympathetic study of that melancholy subject. (For the Conservative party see Robert Blake's account already mentioned.) P. A. Reynolds, *British Foreign Policy in the Inter-War Years* (London, 1954), is a compact but authoritative summary of the subject. F. S. Northedge, *The Troubled Giant: Britain among the Great Powers, 1916–1939* (London, 1966), is a much more detailed study. Christopher Thorne, *The Approach of War, 1938–9* (London, 1967), gives a straightforward account of the events leading to the outbreak of the second World War, while J. W. Wheeler-Bennett, *Munich: Prologue to Tragedy* (London, 1948), is a rather more detailed study of the Munich settlement and its consequences, by a severe critic. A. J. P. Taylor in his controversial *Origins of the Second World War* (London, 1961) takes a very different point of view. For social policy see Bentley Gilbert, *British Social Policy, 1914–1939* (London, 1970), and for an important chapter in British economic history see H. W. Richardson, *Economic Recovery in Britain, 1932–38* (London, 1967).

Of the innumerable books written about the First World War mention may be made of Winston Churchill, *The World Crisis*, 5 vols. (London, 1923–29), readable and informative but semiautobiographical; C. R. M. F. Crutwell, *A History of the Great War* (Oxford, 1934), probably the best single-volume military account from the British point of view; and E. L. Woodward, *Great Britain and The War of 1914–18* (London, 1967), a general survey written long after the event, but colored by personal experience. Arthur Marwick, *The Deluge: British Society and the First World War* (London, 1965), is a critical study of the home front and the social consequences of the war by a younger historian with no personal memories of it. For the Second World War see W. S. Churchill, *The Second World War*, 6 vols. (London, 1948–54), a fascinating and informative personal account written in majestic prose by the man in the center, and E. L. Woodward, *British Foreign Policy in the Second World War* (London, 1962). For a general account see Henry Pelling, *Britain and the Second World War* (London, 1970); and for a very interesting and detailed account of the home front, see Angus Calder, *The People's War: Britain 1939–45* (London, 1969). Of the many volumes in the various official histories of the Second World War mention may be made of S. W. Roskill, *The War at Sea*, 3 vols. (London, 1954–61) and C. K. Webster and N. Frankland, *The Strategic Air Offensive against Germany 1939–1945*, 4 vols. (London, 1961).

Since 1918 politicians have become increasingly addicted to writing their memoirs on retirement. H. H. Asquith, *Memories and Reflections*, 2 vols. (London, 1928), is rather disappointing, but throws some light on the fall of his government in 1916. Lloyd George's *War Memoirs*, 6 vols. (1933–36) and *The Truth about the Peace Treaties* (London, 1938) are highly polemical but contain important documents. L. S. Amery, *My Political Life*, 3 vols. (London, 1953), Duff Cooper (Lord Norwich), *Old Men Forget* (London, 1953), and Hugh Dalton, *Memoirs*, 3 vols., the third post-1945 (London, 1953, 1957, and 1962), are probably the most interesting and informative. Philip Snowden, *Autobiography*, 2 vols. (London, 1934) is long and embittered; Lord Templewood (Sir Samuel Hoare), *Nine Troubled Years* (London, 1954), is an apologia for appeasement; Lord (Sir Herbert) Samuel's *Memoirs* (London, 1945) are useful for the General Strike and the 1913 crisis. The *Memoirs of Anthony Eden, Lord Avon, Facing the Dictators, 1923–1938* (London, 1962) is important for the diplomatic history of these years. *Autobiography of Bertrand Russell* (London, 1967–69) and Harold Nicolson, *Diaries and Letters*, 3 vols. (London, 1966–68), the latter covering the years 1930–1962, should be mentioned as important memoirs of two distinguished, but very different, literary figures—the one an eminent antiestablishmentarian, the other hovering on the fringes of the political world.

The number of good biographies for the period is limited. Sir Harold Nicolson, *King George the Fifth: his Life and Reign* (London, 1952), is a model of its kind and particularly useful for the constitutional crises of the reign. It is solid, but intrinsically less interesting, based on research in the royal archives, as is Sir J. W. Wheeler Bennett's *George VI* (London, 1958). There is as yet no definitive biography of Lloyd George, but Tom Jones' *Lloyd George* (London, 1951) is a penetrating sketch by a man who knew him well. Martin Gilbert, *Winston Churchill*, Volume III, *1914–1916* (London, 1971), covers two and a half years of Churchill's long life in great detail. Keith Middlemas and John Barnes, *Baldwin: a Biography* (London, 1969), is a very long and highly informative, if sometimes partial and inaccurate, biography of a much maligned statesman. Keith Feiling, *Neville Chamberlain* (London, 1946), although an official biography, is better balanced, but it is written too soon after Chamberlain's death to be definitive. Alan Bullock, *The Life and Times of Ernest Bevin*, is a detailed and painstaking biography, two volumes of which have so far appeared (London, 1960, 1967).

1945–1972

There are few books yet published for this period that will be of lasting historical value, except for some memoirs that will be valuable to later historians. There is no general work covering the whole period, although Pauline Gregg, *The Welfare State* (London, 1967), is a useful, if somewhat unbalanced, account of one important aspect of it for the years 1945–1967. J. C. R. Dow, *The Management of the British Economy, 1945–60* (London, 1964), is a more sophisticated, but highly technical, piece of economic history covering much of the period. C. M. Woodhouse, *British Foreign Policy since the Second World War* (London, 1961) surveys that subject up to the late fifties. Hugh Thomas, *The Suez Affair* (London, 1967), is probably the best of a number of books on that melancholy event. M. Sissons and P. French (eds.), *The Age of Austerity* (London, 1961), is a collection of essays dealing with the early postwar years, but there is as yet no satisfactory account of the Labour Government, 1945–51. G. D. N. Worswick and P. H. Ady, *The British Economy, 1945–50* (London, 1952), covers the economic side of these years. Vernon Bogdanor and Robert Skidelsky (eds.), *The Age of Affluence, 1951–64* (London, 1970), is a useful collection of critical essays covering various aspects of the Conservative years in office until more fully researched studies can appear. D. McKie and C. Cook (eds.), *Decade of Disillusion* (London, 1972), is a less satisfactory and more journalistic collection of essays for the years of the first Wilson government. Harold Wilson, *The Labour Government, 1964–70, A Personal Record* (London, 1971), covers the years of his first ministry in great detail and, inevitably, very much from his own point of view. One is struck by the fact that even a socialist government, with all its preconceived plans for achieving the socialist millennium, becomes the prisoner of events once it enters office. Wilson has far more to say about the day-to-day problems that faced him and how he handled them, than about the actual legislative and administrative achievement of his Government. W. Beckerman, *The Labour Government's Economic Record, 1964–1970* (London, 1972), provides a detailed critical appraisal on the economic side. George Melly, *Revolt into Style: the Pop Arts in Britain* (London 1970), is an interesting journalistic account of the "pop revolution" of the 1960s.

Personal memoirs, although inevitably partial, for the time being remain one of the most fruitful sources of political history for the years since 1945. The last volume of Dalton's *Memoirs* (already mentioned) and Herbert Morrison's *Autobiography* (London, 1960) are probably the most useful for Labour, although Lord George-Brown's *In My Way* (London, 1971) is highly readable, if slanted and episodic. Clement Attlee's *As It Happened* (London, 1954) and Francis Williams' interviews with Attlee entitled *A Prime Minister Remembers* (London, 1961) are not very revealing. The Conservatives are readier with the pen. R. A. Butler (Lord Butler of Waldon), *The Art of the Possible* (London, 1971), is a model of a one-volume biography, while Lord Kilmuir (Duncan Fyfe), *A Political Adventure* (London, 1964), is highly informative. The last four volumes of Harold Macmillan's magisterial memoirs, *Tides of Fortune, 1945–1955*, *Riding the Storm, 1956–1959*, *Pointing the Way, 1959–1961*, and *At the End of the Day, 1961–63* (London, 1969, 1971, 1972 and 1973) are highly informative but over long.

Index

NOTE: The following abbreviations are used throughout this index: Col. for Colonel; D., Duke; E., Earl; Gen., General; Ld., Lord; M., Marquis; Pres., President; Vsc., Viscount.

WATERLOO TO THE COMMON MARKET
BY J. B. CONACHER

J. B. CONACHER is Professor of History at the University of Toronto and is chairman of the department there. His specialty is British history since 1815, particularly mid-nineteenth-century politics. He received his M.A. degree from Queen's University in Kingston, Ontario, in 1939 and his doctorate from Harvard University in 1949. He is author of *The Aberdeen Coalition, 1852–1855* (1968) and *The Peelites and the Party System* (1972), and editor of *The Emergence of British Parliamentary Democracy in the Nineteenth Century* (1971). A fellow of the Royal Historical Society, Professor Conacher is currently president of the Canadian Historical Association.

A NOTE ON THE TYPE

THIS old face design, BEMBO 270, has such an up-to-date appearance
that it is difficult to realize this letter was cut (the first of its line)
before A.D. 1500. At Venice in 1495, ALDUS MANUTIUS ROMANUS
printed a small 36 pp. tract, *Petri Bembi de Aetna ad Angelum
Chabrielem liber*, written by the young humanist poet PIETRO BEMBO
(later Cardinal, and secretary to Pope Leo X), using a new design
of type which differed considerably from that of Jenson's. The
punches were cut by FRANCESCO GRIFFO of Bologna the designer
responsible six years later for the first italic types. A second roman
face followed in 1499 and this type design, based on the first, and
used to print the famous illustrated *Hypnerotomachia Poliphili*, was
the one which, after adaptation by Garamond, Voskens and others,
resulted finally in Caslon Old Face.